Dedication

To Robbie and Carlene Hamaty, whose relentless optimism and resilient entrepreneurial spirit defied small island odds and incredible obstacles to make Tortuga Rum Company Ltd. a Caribbean success story. Their enduring can-do attitude has been an inspiration to many.

To my husband Jim and parents, Fred & Billie Currie, who have always encouraged and applauded my literary efforts, regardless of where they took me.

And to my friends throughout the Caribbean, especially the Cayman Islands, Jamaica and the Turks & Caicos Islands, whose resourcefulness, ingenuity and capricious good humor showed me a New World 25 years ago. This remarkable region tugged at my heart and captured my imagination. I have called the Caribbean home ever since.

Preface

Rum Fever, that passion for and fascination with rum, has been around for centuries. Blame it on Columbus. The opportunistic Italian explorer started it with his second voyage to the New World in 1493, when he brought sugar cane cuttings from the Canary Islands to Hispaniola and Cuba. But his "gift" had greedy strings attached. Columbus hoped to plant a fortune's worth of the expensive white substance that fueled Europe's insatiable cravings. Sugar cane thrived in the Caribbean and turned into gold for 17th and 18th century West Indian planters, who discovered rum was the lucrative lagniappe of sugar refining.

Demon Rum quickly became the most powerful and potent liquid on earth. Its colorful and controversial history reached across the Caribbean Sea, which stretches more than 1700, miles from the coast of South America around the Antillean arc to the Yucatan, coddling hundreds of islands and more than 30 countries. But the West Indies was only the tip of the colonial rum trail that flowed north to New England and Canada, east to Europe and all the way to Australia – fueling rebellions along the way. Since then, Rum Fever has spread around the world and back, wherever sugar cane is raised. It has also reached unlikely places where sugar is scarce including three tiny coral outcroppings called the Cayman Islands, my home.

This Western Caribbean destination south of Cuba, famous for offshore banking, beaches and scuba diving, added rum to its list of attractions in 1984. That year Tortuga Rum Company Ltd. launched Cayman's first private label rums and gave a new twist to Caribbean rum's curious and never-ending story – one that inspired this book.

Rum, the legendary potion of romance and enduring seducer, has also been the secret ingredient of island cooks for over 300 years. Many legendary recipes, like West Indian wedding cakes, trifles and Christmas puddings are grand celebrations of rum cooking. For centuries islanders and savvy foreign chefs have known that the judicious use of rum, from a splash to a generous jigger, was a cook's best friend. In the right amount, rum makes a subtle difference in both savory dishes and sweets.

Today rum is conquering the world all over again, creating a new strain of Rum Fever in trendy bars and kitchens as one of the new century's hottest spirits. Regardless of its surroundings and audience sophistication, rum will always be Caribbean magic in a bottle, conjuring visions of romance and sultry nights, and parties with exotic foods and music. All of these will make you happy – and happiness makes you live longer. That may be the best Caribbean recipe of all.

TORTUGA
Rum Fever
& Caribbean Party Cookbook

by Barbara Currie Dailey

Published by

Island Fever Press

PO Box 283 GT
Grand Cayman, Cayman Islands,
British West Indies

TORTUGA RUM FEVER AND CARIBBEAN PARTY COOKBOOK
Revised Edition

Published by

Island Fever Press Ltd.

P.O. Box 283 GT, Grand Cayman, Cayman Islands

British West Indies

Printed and bound in the United States of America by Digital Printers International, North Miami Beach, FL

Book design: DPI

Cover design by Keiron Ng, Digital Printers International, North Miami Beach, Florida

ISBN: 976-95054-1-2 (pbk)

Contents

The Rum Shop

The CookRum

A Tortuga Rum Fête 281

Acknowledgments

On December 12, 1975, on a dare and a rum-fueled impulse, I ran away to the Cayman Islands for a weekend. I slid into the last seat onboard a Red Carpet Flying Service DC-3 in St. Petersburg, Florida at 4 a.m. and arrived in Cayman Brac six hours later. When I stepped onto the tarmac of Gerrard Smith airport, I felt like Alice on the other side of the Looking Glass. Like the fabled Alice, I quickly learned how to believe impossible things before breakfast. It was my first great Caribbean adventure and the experience that launched my freelance writing career. The *Tampa Tribune* published my first travel article, *Serenity on Cayman Brac*, shortly after.

That trip gave me an incurable case of Island Fever. It wasn't just these islands' startling natural beauty and delightful quirkiness, or the paralytic rum punches poured at the Buccaneer's Inn's legendary Holey Hut bar. It was the generosity and kindness of islanders who welcomed me to their islands and into their homes – and kitchens. I owe them tremendous gratitude today. That fateful December visit caused a detour on the road to a reluctant career in newspaper journalism covering an odd combination of police blotters and politics. I have called the Caribbean, especially the Cayman Islands, home ever since.

Red Carpet and the Buccaneer's Inn are long gone, but I want say thanks again to Red Carpet's founder and the Godfather of Tourism in the Sister Islands, Mr. Linton Tibbetts who provided my first wings to paradise whenever I needed them. And to the Scott family of Cayman Brac who owned the Buccaneer's Inn, where I always had a wicked rum punch waiting and a place to lay my head. Thanks to Sammy and Mary McCoy and their family of Little Cayman and Frankie and Jody Bodden and their families, who taught me about bonefish, turtle, conch, wilks, boxfish, coconut and so many wonderful island things. Long overdue thanks to Clarence and Jan Flowers of Grand Cayman, who met this young stranger in George Town and invited me home to share dinner with their Caymanian family – providing my first taste of Cayman stew conch, breadfruit, ackee and other Caribbean delights 25 years ago.

The roots of *Rum Fever* reach back to that very first visit and the idea of doing a rum and Caribbean cookbook has been simmering on the back burner for two decades. But I found the real inspiration for this book right at home in Grand Cayman, from Tortuga Rum Company. Of all the offbeat and improbable island tales I've encountered over the years, this ranks as one of the best. I also owe Captain Robbie Hamaty thanks for the nudge into this book. Awhile back, he suggested I write "a small Caribbean holiday recipe booklet" using Tortuga rums. It was a terrifying idea. I have cooked by instinct from the age of 6 from recipes in my head, but like most Caribbean cooks, I relied on the intuitive "pinch o dis and likkle o dat" method. I have turned out prose by the pound during my eclectic writing career – but only a few recipes in my entire life. At first, it was harder than writing brief and poignant political speeches or honest advertising copy.

Once I got started, this book was like a good West Indian party: it grew much bigger than expected and at times seemed like it would never end. *Rum Fever* evolved into a spontaneous and quirky voyage of discovery, not only through Rum Territory, historic and culinary, but also whole New World of writing and research. My endless thanks to the loyal crew that helped keep this project on course and didn't mutiny when test rations turned out to be ballast. Or when writer's block left me idling in the doldrums at the computer and left them adrift in a sea of convenience foods.

Hugs to my husband Jim, a real Caribbean man, who shared many of the island adventures and remembers the stories that provided material for this book – and never hesitated to remind me of them. My deepest thanks for his humor, patience and incredible depth of institutional knowledge of things Caribbean. And for his tolerance of recipe-testing feasts followed by silent famines of mysteries from the freezer, especially when deadlines swallowed me alive.

An equal measure of gratitude goes to my Mom and Dad for always being there, and for their understanding and encouragement of that 6-year old's precocious culinary instincts – and the literary ones that later evolved. They have always praised the effort even if the results needed work and taught me to clean up the mess as I went along. Good advice beyond the kitchen in later life.

My very special thanks to "Dr." John J. Lucas III of Tradewinds South Nursery in Pembroke Park, Florida whose friendship and enthusiasm for this project pruned away the doldrums many times – and whose spontaneous diagnosis of Rum Fever inspired the title. When writer's block threatened to turn *Fever* into a 10-year plague, his glorious Tradewinds bougainvilleas, Adeniums and other exotic succulent treasures were often the Muses that made ideas flow again.

A tremendous thanks to my "kids," Tim and Stephanie Dailey, for their constant help on the home front in more ways than I can remember and for saving the day during computer crises. And to my relentlessly supportive friends Dr. Lynne Sallot, Gwendy Kerr, and Lorraine Ebanks whose enduring belief in my ability as a writer kept the book fire burning for many years.

And finally, sincerest thanks to Glenn Schmidt and Keiron Ng of Digital Printers International, my irreverent surrogate editors and talented design team who caught Rum Fever from the start. This book would not have been possible without their patience, creative vision, enthusiasm and much-appreciated humor.

Introduction

The Caribbean is Paradise – dazzling beaches, an impossibly turquoise Caribbean Sea, passionate sunsets – and romance on demand. At least that's the fantasy advertising agencies sell us. But for many, it's not those clichés of sun, sand and sea that linger long after the vacation ends – it's memories of the unexpected. The islanders and their offbeat stories; provocative Caribbean music and the contagious *joie de vivre* of festivals and parties. And perhaps most vivid of all: the taste of local rum and exotic island foods.

Whether you're a visitor or fellow islander, you've probably gotten lost trying to create those wicked rum drinks, rum-spiked desserts and spicy West Indian dishes at home. That's what *Tortuga Rum Fever and Caribbean Party Cookbook* is for. It's a tour of culinary territory many would like to explore – but don't know where to start.

In the Caribbean we have a wonderful word, *fête*, which is either a noun or verb, both suggesting a celebration. *Allsopp's Dictionary of Caribbean English Usage* defines *fête* as "A house-party or public dance or jump-up, with much food, rum-drinking and spreeing." It can be any event, from a spontaneous get together to a festival with fireworks. But to Caribbean folk, a Fête is more than just a party, it's a celebration of something special.

Tortuga Rum Fever & Caribbean Party Cookbook is a Fête – celebrating rum, the Caribbean's oldest spirits and first party fuel, and Tortuga Rum Company, one of rum's most unusual modern tales. Established in 1984 on the almost sugar-free island of Grand Cayman, the company introduced the Cayman Islands' first local brand of private label rums and soon took rum beyond its traditional bottled limits. The Tortuga Rum Cake, which has made Grand Cayman the Rum Cake Capital of the World, is the first Caribbean rum confection to become a global hit. Tortuga Rum Company is now Cayman's largest retail and duty free liquor business and their products include 11 quality registered blends of rum and a growing line of gourmet products.

After an overview of rum's fascinating history, you'll find more than 300 very spirited recipes, including rum drinks, native island dishes and rum-laced recipes, from appetizers to decadent desserts – perfect party fare. *Rum Fever* was written with special empathy for visitors to the Caribbean, and those fascinated by this region from afar, who want to taste and understand "native" island dishes and the Caribbean's curious ingredients. It attempts to demystify rum for bartenders and cooks by explaining different blends and their uses. You'll be able to add Caribbean spirit and flair to any affair, from casual meals to parties requiring rum punch for a crowd.

About this Book

Like the Caribbean itself, this book has quirks that will make you laugh at times and scratch your head at others.

Regardless of age or origin, the recipes throughout this book have been "Tortuga-ized" and feature Tortuga rums and gourmet products. You can substitute similar good quality rums and liqueurs if you've run out of Tortuga or can't find it locally. **The Rum Shop** entertains with rum's colorful history and quirky folklore topped off with more than 190 drink recipes. You'll find classic rum cocktails, legendary party punches, seductive tropical drinks and the latest wild rum concoctions -along with invaluable tips on how to become a savvy Caribbean Party Bartender at home.

The CookRum, or Caribbean hearth of yesteryear, raids the island pantry for more rum and exotic Caribbean ingredients for a "Rundown" of more than 150 island dishes and original rum-spiked delights. This is not trendy Caribbean "fusion" cuisine, but a collection of recipes that show off this versatile spirits' magical powers in the kitchen. It opens with **Comfort Food, Western Caribbean Style,** which offers favorites from the Cayman Islands, with important contributions from Jamaica. These culinary sources of *Rum Fever* represent the native soils of Tortuga Rum Company's founders and most important of all, my home.

Servings: For a crowd or him one, Uncle Jimmy?

When I first started collecting recipes from the islands 25 years ago, one of the things I found consistently puzzling was that island cooks and bartenders never mentioned how many servings per recipe. I learned quickly that this was a very silly question and this reply from an old Jamaican cook says it better than my poor presentation of her country patois:

"Don be fool – now how I knows dat? Depends on who deh! You jus eat and drink until it finish. Dey late, dey sorry." Translated, this means: how many servings depends on who's there at the table and how hearty their appetites are.

However modest the party, true Caribbean hospitality still means plates piled high with generous portions -and always the promise of seconds and maybe even take-away plates for snacking on later. With respect to this enduring tradition, I risk the wrath of reviewers and food critics and leave it to you to decide how many of your guests these recipes will serve.

Much traditional Caribbean cooking is not heart smart, but is it delicious. Today forbidden delights, like this region's coconut-rich recipes, horrify the obsessive Health and Fitness Police, who find evil in everything gustatory. I say Phooey on that. I have Caribbean friends in their 80's have more energy-and sharper memories – than I do, and they eat coconut and tipple rum with whenever they want. One 89-year-old retired sea captain I know religiously ends his day with "three fingers of rum, done twice with ice" and white rum twice that amount if the flu grabs hold. He would eat Rundown every day if he could find the conch and fish.

However, in this disclaimer-happy world, here is the obligatory *caveat*. This is a party cookbook and recipes for drinks and food are presented for occasional and responsible consumption. If you try them all in one sitting, they will probably be very bad for you and your guests. Talking on your cell phone while driving is more likely to kill you than sampling the recipes in this book in moderation. I say, *Carpe Diem* and *Carpe Tortuga*. I'd rather go out happy with the taste of jerk, curry and coconut on my tongue. I hope *Rum Fever* inspires you to open the rum bottle, overcome fear of unfamiliar ingredients and enjoy creating a Caribbean fête in your own home.

The Rum Shop

From Sugar Cane to Cask: Rum History & Drink Recipes

In the Caribbean, the Rum Shop is an old tradition: the humble neighborhood or country roadside bar, a place for a sturdy drink of rum, beer or stout and shot of local gossip. You'd never find a **Mudslide** or **Sex on the Beach** here, but you might get three fingers of rum and a Greenie, and strong opinions on which rum is best for curing whatever ails you. Rum shops still dot the Caribbean landscape, but visitors to the Caribbean today are likely to do their rum research at more glamorous resort venues on the beach or at swim up pool bars. Most never realize that same sweet liquor of Caribbean vacation memories once fueled rebellions and kept slave traders and cutthroat pirates in business

Rum Lore is a mix of rum's colorful history and quirky folklore. Tortuga Rums and liqueurs highlight more than 190 libations in **Rum Fete: a 350 Year Celebration of Rum Drink Recipes**. You'll find classic rum cocktails, legendary party punches, seductive tropical drinks and the latest wild rum concoctions – along with tips on how to become a savvy Caribbean Party Bartender at home.

Rum, the western world's oldest liquor is now the New Millennium's hottest spirits. Bartenders everywhere are rediscovering rum's mystique and versatile personality. There are now more than 1000 named rum drinks, with wild new creations frothing out of blenders every day – including ones with names that make even veteran bartenders blush. If you're just discovering the exciting New World of rum refreshers, this section is your travel guide.

Rum Lore

The Curious, Colorful and Controversial History of the New World's Oldest Spirits

R um has subdued and excited, seduced and incited men for centuries. Of all the alcoholic spirits produced during the last 400 years, rum has the most fascinating, volatile – and controversial history, saturated with folklore and myth.

Rum's feverish story is as colorful as the exotic tropical drinks made with it today – but this potion's past was much less glamorous than its current chic global image. Rum was the most plentiful and potent liquor of the New World – as well as one of the world's most powerful influences. In the 17th and 18th centuries, it was linked to everything from religion to economics from the Caribbean to Canada – and caused rebellions as far away as Australia. Privateers and pirates like Edward Teach and Henry Morgan consumed and traded with it. Rum was also the nefarious currency of the 18th century triangular slave trade between New England, Africa and the West Indies.

Rum is now distilled all over the world, from India to Africa, wherever sugar cane grows. But as the birthplace of the world's rum industry, the Caribbean remains the leading producer of fine rums. Today there are more than 95 different brands and 150 varieties of rums produced in the Caribbean region alone. Premium quality brands are manufactured (or blended and bottled from imports) not only in the traditional sugar capitals of Jamaica, Barbados, Puerto Rico and Cuba, but in almost every Caribbean basin country where sugar cane grows, from Mexico to Guyana. Even sugar-impaired countries like Antigua, Bermuda and the Cayman Islands now have their own rums. Grand Cayman is the home of Tortuga Rum Company Ltd. the company that introduced Cayman's first local brand of rums in 1984.

Rum captures the Caribbean spirit in a bottle and its reputation for fueling parties is legendary. Now a new strain of Rum Fever has spread all over the world as sophisticated palates everywhere are rediscovering rum's role as a versatile drink for all seasons. Today rum has almost surpassed vodka as the planet's most popular spirits. This is the newest chapter in rum's history, which stretches over 350 years from the Caribbean's first cane fields to Tortuga Rum Cakes craved around the world.

Highlights of Rum History

Sugar cane was not indigenous to the West Indies – it thrived in Asia and India 2000 years ago and was introduced to Europe by the Moors long before Columbus "discovered" the New World. By the mid-15th century, sugar cane had reached as far west as the Canary Islands, where Christopher Columbus picked up cuttings to carry to the New World. He introduced sugar cane to Haiti and Cuba on his second voyage to the New World in 1493. But it wasn't a gift – it was motivated by greed: Columbus hoped to make a fortune. By then, sugar was one of the most valuable commodities in Europe – so expensive it was sold only by the tablespoon.

Caribbean Gold Was a Different Color. Sugar cane quickly thrived in the Caribbean's hot, humid climate and by the middle of the 17th century, sugar plantations flourished throughout the West Indies from Barbados to Cuba. With them came an unexpected product – a fiery new potion called rum. Caribbean planters soon discovered the residue from sugar making fermented into a whole new commodity. By the mid-1600s rum had surpassed sugar as the fuel of the West Indian economy. The English turned rum into the gold that eluded the colonial Spanish explorers.

Rum's discovery was an accident. Who discovered rum? No one is absolutely sure. Some scholars believe Spanish colonists may have discovered the heady effects of fermented cane juice rum by the early 16th century, 100 years before the English arrived in the New World. Ponce de Leon may have brought a crude form of rum when he traveled to Florida from Puerto Rico.

Cuba was the second island to get sugar cane from Columbus, during his second voyage in 1493. By 1620 Cuba had one of the region's largest sugar cane crops and almost 50 sugar refineries. **Bacardi** and **Ron Matusalem** rums were born here. During Prohibition in the USA (1920-33) Havana became the cocktail capital of the Western World, the playground of America's rich and famous, including Ernest Hemingway and Hollywood stars, who came in search of a stiff drink and heady night life.

How did Rum get its name? The first recorded mention of rum was not very flattering and dates to the 1640's. A a teetotaling Englishman in Barbados named Richard Ligon wrote about "Kill Devil," a drink so strong it could "overpower the senses with a single whiff...It lays them to sleep on the ground." In 1651 another European in Barbados wrote back home, "The chiefe fudling they make in the Island is Rumbullion, alias Kill-Devill, and this is made of sugar canes distilled, a hot, hellish and terrible liquor." Rum could have been derived from rumbullion or rumbustion, 17th century English country slang for a rumpus or public uproar – apt descriptions of rum's aftermath. Or it could have been shortened from the scientific Latin name for sugar cane, Saccarum officinarum.

The Caribbean was the birthplace of the world's commercial rum industry. Barbados has long been labeled the New World birthplace of fine rum and was producing around a million liters of rum a year by 1650. However, Barbados was actually only the first place to produce rum commercially *for export*, not the first to produce it. There were thriving sugar industries in Brazil and Cuba even before the English settled Barbados in

1627. Some believe 16th century Spanish conquistadors may have been the first to make rum in the New World, having learned the techniques of distilling cane back home in Europe.

Barbados Became England's R & R Resort Colony. A colonial joke about the Europeans' priorities during the conquest of the New World went accordingly. Upon arriving, the first thing the Spanish did was build a church; the Dutch built a fort – and the English opened drinking houses. The British declared Barbados a colony in 1627 and within 20 years there were 120 taverns around the port of Bridgetown alone (today the island allegedly has more than 1000.) Its remote location far south and east of the rest of the Caribbean (except for Trinidad and Tobago) made Barbados easy to defend and an ideal place for the Royal Navy to enjoy rest, relaxation and rum. During one spectacular 17th century drinking spree, the Navy, led by William Henry, Prince of Wales, almost demolished a popular Bridgetown rum shop owned by Rachel Pringle. They also skipped on the bill. The Prince finally settled the tab after Miss Pringle chased him back to the ship. It was enough for her to build Barbados' first small hotel.

Rum's reputation for ruin was well deserved. Europeans had never tasted anything so sweet and lethal. By the early 17th century, colonists had Rum Fever and were behaving badly all over the New World. English clergy quickly recognized the Demon in Rum and by 1670 they condemned the potion back home it for rendering men senseless, impotent – or dead. Rum's reputation grew worse in the 18th century with the company it kept. Caribbean privateers, operating with Her Majesty's blessing, traded in rum but many ships' crews corrupted into buccaneers and pirates plundering the Spanish Main. The most feared flag in the Caribbean was not a skull and crossbones, but one with a skeleton brandishing a dagger in one hand and a glass called a "Rummer" in the other. Robert Louis Stevenson sealed rum's misbegotten fate in the legendary *Treasure Island* passage: "Fifteen men on the Dead Man's Chest, yo-ho-ho and a bottle of rum. Drink and the devil had done for the rest – yo ho ho and a bottle of rum."

Rum Almost Scuttled Her Majesty's Royal Navy. In 1655 after the conquest of Jamaica, His Majesty's Royal Navy ships in the West Indies began issuing daily rations of rum to all onboard, at first unofficially. The reason: water became contaminated on long voyages and could not be always be replenished. Beer went sour even faster, but rum stored in casks not only survived at sea – its flavor improved with age. At first, very strong, crude rum replaced the same quantity of beer as the daily ration for sailors. By 1731, the official daily rum ration was a staggering half-pint per sailor, distributed in drams first thing in the morning and in late afternoon. Dubiously, rum became associated with English seafaring valor – the accompanying swagger may have been mistaken for sea legs. It's a miracle the Royal Navy stayed afloat. Rum caused accidents in the rigging at sea and even more problems in port.

Grog: The First Rum Cocktail. By 1740, Admiral Edward Vernon, commander of Her Majesty's fleet in the West Indies recognized this unhealthy English breakfast of champions and ordered the daily ration diluted. The official ration was now a quart of water to every half-pint of rum. He also encouraged ships' pussers to add sugar and limes to the mixture to make the rum more palatable – the Royal Navy version of the first rum cocktail. Vernon's nickname was "Old Grogham," after the unreasonably heavy woolen cloak he wore year-round in the tropics. Sailors called his watered down ration "grog" ("groggy" was derived from it) and the act sparked temporary mutiny throughout the fleet. But the sailors settled down and the Royal Navy continued its twice-daily de rigueur dose of this "tonic" until July 1970.

The Original Flaming Rum Drink was an official Royal Navy ritual. This is a classic tot of rum trivia. In the 17th century, diluting a ship's rum supply was a punishable offense, and the ship's purser or "pusser", was responsible for determining and maintaining the quality. Until 1816, when the Sikes' Hydrometer was invented (the first test to determine the proof of liquor) a Navy pusser relied on this official method, allegedly invented at the Royal Arsenal in London. He mixed pure rum with a small amount of fresh water in a glass and added a few black gunpowder grains. The glass was left to heat in the sun and if the rum was up to proof, the mixture ignited briefly. If it didn't, the pusser was punished for siphoning off nips and watering the rum. Folklore claims that crews anticipated these daily tests in case the crude rum was too strong and exploded, blowing the pusser into space. If so, it was Happy Hour free-for- all around the unguarded rum casks.

The Lord Nelson Myth. "Nelson's Blood" was another rum nickname, coined following the death of Admiral Lord Nelson onboard his ship during the Battle of Trafalgar – of battle wounds, not rum consumption. For years after, rum's fame as a preservative prevailed due to the widespread myth that Nelson's body was returned to England for burial preserved in a cask of rum. In fact, legend says, it was actually brandy and his favorite drink, Marsala wine, which Nelson loved so much, he once bought 5000 gallons for the Royal Navy under his command.

Those Wild 17th Century English Punch Parties. Like early seeds for Monty Python follies, grand and giddy rum punch parties highlighted the English social scene of the late 1600's. Hot rum punch was the rage and parties were thrown to sample the latest rums arriving on ships returning from the West Indies. According to Rum Lore, HM Royal Navy Admiral Edward Russell threw the biggest rum punch party in history in 1694, when 6000 guests emptied a gargantuan vat of punch. The recipe? Eight barrels of rum, 8 barrels of hot water, 80 quarts of lemon juice, 300 pounds of sugar, ten kegs of wine and five pounds of cinnamon. The reason for this spectacularly foggy fête is unknown or perhaps simply blacked out.

Rum Was a Colonial American Passion Too.

"Landlord, to thy bar room skip,
Make it a foaming mug of flip.
Make it of our country's staple,
Rum, New England sugar Maple,
Then Pour more rum, the bottle stopping,
Stir it again, and say it's topping."
—An anonymous 18th century New England ditty

By the mid-1600's rum was flowing from New England distilleries and merchants were importing huge quantities of West Indian molasses to fuel the lucrative industry. The early colonists were besotted by rum and drank it neat (straight), spiced, buttered and nogged – and slipped tots into their sweets and cook pots. By 1654, rum was so important to the economy that Connecticut outlawed the importation of any liquor from the West Indies that might compete with the local product. By 1750 there were 63 distilleries in Massachusetts alone, and colonists were consuming rum at a rate of four gallons per person per year. Demon rum had become Puritan New England's biggest vice and most profitable 18th century industry.

Rum was Many Colonial Cooks' Secret. From Nova Scotia to Barbados, some of the best 17th and 18th century recipes were subtly and sometimes secretly infused with rum – from morning porridge to poultry and puddings. Lots more was probably soaked up by cooks themselves. Even Puritan cooks were known to pour shots of locally distilled rum into their simmering cast iron pots. Rum's versatile nature and culinary *je ne sais quoi* was recognized centuries before it became a hallmark of trendy 1990's "fusion" and "New World" cuisine.

Ethan Allen, hero of the Republic of Vermont, may have invented the Hot Toddy. Historic accounts attribute to Allen a fondness for this winter concoction. His recipe called for a black-walnut size piece of butter, a hickory-nut size serving of maple sugar and a gill (half-cup) of strong rum mixed with a small amount of boiling water.

The Ubiquitous Planter's Punch, the original plantation happy hour libation, has been around since the early 1600's. The most famous of all rum drinks is also a contested concoction – romantics insist it was the favorite dark rum refresher of colonial planters. Others claim it was a cruel liquid diet consisting of crude rum, water and lime mixed in buckets and given to slaves instead of regular food. There is no single correct or authentic "original" recipe for Planter's Punch. I found at least 20 while researching this book – and there are many more. In the French West Indies, Planter's Punch is simply equal measures of white **rhum agricole** and cane syrup, with a squeeze of fresh lime over ice. Even pedantic Rumologists can't precisely define Planter's Punch but insist it includes dark rum and fresh fruit juices. It can have as few as three and as many as nine ingredients.

Rum created the Caribbean's First Dirty Money – and money laundering operation. In the late 17th and 18th century, rum became the nefarious currency of the triangular slave trade for both Mother England and New England. English merchants traded goods for slaves in West Africa, then sold the slaves for rum in the Caribbean – wealthy Europeans had developed a huge taste for the stuff by then.

In New England, it was a little different. Merchants needed West Indian molasses to manufacture rum in local distilleries. The predominantly Puritan New England colonies were rapacious consumers of rum. Much of the local rum, called Yankee Rum or "Stink-e-buss," (to distinguish it from the much more desirable Barbados rums) was shipped to Africa's west coast. There it was traded for slaves, who were crowded onto ships bound for the Caribbean and exchanged for more molasses. That infamous triangular trade made many Yankee and UK merchants filthy rich in the literal sense

Rum was used to "sedate" colonial slaves. While rum was popular with both working class and wealthy colonial New England tipplers, planters in the West Indies preferred European imports like Madeira wine and brandy. They later discovered rum's sweet seductive pleasures, after proper distilling refined its rich taste. But early crude rum was widely given to slaves on West Indian plantations to make them "content and submissive." Many callous plantation masters fed their slaves rum instead of regular food because it was cheaper – even on an empty stomach, slaves could still work fueled by a rum high. French colonial administrators were so concerned about this problem that two sections of France's law governing territorial slave welfare, the Code Noire of 1685, strictly forbade planters to give slaves rum instead of the regular rations of cassava, salt beef and salted fish. Plantation owners found guilty of abuses risked prosecution.

Rum was a Political Ally in Pre-Revolutionary America. Rum Lore contends that after the Revolutionary War, rum flowed heavily throughout colonial politics and was used by politicians to woo voters. "Swilling the planters with bumbo" was the slang term for that practice which actually prompted a Virginia law outlawing plying voters with spirits and declaring elections illegal if won that way. That didn't stop George Washington, who launched his career in 1758 campaigning not with rhetoric, but with rum. He was allegedly elected to the Virginia House of Burgess after doling out gifts to voters in Frederick County, Virginia, totaling 160 gallons of rum, beer, wine and cider – about a quart and a half per voter. This included 28 gallons of rum and 50 gallons of rum punch. Washington was fond of rum himself, and was a pre-Revolutionary regular at Pennsylvania's famous men's club, The State, where Fish House Punch was invented. After he retired, Washington even established his own distillery – but switched to whiskey, capitalizing on the New American taste for grain alcohols.

Rum also Helped Spark – and Fuel a Revolution. The Molasses Act of 1733 imposed a hefty tax on West Indian molasses imported by the American Colonies, where rum had already become an important industry. It provoked the famous New England revolts against "taxation without representation;" planted the seeds of the American Revolution and launched smuggling into full swing. England didn't enforce the tax collection very well, and that law was replaced by the much stricter Sugar Act of 1764. England's militant enforcement of the law and tax collection methods finally halted the New England Colonies' importation of molasses from the West Indies and literally devastated their rum-fueled economy. As recreation, rum was finished – it became so expensive that few could afford it except as "medicine."

Paul Revere's Legendary Ride was Rum-Propelled. Shortly after he started out to warn of the Redcoats' approach on the night of 18 April 1775, Revere was captured but escaped. Trying to elude enemy horsemen, he stopped at the home of friend and rum-maker Isaac Hall, who bolstered the weary hero with several shots of heavy Medford rum. It was then that Paul Revere's famous ride really began – but another legend contends that it was Mary Flint Hartwell, the mistress of a nearby farmhouse, who actually ran the final leg across fields to Captain Smith's place to report the British were coming – while Revere was tippling.

The Ruthless Redcoats Retaliated by Making the Colonies Rum-less. It's amazing what power rum had over men back then – they even went to war over it. The Royal Navy blockaded colonial ports during the Revolutionary War and molasses and rum from the British West Indies became scarce. After the American Revolution, the young country did not entirely restore trade with the British colonies in the Caribbean. In 1807, Congress passed the Embargo Act, outlawing imports from the West Indies. The final cork in the rum bottle came the following year, when Congress made slave trading with Africa illegal. Both molasses and slave smuggling continued for awhile – and didn't end completely until law abolished slavery in 1834 in the remaining English colonies and the French territories in 1848. How curious that Northern Yankees later blamed the South for the evils of slavery in America. However, the unquenchable American thirst for booze prevailed. By the late 1700's, Americans had discovered how to make grain whiskeys including rye and crude bourbon, which replaced rum as the drink of choice by the early 19th century.

The Rum Industry Flourished in the Caribbean. Down south in the tropics, both sugar and rum had become firmly established as mainstays of the Caribbean's economy and the rum industry flourished, exporting shiploads to a booming European market. After the slave revolt in Haiti in 1791, Cuba became the leading sugar producer in the Caribbean and Europeans coveted its fine rums. Barbados, St. Croix and Jamaica also became major sugar centers and rum producers –by 1890 there were almost 150 distilleries in Jamaica alone.

Cuba: Cocktail Capital of the World. By the end of the 19th century ice was available in Cuba, adding a whole new dimension to rum drinking. Cuban bartenders combined ice, rum, abundant tropical fruit juices and coconuts to invent the modern mixed drink. During the 1920's, when Prohibition tried to turn Americans into Teetotalers, Cuba fueled international fantasies of partying and pleasure as the Cocktail Capital of the World. Some of its most famous and enduring drinks were invented later, during the 1940's, including the Saoco (simply coconut milk, ice and rum;) the Mojito (rum, sugar, lime and mint) Ernest Hemingway's favorite Cuban refresher, and the Mulatta, (lime, rum and crème de cacao.) (See recipes in **Rum Fête**)

Rumrunners made the 1920's Roar. Like the forbidden fruit of Eden, rum became the obsession of Americans shackled by Prohibition's ban on liquor from 1920-1933. Why rum? Thank Cuba and the Mob. In 1920's Havana, the spectacular arrival of glamorous resorts, heady nightlife – and rum-based modern cocktails lured wealthy Americans and celebrities down to play. Cocktails captured the nation's imagination and Americans developed a passion for rum drinks like daiquiris and swizzles as a symbol of sophistication. Rum made a stunning comeback in the US and made the Roaring '20s even more outrageous. Reminiscent of the colonial merchants' rebellion against the Molasses Act of 1733, Al Capone and other mobsters thumbed their noses at Government and expanded into smuggling. They made millions bootlegging rum from Cuba and other Caribbean islands, often using Nassau as a transshipment point.

Rum and Coca-Cola was more than a Calypso Hit. An intriguing tale of Rum Lore took place during World War II. In 1943, a little known arrangement with Britain traded 22 US warships for a string of Naval bases in the Caribbean to defend the USA's eastern seaboard. The largest of these, in Trinidad, was the wartime home for over 50,000 American servicemen who soon discovered Trinidad's fine rums which were far superior to anything back home. Coca-Cola, one of the few familiar comforts available in the canteens, was quickly discovered to be the perfect mixer and a military passion for Rum and Coke developed. When the troops returned home in 1946, they introduced their new drink all over the USA. That allegedly was the inspiration for the Andrews Sister's hugely popular calypso hit, *Rum and Coca-Cola*, which sold over a million copies and for a while, created America's National Drink.

While the humble Rum and Coke has long been one of the Western Hemisphere's top ten favorite drinks, rum also became the base for many classic cocktails and traditional tropical favorites including the Daiquiri, Zombie, Mai Tai, Yellowbird and Pina Colada. In the last 20 years, more than a thousand wild rum-fueled concoctions – often with provocative names like Sex on the Beach – have been created.

Mexico's Rum Industry Developed like Molasses, but it made up for it later. In 1519, the infamous conquistador Hernando Cortez introduced sugar cane to "New Spain." But rum manufacturing didn't develop commercially until the 1930's. Today, **Bacardi** and **Seagram's** have major distilleries in Mexico – which is now one of the largest consumers of rum in Latin America. In fact, rum outsells tequila among Mexican drinkers, who are also Jamaica's top rum export market.

Marilyn Monroe Loved Rum Cake. When a large collection of her personal items went on the auction block in 1999, recipes found tucked inside Marilyn Monroe's cookbooks revealed a passion for rum cake.

Cuban-born Bacardi-Martini is now the world's leading rum manufacturer, with sales of over 178 million liters (20 million cases) a year. Its main distillery in Puerto Rico is the world's largest. Family owned for six generations, Bacardi and its trademark bat logo were born in Santiago de Cuba in 1862, in a distillery established by Spanish wine merchant Don Facundo Bacardi y Maso and his sons. They developed the world's first white rum, a completely new taste experience that quickly became Cuba's most popular drink. Bacardi stopped production in Cuba after the 1960 Cuban Revolution, when Castro's government seized more than $76 million in assets. Today, Bacardi's main distilleries are in Puerto Rico and Mexico, but its rums are also manufactured in the Bahamas, Panama and five other Caribbean countries – and rumors, claim, China may be next.

Jamaica's Ghostbusters: J. Wray & Nephew, founded in 1825, is Jamaica's oldest and largest rum producer. Today, it owns and operates three estates, bottling and blending a variety of rums under the **Appleton**, **Wray & Nephew** and **Coruba** labels. It also produces the infamous 126-proof (63 % alcohol) Wray & Nephew White Overproof Rum, locally known as "wine." The world's best selling overproof rum accounts for 90 per cent of the rum consumed in Jamaica. In addition to being Everyman's favorite drink, Jamaicans use white overproof as a remedy and rub for everything from arthritis to the flu. Folklore claims it subdues duppies, or mischievous island ghosts, and exorcises truly evil spirits if sprinkled in the corners of a new room or house. Too much of it will make you see duppies in broad daylight.

Don't Judge a Man by His Rum Bottle. By nature, older Caribbean people are tremendously resourceful, remembering lean times when everything had a use beyond its original purpose. Rum bottles are a good example. Long before plastic was so common it replaced seashells on our coastlines, empty rum bottles were valuable containers for many things. Like a canteen, a rum bottle could hold a day's water supply for a fisherman. Homemade remedies like bush tea keep well in rum bottles. In old times where local shops' supplies of important liquid ingredients were sold by the measure from barrels and gallon containers, rum bottles carried home cooking oil, vinegar and even kerosene. Even today rum bottles are a resource rather than refuse for many Caribbean people.

Rum is a Religious Experience. Rum still plays a role in some Haitian voodoo ceremonies.

Rum Fever Capital of the World? Hold on to your barstool – it's not the Caribbean, it's the Philippines. This county outdrinks everyone as the world's leading consumers of rum. Filipino Rum Fever means knocking off more than 3.5 million cases of rum each year. The country's own flourishing rum industry dates back to 1854. Its oldest brand, **Tanduay** rum, is the country's top seller and a leading export, second only to Bacardi in international volume sales.

Americans are the Biggest Rumheads in the Western Hemisphere. The USA is the world's second biggest rum market overall, downing more than 80 million liters a year. India ranks third, followed by Mexico, Germany and Canada. Rum drinking has been a popular part of European culture since 17th century, when England, France, Spain and Holland established colonies in the West Indies. Surprisingly, Germans now drink more rum than their neighbors, the UK, France and Spain.

A Rum named... Tortuga? Tortuga is Spanish for turtle – but this rum's name isn't referring the turtle's pace of flowing molasses. Las Tortugas is the name Columbus gave to the Cayman Islands when he first sighted the trio in 1503. But he never introduced sugar cane to this Western Caribbean country whose heritage and economy developed around seafaring activities instead. Very little sugar cane has ever been grown in Cayman – but that didn't stop two native Caribbean entrepreneurs from starting Cayman's first rum company. They also dared to "boldly go where no rum company had gone before," expanding the horizons of Caribbean rum with a growing line of rum-infused gourmet products. The story of Grand Cayman's Tortuga Rum Company Ltd. is as unexpected as the variety of recipes in this book using its products.

The Tortuga Rum Cake: More Famous Than Turtles. In October 1987, Tortuga Rum Company Ltd. co-owner Carlene Jackson Hamaty finally gave in to the local demand for her delicious rum cake, made from a 100-year old secret family recipe. The Tortuga Rum Cake was launched commercially in Grand Cayman and was an instant hit. Today, it is the Cayman Islands' top selling souvenir and number one export product, as well as one of the Caribbean's most famous gourmet food items. The cake is now more famous than Cayman's trademark turtles. Read about this unusual Rum Tale in **A Tortuga Rum Fête** later in this book.

How Rum is Made

A little Rum Mathematics:
- One acre of cane fields produces
- 10 tons of sugar cane which gives
- 1 short ton of raw sugar to make
- 32 gallons of rum
- Jamaica produces over 4.5 million gallons of rum annually today
- Grand Cayman's Tortuga Rum Company Ltd. bakes more than 30,000 Tortuga Rum Cakes a week

It's true: Rum actually begins as waste – the byproduct of sugar refining. In sugar production, cane stalks are crushed to extract the sweet cane sap, which is boiled until it crystallizes into raw sugar. The process leaves behind a rich, sticky, dark brown residue of impurities called molasses. For almost 350 years, rum making has involved the same three stages: fermenting, distilling and aging, but each distillery claims its own secret process.

Molasses, Water, Skimming and... Dunder? No, it's not a West Indian law firm; it's rum's key ingredients. The molasses obtained from the boiling process is still too sugar-rich and must first be diluted with water or it won't ferment. Fermentation requires the addition of skimming, the foam that forms on the top when cane sap is boiled, and dunder, the sediment left in the distilling tank from the previous batch. Dunder consists of yeast, bacteria and acids. Both of these additives determine the taste and aroma of the finished rum.

From Fire Water to Fine Premium Rum. Once fermented, the sugar mash must be distilled at high temperatures to evaporate the alcohol and then cooled to form the colorless raw liquid rum. That's the beginning. At this stage, rum is harsh, colorless, 75 per cent alcohol and undrinkable – what the early Spanish colonists called *aguardiente* – literally "fire water." The aging process takes from months to years and is what gives individual rums their distinct flavor. For gold, amber and dark rums, caramel is added to reach the desired color before aging – and aging is what ultimately creates the rich flavor of fine quality rums enjoyed today.

White rums – also called silver or light – go right to aging tanks to maintain their clear color. They don't require extensive aging: six months is often long enough, although a year is standard. (These white rums should not be confused with white overproof rum, which is 126 or higher proof and a completely different product.) Darker rums must be aged longer, generally at least two to four years. The Caribbean's finest rums are still aged in oak barrels for up to 20 years. Dark rums aged over 10 years can be as rich as fine brandy.

While the tradition of aging rum in oak barrels still exists, many commercial distilleries now use stainless steel tanks or vats, and the aging process is generally six months to four years instead of much longer.

In the last 20 years, many specialty rums have been introduced, flavored with coconut, spices or fruit. These flavored rums give cocktails an extra boost, but are not substitutes for the fruit juices and coconut cream needed to make authentic tropical drinks. And overproof rums, including 126 proof White Overproof Rum and 151-proof rum, are in a league by themselves.

There is no such thing as "cooking rum." Unlike cooking wine and sherry, available at most supermarkets, rum has no cheap generic substitute. You must use the real thing in the kitchen. The rule of thumb is don't cook with any rum you wouldn't want to sample while you work: in other words, the best quality rum. For cooking and baking, most chefs recommend dark rum, gold rum or any rum at least 80 proof. For flaming drinks and flambe dishes, you can use lower proof liqueurs, but spirits of at least 80 proof are generally considered the culinary fuel of choice. See **The Caribbean Party Bartender's Guide** for information about different kinds of rums and Tortuga Rum Company's own blends.

A Final Rum Punch Line: More Hot Tots of Rum Lore

Just when you think you've read enough rum lore, here are a few parting shots— an unexpected closing punch line.

Rum wasn't just the spirit of rebellion, pirates and wild parties. Some of the world's most creative artists uncorked casks to find their muse inside, thousands of miles from the West Indies. Wolfgang Amadeus Mozart loved rum punch—in 18th century Germany, "punsch" was a popular hot drink made with strong West Indian rum, fruit and spices. Punch was Mozart's antidote to failure while composing his grueling opera *Don Giovanni* in 1787. According to Austrian lore, steady doses of hot rum punch administered by Mozart's wife Constanze fueled the famous all-nighter during which he finally completed the overture—just in time for the first performance. (A little rum would have eased the audience's pain too.)

Rum punch also inspired 19th century Rome's elite cast of artists and composers, including Hector Berlioz. The famous red-haired French Composer won a music scholarship to the Academie de France's famous Villa Medici in Rome and launched his creative stay during an all night rum punch party thrown by the Academie staff. He recorded what he could remember of the summer 1831 night in his *Memoires*.

And make of this what you will: the Royal Wedding cake created for Prince Charles and Princess Diana on July 29, 1981 was generously spiked with rum—thanks to the pastry chefs at London's Royal Naval School of Cookery.

Rum's influence still rules in surprising places. On March 16, 2001, right here in Grand Cayman, a quart of rum christened the $10 million BritCay House office complex in the capital of George Town. Prominent Caymanian businessman Captain Charles Kirkconnell launched the traditional "roof topping ceremony" by pouring rum down a storm drain. The old custom, which originated in Bermuda, is said to "ward off the duppies (mischievous spirits)." According to the *Caymanian Compass*, the enduring local tabloid-style newspaper, "British Caymanian Insurance Ltd. further raised its profile" by the event, witnessed by Sir David Gibbons, Bermuda's former premier and finance minister.

The Caribbean Party Bartender's Guide

Caribbean bartenders are like magicians, mixing wicked drinks with a sleight of hand that entertains and tames a crowd: a shot of this, a splash of that, a twist of the wrist and a Soca wind of the hips as jiggers fill and empty. With a whir of the blender, another seductive island drink appears.

On your own, you're absolutely lost. How do you make a Cayman Mama or frozen banana daiquiri – much less those really wild concoctions?

No problem! You'll learn how in this chapter.

Some of the best cocktail recipes date back decades – even centuries. Their secret was fresh fruit juices and fine rums in perfect proportions. Use both whenever possible. If you can't find Tortuga rums and liqueurs at home, use the best quality substitutes possible. Then add a splash of memories: romantic island moments, Caribbean sunshine, endless beaches, hypnotic turquoise seas.... and those passionate sunsets. Your rum cocktails just might taste the same back home.

Which Rum Do I Use?

It's important to understand the different kinds of rum.

Gold rum is smooth and versatile. Usually about 86 proof, it is ideal for Planters Punches, Pina Coladas and drinks made with heavier fruit juices.

Light rum (also called white rum – do not confuse it with white overproof rum!) is colorless and lighter, about 80 proof and used for many classic cocktails including daiquiris, collins, sours and martinis.

Dark rum has a richer flavor and higher alcohol content than either light or gold rums, between 90 and 98 proof. It gives a more intense flavor to rum punches and mixed drinks. It is also excellent for specialty coffees and cooking.

Flavored rums, such as coconut, spiced and others – range from 80 proof – 86 proof. The best varieties are gold rum blended with flavorings, originally invented to enhance the flavor of mixed drinks. Some are excellent, with bold, rich flavors. Others are better off left on the shelf. And cheap flavored rums make exceptionally awful drinks.

151 rum gets its name because it is 151 proof. It gives a wicked kick to drinks and is the rum recommended for flambés and other flaming dishes because of its high alcohol content.

White overproof rum should also be approached with caution. It is 126 proof or higher and deceptively smooth and sweet. It is NOT the same as light rum or varieties of white rums from Barbados and other islands, and should not be substituted for them in recipes. This clear liquid is like rocket fuel, a quick ride to oblivion. It's what many islanders claim cures ciguatera (fish poisoning) but that's pure folklore. It's also used as a rub and a vapor to relieve the flu and fevers, and numb the pain of toothaches, employment problems and nagging spouses. The Tortuga Rum Company label does not include white overproof rum.

Tortuga Rum Company's Rums

Established in 1984 when it launched Tortuga Gold and Light Rums, the Cayman Islands' first private label brand, Tortuga Rum Company Ltd. has grown into the largest retail and duty free liquor business in the Cayman Islands. Tortuga Rum Company's line of rums now includes 11 quality registered blends, topped by its Premium Label 12-Year Old Tortuga Rum for rum connoisseurs. Other blends include Tortuga Light, Gold, Dark, 151 Proof, Coconut, Banana, and Spiced Rums and Tortuga Rum Cream Liqueur, Rum Liqueur and Tortuga Coffee Liqueur. Tortuga rums are blended from fine Jamaican rum and bottled exclusively for Tortuga Rum Company. The exception is Tortuga Rum Company's Premium Label 12-Year-Old Rum. This superior, smooth 86 proof rum is blended and bottled for Tortuga from bonded aged rum by one of Barbados' leading rum distilleries.

Here is a brief guide to Tortuga rums and suggested uses.

Tortuga Premium Label 12-Year Old Rum (86 proof / 43% alcohol)

This ultra smooth 86 proof rum is "sipping quality," the ideal choice for true rum connoisseurs. Like fine aged whiskeys, you can enjoy this rum by itself, straight in a brandy snifter or poured over ice. Tortuga Premium Label 12-Year Old Rum is blended from bonded aged private stock and bottled exclusively for Tortuga Rum Company by one of Barbados' leading rum distilleries. Known for centuries as one of the world's finest producers of rum, even Barbados has limited quantities of this kind of fine aged rum. The lengthy, time honored process of bonded aging takes from four to 24 years to achieve premium quality rum, which is in constant demand worldwide. The is the oldest rum bearing the Tortuga label and sold in distinctive, wax-sealed collectible antique-design "foursquare" bottles.

Tortuga 151 Rum (151 proof / 75.5 % alcohol)

With its high alcohol content and intense rum flavor, this rum is ideal for flambés and flaming coffees. In the Caribbean, it's also widely used to give that extra punch to favorite rum drinks like Planters Punch, Zombies and Yellowbirds.

Tortuga Dark Rum (98 proof / 49% alcohol)

Tortuga Dark Rum, a very smooth, rich-flavored rum, is the ingredient in many of Tortuga's gourmet private label products including Tortuga West Indian Rum Plum Pudding; three varieties of Tortuga Rum Flavored Coffee, Tortuga Rum Flavored Bar-B-Que Sauce; Tortuga Rum Flavored chocolate fudge and Tortuga Chocolate Rum Hazelnut Truffles. Tortuga Dark rum is perfect for exotic rum drinks like a Bahama Mama, Long Island Ice Tea and tropical concoctions made with fruit juices. It can be used in flambé dishes, and is the choice cooking ingredient in recipes calling for rum, from custards and trifles to stews.

Tortuga Gold Rum (86 proof / 43% alcohol)

Tortuga Gold Rum has a richly, smooth flavor and is one of the most popular and versatile of all rums on the bartender's shelf. It is used in both traditional rum cocktails and exotic tropical drinks like the Cayman Mama and other signature Tortuga cocktails.

Tortuga Gold rum is also used in cooking, for soups and sauces.

Tortuga Light Rum (80 proof/ 40% alcohol)

This is the perfect rum for mixing classic lighter rum cocktails, including daiquiris, rum swizzles, rum collins – even rum martinis, shaken or stirred. Light rum is often used in combination of two or more rums in creamy exotic drinks like Mudslides. Many rum drinkers prefer this lighter variety to gold rum for drinking straight over ice. Tortuga Light rum can also be used in cooking, for uncooked or frozen desserts and whipped cream recipes.

Tortuga Spiced Rum (80 proof / 40% alcohol) and Banana Rum (60 proof/ 30% alcohol)

These unusual and delicious blended rums were developed as convenient mixers for creating exotic drinks. In all Tortuga flavored rums, the flavors are infused during the blending process, allowing them to mellow and become smooth as the rums age. Tortuga Spiced Rum is a blend of allspice and cinnamon and other island spices – the perfect addition to a party-sized punch bowl. Banana Rum gives extra punch to a Banana Daiquiri and other banana-flavored drinks.

Tortuga Coconut Rum (86 proof /48% alcohol)

Tortuga Coconut Rum was developed to intensify the flavor of Pina Coladas. The easiest Pina Colada is simply two jiggers each of Coconut Rum, pineapple juice and coconut cream shaken with ice. "Coconut rum and pineapple juice" is also popular drink throughout the Caribbean. Innovative island chefs now add coconut rum to many recipes for an unusual flavor boost.

Tortuga Rum Crème (30 proof/ 15% alcohol)

Rum Crème was developed in Jamaica long before Irish Crème and other creamy liqueurs became popular overseas. Tortuga Rum Cream Liqueur is a rich, velvety creamy liqueur, delicious straight or over ice. It is the perfect addition to after dinner coffee. Some prefer to keep the entire bottle in the refrigerator and serve chilled straight up. You can use it to make Mudslides, Grasshoppers and other cream drinks –as well as desserts.

Tortuga Rum Liqueur (56 proof /28% alcohol)

The provocative, heady flavor of Tortuga Rum Liqueur is similar to Jamaica's famous Rumona. It can be served in place of brandy or cognac and sipped straight or over ice. It can also be substituted for brandy in recipes to give an exotic island twist to sauces and desserts.

Tortuga Coffee Liqueur (50 proof/ 25% alcohol)

This smooth blend of fine Jamaican Blue Mountain coffee flavor and premium rum is the ideal ingredient to make Tortuga Cayman Coffee and other fancy coffees. It is also good for sipping and savoring. You can use Tortuga Coffee Liqueur in mixed drinks and any recipes calling for Tia Maria or Kahlua.

Tropical Mixology 101

One of the secrets to making delicious rum drinks is using fresh fruit juices and garnishes whenever possible – and never take shortcuts with liquors. Nothing makes a more offensive drink than using cheap rums, especially flavored ones, which can produce off-tasting, even harsh concoctions. Since you may not be able to find **Tortuga Rums** where you live, choose good quality rums as substitutes.

Measure amounts exactly and use the ingredients recommended in the recipes- experiment later. To do this, know your measures and ingredients

Measures

A part can be any measure, but be sure all "parts" are the same, whether a quart, a jigger or a teaspoon. This is important because confusion still prevails about the amount of liquor in "a shot." Some bartenders use a 2-ounce jigger, while others use 1-1/2 ounces. For that reason, all Caribbean Party drink recipes are given in ounces. If you're collecting recipes on your own, always ask for specific measures!

1 jigger or 1 shot	1/1/2 ounces or 44 milliliters
1 pony	1 ounce
1 glass of wine	4 ounces
1 split	6 ounces
1 pint	16 ounces (2 cups) or 500 ml.
1/2 pint	8 ounces or 200 ml.
1 fifth	4/5 quart – 25.6 ounce or 750 ml.
1 quart	32 ounces or 1000 ml
1 liter	34 ounces
1 splash	1/4 teaspoon
Dash	4-6 drops
Or:	
1 cup	8 ounces
1/2 cup	4 ounces
1/4 cup	2 ounces
2 tablespoons	1 ounce
4 tablespoons	2 ounces
3 teaspoons	1 tablespoon

Citrus measures:

A "squeeze" means a generous squeeze of juice, about 2 teaspoons.

1 medium lemon	2-3 tablespoons juice; 2-3 teaspoons grated rind
1 Persian lime	2-3 tablespoons juice; 2 teaspoons grated rind
1 key lime	1/2-1 tablespoon juice; 1/2 teaspoon grated rind
1 medium orange	1/3 cup juice; 2 tablespoons grated rind

Ingredients

Simple Syrup

Use Tortuga Plain Syrup or buy simple syrup at any liquor store back home. To make your own, combine 2 cups sugar and 1 cup water in a saucepan over medium heat. Stir until sugar is completely dissolved and bring to a boil. Reduce heat and simmer for about 10 minutes, stirring constantly until the mixture resembles light syrup. Remove from heat and cool completely. Store in a sealed container at room temperature.

Sour mix (or Sweet & Sour Mix)

Use commercial bottled Sour mix, available at most liquor stores or make your own.

12 ounces fresh lime or lemon juice, or half of each
18 ounces water
1/4 cup sugar

Combine all ingredients in a blender and blend until sugar is dissolved. Store in a covered container in the refrigerator for up to a week. You can also mix one part simple syrup to one part lemon or lime. Adjust the ratio of syrup to juice to get the tartness you want. If you want to create frothy drinks, add two raw egg whites per quart of mix - because of possible salmonella risk, I don't condone using raw eggs in anything.

Cream of Coconut, Coconut water and Coconut Milk

Cream of coconut, sometimes called coconut cream, refers to Coco Lopez and similar thick, sweetened canned coconut mixes. It is not the same as fresh coconut water or canned coconut milk. These three ingredients have very different flavors and are not interchangeable. Cream of coconut is rich and sweet, the key ingredient in Pina Coladas and most tropical rum concoctions. Coconut water is the clear, salty-slightly sweet liquid from a fresh coconut. Both are delicious when mixed with rum. Coconut milk is coconut water and fresh water that has been mixed with fresh grated coconut and strained, much richer than plain coconut water, and used primarily in cooking.

Orgeat syrup

Orgeat is a non-alcoholic almond flavored syrup unfamiliar to most people today, even though it is still used in many exotic drinks like Mai Tais. Originally, it was made from barley but is now made from almonds, sugar and orange flower water. You can find almond syrup in liquor stores and in many supermarkets, in the coffee and tea section.

Orange liqueurs

Orange-flavored liqueurs are a common ingredient in many exotic drinks and should not be confused with orange-flavored liquors including vodka, gin or even rum. Triple Sec, Curacao (regardless of color-blue, green, orange or clear), Cointreau and Grand Marnier are the most popular orange-flavored liqueurs. However, they vary in alcohol content, so be aware of that when substituting in any recipe:

Triple Sec..46 proof
Curacao ....60 proof
Grand Marnier ....79 proof
Cointreau ....80 proof

Bitters

The bitters referred to throughout this book is Trinidad's **Angostura Aromatic Bitters**, a wonderful secret ingredient in many Caribbean drink and food recipes. Made from gentian and other herbs, bitter bark and roots, Angostura bitters has a surprising 45% alcohol content and a unique flavor no other substance can duplicate. The product is one of few honored by the seal of the **UK's prestigious Royal Warranty**. Angostura Bitters reputedly is a good tonic for a jittery stomach. "Club soda and bitters" on ice in a tall glass is the long-time drink of choice of islanders "on the wagon" or recovering from a grisly hangover.

Pimento Dram and Pimento Liqueur

Pimento dram is a traditional homemade Jamaican liqueur made from allspice berries steeped in white rum. It keeps for years and improves with age. You'll find a recipe for pimento dram in **Rum Fête** under **Old Time Caribbean Favorites**. It is not the same as pimento liqueur, a 60 proof/ 30% alcohol spirits made in Jamaica. This unusual spiced liqueur is very smooth and sweet and makes an interesting substitute for brandy, either straight or in mixed drinks, or in many recipes.

Falernum

Another old Caribbean, Falernum is a sweet liqueur that originated in 18th Century Barbados from a secret recipe blending cane syrup, lime juice, almond, ginger and other spices. It is used to flavor rum drinks and enhance the flavor of fresh fruit salad. There is no substitute for it and many Caribbean folk lament its obscure status today. You can find it at better liquor stores outside the Caribbean.

How to Mix the Perfect Island Drink

● If using a shaker, always put the ice in the shaker first and liquor last. The ice properly chills ingredients and reduces the risk of dilution.

● Some drinks should be stirred with ice rather than shaken – Martinis especially – just enough to mix the ingredients, about 12 stirs. Do not allow ice to melt and dilute liquor mixture.

● Drinks containing soda or carbonated beverages should be stirred just slightly, if necessary, to retain the fizz.

● Drinks that combine cream, fruits juices and eggs should be mixed in a shaker or blender to mix ingredients thoroughly.

● Use a blender to mix frozen drinks or drinks containing fresh fruit, liquor, juices, ice cream and ice to blend smoothly or turn into slush.

● A "Float" means creating separate layer of liquor and this is the last ingredient added to the mixed drink. To do this, hold a teaspoon or demitasse spoon over the glass containing the mixed drink and pour the suggested amount of liquor slowly over it so it trickles on top of the liquid.

● Frosting a glass or mug is easy. Simply dip in water and then put in the freezer for 30 minutes or more.

● To salt a glass or coat it with fine sugar, rub the edge of the rim with fresh lime wedge and then turn upside down in a saucer filled with a layer of coarse salt or superfine sugar. Don't try to sprinkle either directly onto the glass-it won't stick.

● "Muddling" simply means mashing ingredients, such as mint leaves, in the bottom of a glass, usually with sugar. There actually is a bartender's tool made of wood called a muddler, and you can use a bar spoon with a muddler on the end. These won't scratch your glassware. If you don't care about that, then use the back of a regular teaspoon.

The Responsible Rum Drinker

The recipes in this section are presented to help you discover the pleasures of rum and exciting new ways to enjoy it. Rum mixes smoothly with many things – but not scuba diving or driving a car, boat or personal watercraft.

Please be a responsible bartender to your guests and a sensible drinker yourself. Exercise good judgment and common sense whenever consuming rum or any kind of spirits. Whether back home or here in the islands, always appoint a designated driver, on land or sea, when enjoying any drink recipes in this book. And for the sake of your companions, know your saturation point. The only thing worse than cheap rum in a big glass is a loud drunk with a bad attitude.

Rum Fête: A 350-year Celebration of Rum Drink Recipes

Rum is the elixir of tropical romance – no other drink evokes the Caribbean's sensuous pleasures so spontaneously. Rum adds magic to any island vacation, sipped in seductive concoctions like Pina Coladas that conjure illusions of Paradise Found. Rum has also been a favorite party starter for more than 300 years. It has spiked some of history's most famous punch bowls and sparked a spirit of festivity- and in some cases, rebellion-since the 17th century.

What do you call such a multi-century bar menu? Is it a flow, a distillation, a swizzle or an infusion?

How about **Rum Fête**, an old Caribbean word for a spirited celebration, the party that just won't end. Rum's versatile pleasures are now being rediscovered and celebrated around the world. Today there are more exciting and exotic cocktails made with rum than any other spirits and new ones being invented every day. Polish your shot glass, tune up your blender and catch Rum Fever with this collection of Old and New World drink recipes.

Signature Tortuga Cocktails

The Cayman Mama
Here is the most popular Tortuga Cocktail, which is also Grand Cayman's original Hurricane-style beach drink.

1-1/2 ounces Tortuga Gold Rum	1 ounce Tortuga Coconut Rum
2 -1/2 ounces orange juice	2-1/2 ounces pineapple juice
Splash Tortuga Strawberry syrup	

Combine all and shake well. Pour into a chilled hurricane glass over cracked ice and garnish with cherry and slices of lime and orange.

Cayman Papa
This delicious drink almost upstages the Mama's place on the bar menu.

1-1/2 ounces Tortuga Gold Rum   3 ounces mango nectar
2 ounces orange juice   1 ounce Amaretto

Combine rum and fruit juices in a cocktail shaker and shake well. Pour into a tall glass over ice. Float the Amaretto on top.

Tortuga Pina Colada
2 ounces Tortuga Coconut Rum   1 ounce Cream of Coconut
4 ounces pineapple juice

Combine all ingredients in a cocktail shaker with cracked ice and shake well. Pour into a cocktail glass and garnish with pineapple chunk and cherry.

Cayman Sunset
2 ounces Tortuga Gold Rum   2 ounces orange juice
2 ounces pineapple juice   1 teaspoon Tortuga Strawberry syrup or
grenadine

Combine the rum and fruit juices in a glass and stir. Add several ice cubes, and then float the syrup or grenadine on top. It will look just like a famous Cayman sunset!

Tortuga Rum Punch
Tortuga's **Caribbean Rum Punch Mix** is a non-alcoholic blend of mango, orange and pineapple juices, available in 19-ounce cans at all Tortuga outlets. This mix makes perfect rum punch every time. You can vary this recipe by using different Tortuga Rums.

4 ounces Tortuga Caribbean Rum Punch Mix   1-1/2 ounces Tortuga Gold Rum
Squeeze of fresh lime juice   Dash Angostura Bitters

Combine and shake well with cracked ice and pour into a glass. Sprinkle top with nutmeg if desired.

Party-size Tortuga Rum Punch
This recipe makes a gallon of punch.

6 cans Tortuga Caribbean Rum Punch Mix   Juice of 3 fresh limes
1 -750 ml (26 ounce) bottle Tortuga Gold Rum
2 teaspoons Angostura Bitters or 2 teaspoons pimento liqueur

Mix all ingredients in a sealable plastic gallon container and shake well. Pour over ice into individual glasses or a punch bowl.

Tortuga Bloody Mary
4 ounces tomato juice or V-8   1-1/2 ounces Tortuga Light Rum
1/2 ounce sherry   1 teaspoon Tortuga Steak Sauce
1/2 teaspoon seasoned salt   1/2 teaspoon Worcestershire sauce
1/8 teaspoon black pepper   Juice of half key lime
1/2 teaspoon Tortuga Hell-Fire Hot Pepper sauce

Pour all ingredients into cocktail shaker and shake well. Pour over ice into a tall collins glass and serve. Garnish with a cherry tomato, olive and slice of lime on a skewer.

Tortuga Champagne Cocktail

1/2 ounce Tortuga Rum Liqueur
Chilled dry champagne
2 dashes Angostura Bitters
1/2 teaspoon simple syrup
2 dashes Chartreuse

Pour the rum liqueur and syrup into a chilled champagne glass and fill almost to the top with the chilled champagne. Add the bitters and chartreuse and swirl -do not stir.

Tortuga Black Russian

1 ounce Tortuga Coffee Liqueur, Tia Maria or Kahlua
2 ounces Tortuga Light Rum

Mix together and stir. Add ice as desired. Serves one.

Tortuga White Russian

1 ounce Tortuga Coffee Liqueur
2 ounces Half and Half or light cream
2 ounces Tortuga Light Rum

Mix together and stir. Add ice as desired. Serves one.

Tortuga Connoisseur

For the rum drinker who really appreciates the finest!

2 ounces Tortuga Premium 12- Year Old Rum Ice (optional)

Pour the rum over ice or serve straight in a brandy snifter and sip slowly. Repeat.

Tortuga Caribbean Iced Coffee

1 ounce Tortuga Dark Rum
2 tablespoons half and half
4 ounces cold brewed Tortuga Rum Flavored Coffee
1 ounce Tortuga Coffee Liqueur or Tia Maria

Combine all ingredients in a cocktail shaker and shake well. Pour into a tall glass filled with crushed ice and garnish with a sprinkle of ground cinnamon.

Traditional Caribbean Favorites, Classic Rum Cocktails, and Exotic Tropical Drinks

The New World's first rum drinkers nipped their crude rum "neat," or straight. The earliest mixed drinks were simple combinations of rum, fresh fruit juices and sugar in the West Indies, and rum, honey and water – even maple sugar – in colonial New England.

The origin of the word "cocktail", however, is unknown, but it did not originate in the Caribbean. One story traces it to a late 18th century New Orleans apothecary shop, where a Msr. A.A. Peychaud concocted a tonic he called "bitters." He served ailing customers a curative potion of cognac and bitters in an eggcup-which is *coquetier* in French. Understandably, that may have slurred by English-speaking patients to sound like "cocktail."The term "cock tail" first appeared in May 1806, in the *Balance and Columbian Repository*, a local periodical printed in Hudson, New York. The editor defined this strange new idea with an equally strange description: "a stimulating liquor, composed of spirits of any kind, sugar, water and bitters. It is vulgarly called bitter sling and is supposed to be an excellent engineering potion."

Dozens of cock-tall-tales tried to explain the word. The most logical may be a colonial colloquialism, "cocked tail" which meant a horse displaying high spirits. Cocktails were confined to that 1806 recipe until around 1880, when the concept of the cocktail began to change dramatically.

In 1809 Washington Irving, author of *The Legend of Sleepy Hollow*, claimed in *The History of New York* that the Dutch, not the English, "lay claim to be the first inventors of the recondite beverages, cock-tail, stone-fence and sherry cobbler."

During the 1800's grain whiskeys replaced rum in the US as the favorite tipple. But south in the tropics, rum remained the most desirable drink. The arrival of ice in the late 19th century introduced a new age of cocktails, which grow more rococo each decade.

A milestone in "modern" rum mixology took place in the late 1890's in Cuba with the creation of the **daiquiri**, the oldest enduring chilled rum and fruit cocktail and a favorite for over a century. The daiquiri has evolved into many varieties, frozen and straight up, using every tropical fruit juice imaginable – from lychees and mangos to soursop and starfruit.

By the start of the 1900's, rum re- emerged as a socially acceptable, even preferred cocktail ingredient. It became the drink of choice of celebrities in the 1920's, when Havana was in its heydey as the rum and cocktail capital of the western world and Prohibition Era playground. Daiquiris, rickeys, swizzles and rum on the rocks tempted sophisticated palates to flout Prohibition at speakeasies throughout America.

Many of the original "exotic tropical" rum drinks were created far from the sultry Caribbean, often presented as "traditional Polynesian" concoctions. The Zombie and Suffering Bastard originated not in the South Seas or Hawaii – or the Caribbean – but in the mid-1930's at a restaurant called Don the Beachcomber in Hollywood, California. Both of those drinks, according to legend, were created by the owner as hangover remedies for patrons...who felt like the drinks' names not only when they arrived, but even more so after a few of these. Others, like the Mai Tai, are credited to Trader Vic's, another famous Oakland, California bar, and date back to the mid-1940's.

Today, rum's popularity is growing as fast as the variety of flavored rums and exotic new concoctions including them. But many of the best drinks are the oldest and simplest – and some even date back centuries. Those recipes introduce the next section.

The Rum Shop: Old-Time Caribbean Favorites

Rum Neat
This may be the oldest form of rum drinking, as references to "taking rum neat," or straight without water, date back to accounts written in the early 17th century. Later, it referred to three or four fingers of rum followed by a swallow of cold water. In many parts of the Caribbean, this is still considered a working man's relaxer after a hard day.

3 ounces Tortuga Gold Rum   Cold water

Grog
In 1740, when the Royal Navy realized it was about to sink under a rum fog of stupefied crew, Admiral Edward Vernon ordered sailors' daily half-pint rum rations to be diluted four-to- one with water. He also encouraged ships' pursers ("pussers") to add sugar and

limes to the potion to make it more drinkable. Vernon earned the nickname "old Grogram, for the shabby woolen cloak he wore in the tropics, and his unpopular watered down rum was dubbed "grog." Strictly speaking, the Royal Navy may have invented the first mixed rum drink.

Half pint (8 ounces) Tortuga Dark Rum   1 tablespoon sugar
Juice of two fresh limes (2 tablespoons)   1 quart water

Mix all ingredients. Divide in half and drink one ration between 10 a.m. and noon and the second between 4 p.m. and 6 p.m. Do this every day, preferably while at sea.

Orange Shrub

Another colonial drink, reputedly a favorite of Benjamin Franklin. Obviously, this recipe serves more than one.

2 quarts fresh orange juice   2 pounds sugar
1 gallon Tortuga Dark Rum

In a 2-gallon container, combine the sugar and orange juice and stir until sugar is completely dissolved. Add the rum and stir well for several minutes. Cover and let stand at room temperature for a month. Decant with a funnel into smaller bottles and enjoy.

Yard of Flannel

A popular 18th century winter drink believed to have been invented in Boston. It served one.

1 quart ale   4 eggs
4 tablespoons sugar   1 teaspoon grated ginger
1/2 cup dark rum

In a small bowl, beat together the eggs and sugar until smooth, then blend in the ginger and rum. Pour into a heat-proof pitcher. In a medium saucepan, heat the ale until almost boiling. Pour the hot ale , a little at a time, into the egg mixture, stirring rapidly so it doesn't curdle. Pour the mixtures back and forth until it becomes smooth and creamy.

Rum and Coconut Water

Sometime between Columbus and rum, coconut arrived in the Caribbean. This may be the original Caribbean cocktail-and it's still one of the best. This is the perfect island refresher, a traditional "native" drink. Shake the coconut first and listen for the delicious fresh water sloshing around inside.

One green (jelly) coconut per person, preferably chilled
2 ounces Tortuga Light Rum per coconut

Using a machete, carefully remove the top of the coconut to open a 2-inch hole, without spilling the coconut water inside. Take a healthy sip of the fresh coconut water and then add the rum. Swirl around to mix and drink with a straw. When finished, use the machete to cut a larger hole and use a piece of the shell to scoop out the rum-soaked jelly inside. A drink and snack all in one! You can keep a plastic jug of coconut water (NOT coconut milk!) in the refrigerator for up to a week and mix equal parts chilled coconut water and rum and serve over ice.

Rum & Coconut Milk

2 ounces Tortuga Light Rum   1/2 ounce cane syrup or simple syrup
4 ounces coconut milk (not cream)   1/8 teaspoon vanilla

1/2 cup crushed ice   grated nutmeg

Combine all ingredients in a cocktail shaker and shake well. Pour into tall glass and top with grated nutmeg. Serves 1.

Traditional Caribbean Rum Punch

This recipe, without ice of course, dates to 18th century sugar plantations of Barbados and Jamaica and was easily remembered by this rhyme: "One of sour, two of sweet, three of strong and four of weak". This was later amended to include "five drops of bitters and nutmeg spice, serve well-chilled with lots of ice" Translated, this means:

1 ounce fresh lime juice	3 ounces Tortuga Dark Rum
2 ounces Tortuga plain syrup or simple syrup	4 ounces water
Dash of bitters	Grated nutmeg

Combine all ingredients except nutmeg in a shaker with cracked ice. Shake well and serve immediately. Sprinkle fresh grated nutmeg over top of each glass and garnish with fresh pineapple, mango, or lime wedge. Makes one drink.

Planter's Punch (19th Century)

Myer's Rum Distillery opened in Jamaica in 1879, founded by Fred L. Myers. This recipe is attributed to Mr. Myers, and it became a popular drink at Kelly's Bar at the old sugar wharf in Kingston. It remains a popular version today.

1-3/4 ounces Tortuga Dark Rum	3 ounces fresh orange juice
Juice of half a lime	1 teaspoon grenadine
Two dashes Angostura bitters	1 teaspoon superfine sugar

Combine all ingredients in a cocktail shaker and shake well to be sure sugar is dissolved. Pour into a Collins glass filled with cracked ice.

Planter's Punch (20th Century)

Today every bartender in the Caribbean has his own version of this traditional drink. In some parts of the Eastern Caribbean, Planter's Punch is considered the ultimate test of a bartender's talent, a sophisticated, complex and potent drink with nine ingredients. Bartenders jealously guard their recipes and will reveal only that fresh fruit juices is a must and rum is the only liquor used.

1 ounce Tortuga 151 Rum	1-1/2 ounces Tortuga Dark Rum
1 ounce Tortuga Light Rum	1 teaspoon Falernum
1/2 teaspoon Tortuga Strawberry Syrup or grenadine	
Juice of one fresh key lime	3 ounces fresh orange juice
1 ounce fresh pineapple juice	Dash Angostura Bitters

Add cracked ice to a cocktail shaker and pour in all remaining ingredients. Shake for 30 seconds and pour into tall chilled glass. Garnish with a skewer with orange slice, and cherry.

Ginger Beer

Although now widely available in stores, homemade ginger beer is still a traditional favorite.

4 quarts water	1/2 cup lime juice
1 ounce ginger root, grated	1-ounce cake yeast
3 cups sugar	

Grate the ginger into a 6-quart saucepan and add the water, lime juice and 2 cups sugar. Bring to a boil and simmer for 30 minutes. Remove from heat and cool to room temperature. When cool, combine the yeast with remaining 1 cup sugar and 1/2 cup warm water and blend well to make a paste. Stir in the yeast mixture and then pour into a large glass container and cover. Let the mixture ferment for three days. When ready, strain the mixture and decant to glass bottles or jars and then refrigerate. Serve cold.

Goat Hair

You can't go more native than this traditional drink from Barbados-but you must use real cane juice (called *guarapo* in Cuban and Latin markets) and fresh lime. It is sold at the Farmer's market in Grand Cayman and common throughout much of the Caribbean. You can occasionally find it in North American health food or Caribbean specialty stores.

4 ounces Tortuga Gold Rum
Juice of one lime (2-3 tablespoons)
2 cups cane juice
grated nutmeg

Mix the sugar cane juice, lime juice and rum. Pour into glasses and top with grated nutmeg. The traditional recipe does not include ice. Makes 2 drinks.

Carrot Drink

This is an old, but very popular country drink in Jamaica, with just a touch of rum to keep it healthy.

1-11-ounce can carrot juice
2 cups water
1/2 teaspoon vanilla flavoring or extract
2 cups condensed milk
1/2 teaspoon nutmeg
2 ounces Tortuga 151 Rum or Wray & Nephew white overproof rum

Combine all ingredients and blend well. Serve over crushed ice. This recipe should serve four.

Corn and Oil

An old, traditional men's rum shop favorite from Barbados, which is rumored to have more than 1000 rum shops today.

1-1/2 ounces Tortuga Dark Rum
1-1/2 ounces Falernum

Pour both ingredients into a glass and stir lightly. Usually drunk straight, but ice improves the flavor.

Peanut Punch

Long before Mudslides were invented, this rich concoction was downed as a healthy, "energy drink" in many Caribbean islands. Keep this bottle away from children!

1/2 cup creamy-style peanut butter
1 -14 ounce can sweetened condensed milk
1-1/4 cups (10 ounces) Tortuga Dark Rum
2 cups water
1 cup evaporated milk
dash nutmeg

Put all ingredients in blender and blend until smooth. Pour into a bottle or plastic container and seal. Refrigerate until well chilled and shake well before serving. Serve over ice.

Cream Punch (Ponche Crema)

This traditional holiday drink is more popular in the Eastern Caribbean, where it is also considered a "health drink", in spite of the use of raw eggs.

6 eggs	Grated peel of one lime
2-14-ounce cans evaporated milk	1 14-ounce can sweetened condensed milk
1 tablespoon Angostura bitters	1 teaspoon vanilla extract
16 ounces (1 pint) Tortuga Gold Rum	Grated nutmeg

Beat eggs with lime peel until thick, then remove peel. Add both kinds of milk, blending thoroughly. Add rum and bitters, stirring well. Pour into sealable container and refrigerate overnight. Serve over ice with a sprinkle of nutmeg on top

Ponche Crema, Healthy Version

This recipe from St. Croix, USVI cooks the egg and milk punch, eliminating the health risk of raw eggs. Beware, however: this "healthy" version really packs a punch.

6 large eggs, beaten	6 egg yolks, beaten
3 cups condensed milk	1-1/3 cups evaporated milk
1 tablespoon vanilla extract	3-1/2 cups Tortuga Gold Rum
2 teaspoons nutmeg	

In a the top part of a double boiler, combine the eggs, egg yolks and milks and beat with a rotary beater until smooth. Place the pan into the double boiler over medium high heat (the water should be at a low boil but not touch the upper pan) and cook, stirring constantly, for 15 minutes, until mixture is slightly thickened. Stir in the vanilla and pour into a glass container and chill for at least two hours, then stir in the rum and nutmeg. This should serve six.

Soursop Drink

How do you describe a soursop to someone who's never seen one? It's one of the strangest Caribbean fruits, originally from Peru and Ecuador, and a favorite of the Arawak, Ciboney and Carib Indians. It looks like a 2- 3-pound green strawberry covered with soft thorns but inside is creamy white flesh covering dozens of large seeds. It tastes like margarita mix. Many West Indians believe soursop calms the nerves.

2 cups soursop pulp, seeds removed	2 tablespoons sweetened condensed milk
1 cup milk	4 ounces Tortuga Gold Rum
2 tablespoons fresh lime juice	1/2 teaspoon fresh grated ginger
3 dashes Angostura Bitters	Grated nutmeg
Cracked ice	

In a blender, combine the soursop pulp with the condensed milk, milk, lime juice and ginger in a blender and blend 30 seconds, then add rum and bitters and blend until smooth. Pour over ice in tall glasses. Serves 4.

Pimento Dram

In Jamaica a jug of pimento dram is kept in reserve for special occasions. It is a traditional drink, often given as a holiday gift. Pimento, of course, is Jamaican allspice, not sweet red peppers as many North Americans think. This makes about a gallon of dram.

1 quart white overproof rum	1 cup ripe green allspice berries
1-3/4 cups fresh lime juice	10 cinnamon sticks, broken into smaller pieces
8 cups granulated sugar	2 quarts water

Combine allspice, rum and lime juice in a sealable container and let stand at room temperature for four days. Break cinnamon sticks into small pieces. In a 5-quart Dutch oven or large pot, bring the water to a boil and add cinnamon and boil for 10 minutes. Remove from heat and use a slotted spoon to strain out the cinnamon pieces. Return the water to a boil, add the sugar and continue boiling for about 20 minutes or until mixture has the consistency of light syrup. Remove from heat and cool.

Strain the rum mixture to remove the allspice berries and add the rum-lime mixture to the syrup. Stir until well mixed. Pour the pimento dram into glass bottles or a sealable gallon container and let stand at room temperature for a week before sampling. Keeps indefinitely.

Steel Bottom

Years ago I was served the mother of all Boilermakers at a long-gone roadside Montego Bay rum shop. Instead of shots of liquor followed by a swig of beer, this was a single concoction. I'm not sure if it was a real drink, or made up especially for me that afternoon for having the nerve to crash this local fisherman's bar. Or what the name meant, or if I completely misunderstood the barman's cheery but very country Jamaican patois. Nevertheless, I wanted to remember that mystery elixir and scribbled down the recipe, as I understood it, on a piece of paper that managed to survive many years into these pages. Twenty years later, I asked a Jamaican friend and prominent businesswoman if she had ever heard of such an ungodly concoction and she laughed. "Of course! Steel Bottom. It smooth but it knock you down! Soon you don't feel your bottom or your feet! I love them!"

3 shots of J. Wray & Nephew white overproof rum (about 5 ounces!)
1 cold bottle of Red Stripe

or modified significantly for less sturdy nervous systems:
2 ounces Tortuga 151 Rum   1 cold 12-ounce bottle Red Stripe
Combine all ingredients and stir well in a container big enough to hold it. Pour over ice into a tall glass.

Port Maria

An old Jamaican cocktail, named for one of the most romantic areas on Jamaica's north coast. Rum lore claims it was a favorite sunset sip of Noel Coward and his celebrity guests who congregated at FireFly, his splendid garden aerie overlooking the Caribbean.

1-1/2 ounces Tortuga Light Rum   1 tablespoon pineapple juice
2 teaspoons lemon juice   1 teaspoon Falernum
Combine all ingredients in a cocktail shaker with ice cubes and shake well. Strain into a cordial glass and add ice as desired. Garnish with grated nutmeg.

Port Antonio

Another old favorite from Jamaica's north coast.

1 ounce Tortuga Gold Rum   1/2 ounce Tortuga Dark Rum
1/2 ounce fresh lime juice   1 teaspoon Falernum
1/2 ounce Tortuga Coffee Liqueur or Tia Maria
Add three or four ice cubes to a cocktail shaker, then pour in all ingredients. Shake well and strain into a highball glass and fill with ice. Garnish with a slice of lime.

Vanilla Rum Cup

This is not the same as Rum Vanilla used in baking, but an interesting old time Caribbean drink, whose creation is attributed to English planters in Barbados and Jamaica.

1 750 ml. bottle Tortuga Dark Rum   Thin lime slices
6 vanilla beans, split lengthwise   Falernum

Add the vanilla beans to the rum and seal. Chill the bottle in the refrigerator for a week before using. For each drink, fill a wine glass (4-ounce size) with crushed ice and add 1 teaspoon Falernum, a slice of lime and fill with vanilla rum (about 2 ounces) Store the vanilla rum in the refrigerator.

Beer Glow

While this old Jamaican Rum Shop drink may seem like an odd concoction, don't knock it until you've tried it. But don't try too many unless you have a hammock planned for the rest of the day. I was introduced to it at a marlin tournament in Falmouth in 1984 and scribbled the recipe on a napkin that survived all these years.

1 tin pineapple juice (6-ounce can)   3 jiggers rum (4-1/2 ounces Tortuga Gold Rum)
1 bottle Red Stripe (12 ounces)   Pinch of nutmeg and cinnamon

Combine all ingredients and mix well. Pour over ice. (I assumed this was for two drinks, but perhaps not.)

Doctor Bird

From Jamaica, this old cocktail is named after the Doctorbird, the country's national bird, an iridescent green streamer-tailed hummingbird that loves red hibiscus nectar.

1-1/2 ounces Tortuga Light Rum   1 teaspoon half and half or light cream
1 teaspoon Tortuga Wildflower Honey   1/2 cup cracked ice
Two dashes Tortuga Strawberry syrup or Grenadine

Combine all ingredients in a cocktail shaker and shake well. Strain into a chilled champagne glass and garnish with a fresh hibiscus flower.

Rum & Ginger Beer

This is a surprisingly light and refreshing cooler.

2 ounces Tortuga Light Rum   1 12-ounce bottle ginger beer
Lime wedge

Pour the rum over cracked ice in a tall glass and add the ginger beer. Stir and add a squeeze of lime if desired.

Brown Cow

Another old and very simple Jamaican favorite. In Jamaica, this is what you ask for instead of Kahlua and cream.

2 ounces evaporated milk or cream   2 ounces Tia Maria or Tortuga Coffee Liqueur

Combine ingredients in cocktail shaker with 1/2 cup crushed ice and shake until foamy. Pour into glass and serve with a straw.

Coconut Rum & Pineapple Juice

The impatient islander's Pina Colada, now a Caribbean favorite.

2 ounces Tortuga Coconut Rum   4 ounces pineapple juice

Pour rum and pineapple juice over ice into a glass and stir if desired.

Stormy Weather

I discovered this traditional Montserrat drink during a visit 20 years ago, long before Mount Soufriere ravaged that Emerald Isle West. I have never forgotten its startling effects, but not even this sly drink could convince me to betray my favorite creatures and eat Mountain Chicken, Montserrat's national dish – fried giant frogs' legs.

3 ounces Tortuga Dark Rum   6 ounces ginger beer
Lime wedge   Dash of Angostura Bitters

Pour the rum over ice in a tall glass and top with ginger beer, bitters and squeeze of fresh lime juice. Stir lightly.

Rum'N Ting

Ting is Jamaica's refreshing grapefruit soda and nothing the USA has ever produced comes close to this tangy, refreshing drink. Just add rum for an easy, delicious cocktail.

2 ounces Tortuga Gold Rum   1 bottle Ting

Pour the rum over ice cubes in a tall glass and top with Ting. Refill as needed.

Shandy

I was first offered this strange concoction after my first bewildering cricket match on Grand Cayman. I found the drink equally unfathomable. I've never known many native West Indians who actually enjoy this very English thirst quencher, but it remains popular among UK expats today.

1 bottle ginger beer (12 ounces)   Dash or two Angostura Bitters
1 bottle Red Stripe (or other Caribbean light lager)

Take two chilled mugs or glasses and pour half ginger beer and half Red Stripe in each. Add a dash or two of Bitters. Serve immediately (serves 2).

Black and Tan, Jamaica-style

This 100% Jamaican concoction upstages the UK version and could quickly subdue an unruly football crowd.

1 bottle chilled Red Stripe   1 bottle Dragon Stout

Fill a 10-ounce glass or mug half with Red Stripe and half with Dragon stout. Swirl gently to mix. Repeat as necessary.

Salud, Cuba!

Long before Fidel Castro or any trade embargo, Cuba exported many superb cocktail recipes along with fine rum to the US.

Daiquiri

This classic drink with Cuban roots was supposedly created in 1896 by an American mining engineer, Jennings Cox, supervisor of a group of copper mines in Eastern Cuba's Oriente province, outside the town of Daiquiri. One steamy summer day, a group of important visitors arrived unannounced at the site and Cox had only Cuban rum to offer. According to Rum Lore, he was afraid the potent local rum would offend his guests' palates, so he added fresh lime juice and sugar and chilled the concoction-it was an instant hit. He named this new drink after the nearby town and his simple cocktail remains a favorite today.

2 ounces Tortuga light rum	1 tablespoon fresh lime juice
1 teaspoon superfine or powdered sugar	1/4 cup cracked ice

Combine rum, lime juice and sugar with cracked ice in a shaker and shake well. Strain into a chilled champagne or margarita glass. This drink needs no garnish.

Frozen Daiquiri

A mind-fogging variety of frozen daiquiris became the rage beginning in the 1970's and are still popular today. Exotic frozen daiquiris are simple to make. Just add fresh or frozen fruit or juices to this basic recipe and blend away – a ripe banana, a third cup diced mango or fresh lychees or a half-cup of seedless soursop pulp.

1-1/2 ounces Tortuga Light Rum	1-1/2 ounces Tortuga Dark Rum
1 tablespoon fresh lime juice	2 teaspoons simple syrup or powdered sugar
1 cup crushed ice	

Combine all ingredients in a blender and blend until slushy. Pour into a chilled champagne or margarita glass and serve with a short straw.

Coconut Daiquiri

1-1/2 ounces Tortuga Dark Rum	1 ounce Coco Lopez cream of coconut
1 ounce fresh lime juice	1/2 cup crushed ice

Combine all ingredients in a blender and blend until smooth.

Banana Daiquiri

2 ounces Tortuga Light Rum	1/2 ounce Triple Sec
1/2 large ripe banana, sliced	1 ounce lime juice
2 teaspoons simple syrup	1/2 cup crushed ice

Combine all ingredients in a blender and blend at low 5 seconds then at high speed until smooth. Serve with a straw.

Mango Daiquiri

2-1/2 ounces Tortuga Light Rum	1 ounce Triple Sec
1 cup ripe mango, diced	1 tablespoon fresh lime juice
2 teaspoons simple syrup	1-1/2 cups crushed ice

Combine all ingredients in a blender and blend at high speed until slushy. Pour into chilled champagne glasses and serve with a straw.

Carambola Daiquiri

Here's one tropical drink your friends have probably never tried.

2 ounces Tortuga Light Rum	1 cup carambola (starfruit), seeded and
chopped	
2 teaspoons sugar	1/2 ounce Triple Sec
3/4 cup crushed ice	

Combine all ingredients in a blender and blend until slushy. Pour into a chilled glass and garnish with a Carambola "star" slice.

Strawberry Daiquiri

2 ounces Tortuga Light Rum	1/2 ounce Triple Sec

1/2 cup sliced fresh strawberries   1 tablespoon fresh lime juice
2 teaspoons simple syrup   1/2 cup crushed ice

Combine all ingredients in a blender and blend at low 5 seconds then at high speed until smooth. Serve with straw.

El Presidente

This popular Cuban cocktail was created decades ago at the El Presidente Hotel bar in Havana.

2 ounces Tortuga Light Rum   1/2 ounce dry vermouth
1/2 ounce lemon juice   1 tablespoon Curacao
1 dash grenadine

Combine all ingredients in a cocktail shaker with 1/4 cup cracked ice and shake well. Strain into chilled glass.

Cuba Libre

As its name suggests, this drink has political origins. It was allegedly created in 1900 by a band of Teddy Roosevelt's Rough Riders one hot August afternoon in a Havana Bar. They combined a new soft drink, "Coke" with rum and wedge of lime over ice and dedicated it to the cause they were fighting for.

2 ounces Tortuga Gold Rum   Lime wedge
Coke or Diet Coke

Put several ice cubes in a tall glass and pour rum over it. Squeeze lime over rum and drop the lime into glass. Add Coke to desired strength.

Mojito

This Cuban drink whose name means "little sauce" is believed to have been invented in the 1920's in Havana and remains popular today. It gained fame as the favorite refresher of Ernest Hemingway at a small Havana hangout called Bodequita del Medio. A true Mojito is made with yerbabuena, an herb widely used in Cuba, which is slightly more bitter than fresh mint.

2 ounces Tortuga Light Rum   1 teaspoon superfine sugar
6 yerbabuena leaves or 4 mint leaves   1 tablespoon fresh lime juice
3-4 ice cubes   Club soda

Put the sugar and yerbabuena or mint leaves in the bottom of a rocks glass and add the sugar and lime juice Muddle (crush with a spoon or bar muddler) this mixture until the mint leaves are crushed and sugar almost dissolved. Add the ice cubes, then the rum. Top with club soda to fill the glass or to desired strength. Stir lightly again.

Daiquiri Mulata

This is another classic Cuban cocktail – an unusual, but delicious, combination.

1-1/2 ounces Tortuga Gold Rum   1/2 ounce dark crème de cacao
1 tablespoon fresh lime juice   1 cup crushed ice

Combine all ingredients in a cocktail shaker and shake well. Strain into a martini or margarita glass. Or, combine all ingredients in a blender and mix until smooth. Serve in a chilled martini or champagne glass.

La Floridita Cocktail

Named after the famous Havana night spot of the 1920's where it was created.

1-1/2 ounces Tortuga Light Rum	3/4 ounce sweet vermouth
1/2 ounce white crème de cacao	1 tablespoon fresh lime juice
Dash grenadine	

Combine all ingredients in a cocktail shaker with 3-4 ice cubes and shake well. Pour into a chilled rocks glass.

Canchanchara

A traditional Cuban refresher from the country.

2 ounces Tortuga Light Rum	3/4 ounce Tortuga Wildflower Honey
1 ounce fresh lime juice	1-1/2 ounces club soda
Lime slice for garnish	

Combine the rum, honey and lime juice in a cocktail glass and stir to blend. Add several ice cubes and then the club soda. Stir lightly. Garnish with lime slice.

Mary Pickford

Believe it or not, this simple cocktail named after the silent screen star was a 1920's smash, allegedly created at the bar in the Hotel Sevilla in Havana. According to Rum Lore, popular Havana hotel bars created drinks and named them after American screen idols, pandering to-and delighting – tourists.

1-1/2 ounces Tortuga Light Rum	1 tablespoon fresh pineapple juice
3 drops grenadine	3 ice cubes

Combine all ingredients in a cocktail shaker and shake well. Pour into a cocktail glass and garnish with a maraschino cherry if desired

Hemingway Special/ Papa Dobles

This is another double-strength rum drink attributed to Hemingway -allegedly created by a bartender named Constante at La Floridita for his favorite customer. As the Papa Dobles, it became famous with tourists at Key West's famous Sloppy Joe's bar, another legendary Hemingway haunt.

3 ounces Tortuga Light Rum	2 tablespoons fresh lime juice
1 ounce fresh grapefruit juice	1/2 ounce maraschino cherry liqueur
1/2 cup crushed ice	

Combine all ingredients in a cocktail shaker and shake well. Pour into a frosted very tall glass. Makes one drink.

September Morn

The name is a mystery, but this cocktail was created at Havana's Hotel Inglaterra around 1920.

2 ounces Tortuga Light Rum	2 teaspoons fresh lime juice
1 teaspoon grenadine	1 egg white
1 teaspoon superfine sugar	1/2 cup crushed ice

Combine all ingredients in a cocktail shaker and shake well. Rub the rim of a frosted margarita or champagne glass with lime and dip in superfine sugar. Strain drink into the prepared glass.

Classic Rum Cocktails

Rum Bloody Mary

2 ounces Tortuga Light rum	4 ounces tomato juice or V-8
1 teaspoon Worcestershire sauce	Dash or two Tobasco Sauce
1/4 teaspoon celery salt	Ground black pepper to taste
1/2 teaspoon ground horseradish	Squeeze of fresh lime
Ice cubes	

Combine all ingredients in shaker and shake lightly. For extra flavor, rub the rim of the glass with fresh lime and dip into seasoned salt before pouring the drink. Garnish with lime wedge and celery stalk. Serves one.

Between the Sheets

When it was first created decades ago, this drink was considered too suggestive to order aloud. That seems funny today, considering some of the licentious concoctions printed on bar menus.

1 ounce Tortuga Light Rum	1 ounce Grand Marnier
1 ounce brandy	1 teaspoon fresh lemon juice

Combine all ingredients in a cocktail shaker with 3 or 4 ice cubes and shake well. Strain into a cocktail glass.

Columbus Cocktail

The origin of this 1930's classic rum cocktail isn't clear, but it is a very smooth and potent happy hour icebreaker.

2 ounces Tortuga Gold Rum	1 ounce apricot brandy
2 teaspoons fresh lime juice	1/2 cup crushed ice

Combine all ingredients in a cocktail shaker and shake well. Pour into a chilled rocks glass.

Rum Collins

3 ounces Tortuga Gold Rum	1 ounce fresh lime juice
2 teaspoons simple syrup	3 ice cubes
6 ounces club soda	

Combine the rum, lime juice and syrup in a 14 ounce Collins glass and stir well to mix. Add the ice cubes and fill the glass with club soda, stirring lightly. Garnish with a slice of lime.

Rum Fizz

1-1/2 ounces Tortuga Light rum	1/2 ounce cherry brandy
1 ounce sweet and sour mix	Chilled club soda

Combine rum, brandy and sour mix in a cocktail shaker and shake well. Pour into a collins glass filled with ice cubes and top with club soda.

Rum Flip

Once again, a caveat about raw eggs. Thousands enjoyed this for decades and lived to enjoy more.

4 ounces Tortuga Gold Rum	1 egg, lightly beaten
2 teaspoons superfine sugar or simple syrup	

2 dashes Angostura Bitters   1 cup crushed ice
Grated nutmeg

Combine the rum, egg, sugar or syrup and bitters in a cocktail shaker with ice and shake well. Strain into a chilled highball glass and top with grated nutmeg.

Rum Gimlet

2 ounces Tortuga Light Rum   1/2 ounce Roses Lime Juice
Thin slice of lime

Place an ice cube in a small champagne glass and pour in the rum and Roses Lime Juice. Stir and garnish with a thin slice of lime floating on top.

Grasshopper

1 ounce créme de cacao   1 ounce green crème de menthe
3/4 ounce Tortuga Rum Cream Liqueur or half and half
1/2 cup cracked ice

Combine all ingredients in a cocktail shaker and shake well. Strain into martini or 4 ounce cocktail glass.

Harvey Rumbanger

Rum makes a much better version of the Harvey Wallbanger, a 1960's favorite.

1 ounce Tortuga Light Rum   1 ounce Tortuga Rum Cream Liqueur
1 ounce Galliano   4 ounces orange juice

Pour rum, Rum Cream Liqueur and orange juice into a collins glass over ice and stir. Float the Galliano on top. Garnish with orange slice.

Rumhattan

This is the classic Manhattan made with rum instead of whiskey.

2 ounces Tortuga Gold Rum   1 ounce sweet vermouth
Dash Angostura Bitters

Combine all ingredients in a cocktail shaker with cracked ice and shake well. Strain into 4 ounce cocktail glass and garnish with cherry. Variation: for a Dry Rumhattan, substitute 1 ounce dry vermouth.

Rum Margarita

1-1/2 ounces Tortuga Light Rum   1/2 ounce Triple Sec
1 ounce fresh lime juice   Additional lime juice
Coarse salt   Crushed ice

Rub edge of chilled cocktail glass with fresh lime and dip into salt to lightly coat rim. Combine rum, Triple Sec and 1 ounce lime juice in shaker with crushed ice and shake thoroughly until frothy. Strain into glass and serve at once. Makes one.

Rum Martini

Very dry and smooth on a sultry summer eve.

2 ounces Tortuga Light Rum   Drop or two of dry vermouth
Twist of fresh lime   Ice

Mix rum and vermouth in shaker with ice and shake lightly. Serve straight up or on the rocks with a twist of key lime.

Rum Gibson

2-1/2 ounces Tortuga Light Rum
Cocktail onion
1/2 ounce dry vermouth
Ice

Combine rum and vermouth in shaker with ice and shake lightly. Strain and serve straight up or on the rocks with a cocktail onion.

Mint Julep

This famous Kentucky drink probably found its way to the Caribbean along with satellite TV Derby parties-but even deeper south by the 1920's it already had a Cuban rival called the Mojito. Some southerners make this with straight bourbon, but this old recipe is still the best.

4 fresh mint leaves
1 ounce Tortuga Light Rum
Finely crushed ice
1 teaspoon simple syrup or superfine sugar
1 ounce bourbon

Put the mint leaves and syrup or sugar in the bottom of a cocktail glass and "muddle" or crush the leaves to release the oil. Add the ice, bourbon and rum. Stir again and garnish with a fresh mint sprig. Makes 1.

Rum Old Fashioned

2 ounces Tortuga Gold Rum
2 dashes Angostura Bitters
2 ounces club soda
1 teaspoon superfine sugar
2 ice cubes

Combine sugar and Bitters in 4 ounce old-fashioned glass and stir until dissolved. Add club soda, ice cubes and rum. Garnish with cherry and orange slice.

Rum Salty Dog

2 ounces Tortuga Light rum
Lime edge
Ice cubes
4 ounces fresh grapefruit juice
Salt

Rub the rim of a tall glass with the lime wedge and dip in coarse salt (Kosher salt is best). Add ice, rum and grapefruit juice and stir well. Serve with a swizzle stick.

Rum Sazerac

2 ounces Tortuga Light Rum
1 cube of sugar, soaked with 2 dashes Angostura Bitters
Ice water
1/2 ounce Pernod

Put the sugar cube and 3 or 4 ice cubes in an old fashioned glass or short cocktail glass and pour in the liquors. Stir gently, then top with ice water and stir again. Garnish with a twist of lemon.

Rum Screwdriver

This may seem like real no-brainer, but not everyone knows the recipe. It is not, as some veteran island barstool fixtures will claim, equal parts vodka or rum and Tang powder.

2 ounces Tortuga Gold Rum
6 ounce fresh orange juice
Pour rum over ice cubes in tall glass and add orange juice. That's it.

Rum Sidecar

1 ounce Brandy
2 tablespoons Cointreau
1 ounce Tortuga Light Rum
2 teaspoons fresh lime juice
Combine and shake with ice and strain into cocktail glass.

Rum Sour

2 ounces Tortuga Gold Rum
1 teaspoon orange juice
1 teaspoon Tortuga 151 Rum
2 teaspoons lemon juice
1 teaspoon simple syrup

Combine all ingredients in a cocktail shaker with ice cubes and shake well. Strain into a 6 ounce sour glass. Decorate with a 1/2 slice of lemon and a cherry.

Rum Stinger

1-1/2 ounces Tortuga Light Rum
3 ice cubes
1-1/2 ounces white crème de menthe

Combine ingredients in a cocktail shaker and shake well. Strain into a cocktail glass. Serves 1.

Rum Swizzle

2 ounces Tortuga Light rum
2 teaspoons simple syrup
Cracked ice
1 ounce fresh lime juice
Dash of Angostura Bitters
Chilled club soda or seltzer

Combine rum, lime juice, simple syrup, bitters and ice in cocktail shaker. Shake until frothy and pour immediately into tall glass and add chilled club soda. Serve with a swizzle stick, of course.

Tom & Jerry

Another old classic recipe and another caveat. If you are concerned about raw eggs posing a health risk, do not try this.

1-1/2 ounces Tortuga Dark Rum
1 teaspoon superfine sugar
1/3 cup hot milk
1 egg, separated
1-1/2 ounces brandy
Grated nutmeg

Warm an 8-ounce mug. Beat the egg yolk until thick and lemon-colored, and the egg white until stiff peaks form. Carefully fold these two together and whisk in the sugar. Pour the egg mixture into the mug, then add the rum and brandy. Fill with hot milk and top with a sprinkle of nutmeg.

The Beach Bar: Those Wonderful, Wild and Wicked Tropical Drinks

There are hundreds of exotic rum concoctions flowing from bars today, some with ingredients as outlandish as their names. Some were invented decades ago; others only appeared in the freewheeling, "anything goes" 1990's. The variety of exotic rum concoctions grows each year, with no end in sight, and no shame about the combination of ingredients involved. Some, like the unthinkably popular Long Island Ice Tea, seem downright undrinkable. Others are delicious but truly deadly. Once again, I urge discretion and caution when sampling these potions, especially when many kinds of liquor are involved. Hang up your keys and scuba gear until the rum bubbles are long gone from your bloodstream and brain cells.

Acapulco

This old recipe from the Mexican Riviera is a cross between a margarita and a fizz, and must be served in a well-chilled rocks glass.

1-3/4 ounce Tortuga Gold Rum

1 egg white

1/2 teaspoon simple syrup

1/4 ounce Triple Sec

1 tablespoon fresh lime juice

2 mint leaves for garnish

Combine all ingredients except mint leaves in a cocktail shaker with cracked ice and shake well. Strain into a chilled cocktail glass, add ice cubes to fill, and float the mint leaves on top.

Bacchanalian

Also called Purple Passion, this was a lethal concoction from the early 1960's.

2 ounces Tortuga Light Rum

1/2 ounce Yellow Chartreuse

1 ounce orange juice

3 ounces lemonade

1/2 ounce brandy

2 ounces red grape juice

1 tablespoon fresh lime juice

Pour all ingredients into a shaker and shake well. Pour over cracked ice into a tall glass.

Bahama Mama

An old popular drink from Nassau, where a float of Nassau Royale is often an interesting variation.

1 ounce Tortuga Dark Rum

1/2 ounce Tortuga 151 Rum

1/2 ounce lime juice

4 ounces pineapple juice

1 ounce Tortuga Coconut Rum

1/2 ounce Tortuga Coffee Liqueur or Kahlua

1 teaspoon simple syrup

Pour all ingredients into a shaker and shake well. Pour over cracked ice into a tall glass and garnish with pineapple wedge.

Blue Hawaiian

One of the original gaudy umbrella drinks, enjoying a big comeback today.

1/2 ounce Tortuga Dark Rum

1/2 ounce Blue Curacao

1 ounce Coco Lopez

1-1/2 ounces Tortuga Light Rum

3 ounces pineapple juice

1/2 cup cracked ice

Combine all ingredients in a blender and blend for 15 seconds. Pour into a chilled goblet or hurricane glass and garnish with a cherry and pineapple slice. Serve with a short straw.

Caribbean Breeze

1-1/2 ounces Tortuga Dark Rum

3 ounces pineapple juice

2 ounces cranberry juice

1/2 ounce crème de banana

1 teaspoon Rose's Lime Juice

1/2 cup crushed ice

Combine all ingredients in a cocktail shaker and shake well. Pour into a chilled collins glass and garnish with a skewer of banana and pineapple chunks.

Casablanca Cooler

2 ounces Tortuga Light Rum

4 ounces pineapple-orange juice

1 teaspoon grenadine

1/2 ounce coconut rum

1 ounce Coco Lopez coconut cream

1 cup crushed ice

Combine all ingredients except the grenadine in a blender and blend for 20 seconds. Pour into a chilled collins glass and float the grenadine on top. Garnish with a cherry and pineapple chunk.

Castro Cooler

This tropical bar drink was reputedly a favorite of El Presidente Fidel Castro, but its 1970's origin is American, not Cuban and that story is probably Key West bar mythology.

1-1/2 ounces Tortuga Gold Rum
1-1/2 ounces orange juice
2 teaspoons lime juice

3/4 ounce Calvados or apple brandy
1 tablespoon Rose's Lime Juice
1/2 cup crushed ice

Combine all ingredients in a cocktail shaker and shake well. Strain into a collins glass filled halfway with crushed ice. Garnish with a cherry and serve with a straw.

Fog Cutter

1-1/2 ounces Tortuga Light Rum
1/2 ounce brandy
3 tablespoons lemon juice
1 teaspoon sweet sherry

1/2 ounce gin
1-1/2 teaspoons Orgeat syrup
2 ounces fresh orange juice

Combine all ingredients except the sherry in cocktail shaker and shake well. Pour over ice into a tall collins glass. Float the sherry on top and serve.

Goombay Smash

Goombay is the spirited summer festival in the Bahamas. This drink has many variations, but this is believed to be the original recipe created around 1970. It is a deceptively simple and smooth drink whose name indicates caution!

2 ounces Tortuga Light Rum
4 ounces pineapple juice
1 teaspoon simple syrup

3/4 ounce Tortuga Coconut Rum
1 tablespoon lime juice
1/4 cup crushed ice

Combine all ingredients in a cocktail shaker and shake well. Pour into a non-breakable glass or cup and stay out of the midday sun while drinking.

Hurricane

This is similar to the famous party drink served in New Orleans' French Quarter.

1 ounce Tortuga Light Rum
1 ounce Tortuga 151 Rum
1 ounce pineapple juice
Two dashes Angostura Bitters

1 ounce Tortuga Dark Rum
4 ounces passion fruit juice
1/2 ounce fresh lime juice

Combine all ingredients in a cocktail shaker with cracked ice and shake well. Strain over ice into a hurricane glass. Garnish with pineapple wedge, cherry and straw.

Mai Tai

Another "headshrinking" tropical classic, one of the original exotic umbrella-garnished drinks. This is really a recipe for two drinks, but that advice is often ignored.

1 ounce Tortuga Light Rum
1-1/2 ounces Triple Sec
3 ounces lime or lemon juice

1-1/2 ounces Tortuga Dark Rum
1 ounce Orgeat or Almond-flavored Syrup
1/4 teaspoon ground ginger

Combine all ingredients in cocktail shaker and shake well. Pour over cracked ice into chilled tall glass. Garnish with pineapple slice and serve with straw.

Navy Grog

1-1/2 ounces Tortuga Gold Rum
1 ounce fresh orange juice

1 ounce Tortuga Dark Rum
1 ounce pineapple juice

1 ounce passion fruit nectar	1/2 ounce Falernum
1 ounce sweet and sour mix	1/2 cup cracked ice

Combine all ingredients in a cocktail shaker and shake well. Pour into a chilled highball glass and garnish with skewered pineapple chunk and orange slice.

Rum Runner

Rum running was a widespread sport during the Prohibition era from Nassau, Long Island to Nassau, Bahamas. Of course rum is legal today, but this infamous drink, whose creation is credited to Key West, probably should be outlawed. Consume with caution – this sneaky sweet little drink carries a wallop. This recipe is meant to serve two.

1 ounce Tortuga Dark Rum	1 ounce Tortuga Light Rum
1/2 ounce Tortuga 151 Rum	1-1/2 ounce banana liqueur (not rum!)
1 ounce blackberry brandy	1/2 ounce grenadine
1 ounce fresh orange juice	1-1/2 ounces fresh lime juice
1-1/2 cups crushed ice	

Combine all ingredients in blender and blend until smooth. Serve in a tall glass with lime wedge and straw.

Scorpion

1/2 ounce Tortuga Light Rum	1/2 ounce Tortuga Dark Rum
1/2 ounce brandy	1/2 ounce Orgeat syrup
1/2 ounce fresh lime juice	1 teaspoon simple syrup

Combine all ingredients in a cocktail shaker and shake once. Pour over ice into a 6-ounce wine glass or sour glass and garnish with umbrella, cherry and anything else you want.

Shark Bite

1-1/2 ounces Tortuga Dark Rum	3 ounces fresh orange juice
1 ounce Curacao	1/2 ounce sour mix
3/4 ounce Tortuga Strawberry Syrup or grenadine	
1/4 cup cracked ice	

Combine all ingredients in a blender and blend until smooth. Pour into a tall stemmed glass and serve with a straw.

Singapore Sling

It's amazing we survived college in the early 70's, when this party drink was downed like soda pop. If anyone out there knows the origin if its name, I'd like to hear your version.

1-1/2 ounces Tortuga Light Rum	3/4 ounce Tortuga Dark Rum
1/2 ounce Grand Marnier	1/2 ounce Amaretto
1/2 ounce cherry brandy	2 ounces pineapple juice
1 tablespoon fresh lemon juice	

Combine all ingredients in a cocktail shaker with ice cubes and shake until frothy, about 30 seconds. Strain into a wineglass or other long-stemmed glass filled with cracked ice. Garnish with pineapple slice and cherry.

Suffering Bastard

Another one of the original exotic tropical rum drinks, it may seem tame when compared with today's beach bar concoctions. But this simple drink packs a wallop.

2-1/2 ounces Tortuga Dark Rum	3/4 ounce Tortuga 151 rum
1/2 ounce apricot brandy	2 ounces pineapple juice

Juice of half lime

Combine all ingredients in a cocktail shaker with ice cubes and shake well. Pout into a tall collins glass with the ice. Serve with a straw.

Yellow Bird

There are many variations of this famous drink responsible for many romantic nights, but this Tortuga-ized version of a recipe from the old Kittina Hotel on Grand Turk is one of the best. Served only to pedestrians!

1-1/2 ounces Tortuga Light Rum	3/4 ounce banana liqueur
3/4 ounce Galliano	2 ounces pineapple juice
1 ounce orange juice	

Combine all ingredients in a cocktail shaker and shake well. Pour over ice cubes in rocks glass.

Zombie

1 ounce pineapple juice	
Juice of 1 lime	2 ounces fresh orange juice
1 ounce passionfruit juice (optional)	1 teaspoon confectioner's sugar
1/2 ounce Apricot Brandy	2 1/2 ounces Tortuga Light Rum
1 ounce Tortuga Dark Rum	1/2 ounce Tortuga 151 Rum

Blend all ingredients except Tortuga 151 rum at low speed for 1 minute with 1/2 cup crushed ice. Pour into tall glass. Carefully float 151 rum on top and garnish with pineapple slice and cherry. Serve with a straw.

Coladas

According to Rum Lore, the legendary Pina Colada was created at the San Juan Caribe Hilton in 1954 by a bartender named Ramon "Monchito" Marrero, and it quickly became the hottest drink in the Caribbean. Millions of pina coladas have been served since – and its popularity inspired a spring tide of Coladas later. All of these should be made with fresh fruit juices for best results, and served in tall, chilled hurricane glasses.

The Original Pina Colada

2 ounces Tortuga Light Rum	
1 ounce Coco Lopez or coconut cream	6 ounces fresh pineapple juice
1 ounce heavy cream	1/2 cup crushed ice

Combine all ingredients in blender and blend for 15 seconds until slushy. Serve in chilled hurricane glass. Garnish with maraschino cherry and pineapple chunks. Makes one drink.

Banana Colada

1/2 medium ripe banana, sliced	1 ounce Coco Lopez or cream of coconut
3 ounces pineapple juice	1-1/2 ounces Tortuga Light Rum
1 ounce Tortuga Coconut Rum	1/2 cup crushed ice

Combine all ingredients in a blender. Blend until smooth and serve immediately in tall glass. Serves 1.

Guava Colada

1 ounce Tortuga Light Rum	1 ounce Tortuga Coconut Rum

3 ounces Guava nectar   1 ounce Coco Lopez or cream of coconut
1/4 cup crushed ice

Combine all ingredients in a blender and blend 20 seconds. Serve in a tall glass garnished with a cherry.

Mango Colada
1 medium ripe mango, diced into chunks (1 cup)
2 ounces Tortuga Light Rum   2 ounces Tortuga Coconut Rum
4 ounces Coco Lopez or cream of coconut   1 cup crushed ice

Combine all ingredients in blender and blend for 30 seconds. Pour into two chilled hurricane glasses and serve immediately garnished with a chunk of mango and straws.

Mocha Colada
1/2 ounce Tortuga Coffee Liqueur or Tia Maria
1 ounce Tortuga Coconut Rum   1 ounce crème de cacao
2 ounces Coco Lopez   1/4 cup crushed ice.

Combine all ingredients in a blender and blend for 30 seconds. Serve immediately.

Nutty Colada
1 ounce Amaretto   1 ounce Frangelico
1 ounce Tortuga Light Rum   3 ounces Coco Lopez or cream of coconut
1/3 cup cracked ice

Combine all ingredients in a blender and blend 15 seconds or until smooth. Pour into a chilled cocktail glass.

Strawberry Colada
2 ounces Tortuga Coconut Rum   1/3 cup sliced strawberries
1 teaspoon sugar   1 ounce Coco Lopez or cream of coconut
1/2 cup crushed ice

Combine all ingredients in a blender and blend for 30 seconds. Pour into champagne glass and garnish with whole strawberry. Serves 1.

Tropicale Colada
1-1/2 ounces Tortuga Coconut Rum   1/2 ounce crème de banana
1/2 ounce Midori melon liqueur   3 ounces fresh pineapple juice
1-1/4 ounces Coco Lopez   1/2 cup crushed ice

Combine all ingredients in a blender and blend for 20 seconds. Pour into a chilled hurricane glass.

New Millennium Rumbullion: More Wild Island Rum Drinks

AcapulCoco
Rum outsells tequila in the local market in the Mexican Caribbean, where this drink was created.

3/4 ounce Tortuga Dark Rum   1 ounce gold tequila
1 ounce Kahlua   1 ounce Coco Lopez cream of coconut
1/2 cup cracked ice

Combine all ingredients in a cocktail shaker and shake well. Strain into a martini glass garnished with a chunk of fresh coconut.

Another Day in Paradise

Pisang means banana in Indonesian and Pisang Ambon is a potent Indonesian liqueur that tastes like a blend of green banana and spices. Coconut, banana and almonds -the flavors of paradise.

1-1/2 ounces Pisang Ambon	1-1/2 ounces Tortuga Coconut Rum
1/2 ounce Amaretto	1-1/2 ounces half and half or light cream
3 ice cubes	

Combine all ingredients in a cocktail shaker and shake well. Strain into a chilled margarita or champagne glass and garnish with a slice of banana and maraschino cherry.

Bashment Juice

A "bashment" is a "big island fête" or outdoor party with lots of music and dancing. Don't plan serious conversation or action after this concoction. Share it with someone you'd like to know better.

1 ounce Tortuga Coffee Liqueur or Tia Maria	
1 ounce Tortuga Spiced Rum	1 ounce Tortuga Coconut Rum
1 ounce Banana Liqueur	1 ounce Tortuga Rum Cream Liqueur
4 ounces milk	

Combine all ingredients in a cocktail shaker and shake well. Pour over cracked ice in tall glass. Serve with two straws and caution

Bee Sting

2 ounces Tortuga Light Rum	1 teaspoon Tortuga Wildflower Honey
1 teaspoon heavy cream	

Combine all ingredients in a cocktail shaker with ice and shake well. Strain into a chilled cocktail glass.

B-52

The original recipe for this infamous drink calls for the 151 rum to be added last and the drink ignited. The glass is immediately slammed on the counter to extinguish the flame, and then drunk straight as a single shot. Unless you crave such dramatic special effects, try this:

2 ounces Amaretto	1 ounce Bailey's Irish Cream
1 ounce Tortuga 151 Rum	

Pour the Amaretto, then the Bailey's into a rocks glass. Float the 151 rum on top. Sip slowly to prevent vertigo.

Bird of Paradise

1 ounce Tortuga Banana Rum	1-1/2 ounces Absolut Citron vodka
2 ounces Ruby Red Grapefruit juice	1 ounce cranberry juice
2 ounces mango nectar	Splash of Sprite or 7-up

Combine all ingredients except Sprite in a cocktail shaker and shake well. Pour into a tall glass and add a splash of Sprite or 7-up (diet if preferred) and stir once.

Blasted Parrot

Cayman parrots are magnificent birds, but noisy and a nuisance, especially if you have a hangover and they are outside your window. Farmers use stronger words to describe them, since the birds particularly love mangos, and nibble just enough to ruin the fruit. Too many of these will make you resemble the drink's name.

1-1/2 ounces Tortuga 151 Rum	1 ounce banana liqueur
1/2 ounce peach schnapps	1/2 ounce Curacao
2 ounces mango-orange juice	2 ounces guava nectar
1 teaspoon fresh key lime juice	1 teaspoon strawberry syrup

Combine all ingredients except the strawberry syrup in a cocktail shaker with cracked ice and shake well. Pour into a tall collins glass and float the syrup on top. Garnish with a mango chunk and serve with a straw.

Blue Iguana

There really is a Blue Iguana you can see without drinking this concoction, a species found only on Grand Cayman.

1-1/2 ounces Tortuga Light Rum	1 ounce Blue Curacao
1/2 ounce Absolut lemon vodka	1 ounce fresh grapefruit juice
7-up or Sprite	

Combine all ingredients expect 7-Up or Sprite in a cocktail shaker and shake well. Pour over ice in tall glass and top with Sprite or 7-Up.

Bullfighter

1-1/2 ounces Tortuga Gold Rum	1/2 ounce dry sherry
1/2 teaspoon Tortuga Hellfire Pepper Sauce	
Dash of Worcestershire sauce	1/2 teaspoon Pickapeppa Sauce
4 ounces canned beef broth or bouillon, chilled	

Pour the rum, sherry, pepper sauce, Worcestershire sauce and Pickapeppa sauce over cracked ice into a glass. Add the chilled beef broth and stir well.

Bush Pilot

I feel safe flying in small planes throughout the islands with our "bush pilots" who know local tropical skies, but many tourists would need one of these before and after take-off. This recipe is meant to serve two nervous flyers. The "healthful" stomach soothing ingredients of bitters and ginger alone over ice would suit the teetotaler.

1 ounce Tortuga Spiced Rum	1 ounce Tortuga Coconut Rum
1 ounce Tortuga Banana Rum	1 ounce Tortuga 151 Rum
2 ounces orange juice	2 ounces pineapple juice
1 teaspoon pimento dram or Pimento liqueur	
1 teaspoon Angostura Bitters	Ginger beer or ginger ale

Fill a 12-ounce plastic cup half with ice cubes. Pour rums over ice, then juices, grenadine and bitters. Stir well and fill to top with ginger beer. Stir again. Drink slowly.

Carib Bushwacker

This recipe is meant for 2-3 drinks-NOT one!

1 ounce Tortuga Dark Rum	1 ounce Absolut vodka
1 ounce Tortuga Coffee Liqueur or Kahlua	
1 ounce Tortuga Rum Cream Liqueur	1 ounce Amaretto

46

1 ounce Frangelico   1 ounce dark Crème de Cacao
6 ounces milk or half and half

Combine all ingredients in a shaker with cracked ice. Shake well and strain into short cocktail glasses. You can also make a frozen version by combining all ingredients in a blender with 2 cups of crushed ice.

Coconut Bushwacker

What a difference coconut makes! This is for two drinks.

2 ounces Coco Lopez   1 ounce Tortuga Coffee Liqueur or Kahlua
1 ounce Tortuga Coconut Rum   1 ounce Crème de cacao
1 ounce Amaretto   2 ounces half and half
1 cup cracked ice

Carambola Quencher

I'll guarantee you've never tried one of these before – the tartness of the carambola or starfruit makes a perfect complement to the liquors.

2 ounces Tortuga Light Rum   1/2 ounce Grand Marnier
1/2 ounce Chambord raspberry liqueur   Club soda
2 carambola "star" slices, seeded about 1/4 inch thick.

Remove the seeds from the carambola slices and place one slice on the bottom of a rocks glass. Muddle the carambola until pulpy and juice is released. Add the rum, Grand Marnier and Chambord and 2 or 3 ice cubes. Fill with club soda and top with remaining carambola slice.

Caribbean Lullaby

1-1/2 ounces Tortuga Light Rum   1/2 ounce Tortuga Banana Rum
1/2 ounce tequila   1/2 ounce apricot brandy
1 ounce orange juice   1/2 ounce pineapple juice
1/2 ounce cranberry juice   1 tablespoon Amaretto
1/2 cup cracked ice

Combine all ingredients in a cocktail shaker and shake well. Pour into a chilled Collins glass and garnish with an orange slice and cherry.

Cayman Sunburn

This drink goes down so easily, be careful you don't nod off in the sun so your skin becomes deep-fried!

2 ounces Tortuga Coconut Rum   1 ounce crème de banana or banana liqueur
1 ounce Galliano   1/2 ounce fresh lime juice
1/2 ounce cranberry juice   1 ounce pineapple juice
1 ounce grapefruit juice   1 ounce orange juice

Combine all ingredients in a cocktail shaker with ice cubes and shake well. Pour with the cubes into a tall plastic traveling cup and take to pool chaise or beach towel.

Coconut Ecstasy

This is a coconut lover's dream.

1-1/2 ounces Tortuga Light Rum   1 ounce Tortuga Coconut Rum
2 teaspoons fresh lime juice   2 teaspoons simple syrup
1 ounce Coco Lopez   2 teaspoons heavy cream
2 teaspoons Tortuga 151 Rum

Combine all ingredients except the 151 Rum in a cocktail shaker and shake well. Pour into a hurricane glass or large wineglass filled with cracked ice. Float the 151 Rum on top. Garnish with a cherry, slice of fresh coconut and serve with a straw.

Duppy Milk

In Cayman, a duppy is a mischievous spirit, akin to the Chicharney of the Abacos – something you might see after too many of these.

1/2 ounce Tortuga 151 Rum	1 ounce Tortuga Light Rum
1 ounce banana liqueur	1/2 ounce Galliano
1 ounce Tortuga Rum Cream Liqueur	1 ounce Coco Lopez
1 cup cracked ice	

Combine all ingredients in a blender and blend until smooth. Serve in a margarita glass.

Fantasy Island

1 ounce Tortuga Dark Rum	1 ounce crème de cassis liqueur
1 ounce apricot brandy	1/2 ounce passion fruit nectar
1/2 ounce pineapple juice	1 ounce orange tangerine juice
1 teaspoon fresh key lime juice	1 ounce club soda

Combine all ingredients except club soda in a cocktail shaker and shake well. Pour over cracked ice into a tall collins glass and top with club soda.

Gold Doubloon

1-1/2 ounces Tortuga Spiced Rum	1 ounce banana liqueur
1 ounce Galliano	6 ounces pineapple juice

Pour all ingredients into shaker and shake well. Pour over cracked ice.

Gorilla Milk

This drink is the only way you'll see any gorillas in the Caribbean.

1 ounce Tortuga Gold Rum	1/2 ounce Tortuga Coffee Liqueur
1/2 ounce Bailey's Irish Cream Liqueur	1/2 ounce Creme de Banana
1 ounce milk	

Combine all ingredients in cocktail shaker and cracked ice and shake well. Strain into a glass and Garnish with a banana slice.

Green Flash

This shooter was invented at a Seven Mile Beach bar many years ago to help tourists see the legendary Green Flash -even if it was long after sunset.

1 ounce green Chartreuse	1/2 ounce Tortuga 151 Rum

Combine both liquors in a cocktail shaker with several ice cubes. Shake well to chill ingredients, then pour into a shot glass. Drink as you would any shooter, in one swallow.

Guanabana Banana

See how fast you can say that after a few of these.

1 ounce Tortuga Light Rum	1 ounce Tortuga Banana Rum
1 ounce crème de banana	3 ounces guanabana (soursop) nectar
1/3 cup cracked ice	

Combine all ingredients in a cocktail shaker and shake well. Pour into a cocktail glass and garnish with a two or three round banana slices.

Guava Slider

The sweet, pungent flavor of guava makes an unusual drink. It tastes completely different from the way it smells!

1-1/2 ounces Tortuga Dark rum   1-1/2 ounces currant flavored vodka
Pulp of one fresh ripe guava, peel and seeds removed
2 ounces coconut cream   1 ounce fresh orange juice
1/2 cup cracked ice

Combine all ingredients in a blender and blend until smooth. Serve in a chilled cocktail glass with a straw.

Hair of the Turtle

Hair of the dog? Not in Cayman, where years ago, a friend tried to cure a very fuzzy sunrise and invented this brunch or midday refresher.

2 ounces Tortuga Light Rum   4 ounces bloody mary mix
Squeeze of fresh lime   Seven-up or Sprite

Fill an 8-ounce glass with ice and add the rum, bloody Mary mix and lime and stir well. Fill with regular or diet 7-up or Sprite and stir again. Serve with salted pretzels to settle stomach faster.

Hobbled Grasshopper

No wonder you never see grasshoppers in the Caribbean.

1 ounce Tortuga Light Rum   1/2 ounce Tortuga 151 Rum
1/2 ounce Creme de cacao (brown)   1/2 ounce Creme de Menthe (white)
1 ounce half and half

Combine all ingredients in cocktail shaker with ice and shake well. Strain into rocks glass.

Jamaica Me Crazy

There have been several drinks created with this name, allegedly created to expedite sunbathing *au naturale*, a tradition in many parts of Jamaica's silver coast along Negril.

1 ounce Tortuga 151 Rum   1 ounce Tortuga Coconut Rum
1 ounce banana liqueur   1/2 ounce Triple Sec
1/2 cup diced fresh mango   1 ounce fresh orange juice
2 ounces passion fruit juice

Combine all ingredients in a blender with 1/2 cup crushed ice and blend until slushy. Serve with a straw and share with a friend.

Kamikaze

This drink earned its name because it's supposed to be drunk shooter-style, in one swallow, bottoms up. Good luck.

1 ounce Tortuga Light Rum   1 ounce Triple Sec
1/2 ounce lime juice

Combine ingredients in cocktail shaker with ice and shake well. Strain into a glass.

Last Fling

Don't take this literally and fling back too many the night before you leave. Plane rides and rum hangovers are bad seatmates.

1 ounce Tortuga Light Rum	1 ounce Chambord
1 ounce Grand Marnier	1/2 ounce peach schnapps
2 ounces fresh orange juice	2 teaspoons fresh lime juice
1 teaspoon simple syrup	1/2 cup cracked ice

Combine all ingredients in a cocktail shaker and shake well. Strain into a champagne glass and serve immediately

Little Cayman Lemonade

1-1/2 ounces Tortuga Light Rum	1 ounce Triple Sec
1 ounce sweet sour mix	Sprite

Fill a collins glass with cracked ice and pour in the rum, Triple Sec and sweet and sour mix. Stir to mix and then fill with Sprite. Garnish with a lemon or lime slice and maraschino cherry.

Little White Lie

This renamed drink was a fashionable lunch sip with Cayman's English ladies of leisure some years ago who discreetly ordered "ginger and lime" from the cued-in barman. Many skipped the last three ingredients after the first drink.

1 1/2 ounces Tortuga Light Rum	1 ounce Sweet Sherry
1 teaspoon fresh lime juice	Ginger Ale
Dash grenadine	

Pour rum, sherry and lime juice into highball glass over ice cubes and stir. Fill with ginger ale, and add dash of grenadine.

Marlin Strike

The vivid iridescent color of a marlin when it "lights up" when fighting a line earned this drink its name. It was created by the pitcherful, one June during Cayman's Million Dollar Month fishing tournament, by the captain of a luxurious but luckless Texas boat to sedate the owner while waiting for the strikes that never came.

1 ounce Absolut Citron vodka	1 ounce Tortuga Light Rum
1/2 ounce Cointreau	1 ounce Blue Curacao
2 ounces pineapple juice	1/2 ounce Rose's Lime Juice
1 ounce Coco Lopez	Ice

Combine all ingredients in a cocktail shaker, mason jar or anything else you have that works in 3-foot seas and shake well. Pour into a plastic cup. Repeat until you get a marlin strike.

Mayan Ruins

Too many of these and that's what you'll feel like.

2 ounces Cuervo Gold Tequila	1 ounce Tortuga Coffee Liqueur or Kahlua

Pour both liquors over ice cubes into a cocktail glass and stir. Sip slowly and hang on to your seat.

MelonBerry Blast

The best way to make this drink is to use frozen fruit, which eliminates the need for ice. Plan ahead and freeze zip-top bags of 1/2 inch watermelon chunks and fresh strawberries at least four hours ahead of party time.

1 cup chopped seeded watermelon   1/3 cup sliced strawberries, unsweetened
2 ounces Tortuga Light Rum   1 ounce Triple Sec or Curacao
1 tablespoon fresh lime juice   2 teaspoons simple syrup

Combine all ingredients in a blender and blend until smooth. Serve in a champagne glass and garnish with a chunk of fresh watermelon

Me Meloncholy No More

No wonder. This drink would lift anyone's spirits, especially if sipped in frosty glass, in a hammock on the beach.

1 1/2 ounce Tortuga Gold Rum   1 ounce Midori melon liqueur
1/2 ounce Curacao   1/3 cup diced fresh cantaloupe
2 ounces papaya nectar   1/2 cup crushed ice
1/2 teaspoon Tortuga Strawberry Syrup or grenadine

Combine all ingredients in blender and blend until slushy. Pour into margarita glass and garnish with fresh cantaloupe chunks on a spear.

Milky Way

Like the popular candy bar, this was around long before mudslides took over the tropical bar scene.

1/2 ounce Tortuga Dark Rum   1/2 ounce bourbon
1/2 ounce brandy   1/2 ounce crème de cacao
1/4 teaspoon vanilla extract   6 ounces milk
1 cup cracked ice

Combine all ingredients in a blender and blend until slushy. Pour into a 10-ounce glass and serve with a straw. You can also make this drink in a cocktail shaker like an exotic milk punch.

Monkey Business

Like its name suggests, this is a group activity. Chill four hurricane glasses in advance.

4 ounces Tortuga Banana Rum   2 ounces banana liqueur
4 ounces Tortuga Rum Crème   1 medium ripe banana, sliced
1 cup Coco Lopez   1 8-ounce can crushed pineapple, undrained
1/3 cup orange juice concentrate   Cracked ice

Mix all ingredients together in blender with cracked ice. Blend until smooth and serve immediately in four chilled hurricane glasses.

Mudslide, Island Style

Here is the traditional mudslide with a delicious surprise hint of orange from the islands.

1 ounce Stolichnaya Vodka   1 ounce Bailey's Irish Cream
1 ounce Tortuga Coffee Liquor or Kahlua   3/4 ounce Curacao or Cointreau

Combine all ingredients and pour over ice in a tall glass. For a frozen drink, combine all ingredients in a blender with 1/2 cup crushed ice and blend until smooth.

Mustique Whammy

Considered one of the finest champagne cocktails ever invented, this creation is from Basil's Bar in Mustique, the Grenadines.

1 ounce Tortuga Gold Rum   3-1/2 ounces very cold champagne

1 ounce fresh orange juice   1/2 ounce lemon juice
1/4 ounce grenadine

Combine all ingredients in a chilled champagne glass and stir gently to mix. Sip slowly to savor every drop.

Nectar of the Gods

Anything with fresh strawberries deserves this description in the Caribbean, where they are a luxury and extravagance. Beware, this is a potent potion.

1-1/2 ounces Tortuga Gold Rum   1/2 ounce Tortuga Banana Rum
1 ounce Grand Marnier   2-1/2 ounces orange-passion-guava juice blend
1/3 cup sliced fresh strawberries   1 ounce Coco Lopez
1 tablespoon half & half   1/2 cup cracked ice

Combine all ingredients in a blender and blend until smooth. Pour into tall glass and serve with a straw. Garnish with a fresh whole strawberry, if you have any left.

Paradise Creamsicle

It's a good thing real Creamsicles weren't this potent or many of us would never have survived our 1950's childhoods.

1 ounce Galliano   1 ounce Tortuga Coconut Rum
1 ounce Grand Marnier   1 ounce white crème de cacao
2-1/2 ounces Coco Lopez   2 ounces fresh orange juice
1 cup cracked ice

Combine all ingredients in a blender and blend until smooth. Pour into a chilled highball glass. Makes one drink.

Rasta Russian

Here is a White Russian transformed by the tropics.

1 ounce Tortuga Coffee Liqueur (or Tia Maria or Kahlua)
1 ounce Tortuga Dark Rum   1 ounce Tortuga Rum Cream Liqueur
1 ounce dark crème de cacao

Pour all ingredients into cocktail shaker with cracked ice and shake well. Strain into cocktail glass over cracked ice. Serves two, ha ha.

Rum Buzz

A fizz with more punch is a buzz.

1-1/2 ounces Tortuga Dark rum   1/2 ounce peach brandy
1/2 ounce blackberry brandy   1 ounce fresh lemon juice
1/2 teaspoon superfine sugar   Chilled club soda

Combine rum, brandies, lemon juice and sugar in a cocktail shaker and shake well. Pour into a collins glass over several ice cubes and top with club soda.

Rumslide

It's a Mudslide made with rum, of course-and therefore, better!

1 ounce Tortuga Light Rum   1 ounce Tortuga Rum Cream Liqueur
1 ounce Tortuga Coffee Liqueur or Kahlua
1 ounce Bailey's Irish Cream   1/4 cup cracked ice
Ground cinnamon

Combine all ingredients in a cocktail shaker with cracked ice and shake well. Pour into a tall glass and sprinkle lightly with cinnamon.

Rum Truffle

1 ounce Tortuga Rum Cream Liqueur   1 ounce Tortuga Dark Rum
1/2 ounce Frangelico hazelnut liqueur   1/2 ounce crème de cacao
Pour all ingredients into a cocktail shaker with cracked ice and shake well. Strain into a cocktail glass.

Rusty Screw

1-1/2 ounces Tortuga 151 Rum   1 ounce Grand Marnier
2 ounces milk or half and half   1/2 cup cracked ice
Combine all ingredients in a cocktail shaker and shake well. Pour into a chilled rocks glass.

Seven Mile Tango

There are two different explanations for this one. It takes two to tango – this is meant to be shared. Or if you drink this alone, you may try to tango all the way up Seven Mile Beach.

1-1/2 ounces Tortuga Banana Rum   1 ounce Amaretto
1 ounce Galliano   1 ounce Godiva Chocolate Liqueur
1 ounce Coco Lopez coconut cream   1/2 cup crushed ice
Nutmeg
Combine all ingredients in a blender and blend until smooth. Serve in two chilled rocks glasses and sprinkle tops with nutmeg.

Sex on the Beach

Yes, there really is a drink by this name-in fact, there are several variations and they've been around awhile. It's not just a pick up line around beach bars.

1/2 ounce Tortuga Light Rum   1/2 ounce Midori melon liqueur
1/2 ounce Chambord raspberry liqueur 1/2 ounce Absolut vodka
3 ounces cranberry juice   1 ounce grapefruit juice
Pour the liquors over ice cubes in a tall glass. Add the cranberry juice and top with grapefruit juice.

Shooting Star

Its name suggests what you'll see in the Caribbean sky-day or night – if you have too many of these.

1 ounce Wray & Nephew White Overproof Rum   1/2 ounce white crème de cacao
1/2 ounce white crème de menthe   1 ounce light cream or milk
1/2 cup cracked ice   1/2 ounce Tortuga 151 Rum
Combine all ingredients except the 151 rum in a cocktail shaker and shake well. Pour into a brandy snifter or margarita glass and float the 151 rum on the surface. Garnish with nutmeg, freshly grated if possible. Sip slowly.

Slippery Banana

1-1/2 ounces Tortuga 151 Rum   1/2 ounce Crème de banana
1 ounce Tortuga Rum Cream Liqueur   1/2 ounce Amaretto
2 ounces half and half   1/2 cup cracked ice

Combine all ingredients in cocktail shaker and shake well. Strain into a chilled champagne glass.

Slithering Lizard

What you might turn into after too many of this pretty green but mostly-liquor refreshment.

1-1/2 ounces Tortuga Banana Rum   1/2 ounce Blue Curacao
1/2 ounce Midori melon liqueur   1/2 ounce Galliano
Sprite

Pour the four liquors over ice cubes into a collins glass and fill with Sprite. Stir and serve with a straw.

Small Island Ice Tea

This is yet another variation of Long Island Ice Tea, that "over the edge" concoction. I'm still trying to figure out how it got its name or why anyone would drink it. Maybe no one has recovered long enough to explain its popularity, as this recipe makes only one drink.

1 ounce Absolut Citron vodka   1 ounce tequila
1 ounce Tortuga Light Rum   1 ounce Tortuga 151 Rum
1 ounce Curacao   1 ounce sweet and sour mix
Cola

Combine all ingredients in a cocktail shaker with ice and shake lightly. Pour with ice into 12-ounce glass and fill to top with cola. Garnish with lemon slice.

Spring Breaker

This may seem like a real sissy drink but it carries a serious kick. Ting is Jamaica's famous grapefruit soda, the perfect tropical twist for this combination.

2 ounces Tortuga Light Rum   1/2 ounce peach brandy
1/2 ounce cherry brandy   1 teaspoon lime juice
1/2 bottle chilled Ting

Filled a tall glass with ice cubes. Pour in the rum, then the brandies and lime juice. Fill with Ting and stir slightly. Top with a cherry and orange slice.

Storm Warning

2 ounces Tortuga Dark Rum   1 ounce sweet vermouth
1 ounce apricot brandy   1 teaspoon pimento dram
1 teaspoon fresh lime juice

Pour all ingredients into a glass, in order, and then add ice cubes. Stir lightly and sip slowly.

Sunset Passion

1 ounce Tortuga Spiced Rum   2 ounces Tortuga Dark Rum
1/2 ounce Chambord raspberry liqueur 1/2 ounce peach brandy
1/2 ounce fresh lime juice   1 ounce orange juice
2 ounces passion fruit nectar   1/2 cup cracked ice

Combine all ingredients in blender and blend 20 seconds. Pour into glass and garnish with cherry and straw.

That's A Moray

A moray, amore....who cares after a few of these?

1-1/2 ounces Tortuga Dark Rum   1 ounce Tuaca (Italian vanilla-orange liqueur)
2 ounces Tortuga Rum Cream Liqueur

Pour all ingredients into a rocks glass and stir. Add ice if desired.

Turtle Crawl

This fruit salad combination of flavors masks its almost pure alcohol content and goes down quickly-don't get caught by surprise.

1 ounce Tortuga Light Rum   1/2 ounce Absolute Currant vodka
1/2 ounce peach schnapps   1/2 ounce Galliano
1/2 ounce Blue Curacao   3 ounces pineapple juice
1/2 teaspoon Tortuga Strawberry syrup   1 cup cracked ice

Combine all ingredients in a blender and blend until smooth. Pour into a hurricane glass and serve with a straw and seatbelt for the barstool. This makes one or two drinks, depending on the person.

West Indian Red Eye

Some swear this is the best eye-opener in the tropics.

1/2 chilled bottle Red Stripe beer   2 ounces Tortuga Light Rum
2 ounces chilled tomato juice   Squeeze of fresh lime

Pour the rum into a tall glass, then add the tomato juice. Fill 3/4 of the way with Red Stripe. Drink. Top with squeeze of lime juice. Drink. Repeat if necessary.

Drinks with a History

White Witch

Some claim this old potion keeps the ghost of Annie Palmer, the infamous White Witch of Rose Hall, Jamaica, at bay after dark. Considering the ingredients, it would seem to conjure apparitions instead.

2 ounces Tortuga Light Rum   1 ounce Cointreau
1 ounce white Crème de Cacao   4 teaspoons lime juice
Club soda

Fill a tall cocktail glass with ice cubes and add the lime juice, then the remaining ingredients. Fill with club soda and stir.

The Big Bamboozle?

Errol Flynn, the swashbuckling screen idol of the 40's, led a wild and wicked not-so-private life in Port Antonio, Jamaica. In tamer moments, he helped turn rafting on the Rio Grande into a popular tourist attraction, organizing the first bamboo river raft races. I've met a few of his Jamaican contemporaries and partymates who survived to share fascinating stories about that era of Port Antonio's wildlife. But his observers laugh at the idea that Flynn invented this famous old tropical drink attributed to him. The "Big Bamboo" is an expression that has nothing to do with rafting. Besides, they claim Flynn's drink of choice was rum straight up, from breakfast on. So the legendary Big Bamboo was probably pure folklore and the Rum Tourist Drink of 1940's Jamaica. But the romantic myth is worth preserving, more than 50 years later.

Big Bamboo

One of the original exotic tropical drinks that caused the sun to set early.

1 ounce Tortuga Dark Rum   1 ounce Tortuga Gold Rum
1/2 ounce Tia Maria or Tortuga Coffee Liqueur
1/2 ounce lime juice   1/4 ounce simple syrup
3 ounces pineapple juice   1 teaspoon Falernum

Combine all ingredients in a cocktail shaker with 1/2 cup crushed ice and shake well. Serve in tall glass with ice, garnished with fresh orange slice, pineapple chunk and cherry.

Firefly

Legend says this was a favorite sip of the celebrated author, playwright and bon vivant Noel Coward, named after Firefly, his Port Maria, Jamaica aerie overlooking the Caribbean.

2 ounces Tortuga Light Rum   1 ounce brandy
1 teaspoon lemon juice   1 teaspoon grenadine

Combine all ingredients in a cocktail shaker with ice and stir. Strain into a cocktail glass.

Rhapsody on the Rocks

Along Seven Mile Beach, several drinks by this name were created after a historic 1982 event off Grand Cayman's west coast, when the cruise ship *Rhapsody* went aground on a reef for several months. This drink wrecked a lot of people ashore who tried to refloat the cruise liner every day by lifting glasses.

1 ounce Tortuga 151 Rum   1 ounce Vodka
1 ounce Tequila   1 ounce Blue Curacao
1/2 tablespoon Cherry Brandy   3 ounces Sour Mix
3 ounces orange juice

Combine all ingredients in cocktail shaker and shake well. Pour on the rocks into a hurricane glass. Garnish with a compass to help navigate the way home.

The Firm Turns Cayman Giddy

In February 1993 Grand Cayman turned even giddier when Director Sydney Pollack and Paramount Pictures flew into town for the filming of John Grisham's *The Firm*. With a crew of 90 and cast of stars that outdazzled even the tropical winter sky, Paramount's arrival turned Cayman into a frenzy of Hollywood wannabees. Paramount's casting call for extras drew 1200 of the 32,000 residents – in Manhattan, a similar mega star movie casting call would have lured about 500. The famous seduction scene on Seven Mile Beach was filmed under tight security, but the under-the stars dance segment at the old Holiday Inn titillated lucky visitors and local gawkers alike.

Everyone had a Cruise or Hackman story after Paramount departed, most of them pure fiction, like most island bar tales. Scores of star-struck residents claimed to be "close personal friends with Tom Cruise and Nicole Kidman," or "taught Gene Hackman how to dive." (However, I know for a fact that the crew ate a lot of original Tortuga Rum Cakes, because I delivered them into their hands.)

But whether these cocktails that surfaced as "drinks of the stars" ever touched any celebrity lips is a secret that rests in the sands of that venerable Seven Mile site where the Holiday Inn once stood.

Paramount's Roman Holiday Inn Fizz

4 ounces Ting grapefruit soda   2 ounces Tortuga Light Rum
1 ounce Grand Marnier   1/2 ounce crème de cassis
Squeeze of fresh lime

Pour the three liquors over ice into a 12-ounce plastic cup. Top with Ting and stir lightly.

Mitch's Seven Mile Indiscretion

3 ounces passion fruit nectar   2 ounces Coco Lopez
2 ounces Tortuga Gold Rum   1 ounce Absolut vodka
1/2 ounce Amaretto   Dash bitters
1/2 cup cracked ice

Combine all ingredients in a blender and blend 30 seconds or until slushy. Pour into 12-ounce plastic carry-away cup and wander up the beach.

Avery's Cayman Amnesia

No wonder he passed out on Abby in the Great House condo – he got his Cayman bar bill! Don't try this nuclear version of a Mimosa at brunch if you want Cayman memories later.

1 bottle well chilled Dom Perignon champagne
4 ounces fresh orange juice   2 ounces Grand Marnier
1 ounce Chambord Raspberry liqueur   2 ounces Tortuga Gold Rum

Combine all ingredients except champagne and shake well. Divide between two champagne flutes. Add enough Dom to fill each flute. Keep refilling flutes with liquor mix and champagne until bottle is empty or your clothes come off. Take proper action accordingly.

Party-size Rum Potions

Some of the most potent party punches ever created originated not in the sultry, carefree Caribbean, but in Dixie, the region comprising the Deep South USA. Part time residents and visitors introduced some of these to the islands during their holiday celebrations, proof that rum remains a favorite far from sun, sand and sea-drenched shores. You will have to use ingenuity or imagination to find containers large enough for most of these recipes.

Tortuga Party Watermelon

This is exactly what it says and makes a great hit at beach parties. The secret is letting the watermelon chill a long time.

1 large watermelon   1 quart Tortuga Gold or 151 Rum

Cut two 1-1/2 inch diameter plugs from the same side of the watermelon and remove. Slowly pour the rum into the holes in the melon. When all rum has been absorbed or the melon will not absorb any more, plug the holes, seal with duct tape. Refrigerate or chill the watermelon in a big cooler on ice for at least 12 hours-longer if possible. Cut into wedges and serve. Warn unsuspecting guests first, please.

Buccaneer's Rum Punch

My first trip to the Cayman Islands in 1975 planted me at the old Buccaneer's Inn in Cayman Brac. Generously dispensed welcome rum punch was the best thing I'd ever tasted. It looked just like the incredible sunsets from the Holey Hut bar, and turned even white tourists into calypso demons on the sandy dance floor. I was told by Brackers that while the ingredients sometimes varied according to supplies on hand, at least three fingers of rum per person was the rule of thumb.

1 32 ounce can pineapple juice	1 32 ounce can orange juice
1 32 ounce can pink grapefruit juice	1 cup grenadine syrup
1/2 cup fresh lime juice	1 quart Tortuga Gold Rum
1 quart Tortuga Coconut Rum	Fresh hibiscus blossom or bougainvillea sprig
Aspirin	

Mix all in a container big enough to hold it, then add a big chunk of ice. Or decant into plastic gallon jugs and shake well. Keep chilled and pour over ice when ready to serve. Serve in tall glass over ice, garnished with fresh hibiscus or bougainvillea sprig. Have aspirin handy for the next morning.

Point of Sand Crusoe's Punch

Back in the 70's, Crusoe-style beach picnic day trips by boat to then-isolated Point of Sand on Little Cayman were an unforgettable highlight of a Brac visit. At least two gallon jugs were essential for each party of 10 or 15. It's a wonder we ever made it back.

1/2 quart Tortuga Gold Rum	1/2 quart Tortuga Coconut Rum
2 quarts orange juice	1 quart pineapple juice
Splash grenadine syrup	One brown coconut

Combine all in gallon jug and put in cooler with ice. After arriving in Little Cayman, find, husk and crack fresh coconut add the coconut water to punch mix. Pry out the coconut meat and chop up to pass around. Serve in plastic cups with ice.

Wreck of the Ten Sail Punch

I shouldn't have to state the obvious but strange things happen on small islands. This recipe is not for one drink, but enough to shipwreck a party.

1 gallon fresh orange juice	1 quart Tortuga Banana Rum
12 ounces apricot brandy	8 ounces Galliano
4 ounces Roses Lime Juice	4 ounces fresh lime juice
4 ounces Tortuga Strawberry Syrup	1 quart chilled club soda or seltzer

Combine all ingredients except soda in a punch bowl and mix with large spoon. Add a solid chunk of ice and soda water. If you want a very potent punch, use half the soda water.

Bride's Punch Bowl

In late 18th century New England, rum manufacturing was King of the economy and rum punch was considered an important society wedding tradition. The toast to the bride was called "Drinking the Bride's Bowl." That recipe has been adapted slightly over the centuries, but for a long time, this was considered America's traditional wedding punch.

1- 15 ounce can pineapple chunks, drained	1-6 ounce can frozen lemonade
concentrate	1-1/2 750 ml bottles Tortuga Gold Rum

4 ounces peach brandy
1 quart strawberries, hulled and sliced or 1-pound package frozen sliced strawberries
2 quarts club soda

Combine the pineapple, lemonade concentrate, rum and brandy in a half-gallon container and mix well. Refrigerate for two hours or longer. Place a block of ice or ice ring in a large punch bowl and pour in the rum fusion. Add the strawberries and club soda and stir well. This recipe is meant to serve 20 guests.

Cape Fear Punch

This recipe's roots are in 18th Century North Carolina and ingredients vary slightly according to the host. With US Airways flying into the Cayman Islands from Charlotte every day, no wonder generations-old recipes like this made their way into the Cayman holiday circuit. This recipe makes about 11 quarts, but how many it serves depends on "who dere." You need to begin making this at least a month in advance – tradition says three months is right.

6 tablespoons light brown sugar	2 cups lemon or lime juice
1 quart strong green tea	1 quart Tortuga 151 Rum
4 quarts bourbon	1 quart good quality brandy

Combine all ingredients in a container large enough and mix well. Cover but do not seal tight, and let this mixture age for one to three months in a cool place. When ready, decant into 1-gallon jugs or bottles and seal until ready to use. To prepare the finished punch, combine with an ice ring or chunk in large punch bowl:

1/2 gallon aged punch base mixture	2 -32 ounce bottles chilled champagne
2-24-ounce bottles sparkling water	
2 oranges, sliced	2 lemons, sliced

The Five Gallon Docktail

An avid saltwater angler from Houston came up with a big Lone Star way to celebrate any occasion, from another sunrise to a triumphant day trolling for tuna on the banks. This was served dockside at his "tricked out to the max," Texas-size Hatteras.

1 quart Absolut vodka	1 quart Tortuga Light Rum
1 fifth Southern Comfort	1 gallon lemonade
1 gallon cranberry juice	1 gallon guava orange juice drink

Pour all ingredients into a clean five-gallon bait bucket and stir. (Be sure all bait and chum have been removed.) Have a cooler of ice nearby and 12-ounce plastic cups. Dip cups into the bucket and add ice if desired. You can also double the recipe and mix it in a 48-qt cooler instead of a bucket.

Pirate's Party Punch

Cayman's Pirates Week Festival and its colorful Pirates invasion of George Town Harbor attracts several thousand visitors each October. This party-size recipe goes well with the spirit of the festival – but should only be consumed when safely ashore!

1 pint Tortuga Coconut Rum	1 pint Tortuga Banana Rum
1 pint Tortuga 151 Rum	4 ounces Triple Sec
2- 11.5 ounce cans papaya nectar	2-11.5 ounce cans guava nectar
1-15 ounce can Coco Lopez	5 cups fresh orange juice
1/2 cup fresh lime juice	

Combine all ingredients in a gallon jug and shake well. Serve over ice in plastic cups.

Chatham Artillery Punch

Like Philadelphia's Fish House Punch, there are as many recipes for this 19th century "military strength" concoction from the pre-Civil War south as there are stalks in a canefield. However, history attributes the original recipe to Savannah, Georgia's Chatham Artillery National Guard unit, which allegedly created this incredible recipe in May 1819 in honor of the visit of President James Monroe. The punch's reputation as liquid dynamite had one purpose: to remove all inhibitions. In those days, served about 200. The challenge today is finding a container large enough for this punch as it ages.

2 gallons strong brewed tea (one pound of tea brewed with 2 gallons water)
1 pound sugar or more, to sweeten to taste

2 quarts maraschino cherries	2 large pineapples, peeled and cut into cubes
8 quarts Tortuga Dark Rum	4 quarts Hennessey's 3-Star brandy
4 quarts gin	4 quarts rye whiskey

Combine all of these ingredients in a 10-gallon container and stir well. Sample and add a pound or more of sugar to sweeten to taste. Cover and let rest undisturbed for two weeks. When ready to serve, place a large ice block in the punch bowl and pour in the punch, refilling as needed. Serve in champagne glasses.

Old Fashioned Eggnog

Originally a variation of a 17th century English drink called posset, egg nog in the early American colonies and West Indies was originally made with ale – nog was British slang for ale. In the American colonies, this concoction wasn't originally a holiday punch, but considered a nourishing health drink prescribed for "debilitated persons and consumptives." Again, the caveat about consuming raw eggs today.

14 eggs, separated	1 cup sugar
1 whole nutmeg, freshly grated	2 cups Tortuga Dark Rum
1 cup bourbon	3 quarts half and half

In a large bowl, beat the egg yolks until thickened, then gradually beat in the sugar until mixture is smooth. Blend in the grated nutmeg, rum and bourbon. Beat the egg whites until stiff peaks form, and fold into the yolk mixture. Stir in the half and half and pour into a large chilled punch bowl.

Fish House Punch

There are many variations of this 18th century punch recipe that, according to Rum Lore, was created during the reign of King George II in 1732 by Captain Samuel Morris at the "State in Schuylkill," an elite men's fishing and social club near Philadelphia, Pennsylvania. Members met there to fry fish and imbibe. George Washington allegedly warmed himself with this punch on several wintry occasions. The most famous account of this concoction was penned by a William Black in 1744. The astounded visitor wrote in his journal that his party was greeted at the club with "a bowl of punch large enough to have swimm'd half a dozen young geese." Well, obviously, this makes enough for a party – you can double the recipe for a large fête.

1 quart fresh lemon or lime juice	1 pound sugar
peel of 6 lemons	2 quarts Tortuga Dark Rum
1 quart cognac or fine brandy	1/2 pint peach brandy
1 quart sparkling water or club soda	

Combine the sugar and lemon juice in a large bowl and stir until sugar is dissolved. In a

5-quart container with a cover, combine the lemon-sugar mixture, lemon peel, rum, brandy and peach brandy. Stir well to blend, then cover and refrigerate for several days. An hour before serving, strain the punch into a large punch bowl with a block of ice in the center. If desired, dilute with club soda or sparkling water. Serve in chilled 4- ounce punch cups.

Blue Mountain Coffee Syllabub

This is a variation of an old Colonial Christmas drink, from 18th century Williamsburg, Virginia and makes wonderful brunch or after dinner drink.

3 cups brewed Blue Mountain Coffee, chilled
2 cups heavy cream   1 cup milk
2 cups Tortuga Dark Rum   1 cup sugar
4 egg whites   nutmeg

Combine all ingredients except egg whites and nutmeg in a large bowl and beat with hand mixer until sugar is dissolved and mixture is smooth. Chill the syllabub thoroughly, several hours in the refrigerator or an hour in the freezer. When ready to serve, beat the egg whites with 3 tablespoons sugar until stiff peaks form. Beat the coffee mixture in the bowl once again for about 15 seconds and top with dollops of egg white sprinkled with nutmeg. Ladle into sherry glasses or punch cups. When served this way, this recipe makes about 16 servings.

West Indian Regiment Artillery Punch

1 quart Tortuga Dark Rum   8 ounces Pimento dram or pimento liqueur
1 quart bottle red wine   1 pint peach or apricot brandy
2 quarts fresh orange juice   1/2 cup simple syrup
Juice of six large limes   2 tablespoons Angostura Bitters
2 quarts club soda

Combine all ingredients in a large punch bowl and stir well. Add a block of ice and chill well. Conquers approximately 20 people.

Hot Rum Drinks

When it gets really cold in Cayman, down to about 72 degrees, these drinks are perfect chill chasers.

Hot Rum Toddy

1 teaspoon dark brown sugar   1-1/2 ounces Tortuga Spiced Rum
Lemon slice studded with two cloves Boiling water

Mix the sugar and rum in a coffee mug. Add the lemon slice and cloves. Pour in boiling water to fill the cup. Let steep until cool enough to drink.

Tortuga Toddy

2 ounces Tortuga Dark Rum   4 tablespoons Tortuga Wildflower Honey
1-1/2 tablespoons lemon juice   6 ounces water
1 tablespoon butter   Grated nutmeg

Combine water, honey and lemon in a mug and microwave 60 seconds on high. Add the rum and stir. Float the butter on top and sprinkle with nutmeg.

West Indian Hot Toddy
This old remedy is also called a Hot Jamaican.

2 ounces Tortuga Dark Rum
3/4 ounce fresh lime juice
2 whole cloves
1 cinnamon stick, broken into two pieces
3 ounces boiling water
1 tablespoon simple syrup
Lime wedge

Push the cloves into the lime wedge and place in the bottom of a mug or heat-proof glass. Combine the sugar, lime juice and rum in a small saucepan and bring almost to a simmer. Remove from heat and pour unstrained into the mug or heat-proof glass. Fill with boiling water and stir occasionally with cinnamon stick until cool enough to drink.

Hot Buttered Rum
2 ounces Tortuga Dark Rum
1 tablespoon butter
Pinch nutmeg or ground allspice
1 teaspoon butter
1 teaspoon light brown sugar
Pinch powdered cloves
Cinnamon stick
Boiling water

Combine rum, brown sugar, rum, cloves and nutmeg in a warm coffee mug and stir until the sugar is dissolved. Add the cinnamon stick and fill the mug with boiling water. Add boiling water and stir with cinnamon stick. Top with butter and serve.

Flu Shot
1 tablespoon Tortuga Citrus Honey
2 ounces orange juice
2 dashes Angostura bitters
1-1/2 ounces Tortuga Spiced Rum
2 dashes Tortuga Hell-Fire Hot Pepper sauce

Combine all ingredients in a coffee mug and heat in microwave 40 seconds or until very hot but not boiling. Sip slowly and repeat if necessary.

Tortuga Coffee Royale
2 ounces Tortuga Rum Cream Liqueur   1 ounce Tortuga Coffee Liqueur
5 ounces freshly brewed Tortuga Blue Mountain Blend Coffee

Pour liqueurs into coffee glass or mug and fill with steaming freshly brewed Blue Mountain coffee. Top with whipped cream and freshly grated nutmeg.

Tortuga Cayman Coffee
1 ounce Tortuga Dark Rum   1-1/2 ounces Tortuga Rum Cream Liqueur
6 ounces freshly brewed Tortuga Blue Mountain Blend coffee

Pour both rums into an 8-ounce coffee glass or mug and fill with steaming freshly brewed Blue Mountain coffee.

Tortuga Calypso Coffee
1 ounce Tortuga Coffee Liqueur
1/2 ounce Curacao
6 ounces freshly brewed coffee
1/2 ounce crème de cacao
1/2 ounce Tortuga Dark Rum
Whipped cream

Pour the liquors into an 8-ounce coffee mug or glass and fill with hot coffee. Top with whipped cream if desired.

Café Banana
1-1/2 ounces Tortuga Dark Rum
6 ounces freshly brewed coffee
1/2 ounce crème de banana
Whipped cream

Pour the liquors into a coffee mug and fill with hot coffee. Top with whipped cream.

Toasted Coconut Coffee

1 ounce Tortuga Rum Cream Liqueur   1/2 ounce Amaretto
1 ounce Tortuga Coconut Rum   6 ounces hot coffee
Whipped cream

Pour the liquors into a coffee mug or glass and fill with hot coffee. Top with whipped cream.

Café Don Juan

3/4 ounce Tortuga Dark Rum   3/4 ounce Tortuga Coffee Liqueur or Kahlua
5 ounces hot coffee   Lemon wedge and sugar

Rub the rim of the coffee glass or mug well with the lemon and then invert onto a small plate lined with sugar. Twist until rim is coated with sugar. Pour the liquors into a coffee mug or glass and fill with hot coffee. Top with whipped cream.

Rumba Coffee

3/4 ounce Bailey's Irish Cream   3/4 ounce Tortuga Dark Rum
4 ounces hot coffee   Whipped cream

Pour the liquors into a coffee mug and add the coffee. Stir lightly, then top with whipped cream

Tortuga Hot Cocoa

Not meant for the kiddies!

1-1/2 ounces Tortuga Coconut Rum   2 ounces Tortuga Rum Cream Liqueur
6 ounces hot cocoa   Whipped cream

Pour the rums into an 8-ounce mug and then add the hot cocoa. Top with whipped cream.

Drinks Afire

If you want to serve flaming coffees or drinks as a special touch, read this section – and practice first. Nothing is more dramatic than a flaming postprandial drink or coffee served by candlelight. Most spirits will ignite, but there is a proper technique to be sure the drink, and not the host, ignites. To flame a drink, follow these steps:

▲ Float a top layer of liquor (about 2 teaspoons) on each drink that is least 80 proof spirits and make sure the top layer reaches the edge of the glass, not just the center.

▲ Warm additional liquor, so that you will have about 1 teaspoon per drink, in a small saucepan. Take the warm liquor to the serving area. For each drink, fill a long-handled bar spoon with the same spirits, hold over the glass or mug, and carefully ignite.

▲ Quickly, but gently, float the flaming alcohol on the surface of each drink.

▲ Do not let the drink burn more than about 20 seconds, or the glass could crack.

The CookRum

Western Caribbean Cooking and Spirited Rum Recipes

It is pronounced " CookRum" but was actually the cookroom, a small outer building behind the kitchen that housed the caboose (fire hearth, a wooden box filled with sand and firewood) or wood stove in Cayman and the Caribbean of yesteryear. It had nothing to do with "cooking rum" or the rum-making process. This was where resourceful cooks labored long hours to turn simple ingredients into culinary delights like conch stew and heavy cakes. It's a wonder how weddings and parties ever took place in those days when even simple meals often required an all-day effort.

While the cookroom has almost vanished from the islands' landscape, many of the traditional dishes created there are foods we still cherish – and miss most today, in spite of our sophisticated tastes. Modern conveniences like food processors and canned coconut milk have simplified many time-consuming recipes. But today many islanders have little time to cook – or may never have learned those traditional recipes.

The **CookRum** opens with **The Island Pantry**, **The Caribbean Market** and **Going Coconuts**, which present an introduction to the spices, fruits, vegetables and language of Western Caribbean cuisine – including cooking with rum. Some of our most important island ingredients like mango and conch are highlighted in individual chapters that follow.

Comfort Food, Western Caribbean Style serves up favorite traditional dishes from the Cayman Islands, with important contributions from Jamaica. The culinary roots of Rum Fever lie in these Western Caribbean countries – the native soils of Tortuga Rum Company's founders. Cayman is also the birthplace of Tortuga Rum – and most important of all, it is my home and where my heart lies.

Caribbean parties today can dazzle and display a wide tropical latitude of dishes – but a taste of these traditional "comfort foods" is still a must for any menu. It may take you many attempts to get rice n peas or conch stew just right – but that's true here in the Caribbean too. No matter how hard you try to create authentic Caribbean dishes from these recipes in your own kitchen, they will never taste as good as they do fresh from the well-seasoned pots of Caymanian and Jamaican cooks. And their recipes, part intuition, are always in their heads.

The remaining chapters tempt with more Caribbean party food: Tortuga Rum-spiked and Caribbean-spiced recipes from both Old World and contemporary kitchens – including my own. Just remember that the rum in these recipes is for the dish, not the cook. You'll have to pour that separately!

Caymanian Cookery: A Very Curious Cauldron

"Where can we find native food?"

Hooray for those visitors to our islands who still make the effort to discover traditional Caribbean cooking. But "native food," is a confusing term today, especially in a melting pot population like the Cayman Islands. It depends on how you define native.

If you mean indigenous, truly Caymanian, that's a unique cuisine in itself, which like the islands' culture, centered around the sea. Caymanians by tradition are an independent people whose resourcefulness and seafaring ability helped them survive the kind of isolation that earned the country the media moniker "Islands Time Forgot" as late as the 1960's. Cayman's original settlers arrived in the late 1600's and early 1700's from the British Isles via Jamaica. They adapted to nature and survived hardships on these flat coral islands. Caymanians had limited staples and almost non-existent luxuries before the 1960's. But they did have abundant turtle, fish, conch, coconut and a variety of "ground provisions," primarily starchy root vegetables, with very basic seasonings of onion, scallion, sweet pepper and hot pepper. These are the ingredients of traditional Caymanian cookery, which includes some of the most delicious dishes ever created in Caribbean kitchens. You haven't lived until you eaten conch stewed in coconut or Rundown, Cayman style. That's an example of what we consider "native food."

If "native" means "local food" including Caymanians and Cayman's other West Indian residents, then you'll discover culinary influences from Honduras, Nicaragua, Costa Rica, Belize, Cuba and Jamaica, countries with strong trade ties with Cayman. During the last century, people from these countries have become part of the Cayman community. Those influences show clearly in "local" recipes today.

And if "native" simply means "residents", you'll be overwhelmed. Today this sophisticated international financial center is home to more than 80 nationalities. Cayman's restaurants reflect this extraordinary ethnic melting pot: German, Indian,

Italian, Tex-Mex, Chinese, Thai, Mediterranean, "Spanish" (meaning Honduran) and American bistro. Our supermarkets are stocked with an international festival of foodstuffs. You can find exotic local and imported produce and products catering to a cultural blend that includes American, Italian, English, Canadian, Filipino, Indian, UK and Middle Eastern residents.

Stand in line in a Grand Cayman supermarket and observe this culinary diversity: a simple box of frozen squid is one man's calamari – and another man's wahoo bait!

The Island Pantry

This section is by no means a complete glossary or inventory of the multinational West Indian pantry, which is a book in itself. But it will help you know the basics of cooking with rum and understand the most important seasonings, spices and staples of West Indian cookery. Many American, Canadian and European markets now carry West Indian spices and sauces in their ethnic foods sections. If you can't find Caribbean products, refer to the Caribbean Spice Finder section of this chapter.

Cooking with Rum

Cooking Rum

Unlike wine and sherry, there is no such thing as cheap "cooking rum." You should use good quality rums and liqueurs in all recipes – don't cook with anything you wouldn't also enjoy drinking. Dark rum and 151 proof rum are best for flambés and flaming dishes because of their high alcohol content. Dark rum is the best all around rum for cooking and baking. "Seasoned" rum is another matter. Caribbean recipes for Pepper Wine and Rum-Peppers date back centuries. A drop or two of these fiery infusions is flavoring for soups and other dishes. See **Caribbean Heat** for recipes.

Which Rum to Use?

Knowing the right kind of rum for recipes is important and each has a different alcohol content and flavor.

Tortuga 151 Rum (151 proof / 75.5 % alcohol)

With its high alcohol content and intense rum flavor, this rum is ideal for flambé dishes.

Tortuga Dark Rum (98 proof / 49% alcohol)

Tortuga Dark Rum, a very smooth, rich-flavored rum, with a high alcohol content. It too can be used in flambé dishes, and is the ideal rum for most recipes, savory or sweet, calling for rum, from custards and trifles to stews. It can also be substituted, measure for measure, for vanilla extract or other flavoring.

Tortuga Gold Rum (86 proof / 43% alcohol)

Tortuga Gold rum is another good choice for using in sauces, soups and savory dishes.

Tortuga Light Rum (80 proof/ 40% alcohol)

Tortuga Light rum can be used as a substitute for dry sherry or white wine in lighter cream sauces. It is often used in frozen desserts and whipped cream recipes.

Alcohol-free Cooking

You bought the wrong cookbook. However, for those who prefer not to cook with alcohol, many of these recipes can be made without rum by substituting the same measure of apple juice, broth or compatible flavored liquid. The flavor will NOT be identical; that subtle difference rum makes will be missing. Obviously some recipes absolutely require rum – you can't make rum balls or rum cake with fruit juice.

Rum Extract, Rum Vanilla and Vanilla Rum

Rum Extract

There is no such thing. This concoction is actually "Imitation Rum Extract" and 35% alcohol, but it's not made from rum. The ingredients commonly listed are corn syrup, propylene, glycol, water, ethyl acetate and other esters, oil of cassia, other "essential oils" (?), acetic acid and other organic acids and artificial color. Why not simply use a teaspoon of Dark Rum, which is 98 proof or 49% alcohol without all those inscrutable ingredients?

Vanilla extract is actually 35% alcohol, the combination of vanilla beans soaked in grain alcohol. Centuries before vanilla extract was created commercially, brandy was used in baking cakes and other confections – not only for flavor, but also for its unique leavening ability, creating a lighter baked product. Cognac vanilla was an old recipe created in the early 19th century American South and the inspiration for Rum Vanilla.

Rum Vanilla

This unusual infusion is better than any vanilla extract you can buy. Tortuga Dark Rum is 46% alcohol – you can actually use it instead of vanilla, but the rich flavor of this blend is superior for cooking. You can make it in any quantity desirable, but the recommended proportion is:

4 whole vanilla beans
1 pint Tortuga Dark Rum

You will need a sterilized jar or bottle tall enough to hold the length of the vanilla beans and one that can be closed, airtight. Carefully split the vanilla beans lengthwise, exposing the black seeds. These are the real source of that rich, intense vanilla flavor. Place the bean halves with seeds in the prepared container and cover with the rum. Seal the container and shake well. Store at room temperature for a week or longer before using. The real flavors will come out while baking.

Vanilla Rum

This is not the same nor as richly flavored as Rum Vanilla, but is another substitute for vanilla extract. It makes a delicious flavored rum and drink mixer. Take a liter bottle of Tortuga Dark Rum and add 6 split vanilla beans. Seal the bottle and turn upside down several times before setting on the shelf to age for a month. As the bottle empties, the rum will become more richly flavored unless you replace the amount used. I don't recommend this as the vanilla beans lose their flavor.

Our Special Caribbean Ingredients

Many of our Island visitors are not familiar with the common seasonings and tropical ingredients we take for granted. Here are some of the most common ones, with tips on how to use them or make substitutions if appropriate.

Coconut

See **Going Coconuts** for complete information about this key island ingredient, including how to make fresh coconut milk.

Saltfish

Salt cod became part of Caribbean cookery during the plantation era, when European masters preferred expensive imported dried fish to anything caught locally. Nova Scotia developed a huge and enduring thirst for rum received in trade for this product. It has a very strong flavor and before using, must be soaked and picked over to remove bones. Still a popular ingredient in many Caribbean dishes, salt cod is now widely available in North American supermarkets.

Allspice *(Pimenta dioica)*

This is not the popular men's aftershave, but a native West Indian spice first used by the Arawak Indians as a meat preservative. Also called pimento, it is one of the Western Caribbean's most important seasonings. Allspice is the ripe reddish-brown berry of the allspice tree that grows primarily in Jamaican and Cuba. It gets its name from its flavor, which seems to blend cinnamon, cloves, nutmeg and black pepper. Ground allspice is an important ingredient in jerk seasoning. The leaves and wood are used in the jerk fire and infuse meat with a flavor that can't be duplicated with charcoal or other woods. Whole allspice is a key ingredient in traditional pickling spice blends. Jamaica is the world's leading producer and exporter of allspice.

Thyme

One of the most common herbs used in Caribbean cooking, thyme remains an unfamiliar seasoning to many foreign cooks. Its pungent almost lemony-pepper flavor is easy to recognize once you know it. You probably won't be able to find fresh thyme, the preferred seasoning, but a teaspoon of dried thyme provides about the same flavoring as a large fresh sprig.

Scallions (or escallions)

Also known as green onions or spring onions, scallions are another important Caribbean seasoning found in supermarkets worldwide. After cutting off the roots and removing the paper-like outer skin, chop and use the entire scallion in recipes, not just the white part.

Ginger

Ginger is an important spice in Caribbean cooking. Today, fresh gingerroot from Jamaica and Costa Rica is available in the produce section of many supermarkets overseas. It should have a smooth skin and pale buff or tan color. Use a vegetable peeler to peel away the thin skin and then grate, slice or mince to use in recipes. Cooks also disagree on the proper amount of powdered ground ginger to substitute for fresh grated ginger – it varies from 1/4 teaspoon to 1 teaspoon powdered ground ginger for 1 tablespoon grated fresh ginger. The flavors are very different anyway, so I don't advise you to substitute one for the other unless the recipe states this. A little ginger helps eliminate the fishy taste when added to fish tea and seafood chowders. Ginger tea is a West Indian remedy for head colds, bronchitis – and upset stomachs. And, many islanders swear ginger beer can help cure a hangover – fishermen and sailors stock ginger beer or ginger ale in coolers in case of seasickness.

Curry Powder

Caymanians, Jamaicans and many West Indians generally like their curry spicy rich and "flavorful," but not fiery hot, and add Scotch Bonnets or other local hot pepper or hot sauce to the curry to suit individual taste. Jamaican and Trinidadian curry powders are now widely available in overseas market. My favorite is any blend of **Trinidad's Chief Curry Powder**, which contains a very flavorful combination of spices, nicely balanced with hot pepper. You can make your own curry powder – here is one suggestion:

4 teaspoons ground ginger
4 teaspoons ground turmeric
4 teaspoons ground black pepper
1 teaspoons ground cinnamon
1 teaspoons ground cardamom
1/2 teaspoon ground nutmeg
1 teaspoon ground allspice
1 teaspoons ground fenugreek
2 teaspoons ground cumin
2 teaspoons garlic powder
4 teaspoons ground coriander

Mix ingredients together in zip-top plastic bag and blend thoroughly. Store in the refrigerator for maximum shelf life.

Seasoning

"Seasoning" is a unique feature of Caribbean cooking – here, the word means a blend of spices and herbs used in Caribbean cooking, almost always with hot pepper of some kind. There are many different seasoning blends, from Jamaica's fiery Jerk seasoning (for recipe see **The Great Caribbean Cookout: Jerk & Barbecue**) to "green seasonings" from Trinidad, and Barbados' equally spicy Bajan seasoning. (See **Rum Sauces and Uncommon Condiments** for rub and marinade recipes and **Caribbean Heat** for pepper sauces.)

Jamaican All Purpose Seasoning is a favorite of mine and used in several recipes in this book. Grace, Kennedy & Co. of Jamaica bottles this wonderful aromatic blend of 11 spices, salt, sugar and citric acid. It's a unique mix of allspice, coriander, garlic, paprika, onion, ginger, celery salt, thyme, oregano, black pepper, cumin and hot red pepper in 6 ounce plastic jars. You can find it in the spice sections of supermarkets in Jamaica and Grand Cayman. There really is no exact substitute for it. However, you can make an acceptable substitute and adjust the seasonings to your own taste:

1 – 3.5 ounce bottle Spice Island Beau Monde seasoning
1 teaspoon ground allspice
1 teaspoon ground coriander
1/2 teaspoon ground cinnamon
1/2 teaspoon garlic salt
1/4 teaspoon ground cayenne pepper
1/2 teaspoon sweet paprika
2 teaspoons sugar
Combine all ingredients and blend well. Store in tightly sealed container in a cool place.

Pickapeppa Sauce®

No Caribbean kitchen or table is complete without this delicious sauce and seasoning. Many have tried to duplicate it, but there simply is no substitute for this famous tangy, mildly hot sauce created by a Jamaican named Norman Nash in 1923. Pickapeppa Sauce has become one of the Western Caribbean's most popular seasonings. This blend of tamarind, cane vinegar, mango, raisins, onions, tomatoes, Scotch bonnet pepper and spices is aged in oak barrels for a year before bottling. Pickapeppa Sauce is a key ingredient in Jamaican and Caymanian cooking and now available in many US supermarkets. **Pickapeppa Meat Seasoning**, a spicier seasoning concentrate and meat rub, is based on the original sauce recipe and makes delicious roasts, grilled meats and poultry.

Rose Water

Another ingredient in old-time West Indian, Middle Eastern and Asian recipes, primarily sweets, rose water is sold in West Indian markets alongside vanilla and other flavorings. As its name and flavor suggest, it is the extract of distilled rose petals, about 5% alcohol.

Browning

Browning is similar to Kitchen Bouquet and Gravy Master and sold in 5-ounce bottles. It is an important, versatile ingredient in Caribbean cooking. You can find it in any Caribbean supermarket, from Trinidad to Grand Cayman, and in many foreign supermarkets. This caramelized sugar-based flavoring is frequently used in soups, stews and meat dishes as well as sauces and gravies. Use either of the other products if you can't find browning.

Evaporated and Condensed Milk

Evaporated milk and sweetened condensed milk are common ingredients in Caribbean cooking, but they not the same thing and not interchangeable. Evaporated milk is unsweetened milk with 40% of the water removed, often used in place of light cream on the table or in recipes. Mix equal parts water and evaporated milk as a substitute for the same measure of regular milk. Sweetened condensed milk, invented around 1860, has half the water of whole milk and a lot of sugar. A 14-ounce can contains the fat equivalent of 2-1/2 cups milk, before the water is removed, and 1/2 cup sugar. It is used in baking as a sauce or sweetener in place of cream and sugar combined

Thickeners for Gravy or Sauces

Arrowroot is still the preferred thickener of many Caribbean cooks. If your sauce, stew or gravy is not thick enough and you're afraid you won't have enough of it if you reduce it by boiling longer, use arrowroot, flour or cornstarch to thicken.

The rule of thumb: 1 tablespoon cornstarch or arrowroot will thicken 2 cups liquid. Mix either with a tablespoon or two of cold water to make a paste, then stir into the sauce. Cook over low heat to remove any starchy flavor and thicken the sauce.

You can also use flour, mixing one part flour to two parts water or stock to form a paste. Use about the same proportion as cornstarch – 1 tablespoon will thicken 2 cups but you must cook the sauce or stew at least three minutes after adding the flour paste, stirring with a wire whisk, to blend smoothly and avoid lumps, to cook out the raw floury taste.

Adding peeled and sliced breadfruit to stews and soups will help thicken the broth but this requires longer cooking.

The Caribbean Spice Finder

You'll discover a New World of exotic spice blends and sauces when visiting the Caribbean—but look for them in island supermarkets where the local people shop. Large and small, they offer greater variety and cheaper prices for spices and sauces than souvenir shops and resort boutiques catering to tourists. Back home, those essential spices you may overlooked before, like allspice, thyme, coriander and curry powder are easy to find in any supermarket. You'll probably also find fresh ginger, cilantro, scallions and other Caribbean essentials in your local produce sections. Look for exotic Caribbean sauces and seasoning blends in the specialty or ethnic foods sections of supermarkets, or in stores specializing in Caribbean and West Indian products. Today, there are large Caribbean communities in many areas throughout the US, Canada and Europe and neighborhood stores catering to them are growing more common each year.

If you can't find Caribbean products locally, there's no need to suffer! Try these websites to order online or locate sources in your area.

Tortuga Rum Company's growing line of sauces, seasonings and gourmet products are available from www.tortugarums.com. The site is updated regularly with new products.

Jamaica Place Inc., www.jamaicaplace.com is an excellent resource and reference guide for learning about the variety of Caribbean seasonings available and ordering them online. The site provides links to leading Caribbean food sites, including Grace Foods at www.gracefoods.com. The site offers many other "tings Caribbean," from books and music to Easter Buns and other baked goods.

Learn about the complete line of **Walkerswood's Caribbean Foods** (and download more Caribbean party recipes) at www.walkerswood.com. The site features a Find It In Your Town page that tells where to buy their products in the USA and Europe. **Caribbean Place**, www.caribplace.com, is a good source of 100% Jamaican Blue Mountain Coffees, Jamaica's **Busha Browne** sauces and jams and **Baronhall Farms** hot sauces and exotic spice blends. And **Caribbean Island Imports**, www.caribimports.com is another source for Caribbean gourmet foods and gifts.

Ocho Rios brand Jamaican and Caribbean seasonings and products are another good choice, now available in South Florida Publix supermarkets. Contact: Ph: (305) 326-1734/8899; Fax: (305) 324-1362.

Weights and measures

Liquid measures (US):

3 teaspoons	1 tablespoon
1 tablespoon	1/2 fluid ounce (oz.)
2 tablespoons	1 fluid ounce or 1/8 cup
4 tablespoons	2 fluid ounces or 1/4 cup
8 tablespoons	4 fluid ounces or 1/2 cup
16 tablespoons	8 fluid ounces or 1 cup
1 cup	1/2 pint or 8 fluid ounces
1 pint	2 cups or 16 fluid ounces
1 quart	4 cups or 32 fluid ounces
1 gallon	4 quarts or 128 fluid ounces

Liquid measures (UK):

1 Imperial pint	20 ounces
1/2 pint	10 ounces
1/4 pint	5 ounces
1 Imperial quart	40 ounces or 4.227 cups
1 Imperial Gallon	160 ounces

Dry measures:

"Pinch"	a scant 1/8 teaspoon
1 teaspoon	1/3 tablespoon
3 teaspoons	1 tablespoon
1 dessertspoon	1 scant tablespoon
1/2 tablespoon	1/2 ounce
2 tablespoons	1 ounce
4 tablespoons	2 ounces or 1/4 cup
8 tablespoons	4 ounces or 1/2 cup
12 tablespoons	6 ounces or 3/4 cup
16 tablespoons	8 ounces or 1 cup

Dry Ingredient Measures:

1 pound granulated sugar	2 cups
1 pound brown sugar	2-1/4 cups packed
1 pound powdered sugar	3-1/2 cups
1 cup honey	1-1/4 cups white sugar plus 1/4 cup liquid
1 pound all purpose flour	3-3/4 cups
1 pound rice	2 cups dry, or 4 cups cooked
1 pound loaf bread	12-16 slices
1 cup soft breadcrumbs	1-1/2- 2 slices bread

Dairy and canned milk products:

1 pound butter or margarine	2 cups or 4 sticks
1/2 pound butter	1 cup or 2 sticks
1/4 pound butter	1/2 c or 1 stick, or 8 Tablespoon
1 –14.5 ounce can evaporated milk	1-2/3 cups
1- 14 ounce can condensed milk	1-1/4 cups
1 cup heavy cream	2 cups whipped cream

1 14-ounce can coconut milk ....1-3/4 cups

Fruits and vegetables:
1 pound tomatoes ....2 large ripe (3 inches in diameter) or 3 medium
1 pound bananas ....3 medium
1 pound apple bananas ....8-10- 3-inch fruits
1 average brown coconut.........................1-1/2 pounds, 3 -3-1/2 cups coarse grated meat
1 average brown coconut.........................1/2 - 1 cup coconut water
1 medium pumpkin (calabaza) 5 pounds or about 4-1/2 cups cooked mashed
1 large soursop..1 quart pulp, seeds removed
1 medium mango ....3/4 to 1 pound, 1-1/2 cups peeled and diced, 1 cup puree
1 medium orange ....1/3-cup juice, 2 –2-1/2 tablespoons grated peel
1 medium lemon..2-3 tablespoons juice, 1-1/2 -2 teaspoons grated peel
1 medium Persian lime ....2-3 tablespoons juice, 1-1/2 – 2 teaspoons grated peel
1 key lime ....2 –3 teaspoons juice, 3/4-1 teaspoon grated peel
1 quart strawberries ....4 cups hulled berries
1 medium onion...1 cup chopped
1 medium green pepper ....1 cup chopped (seeded and cored)
3 medium white potatoes........................2 cups peeled and diced
1 pound dry red or kidney beans ....2-1/2 cups dry or 6 cups cooked
1-1/2 inch piece* gingerroot ....1 ounce or about 1-1/2 tablespoons grated
(*called a "thumb")

Seafood
1 pound cleaned conch ....7-8 average or 4 large, 2- 2-1/4 cups ground
1 pound Caribbean lobster ....2 medium (8 oz.) tails, including shell weight
1 pound shrimp..12-14 jumbo; 21-30 large; 31-40 medium

The Caribbean Market

Amazing Fruits, Curious Vegetables and Formidable Tubers

Caribbean markets are a real adventure, filled with exotic spices, amazing fruits, curious vegetables and formidable tubers. Some of these are so funny-looking they leave visitors staring and scratching their heads. West Indian yams look like you'd need a chainsaw to peel them. What on earth do you do with a breadfruit? Soursop evokes amazement – is it a huge green strawberry on steroids? And we won't even get into those deceptive, pretty –and near-lethal little West Indian chiles – they're covered in a special chapter of their own.

Tropical fruits often have dual personalities. When green, some fruits are eaten as vegetables – plantain and papaya for example. Others, like breadfruit, ackee and avocado are served as vegetables when ripe.

Many of the Caribbean's most popular fruits and vegetables were enjoyed long before white men, sugar cane or rum arrived in the West Indies. The Arawak Indians introduced the Europeans to corn, sweet potatoes, cassava, eddos and other roots, as well as tomatoes, avocados, papaya, beans, pumpkin, chili peppers and vanilla. The Spaniards and English brought to the feast sugar, rice, breadfruit, plantain, banana and mango. African slaves brought yam, taro, gungo peas, ackee and okra. Today all of these are popular wares of the Caribbean market. Here is a short introduction to our most popular Western Caribbean vegetables.

Ackee *(Blighia sapida)*
Imported from Africa to the Caribbean during the mid-18th century slave trade, this unique fruit, often mistaken for a vegetable, resembles a ripe red bell pepper when hanging on the tree. You have to be careful: ackee is poisonous when unripe. When edible, the fruit turns red and splits open to reveal 3 or 4 edible fleshy yellow lobes

clinging to large glossy black seeds. When cleaned and boiled or sautéed, they taste somewhat like avocado, but look like scrambled eggs. Ackees are relished in Jamaica and Cayman – in fact, ackee and saltfish (dried salted cod) is Jamaica's national dish and a popular breakfast entrée in Cayman too. But the rest of the Caribbean has never really been interested in this curious fruit.

Ackee Sauté

1 dozen fresh ackees or 1 can (18 ounces) ackees, drained
1/4 pound bacon
2 medium onions, diced
1/2 cup green pepper, diced
3 scallions, chopped
1/2 teaspoon dried thyme
1 teaspoon Worcestershire sauce
2 large fresh tomatoes, diced
1 teaspoon garlic salt
1 teaspoon ground black pepper
1 teaspoon Tortuga Hell-Fire Hot Pepper sauce

If using fresh ackees remove seeds and pink membranes and place cleaned ackees in saucepan. Add enough water to cover and add 1/2 teaspoon salt. Bring to boil then reduce heat to low and simmer for 6-7 minutes, then remove from heat and drain. If using canned ackees, simply drain well. Set ackees aside. Never overcook ackees or they will become mush.

In a frying pan or large skillet, cook bacon until almost crisp. Remove bacon and drain on paper towels. Drain off all but 2 tablespoons bacon fat from pan; add onion and green pepper, cook over medium heat until vegetables are soft. Add tomatoes, scallions, thyme, Worcestershire, garlic salt, pepper, and pepper sauce and stir well. Cook for three minutes, then gently add ackees and bacon – be careful not to mash ackees. Reduce heat to low and cook 3 minutes more until heated through and serve warm.

Avocado *(Persea gratissima or Persea americana)*

Throughout most of the Caribbean, avocados are called "pears," except in Cuba and Spanish-speaking islands, where they are *aguacate* – derived from the Aztec name for the fruit. There are more than 100 varieties of this bright green native South American fruit, actually a cousin of cinnamon from the laurel family. The first mention of this delicacy dates to 1526 when Spanish explorer Gonzalo Oveido saw the tree near the Isthmus of Panama in Colombia. The fruit was first introduced to the West Indies in Jamaica about a century later. When choosing pears, ripe ones will give slightly to a thumb's pressure but should not be soft all over. That's when the slightly nutty flavor and buttery but slightly firm texture are best. While contemporary chefs use avocados in everything from cold soups to ice cream, most Caribbean people eat pears plain, sliced as a side dish or stuffed with seafood as a salad. They are delicious eaten with a spoon, some lime juice and salt all by themselves.

Bananas *(Family Musacae)*

Few things say "Caribbean" more visually than the huge, broad leaves and dangling fruits of a banana plant. Once you've eaten a fresh ripe banana, you'll never be content with supermarket fruits again. Although bananas have been a major Caribbean crop for decades, the fruit was another 18th century European import during the slave trade. There are several varieties in the Caribbean, but the absolute treasure in the Caribbean banana collection is the small, 3 inch sweet finger banana, or "apple banana", named for its slightly-tart flavor. These are often hard to find –islanders gobble them up in markets as soon as they appear, and these bananas are seldom seen outside the Caribbean.

Green bananas are simply very unripe bananas. You'll see clusters of these bananas in island markets – but don't buy and expect them to ripen. Green bananas are peeled, boiled in salted water and served at any meal as a vegetable.

Green Banana Pudding

6 large green bananas
1/4 cup margarine
1 large egg
1 cup sugar
1/4 teaspoon salt
2 cups flour
2 teaspoons baking powder
1/2 teaspoon nutmeg
1/2 teaspoon cinnamon
1/2 cup milk
1/2 cup fresh coconut, grated or chopped fine
1 tablespoon Tortuga Dark Rum

Preheat oven to 375. Grease a 2-quart baking dish. Boil the bananas until soft. Drain and add margarine and mash well. Beat the egg, salt and sugar until light. In separate bowl, sift together the flour, baking powder, cinnamon and nutmeg. Add to the egg mixture alternately with the milk and blend well. Stir in the rum, bananas and coconut and pour into the prepared baking dish or pan. Bake until pudding is lightly browned set in the center, about 30 minutes. Serve warm.

Beans and Peas

Beans are not always beans: often they're called peas or frijoles. But the legumes Caribbean people call peas should not be confused with English peas, the small sweet green vegetable from a pod. Since the days the Amerindians, beans have endured as one of the most important staples of Caribbean diets. Every country from Guyana to Honduras has different recipes, often marrying beans with rice in entrees and sides dishes. The favorites are red beans (red kidney beans) gungo peas (pigeon peas or gandules), black beans (turtle beans) and small Honduran red beans, whose name I have not yet learned. I could devote an entire book to Carib-Bean cookery. Instead, here are essential bean cookery tips and recipes to surprise guests at your next Fête.

Soaking Dry Beans: A pound of dried beans equals about 2 cups and gives you 6 cups cooked. For every pound of beans used, add 8 cups of hot water to a large pot. Stir and bring the beans to a full boil over high heat, then turn off the heat. Cover the pot and soak beans for 1 to 2 hours. You should always soak beans this way before cooking. It returns moisture, softens them and reduces cooking time. But there's another secret to soaking: it draws out and dissolves some of the beans' gas-inducing substances.

Cooking Beans: After soaking, you can cook the beans in the soaking liquid, but if you strain the beans and discard the water it will help reduce their gassy effects. Many Caribbean cooks swear that adding few slices of fresh ginger to the cooking liquid does the same thing. If you drain, add fresh water to cover beans and desired spices or seasonings like garlic and onion – except salt or acidic ingredients like vinegar, lime juice, wine or tomatoes (add these after the beans are tender.) Bring beans to a boil and boil for 10 minutes, then reduce heat to a simmer and cook for 1-1/2 to 2 hours, until beans are soft but not mushy, adding more water if necessary to keep beans from drying out. Cooked beans can be stored in the refrigerator for up to 5 days.

Honey Rum Spiced Beans

1/4 pound salt pork or 8 slices bacon, cut into 1-inch pieces
1 pound dried kidney beans
7 cups water
2 large red onions, chopped
10 cloves garlic, minced
2 stalks celery, sliced in crescents (not chopped)
1/4 cup Tortuga Wildflower Honey or other honey
1 teaspoon fresh grated gingerroot
4 teaspoons ground cumin
1 tablespoon ground coriander
1 tablespoon chili powder
1 tablespoon Worcestershire sauce
1 teaspoon Tortuga Hell-Fire Hot Pepper Sauce
1 can diced tomatoes with juice
1 cup Tortuga Dark Rum
1 teaspoon seasoned salt
1 teaspoon ground black pepper

This dish is best if made a day or two ahead and allowed to "age" in the refrigerator. Pick over beans and place in large saucepan and add water. Bring to a boil and continue boiling for 2 minutes. Remove from heat and let soak, covered, for an hour. Cook salt pork or bacon in 5 quart or larger saucepan or Dutch Oven over medium heat until almost crisp. Remove pork pieces and drain on paper towels. Reserve 1 tablespoon of drippings and add onions, celery and garlic. Cook over medium heat for two minutes but do not allow to brown. Add beans with liquid and cooked pork pieces and bring to a boil, then reduce heat and cook over medium-low for 30 minutes. Add honey, cumin, coriander, chili powder, Worcestershire sauce and pepper sauce. Cover partially and simmer for an hour longer, stirring occasionally to prevent beans from sticking. Remove from heat and add diced tomatoes and 3/4 cup Tortuga Dark Rum and stir well, cover partially and simmer another 45 minutes. Then uncover and add the remaining 1/4 cup rum and simmer until beans are very tender, liquid is reduced and mixture is thick. Add the salt and pepper last, to taste.

Black Beans "Borracho" With Sour Cream

The Cayman Islands lie only about 130 miles south of Cayo Largo, Cuba and the Caymanian connection to the Isle of Pines dates back over a century. This "drunken" spicy adaptation of the traditional Cuban dish, Moros y Cristianos (Moors and Christians) goes well with Caribbean-style pork of any kind.

2 –15 ounce cans black beans, drained
6 slices bacon, cut into small pieces
2 tablespoons olive oil
1 medium onion, chopped (1 cup)
1 stalk celery, diced
4 large cloves garlic, minced
1 teaspoon oregano
1 10-ounce can diced tomatoes & green chilies
1/2 cup Tortuga Dark Rum plus 2 tablespoons
1/2 teaspoon allspice
1 teaspoon ground cumin
2 teaspoons black pepper
1 teaspoon Tortuga Hell-Fire Hot Pepper Sauce
1 tablespoon Worcestershire sauce
1 teaspoon salt

In a large skillet or Dutch oven, cook the bacon over medium heat until crisp. Remove bacon and drain on paper towels. Reserve 1 tablespoon bacon fat and add the olive oil. Heat over medium heat and add the onion, celery and garlic and cook until onion is soft but not brown. Add bacon pieces and remaining ingredients, except for 2 tablespoons rum, and stir well. Bring to a boil, then reduce heat to low. Cover and simmer 30 minutes, stirring occasionally, then adjust seasonings to taste and stir in the remaining 2 tablespoons rum right before serving. Serve with white or yellow rice or as a side dish, garnished with sour cream and chopped scallions. For best flavor, refrigerate overnight and reheat. If reheating, wait to stir in the remaining 2 tablespoons rum until beans are hot and ready to serve.

Breadfruit *(Artocarpus altilis)*

"Conch don't run and breadfruit always ripe" is an old Caymanian saying. Years ago, it meant food was always plentiful and literally, there for the picking. While still abundant on Grand Cayman, breadfruit isn't as widely eaten and appreciated today. Today these delicious, lovely bright green fruit resembling monstrous golf balls fall from trees and often lay ignored.

The humble breadfruit is one of the most interesting of all Caribbean fruit stories. According to history tinged with legend, a British Botanist named Joseph Banks discovered the "rich and abundant food stuff" while traveling the Pacific with Captain Cook in the late 18th century. British Colonial officials in the Caribbean heard this, and sent for the plant – for the sole purpose of providing cheap food for slaves. In April 1789, Captain William Bligh left Tahiti with over 1000 breadfruit cuttings onboard the *H.M. S. Bounty*, bound for the West Indies. But Bligh watered his plants instead of the crew with the sparse water rations during the grueling voyage. This caused the parched sailors to stage the infamous *Mutiny on the Bounty* and the plants never reached the Caribbean.

King George III supported Bligh's second attempt three years later and he returned to Tahiti onboard the *H.M.S. Providence*. This time, he succeeded and sailed into Port Royal, Jamaica in January 1793 with a shipload of 2,126 breadfruit plants which were shared with the rest of the British colonies. Breadfruit soon spread, thrived and many years later became an important part of the West Indian diet.

Breadfruit is a key ingredient of a traditional one-pot meal called **Rundown** in Jamaica and Cayman, and "oil down" in other Caribbean countries (See **Comfort Food, Western Caribbean Style**.) In spite of its odd-pockmarked skin and intimidating size, a ripe or "fit" breadfruit is easy to cook and can be prepared and used just like potatoes in recipes.

For boiled breadfruit, cut the whole fruit into pieces and peel off the green skin with a sharp knife. Boil in salted water until tender – about 15 minutes. Save the water for soup stock – or add chicken bouillon granules and hot sauce and drink immediately like tea. **Roast breadfruit** is even more delicious. Select a fit breadfruit and rub well with vegetable oil. Set the breadfruit on a gas grill or on a grate over hot coals for about an hour, turning several times so the skin is blackened evenly. Steam should come out of the stem end when the breadfruit is ready. **For baked breadfruit**, oil the breadfruit as you did above and preheat oven to 400F. Place the breadfruit on the top oven rack with a pan or aluminum foil directly underneath to catch any oozing juice. Bake for an hour or until the outside yields a little when pressed. Remove from oven and cool for 30 minutes or until easy to handle, then peel and slice or mash with milk and butter.

Breadfruit Chips

1 half-ripe breadfruit
Coconut or peanut oil
Salt

Peel the breadfruit, cut into quarters lengthwise remove the core and parboil in salted water for about 5 minutes. Remove from pot and cool. Pat the pieces dry. Cut each piece in half and slice into thin slices. Heat an inch of oil until hot and fry the pieces, turning once, until golden on both sides. Remove with slotted spoon and drain on paper towels and sprinkle with salt. Serve warm.

Callaloo *(Ameranthus)*

Callaloo is the Caribbean's equivalent to spinach or turnip greens. To some, it is the leaves of the taro root or dasheen. In Cayman and Jamaica, callaloo is a 3-foot dark green leafy vegetable some dismiss as "weeds." It is the key ingredient in Pepperpot Soup (**see Soup Pot**.) Throughout the Caribbean, the word callaloo itself means different things. In Cayman and Jamaica, it is a steamed spiced breakfast dish (see **Comfort Food, Western Caribbean Style**.) In St. Lucia, it is a thick soup with okra and meat. In Trinidad, it becomes a rich one pot meal made with coconut milk, shrimp and spices.

Callaloo or Spinach in Coconut Milk

A delicious island variation of creamed spinach.

3 slices bacon
1 medium onion, diced
1 cup coconut milk

2 pounds chopped callaloo or spinach, rinsed and drained
1 teaspoon lime juice
1 tablespoon Tortuga Dark Rum
1 teaspoon ground black pepper
1/2 teaspoon nutmeg

In a large skillet over medium heat, fry the bacon until crisp. Drain on paper towel. Reserve 1 tablespoon of the bacon fat and sauté the onion until softened. Add the callaloo, coconut milk, rum, lime juice and seasonings. Cover and cook over low heat for 20 minutes. Crumble bacon and mix with callaloo just before serving.

Carrots

The humble, versatile carrot is another favorite vegetable in the Caribbean.

Rum Glazed Carrots

1 pound carrots, peeled
1 tablespoon sugar
1/4 cup unsalted butter, divided
1/2 teaspoon salt
1-1/2 cups water
2 tablespoons dark brown sugar
3 tablespoons Tortuga Dark Rum
1/2 teaspoon ground coriander
1/2 teaspoon nutmeg

Slice the carrots diagonally into 1/4 inch pieces. In a 3-quart saucepan, combine the carrots, 1 tablespoon sugar, 2 tablespoons butter and 1/2 teaspoon salt. Add the water and bring to a boil. Reduce heat to simmer and cover. Cook until the carrots are almost tender, about 10 minutes. Drain and set aside.

In a large skillet over medium heat, melt the remaining butter and stir in the brown sugar. Stir until the sugar has dissolved, then add the carrots and stir again. Sauté until they are evenly coated with the glaze and heated through. Add the rum, coriander and nutmeg and cook another 2 to 3 minutes. This dish can be refrigerated to let flavors blend and reheated over medium heat later.

Carrot Pudding with Rum Sauce

This unusual side dish is an old recipe once popular in the Caribbean's English territories. You seldom see it today.

1/2 cup butter
1/2 cup granulated sugar
1/4 cup light brown sugar, packed firmly
3/4 cup raisins
10 tablespoons Tortuga Dark Rum
2 tablespoons water
1-1/2 cups grated or finely chopped carrot (use a food processor)
1 large eggs, beaten
1 cup flour
1 teaspoon baking powder
1/2 teaspoon salt

1/2 teaspoon cinnamon
1/2 teaspoon nutmeg
Rum Pineapple Sauce (recipe follows)

Preheat oven to 350 F. Grease and flour (or spray with Baker's Joy) an 8-inch square or 1 quart baking dish. Cream together the butter and sugars until smooth, then stir in the eggs, raisins and carrot and blend well. In a separate mixing bowl, combine the flour, baking powder, salt and spices. Gradually add to the carrot mixture and mix well. Combine the rum and water and add to the batter, blending well. Spoon the batter into the prepared dish and bake for 35 –40 minutes or until a toothpick inserted in the center comes out clean. Pudding and sauce can be served warm or chilled.

Rum Pineapple Sauce

2 tablespoons cornstarch
1 cup cold water
1/4 cup sugar
1 cup unsweetened pineapple juice
1 cup Tortuga Dark Rum

In a medium saucepan, combine the cornstarch and cold water and stir until cornstarch dissolves. Add the sugar and cook over medium heat, stirring constantly, until sugar is dissolved and sauce begins to thicken. Remove from heat and stir in the pineapple juice and rum, then return to heat and continue cooking for five minutes, stirring, until the sauce has reduced and thickened slightly.

Cashews (Anacardium occidentale)
If you going to cook absolutely native Caribbean, you'll use cashews instead of walnuts or pecans. Also called cashew apple, the tree originated in South America and arrived in the Caribbean sometime before Columbus. Freshly roasted cashews are a favorite treat in Jamaica – but the tree is not common in Cayman. Cashew wine is a traditional West Indian drink, made from the ripe red fruit. The nut is hidden deep inside and harvesting cashews is a labor-intensive feat.

Cassava Manioc or Yuca (Manihot dulcis – sweet, Manihot esculenta – bitter)
This tough-looking root vegetable, called yuca in Cuba, has been an important part of Caribbean diets since Pre-Columbian times. The Arawak and Carib Indians revered this root as the staff of life – cassava bread was sacred to Carib religious ceremonies.

There are two kinds of cassava, bitter and sweet. Both contain contain prussic acid, a poison removed by cooking – but the bitter cassava root contains so much of this poison that eaten raw, it can kill you. Cassava is grated and made into a popular fried flat bread called **bammy**; peeled and boiled and eaten with butter and garlic, or added to soups and stews.

Like other favorite West Indian tubers, cassava requires effort to prepare. First you must peel away the thick (and sometimes waxed) skin with a heavy sharp knife. But added to soups, and stews or just boiled and covered with the garlicky Cuban mojo or butter sauce, it's delicious. You can now buy frozen peeled cassava in many supermarkets in the US, but it's just not the same as fresh, so make the effort.

Plain Old Cassava

Peel the amount of sweet cassava you want to cook and slice into rounds about 1/2 inch thick. Add to soup or stew at least an hour before serving time. If using as a side dish, cut into larger pieces, cover completely with water and bring to a boil. Reduce heat to a simmer and cook for about 45 minutes, or until the cassava is sticky and tender but still holds its shape. Drain, cool slightly and remove the tough center membrane. Serve with salt and butter or garlic mojo.

Bammy

What Caribbean folks call "bammy" today is very close to the traditional Carib Indian flat cassava bread that sustained the original Spanish settlers. Making bammy from scratch is a time-consuming tradition. You have to peel and grate several pounds of raw bitter cassava, wrap it tightly in cheesecloth and squeeze out all the juice, leaving cassava meal or "bran." According to bammy experts, the best is made in St. Elizabeth parish in Jamaica. Today, you can buy refrigerated or frozen, ready to fry bammy in many Caribbean and US supermarkets, often in the same section as tortillas.

Cho-Cho (Christophene, chayote, vegetable pear or mirliton) *(Sechium edule)*

This bland, innocuous little squash has been a favorite West Indian food dating to the Arawak Indians. The pale green wrinkled lobes grow on lush vines, causing some to mistake them for tiny melons. Cho-chos have more names than uses and can be eaten raw or cooked, peeled or unpeeled. They are added to pickles and pepper sauces, escoveitched fish, soups and stews. Usually, cho-chos are boiled and served with butter and grated cheese as a side dish. Some like them baked them stuffed with ground beef and breadcrumbs. Here's a tidbit of odd insider information: when visiting Costa Rica, please be aware that "chocho" is a rude word, referring to a lady of questionable reputation. Unless you know what you are ordering, be prepared for the consequences. This is undoubtedly more exotic than the vegetable itself, whose appeal I have never quite understood. Nevertheless, here is a popular recipe for cho-cho.

Cho-Cho Au Gratin

I added a hint of rum to this traditional Caribbean favorite, just to add a little zip. You could drink the rum instead, which would make anything more palatable.

3 large cho-chos (about 12 ounces each)
2 tablespoons Tortuga Gold Rum
5 tablespoons butter
2 cups chopped onion
3 cloves garlic, minced
1 teaspoon salt
1 teaspoon black pepper
1-1/2 cups grated parmesan cheese

Preheat oven to 350 F. Line a 9 x12 pan with aluminum foil. In a large pot or Dutch oven, boil the whole, unpeeled cho-chos for 30 minutes, or until tender and a fork pierces the skin easily. Remove from pot and cool 30 minutes. Cut the cho-chos in half and scoop out the pulp and place in a large bowl. Save the skin halves. Mash the cho-cho with the rum and set aside. In a large skillet, melt 3 tablespoons butter over medium heat and sauté the onion and garlic until the onion is soft but not browned. Stir in the mashed cho-cho, salt and pepper and cook two minutes longer. Remove from heat and stir in 1 cup of the grated cheese, mixing well. Divide the mixture and stuff the six cho-cho shells and top each with 1 teaspoon butter and some of the remaining cheese. Arrange in the baking dish and bake for 15-20 minutes, until tops are just lightly browned.

Cocos, Eddoes – Other Hairy, Scary Roots

Along with yams, there are many other intimidating-looking but interesting tropical root vegetables which Caribbean people love. Some of these have a tough, bark-like skin and look like you need a chainsaw to peel them. However a sharp, heavy paring knife will do, but forget using a vegetable peeler. Cocos are also called eddos in Barbados, Cayman and Jamaica – the leaves of this plant are called callaloo, and eaten as greens. Taro and dasheen are other names for this tuber. With the exception of cassava, most of these hairy roots are peeled, chunked and added to soups or stews, not served as side dishes.

Corn

Corn was one of the Amerindians' most important crops yet it never became as important in the Caribbean as it did in North America and is not a major ingredient of Caribbean cooking today. Cornmeal however, is another story. Cornmeal creations are among the Caribbean's oldest and most unusual traditional dishes. In the Western Caribbean, cornbread, corn pudding, such as Cayman's custard topped cornbread and cornmeal custard are old time favorites. West Indians like corn on the cob roasted in the husk over hot coals or boiled with spices. Off the cob, it usually appears in soup or corn pudding.

Spiced Corn, Caribbean Style

8 ears corn, shucked
1 Scotch Bonnet pepper, seeded, deveined and chopped
4 whole allspice berries
1 large yellow onion, chopped
4 cloves garlic, chopped
1 teaspoon dried thyme or 1 sprig fresh thyme
2 tablespoons sugar

Combine all ingredients except corn in a large steamer pot or pan large enough to cover corn with water, about 6 quarts. Bring the water to a rolling boil for three minutes and then add the corn. Reduce heat to simmer and cook for about 7 minutes, or until corn kernels are soft. Serve hot with butter, seasoned salt and pepper.

Corn Pudding

A colorful variation of a traditional favorite.

1 15-1/4 ounce can whole kernel corn, drained
1-15-1/4 ounce can cream-style corn

1 tablespoon butter
2 tablespoons chopped onion
2 tablespoons diced red sweet pepper
1 teaspoon Tortuga Hell-Fire Hot Pepper sauce
1 tablespoon yellow cornmeal
1/4 cup flour
1 teaspoon salt
2 tablespoons sugar
1 teaspoon garlic pepper
1/4 cup butter or margarine, melted
2 tablespoons Tortuga Dark Rum
1 cup evaporated milk
2 large eggs, lightly beaten

Preheat oven to 350 degrees. Spray 2-quart baking dish with nonstick vegetable spray. In a medium saucepan, melt 1 tablespoon butter over medium heat and sauté the onion and red pepper until soft, about three minutes. Remove from heat and stir in both kinds of corn, pepper sauce and garlic pepper. In a small bowl stir together the flour, cornmeal, salt and sugar. In a large mixing bowl, whisk together the milk and eggs until well blended and stir in the rum and melted butter. Gradually stir in the flour mixture and mix until smooth, then stir in corn mixture. Pour into prepared dish and bake for 35 minutes or until center is set and top is pale golden. Cool 10 minutes before serving.

Grapefruit and Uglis

Grapefruit have never been important in Caribbean cooking and I feel sorry for this under-appreciated West Indian creation. According to culinary historians, grapefruit did not exist until the 18th century. In the late 1600's, an English Navy captain sailed into Jamaica from the South Pacific an introduced a large citrus fruit with a thick rind and orange pulp: the shaddock or pomelo. During the next 50 years, somehow an ambitious bee or other act of nature hybridized this mildly bitter fruit and a different species appeared: the grapefruit. It had a thinner rind and much sweeter flavor. The lumpy ugli fruit (pronounced Hooglee) also originated in Jamaica, but it was a deliberate effort. Its pulp is almost seedless and even sweeter than most grapefruit.

Guava *(Psidium Quajava)*

Guavas are another small round fruit native to South American, whose European discovery dates to 1526. Their pungent smell startles many people at first, but the ripe pulp is sweet and exotic-flavored, and makes delicious jelly and paste for desserts.

Lime *(Citrus aurantifolia)*

When Spanish explorers arrived in the New World, they found Amerindians liberally using lime and chile peppers to season seafood. Caribbean limes, or key limes, are smaller, sweeter and juicier than Persian limes and have pale yellow skins when fully ripe. These limes average only about 1-1/4 inches in diameter, but they pack more vitamin C per drop than any other fruit. The Royal Navy picked up supplies of them to prevent scurvy among the crew – coining the term "limey," the West Indian nickname for Englishmen. Limes are one of the most important ingredients in Caribbean sauces, marinades and drinks. Any recipe calling for lemon juice is improved by using key lime juice instead.

Papaya or Paw-Paw *(Carica papaya)*

Called the 'Fruit of Angels" by the early Spanish explorers, papaya, or "paw paw" as it called in Cayman and Jamaica, is a native Caribbean fruit with an amazing variety of uses. The Amerindians considered the plant almost sacred and learned before anyone else that it's one of nature's greatest health foods. Medicinal and healing qualities are attributed to the entire plant, from the stem and roots to the fruit, green or ripe. The fruits can grow to weigh more than five pounds, and the skin contains papain, en

enzyme used in meat tenderizers. Green papaya is eaten boiled or baked as a vegetable, and peeled and sliced raw in salads.

Plantain *(Musa paradisiaca)*

No one is certain about the plantain's origin. Some claim it thrived in Mexico and parts of Central America long before Europeans arrived. Other historians claim it made its way from India to Southern Europe with Arab traders, and from there to the West Indies with a Spanish missionary in 1516.

This bulkier relative of the banana is a fruit commonly eaten as a vegetable and goes with any Caribbean meal, especially breakfast. But plantain confounds many visitors, who don't understand its moody color changes, or which stage is best boiled, fried or baked. Green plantain are cut into 2-inch pieces, boiled for 15 to 20 minutes and eaten with butter and salt, or added to soups or stews. Ripe yellow plantain with dark brown spots and slightly soft when squeezed, makes the sweetest fried plantain.

Here's helpful tip on handling plantains, which are harder to peel than bananas. Plunge the plantain into a pot of warm water for a minute, or hold it under warm running water. This will loosen the skin and make peeling easier.

Fried Plantain

2 large ripe plantains, peeled   1/4 cup peanut oil
1 teaspoon salt

Cut plantains crosswise on the diagonal into pieces about 1/4 inch thick. Sprinkle plantains lightly with salt on both sides. In a large skillet, heat the oil over medium high heat until hot but not smoking. Fry the plantain slices until golden, about 2 minutes on each side. Drain on paper towels and serve hot.

Pumpkin *(Cucurbita sp)*

In the Caribbean, we eat "pumkin" year round. The West Indian pumpkin is actually one of the largest fruits on earth, a member of the gourd family. This pumpkin is called *calabaza* in many Latin countries and sold under that name in US supermarkets. An average pumpkin weighs about 5 pounds. and is seven inches across, with a green and white mottled skin, bright orange flesh and a wonderful, sweet nutty flavor. However, monster pumpkins are common, and can weigh several hundred pounds. It is sweet and delicate enough to make wonderful soups; is a tasty addition to stews and is a favorite side dish, boiled or baked and served with butter and a sprinkle of nutmeg.

Spiced Pumpkin

2 pounds pumpkin, peeled and cut into large cubes
1/2 cup chopped onion
3 cloves garlic, chopped
1 quart chicken broth
2 teaspoons Grace All Purpose Seasoning (see **Island Pantry**)
1 teaspoon black pepper
1 teaspoon Tortuga Hell-Fire Hot Pepper Sauce
2 tablespoons butter

In a large saucepan or Dutch oven, combine the pumpkin, onion, garlic and chicken broth and bring to a boil. Reduce heat and cover, simmering until pumpkin is tender, about 20 –25 minutes. Strain the pumpkin, onion and garlic and pour into a bowl and save the broth to use as soup stock – or drink while warm. Add the butter, seasoning, black pepper and pepper sauce and toss gently or mash if desired. Serve hot.

Pumpkin Pudding

This favorite special occasion side dish could double as dessert or breakfast fare.

2 pounds pumpkin, peeled and cut into cubes
2 cups flour
2 cups light brown sugar
2 large eggs, beaten
2 tablespoons fresh lime juice
1 teaspoon vanilla extract
1/4 cup butter or margarine, melted
3 tablespoons Tortuga Dark Rum
1-1/2 cups coconut milk

Preheat oven to 350 F. Grease or spray with nonstick vegetable spray a 3-quart. baking dish. In a large saucepan, boil the pumpkin in enough salted water to cover it until pumpkin is soft, about 20 minutes. Drain pumpkin and save water for soup stock if desired. Place the pumpkin in a large bowl and add the flour and sugar, beating until smooth. Gradually add the beaten eggs, mixing until smooth. Add the coconut milk, lime juice, vanilla and rum and blend well. Pour mixture into the prepared baking dish and bake at 350F for 45 –50 minutes, until top is golden and slightly puffed. Remove and cool for 10 minutes before serving.

Sweet Potatoes (Ipompea batata)

There are several varieties of West Indian sweet potato, whose botanical name sounds like a Latin epithet, *Ipompea batata*. These are different from Louisiana "yams" or soft skinned sweet potatoes, which we call American Sweet Potatoes. In the Western Caribbean, our locally grown sweet potato is drier and has yellow or white flesh and is usually eaten boiled, added to soups or stews or baked. Cubans love **boniato**, another variety of sweet potato, which has bumpy, reddish skin and white, slightly sweet flesh – it is also delicious when baked.

Sweet Potato Pone

2 pounds West Indian white sweet potatoes, peeled and grated (or chopped fine in food processor)
1/2 cup grated or finely chopped fresh coconut
1-1/4 cups dark brown sugar, firmly packed
3 cups coconut milk (freshly made if possible)
1 cup evaporated milk
1/2 cup raisins
1 tablespoon currants
2 tablespoons butter, melted
2 teaspoons vanilla extract
1/2 cup Tortuga Dark Rum
1/2 cup flour
1/2 teaspoon salt
1 teaspoon baking powder
1/2 teaspoon nutmeg
1 teaspoon cinnamon
2 teaspoons grated fresh gingerroot

Butter the inside of a 10-inch springform pan, and wrap outside with aluminum foil. In a large mixing bowl, combine the sweet potato, coconut, both milks, sugar, raisins and currants. Stir well, then add the vanilla, rum and butter. In a separate bowl, combine the flour, salt, baking powder and spices. Stir to blend, then add to the sweet potato mixture. Stir until well blended. Pour into the prepared pan and let sit for 30 minutes. Heat oven to 350F. Bake the pudding for 1-1/4 to 1-1/2 hours, or until the center is set. Remove from oven and cool on wire rack until pudding reaches room temperature.

Soursop *(Annona muricata)*

This weird fruit migrated to the West Indies from Peru and Ecuador and was another surprise that greeted the Europeans, who were probably frightened by its bizarre appearance. The fruits can weigh several pounds when ripe and look like huge green strawberries with soft bristles. It was a favorite treat of the Arawak and Ciboney Indians who made medicinal tea from the leaves and knew that nature's lemon custard was inside the rugged green skin. After peeling and removing the seeds from the creamy white pulp, you can chill the fruit and eat it like pudding or use it in drinks or, ice cream. (See the **Rum Shop** for recipes for traditional soursop drinks.)

Tamarind *(Tamarindus indica)*

Originally from India, towering tamarind trees have grown on most Caribbean islands for over two centuries. Caribbean islanders know when to pick the wrinkled brown pods to get the tamarinds at the peak stage of ripeness. These pods are filled with seeds surrounded by tart pulp, a key ingredient in **Pickapeppa Sauce®**, a Caribbean favorite; chutneys and Worcestershire Sauce. Many suspect tamarind is also the secret ingredient of Trinidad's **Angostura Bitters**. Pucker-producing tamarind balls are a favorite Caribbean sweet. Fresh tamarinds are hard to find outside the Caribbean, but canned tamarind nectar is now widely available.

Tamarind Balls

1 quart water
1-1/2 tablespoons salt
3 cups tamarind pulp, seeds removed
3 cups granulated sugar
1/4 teaspoon finely chopped, seeded and deveined hot chile pepper (bird or Scotch bonnet)

In a large saucepan or heavy pot, combine the water and salt and stir well. Add the tamarind pulp and bring to a boil, cooking until pulp is soft. Strain off the water and add the pepper and sugar, a little at time, until the mixture is firm enough to shape into balls. Roll mixture into 1-inch balls and roll in additional sugar. Wrap in wax paper and chill until ready to eat.

Tomatoes

You're probably saying: "Come on, this isn't "native Caribbean!" Oh yes it is!

When the Spanish explorers arrived seeking gold in the New World, they instead discovered edible treasures instead to take home. Corn, squash, pineapples, avocados, chiles – and tomatoes were among that 15th century cache of culinary gems. The modern tomato began as a Pre-Columbian weed that spread from Peru throughout tropical America, and was later cultivated in Mexico. Off all the exotic ingredients exchanged between old and new worlds, the tomato became the darling of European society – adored much more there than in its native region.

I have come across few English-speaking Caribbean recipes which celebrate the use of tomatoes the way the French and Spanish Caribbean countries do. Small plum tomatoes, often imported, are used to season some dishes, from **Fish Cayman Style** to steamed callaloo. But ripe fresh local tomatoes, many grown in hydroponic farms, are still an expensive delicacy in Cayman. Cooking with them would be blasphemy.

Yams (Dioscorea sp)

The name "yam" has confused many people. Botanically speaking, West Indian yams are the edible roots of the Dioscorea family. The small orange lobes relished in the Southern USA are sweet potatoes, not yams, and belong to a different family entirely. Yams traveled with the slave trade from Africa to the Caribbean. There are several varieties: the most common have white or yellow flesh. Yam pieces can be as big as firewood – whole yams can grow over 100 pounds. They have a tough brown skin and must be peeled with a sharp, heavy knife before cooking. West Indian yams have slightly sweet, nutty flavor and are usually boiled like a potato, but are also delicious roasted, baked or made into yam chips. More odd trivia: succulent plant enthusiasts in Europe and South Africa prize members of this family as botanical showpieces and would be shocked to find them in a pot.

Baked Yams Caribe

3 pounds yellow yam, peeled
2/3 cup evaporated milk
2 tablespoons butter, softened
1 large egg, beaten
2 tablespoons Tortuga Gold Rum
2 cloves garlic, minced
1 teaspoon salt
1 teaspoon ground black pepper
2 cup shredded or grated cheddar cheese, plus 3 tablespoons
1 teaspoon grated nutmeg

Clean the yams and remove any coarse fibers running through the flesh and cut into 1-inch pieces. In a large saucepan, boil the yams in salted water until soft, then drain and cool slightly. Preheat oven to 350 F. Lightly grease a 2-quart baking dish. Mash yams lightly with fork then use an electric mixer to beat with the milk, butter, rum and egg. Mix in the garlic, salt and pepper, then add the 2 cups cheese. Spoon the yam mixture into the prepared baking dish and sprinkle with remaining grated cheese and nutmeg. Bake for 25-30 minutes until golden brown on top. Serves 4 to 6.

Comfort Food – Western Caribbean Style

No matter how affluent or sophisticated we become, our palates long for traditional dishes, our comfort food: things like turtle stew, conch stewed in coconut milk and cassava heavy cake. Other Cayman favorites, like ackee and saltfish, jerk pork and rice 'n peas, reflect the influence of Jamaica and other Caribbean cultures.

Rum and Red Stripe may get things started, but the heart of Caribbean parties is food. The menu should include at least a taste, if not a feast, of favorite local dishes – what some call "native food". Start with generous portions of meat, chicken or seafood – sometimes all three – and then add side dishes. Coleslaw, breadfruit salad and two or three additional kinds of starch: rice and peas, macaroni and cheese and boiled or baked cassava, breadfruit, yam or sweet potato –or maybe all of the above. Bread is a must, whether you serve johnnycake, hard-dough bread, coco bread or cornbread. And then start another plate for those wonderful sweets...

Then step up the beat with a pulse of provocative rhythms – **Byron Lee and the Dragonnaires**, **The Mighty Sparrow**, the **Tradewinds** and **Cayman's Barefoot Man and Band** , start dancing and work off all that delicious food.

Like many Caribbean dishes, traditional Caymanian cooking is not very heart-smart. You may wish to lighten recipes I've preserved in their original form. Many require some form of coconut, including pure coconut oil. Before trying recipes requiring coconut milk, refer to **Going Coconuts** for an explanation of this traditional Caribbean ingredient. Since the foreign Cholesterol Police banned coconut as a catalyst to cardiac arrest years ago, the oil is now hard to find especially outside the Caribbean. It makes a huge flavor difference – and many islanders have lived long healthy lives that included a coconut-rich diet.

Breakfast

Once you've eaten breakfast, Caribbean-style, you'll never think of this meal the same way again. A healthy helping of soup for breakfast is still a Saturday morning tradition in many parts of the region, especially Jamaica. Some claim this custom started as the cure for Friday night "fête head" or the jitters from a rum shop marathon. Soup restores the body's balance of "normal- proof" fluids and nutrients. Caribbean soups are eaten any time, from breakfast until the after-party hours. You'll find Caribbean folk enjoying soup when most people are sleeping or drinking their morning coffee. (See the **Soup Pot** for more recipes.)

Some soups are reputedly aphrodisiacs – conch chowder tops the list (see **Conch Pearls** for recipes). Jamaica's famous Mannish Water and Bullfoot Soup (Cowfoot) are others, but the ingredients might overwhelm **Rum Fever** readers, so I'll let you enjoy them in ignorance when visiting the islands.

Fish Tea

In Cayman, it's agreed that West Bay captains and fishermen make some of the country's best fish tea, especially in crowd-size quantities. There are many different recipes, but all begin with a fish head, the bigger the better and a very large, well-seasoned pot. For smaller quantities, divide by half or quarters.

4 pounds fresh fish, including head and backbone, cut up
8 quarts water
1/3 cup salt or more to taste
2 large sprigs fresh thyme
10 allspice berries
2 bay leaves
2 tablespoons ground black pepper
5 large onions, chopped
8 large scallions, green tops and white part, chopped
6 stalks celery, diced
3 teaspoons Tortuga Hell-Fire Hot Pepper Sauce or 1 whole Scotch Bonnet
6 cup white potatoes, peeled and diced
2 tablespoons fresh ground black pepper or more to taste
1/3 cup fresh lime or lemon juice

Clean and gut the fish and remove any scales and fins; wash thoroughly with water and fresh lime juice. Combine the fish, water, salt, thyme, onion, scallion, peppercorns, allspice, bay leaves and whole Scotch bonnet pepper, pierced once. Bring to a boil. Reduce heat and simmer uncovered for 45 minutes, stirring several times, then remove from heat and cool. Strain the fish tea to remove fish skin, bones and meat and seasonings, leaving the fish stock in the pot. Save the strained solids. There are two ways to finish the tea:

The **Caymanian way** is to pick over the fish carefully and remove all edible meat. Save the eyeballs – these are special. Discard the skin, bones and waste and return the eyeballs and edible chunks of fish to the pot.

Jamaican-style is much closer to a fish broth. After straining out the fish and seasonings, remove the bay leaves and Scotch bonnet, and pick over the fish, saving the meat. Combine the other seasonings and fish meat in the sieve and press and rub through. You should have fine seasoned fish flakes in the broth.

To the original stock pot, add the potatoes and any other desired vegetables, such as peeled yam, cho-cho or green banana, and lime juice. Bring to a boil, then reduce heat to low and simmer for 15 minutes or until potatoes are tender. Stir well and add the lime juice and season with more salt and pepper to taste. Serves 20, more or less, depending on their passion for fish tea.

Red Bean (Peas) Soup

A favorite in Cayman and Jamaica and every cook's recipe is slightly different – mine adds a hint of dark rum and ginger.

2 cups dried red beans or kidney beans
2-1/2 quarts water
1-1/2 pounds beef stew meat, trimmed of excess fat
3/4 pound salted pig's tail or chopped cooked ham
3-3/4 quarts water
1 cup Tortuga Dark Rum
1 large onion, chopped
4 scallions, chopped
1 large sprig fresh thyme or 1 teaspoon dried thyme
2 cloves garlic, minced
1 tablespoon ground black pepper
1 whole Scotch bonnet pepper, unpierced,
OR 1 tablespoon Tortuga Hell-Fire Hot Pepper Sauce
1 tablespoon fresh grated gingerroot
1 tablespoon chicken bouillon granules or salt, more to taste
3/4 pound West Indian yellow yams or cocos, peeled and diced
Dumplings (Spinners – recipe follows)

Soak the pig's tail in cold water for 4 hours to remove some of the salt. Rinse the beans and add to 2-1/2 quarts of hot water in a large pot. Stir and bring the beans to a full boil over high heat, then turn off the heat. Cover the pot and soak beans for 2 to 4 hours. Drain both the pig tail and beans (if using ham, add here) and transfer to an 8-quart pot or Dutch oven, and add the remaining 4 quarts water, rum, beef and all remaining ingredients except yam and dumplings and bring to a boil, stirring several times. Reduce heat to low, cover and simmer for 2-1/2 hours or until beans are turning soft and meat is almost fork tender. Add the chicken bouillon or salt, yams and dumplings and cook another 20 minutes until all ingredients are soft and dumplings are cooked. Remove whole Scotch bonnet pepper and adjust seasonings as desired. If you want a smoother soup, puree half the soup or more in a food processor and return to the pot.

Plain Flour Dumplings

In Jamaica, these are also called "spinners."

1-1/4 cups flour
1/2 teaspoon salt
Water

Combine the flour and salt and add enough water to make a stiff dough. Measure out about 2 tablespoons for each dumpling onto floured surface and roll into two-inch lengths. Add to the simmering Rundown, soup or stew during the last 15-20 minutes.

Cornmeal Dumplings

This recipe makes about two dozen.

1/4 cup yellow cornmeal (not self rising)
1 cup flour
1 teaspoon sugar
1 teaspoon salt
2 tablespoon butter
Water

Combine the cornmeal, flour, sugar and salt and stir well or whisk with a wire whisk until blended. Using two knives or a pastry blender cut in the butter until the mixture is crumbly. Add just enough water to form a stiff smooth dough, blending all ingredients. Flour your hands and pinch off chunks of dough and roll into 2-inch oblongs about 1/2 inch thick and tapered at the ends. Drop into hot soup or stew and boil until done, about 15-20 minutes.

Pepperpot Soup

A delicious blend of flavors – and another recipe that varies throughout the Caribbean. It's often a meal in itself. You can substitute fresh spinach, kale or collard greens if you can't find callaloo locally.

2 quarts water
1 pound beef stew, cut into 1-inch chunks
1/2 pound lean salt pork, diced fine
2 medium onions, diced
2 medium green peppers, seeded and diced
2 large cloves garlic, minced
4 scallions, chopped
2 pounds callaloo, washed and chopped fine
1 teaspoon dried thyme
1 whole Scotch bonnet pepper, unpierced
OR: 1 tablespoon Tortuga Hell-Fire Hot Pepper Sauce
1/2 pound West Indian yellow yam, peeled and cubed
1/2 pound coco, dasheen or other white tuber, peeled and sliced
1 dozen fresh okras, washed and sliced
2 tablespoons vegetable oil
2 teaspoons black pepper
1-1/2 cups coconut milk

In a 6-quart pot or Dutch oven, combine the water, beef, salt pork, thyme, onion, garlic and scallions and bring to a boil. Reduce heat to low, cover and simmer for an hour. Add the callaloo, green pepper, Scotch bonnet pepper or sauce, yam and coco and stir well. Bring to a boil, then reduce heat to low, cover and simmer for 45 minutes adding more water if necessary. Cook until vegetables are soft and meat is falling apart tender. If you want dumplings, add them during the last 20 minutes. In a small skillet, heat the oil over medium heat and sauté the okras until lightly browned and slime is cooked out, about

3 minutes. Add the okra and coconut milk to the soup and stir well. Cook five minutes longer and adjust seasonings as desired.

Pumpkin Soup

This rich, thick soup is one of my favorites, adapted from a recipe given to me in Nevis 20 years ago.

1/2 pound bacon or salt pork, diced
1/4 cup butter or margarine
3 medium onions, chopped
3 large cloves garlic, minced
2 medium green peppers, seeded and chopped
1 small eggplant, peeled and cubed (2 cups)
6 cups chicken broth
2 cups coconut milk
2 pounds peeled and diced West Indian pumpkin (calabaza)
2 teaspoons Tortuga Hell-Fire Hot Pepper Sauce
1 teaspoon ground cumin
1 teaspoon thyme
2 teaspoons sugar
2 teaspoons black pepper
2 teaspoons seasoned salt
1/2 cup Tortuga Dark Rum
2 cups canned cooked pigeon peas, well drained

In a large pot or 8- quart Dutch oven, cook the bacon or salt pork until firm and browned but not crisp, then remove and drain on paper towels. Reserve 3-4 tablespoons of drippings and add the butter or margarine. Heat over medium heat and add the onion, peppers, garlic and eggplant and stir well. Cook the vegetables, stirring frequently, for 10 minutes until turning soft, then add the chicken broth, coconut milk pumpkin, pepper sauce, bacon or salt pork pieces, cumin, thyme, sugar, rum, salt and pepper and bring to a boil. Reduce heat to low, cover and simmer 30 minutes, stirring occasionally, until vegetables are very soft. Add more chicken broth if necessary, but vegetables should cook down to provide enough liquid. Stir soup well to mash vegetables. At this point, if you want a smoother soup, puree half the amount in batches in a food processor and return to pot. Stir in the pigeon peas and cook another 15 minutes until hot. Adjust seasonings to taste.

Ackee & Saltfish

Although actually the National dish of Jamaica, this is widely enjoyed in Cayman too, especially for breakfast. Chances are unless you live in South Florida, you won't find fresh ackees available. Look for canned ackees at any Caribbean market.

1 pound saltfish (salted cod)
1/4 cup olive oil
1/2 pound salt pork, diced or 8 slices bacon, cut into small pieces
4 scallions, trimmed and minced
1 medium onion chopped
1 clove garlic, minced
1/2 teaspoon dried thyme
1 teaspoon Tortuga Hell-Fire Hot Pepper Sauce

OR 1/16th –1/8th teaspoon minced, seeded Scotch Bonnet pepper
3 medium tomatoes, chopped
2 cans drained or 2 dozen fresh ackees
1 teaspoon Worcestershire sauce
1 teaspoon seasoning salt
fresh ground black pepper to taste.

Place salt cod in saucepan and cover with cold water. Soak for 30 minutes, then drain and add a quart of fresh water. Bring to a boil and cook for 10-12 minutes. Drain the fish and rinse under cold water. When cool enough to handle, pick over to remove any skin and bones and flake the fish.

If using fresh ackees, remove seeds and pink membranes and place in saucepan. Add enough water to cover and 1/2 teaspoon salt. Parboil the ackees: bring to boil then reduce heat and simmer for 5 minutes, then remove from heat and drain. If using canned ackees, simply drain well. Set ackees aside. Never overcook ackees or they will become mush.

Fry salt pork or bacon in frying pan until crisp – remove pieces from pan. Reserve 2 teaspoons fat. (You can omit the salt pork and pork fat and increase oil by 2 teaspoons.) Add oil to remaining pork fat and heat over medium heat. Add the scallions, onion, garlic, Scotch Bonnet, thyme and tomatoes and sauté until onion is soft, about five minutes. Reduce heat to low and stir in the flaked saltfish until mixed with vegetables. Gently stir in ackees so they remain in large pieces and top with salt pork pieces and bacon. Cook over low heat about 5 minutes longer, until heated. Sprinkle black pepper over mixture and serve hot.

Ackee and Shrimp

I risk blasphemy by admitting I prefer my ackee without saltfish and this dish, with a side of boiled green bananas and callaoo is my idea of a heavenly brunch.

2 dozen fresh ackee or a 1-pound can, well drained
1 pound medium to large shrimp, peeled
2 tablespoons butter
1 large onion, chopped
3 cloves garlic, minced
2 tablespoons Tortuga Gold Rum
1 teaspoon Tortuga Hellfire Pepper Sauce
1 cup clam juice or chicken broth
2 ripe plum tomatoes, chopped
1/2 teaspoon thyme
2 teaspoons Pickapeppa Sauce
1 teaspoon seasoned salt
1 teaspoon ground black pepper

If using fresh ackees, remove seeds and pink membranes and place in saucepan. Add enough water to cover and add 1/2 teaspoon salt. Parboil the ackees: bring to boil then reduce heat and simmer for 5 minutes, then remove from heat and drain. If using canned ackees, simply drain well. Set ackees aside. Never overcook ackees or they will become mush.

Heat the butter over medium heat in a large skillet and add the onions and garlic, sautéing over medium heat until onions are soft, stirring frequently. Do not let onions or garlic brown. Add rum, clam juice or broth, pepper sauce, tomatoes and remaining seasonings and simmer another 5 minutes, then gently stir in the parboiled ackee and shrimp and cook another 3 minutes until shrimp turn pink. (If using canned ackees, add them last, gently stirring into the hot shrimp mixture just until mixed and heated through)

Steamed Callaloo

"Spinach" for breakfast? You bet! In my opinion, this dish stands alone as the breakfast of champions. It goes well with a side of grits or scrambled eggs too.

2 pound callaloo or spinach, washed and chopped (including stems)
6 slices bacon
1 medium onion, chopped
2 scallions, chopped
1 teaspoon Tortuga Hell-Fire Hot Pepper Sauce
OR 1/16th teaspoon minced, seeded Scotch Bonnet pepper
1 clove garlic, minced
1 teaspoon black pepper
2 teaspoons salt
1 medium tomato, or 2 plum tomatoes, chopped
1 tablespoon olive or vegetable oil

In a large skillet, fry the bacon until almost crisp and remove and drain. Reserve 1 tablespoon bacon fat in skillet and add the vegetable oil, Heat over medium heat and add the onion, scallion, pepper sauce or Scotch Bonnet and garlic and cook until onion begins to turn soft, about 3 minutes. Add the callaloo and tomato and stir well, then the salt and pepper. Stir and cover, reduce heat to low and simmer for about 10 minutes, stirring occasionally, or until the callaloo is tender. Stir in reserved bacon pieces and serve.

Mackerel Rundown

Hold on, you say: this dish can't be "what it's name suggests!" It sounds like roadkill! But this Jamaican favorite, also called "Dip and Fall Back" lives up to its name. All the ingredients are put into a big pot on the stove and cooked over low heat until it "runs down", or cooks away to a savory coconut fish stew. This is another favorite dish that varies from cook to cook. Some like to add boiled flour dumplings with the variety of "ground provisions:" local roots and vegetables, such as plantains, cassava, yam and breadfruit.

1 quart fresh coconut milk or 4 cups canned coconut milk
2 pounds salted mackerel
1 tablespoon fresh lime juice
2 tablespoons oil
3 medium onions, chopped (about 1-1/2 cups)
2 cloves garlic, minced
3 large stalks scallion
2 medium tomatoes, chopped
1 medium green sweet pepper, diced

1 teaspoon vinegar
1 teaspoon Tortuga Hell-Fire Hot Pepper Sauce
OR 1/16th teaspoon minced, seeded Scotch Bonnet pepper
1 large sprig fresh thyme or 1 teaspoon dried thyme
Peeled and sliced breadfruit, green plantain, yam as desired

Wash the mackerel in fresh water and lime juice and place in a 3-quart pot. Cover with water and bring to a boil. Cook until fish begins to fall off the bone and remove from heat. Carefully pick over to remove the bones and reserve the cleaned fish.

In a Dutch oven or large pot, heat the oil over medium heat and add the onions, scallion, green pepper and garlic and cook until onions are soft – do not let vegetables brown. Add the coconut milk, tomatoes, vinegar, pepper sauce or whole pepper, thyme and about 2 cups of breadfruit or other vegetables as desired. Stir well and bring the mixture to a boil, then reduce heat, cover and simmer for 30 minutes until the breadfruit is tender and coconut milk has "run down" to form a thin layer of oil on the surface. Stir in the mackerel and heat thoroughly. Remove the whole pepper and add more salt and black pepper to taste. At this point, the stew is "run down" and ready to serve. Serve with rice and peas and additional roasted breadfruit slices.

Rundown, Cayman Style

Rundown is a favorite dish in many Caribbean countries, where it is also called Oiled Down. Along with Turtle Stew and conch stew, Rundown is considered a favorite traditional dish in the Cayman Islands. However, Caymanians like their Rundown with either salt beef or fresh fish rather than salted mackerel. It will take some practice to get this right.

1/4 cup butter (1/2 stick)
1/4 cup flour
1 quart coconut milk (fresh, if possible)
2 pounds fresh fish steaks or filets
1 tablespoon fresh lime juice
3 medium onions, chopped (about 1-1/2 cup)
2 cloves garlic, minced
1 teaspoon Tortuga Hell-Fire Hot Pepper Sauce
OR 1/16th teaspoon minced, seeded Scotch Bonnet pepper
3 large stalks scallion
1 medium green sweet pepper, diced
2 stalks celery, diced
1 large sprig fresh thyme or 1 teaspoon dried thyme
Peeled and sliced breadfruit, green bananas or plantain, yam, as desired
Dumplings (recipe in this chapter)

Wash the fish in fresh water and lime juice and season with seasoned salt and pepper. In a Dutch oven or large pot, melt the butter and stir in the flour to blend well. Cook over low heat, stirring constantly, until the mixture bubbles and turns light colored but not brown. Pour in the coconut milk and stir well, then stir occasionally as mixture comes to a boil. Add the chopped onions, garlic, hot pepper, scallion, sweet pepper, celery and thyme and simmer 10 minutes. Next add the amount of vegetables desired, peeled and cut into serving pieces. Let the rundown return to a boil then reduce to simmer, cover and cook for 5 minutes. Remove cover and place the fish on top of the mixture and add the dumpling dough at this time. When mixture returns to a simmer, cover again and cook until oil appears on the surface and meat or fish is cooked, about 20 minutes.

Boiled Green Bananas

Green bananas are a popular breakfast dish, often served on the side as a vegetable or added to soups, stews and dishes – like Mackerel and Green Banana. Cut the ends of each banana and slice the skin along the length on the ridges, but leave skins on. Cover with salted water and bring to a boil for 10 minutes. Peel and serve warm.

Liver and Onions

This is another popular breakfast dish – nothing like liver and onions American style.

2 pounds beef liver
1/4 cup Tortuga Gold Rum * (Optional, but gives a delicious flavor)
1 medium onion, chopped
3 cloves garlic, minced
3 scallions, chopped
1 teaspoon Tortuga Hell-Fire Hot Pepper Sauce
OR 1/16th teaspoon minced, seeded Scotch Bonnet pepper
1 teaspoon dried thyme
2 tablespoons Pickapeppa Sauce
1 tablespoon browning
2 teaspoons black pepper
1 teaspoon seasoned salt
1 large tomato, chopped
1/4 cup vegetable oil
1/4 cup beef broth

Slice the liver across the grain into strips and then slice again, so pieces are about and inch and a half long. In a plastic or glass bowl, combine the meat and all ingredients except the tomato, oil and beef broth. Let the mixture marinate for several hours.

Heat the oil in a large skillet and remove the liver pieces from the marinade. Reserve the marinade. Sauté the liver in batches, until browned, removing each batch so it doesn't overcook. When all liver is browned, return to pan and add the reserved marinade and vegetables and beef broth, tomato, and stir well. Reduce heat to low, cover, and simmer for about an hour or until liver is fork tender. Check the liver and stir occasionally, and if needed, add a little more beef broth if mixture appears too dry.

Johnny Cakes

These little dough balls are a popular breakfast side with ackee and saltfish, mackerel and banana and just about anything. In Barbados, a similar dish is called Bakes.

2 cups flour
1 tablespoon baking powder
1/2 teaspoon salt
1 teaspoon sugar
2 tablespoons lard (yes, lard!) or vegetable shortening
About 1/2 cup water

Sift the flour, baking powder, salt and sugar into a medium mixing bowl. Using a pastry blender or your fingers cut or rub in the lard until the mixture resembles fine crumbs. Add enough water, a little at a time, to form a soft dough. Turn the dough onto a lightly floured surface and flour your hands. Knead the dough until smooth, adding a little more flour if necessary to work easily. Pinch off pieces of dough (about 2 tablespoons each) and roll into 2-inch balls. Flatten into 1/2 inch thick circles. Heat enough vegetable oil to cover cakes completely in a large heavy skillet until hot (375 F) Fry cakes until golden on each side, and then remove and drain on paper towels. This makes 12 cakes. Serve warm

Escoveitched Fish

This delicious, spicy fish dish is a traditional Jamaican dish and also part of "Caribbean breakfast" in Cayman, whose "native cuisine" is heavily influenced by Jamaica. While cleaned, small whole grunts or snappers are best, you can use any kind of fish steaks, such as kingfish or dolphin instead. It can be prepared a day ahead of time and refrigerated to get the maximum flavor from spices, but should be served at room temperature.

6- small whole, cleaned grunts or snapper or 6-6 ounce fish steaks (wahoo, kingfish, dolphin)
3 limes
1/2 cup flour
1-1/2 tablespoons fresh ground black pepper
4 teaspoons seasoned salt
1/2 cup peanut oil (for frying)
Marinade:
2 cups white vinegar
1 teaspoon Tortuga Hell-Fire Hot Pepper Sauce
OR 1/16th teaspoon minced, seeded Scotch Bonnet pepper
1 carrot, cut into julienne strips
1 cho-cho (Chayote), peeled and cut into strips
2 medium onions, sliced into thin rings
1 green pepper, sliced into thin rings
4 cloves garlic, sliced thin
1 tablespoon allspice berries
8 whole black peppercorns

Rinse the cleaned whole fish or steaks with water and sprinkle with lime juice. Pat dry and sprinkle each with seasoned salt and black pepper. Pour the flour into a small bowl and dredge each fish or steak lightly in flour, shaking off excess. Set aside. Heat the oil in a frying pan until very hot and fry fish immediately until golden brown, about 3 -4 minutes per side. Remove fish and drain on paper towels, then arrange in a single layer in glass or plastic dish.

Marinade: Combine all remaining ingredients, from vinegar to black peppercorns, in saucepan and bring to a boil over medium heat. Reduce heat and simmer until vegetables are tender, about 4-5 minutes. Remove from heat and cool 10 minutes, then pour the marinade over the fish and arrange fish so all pieces are evenly covered with mixture. Allow to stand for at least an hour, or refrigerate until ready to serve. Allow fish to return to room temperature before serving.

Snacks & Street Food

Meat Patties

They been around for decades and are still the most popular savory snack in Cayman and Jamaica. Be careful – these Caribbean meat pastries are addictive. You can adjust the amount of hot pepper to taste. Both the filling and the pastry should be made a day ahead.

Filling:
1 tablespoon vegetable oil
3/4 pound ground beef or chicken
2 teaspoons curry powder
1 teaspoon ground black pepper
2 large scallions
1 medium onion
1 teaspoon Tortuga Hell-Fire Hot Pepper sauce
OR about 1/16th teaspoon finely minced, seeded Scotch bonnet
2 cloves garlic
1 teaspoon seasoned salt
1/2 teaspoon dried thyme
1 teaspoon ground allspice
1/4 teaspoon ground cumin
3/4 cup dry unseasoned bread crumbs
1 tablespoon Tortuga Dark Rum

Use a food processor to chop finely the onion, scallion, garlic and hot pepper or pepper sauce. In a large skillet, heat the oil over medium heat and add the ground beef or chicken, breaking up so it's crumbly. Sprinkle with the curry powder and black pepper and cook until browned, about 10 minutes. Stir in the remaining ingredients and cook over medium heat, 25 minutes, until all liquid has evaporated and meat mixture is thick. Remove from heat and transfer filling mixture to a bowl, cover and chill overnight.

Pastry:
2 cups flour
4 tablespoons lard, chilled
4 tablespoons unsalted butter, chilled
1/2 teaspoon salt
1 teaspoon curry powder or ground turmeric (for color)
About 2- 3 tablespoons ice water

Sift together the flour, curry powder and salt into a large bowl. Using a pastry blender, cut the lard and butter into the flour until it resembles coarse meal. Add enough water to make a soft dough you can work with. Flour your hands and form the dough into a large ball and place on a floured surface. Knead, turning once or twice, until it is smooth. Wrap the pastry in wax paper or plastic wrap and chill overnight or at least 12 hours.

To make the patties: Preheat oven to 400. Line a baking sheet with aluminum foil and grease lightly. When ready to make the patties, divide the dough into about 24 pieces, each enough to roll out into 6 inch circles. Place about 2 tablespoons of meat filling on one side of each circle and fold dough over to form a semi-circle. Crimp and seal edge by flattening with a fork. Transfer to baking sheet and bake at 400F for 25-30 minutes, or until pastries are golden brown.

Stamp & Go (Salt Cod Fritters)

A traditional snack that originated in Jamaica.

1/2 pound saltfish (salted codfish)
1 cup flour
1 teaspoon baking powder
1/2 teaspoon seasoning salt
1/2 teaspoon ground black pepper
1 egg, lightly beaten
3/4 cup milk
1 tablespoon vegetable oil or melted butter
1 small onion, chopped fine
1 clove garlic, minced or 1/4 teaspoon garlic powder
1 teaspoon Tortuga Hell-Fire Hot Pepper sauce
OR about 1/16th teaspoon chopped Scotch bonnet
1 scallion, finely chopped
1/2 teaspoon dried thyme
Vegetable oil for frying

Pour boiling water over codfish and let soak overnight. Drain, rinse under cold water and combine in saucepan with enough fresh cold water to just cover and simmer over medium heat under tender, about 15-20 minutes. Drain thoroughly and when cool, pick through to remove any bones or skin. Flake fish very fine and set aside.

Combine flour, baking powder, salt and pepper in bowl and blend. Make a hole in center and pour in the milk, egg and oil. Mix with large spoon until smooth. Stir in fish, onion, pepper sauce or minced pepper, garlic, thyme, scallion, and mix well.

Heat about 1/2 inch of oil in frying pan until hot but not smoking. Drop mixture by tablespoonfuls into hot oil, leaving plenty of room between. Flatten with spatula if necessary and cook until golden brown on both sides. Remove with slotted spoon and drain on paper towels. Keep warm in oven and serve hot. Makes about 24 fritters.

Bun N Cheese

The beloved Easter Bun, also called bun, is a dense, spiced loaf that appears around Easter Time, always prompting discussions over who makes the best, and whether bun should be made with yeast, Dragon stout, baking soda or baking powder. Although a holiday treat, many love these as an anytime snack and stash buns away in the freezer to nibble on year-round. The cheese you MUST use for this is **Tastee** processed cheese sold in chunks cut from 2 kg. tins in Jamaican and Cayman supermarkets. A thick slice of cheese between two slabs of Easter Bun will sustain anyone through a hard morning – maybe even all day.

Easter Bun (Baking Powder)

This is an easy recipe for bun lovers who don't want to fool around with yeast. The rum-soaked fruit is not traditional –you can leave out the rum if you want and make a strong drink instead.

1 cup raisins or currants
3 tablespoons Tortuga Gold Rum (optional)
1 large egg, beaten
1 3/4 cups light brown sugar, firmly packed
1 tablespoon Pure Cayman Honey
2 tablespoons butter, melted
1 cup milk or Dragon stout
3 cups flour
1 tablespoon baking powder
1/2 teaspoon salt
1 teaspoon nutmeg or mace
1 teaspoon cinnamon
1/4 teaspoon ground cloves
Sugar glaze (recipe follows)

Combine the raisins and rum and let soak for several hours or overnight. Drain any unabsorbed rum and drink or set aside for another use. Preheat oven to 350 F. Grease lightly 2 - 8 1/2 x 4 loaf pans and line with lightly greased wax paper. In a small mixing bowl, beat the egg, sugar, and honey until smooth, then blend in the melted butter and milk or stout. In a large mixing bowl, combine the flour, baking powder, salt and spices and stir with a wire whisk to blend. Gradually pour the milk mixture into the dry ingredients and beat until smooth. Stir in the raisins. Spoon the batter into the prepared pans and bake for an hour or until toothpick inserted in center comes out clean. Remove from oven, spread glaze over top and bake another five minutes.

While bun is baking, make the glaze:

1/3 cup light brown sugar
1/3 cup water
Combine the sugar and water in a small saucepan and bring to a boil, then lower heat to medium and continue to cook at a low boil for 4-5 minutes, until thick.

Lunch & Supper Dishes

Festival

In Cayman and Jamaica, these little fried cornmeal snacks are eaten with soups and jerk pork or chicken. A Caribbean hush puppy, if you prefer.

1 cup yellow cornmeal
3/4 cup flour
3 tablespoons light brown sugar
1/2 teaspoon salt
1-1/2 teaspoons baking powder
1 egg, beaten
Ice water

Stir together the cornmeal, flour, baking powder, salt and sugar with a wire whisk until blended. Add egg and enough water to make dough that is stiff enough to knead and roll. Knead the dough lightly and divide into six portions. Roll each portion into 2 in. x

6 in. long strips, flattened in the middle. Fry a few festival at a time in hot oil (375 F) at least an inch deep until golden brown. Drain on paper towels and serve hot. Makes 6.

"Salad" or traditional Cole Slaw

When I arrived in the islands 25 years ago, fresh produce was a rare luxury and "salad" was shredded green cabbage and if lucky, carrots mixed with a little oil and vinegar or mayonnaise. Cole slaw is a step above that, and popular today throughout the islands.

3 cups shredded green cabbage
1 cup shredded carrots
1/2 cup chopped onion (red is best)
1/2 cup chopped seeded green sweet pepper
1/3 cup sugar
1 cup vegetable oil
1/2 cup vinegar or lime juice
2 teaspoons ground black pepper
1 tablespoon seasoned salt
1 tablespoon Tortuga Hell-Fire Hot Pepper Sauce, if desired

In large bowl, combine the cabbage, carrots, onion and green pepper and mix well. Combine the oil, vinegar, sugar, salt and pepper and hot sauce if desired. Mix until sugar is dissolved and pour over cabbage mixture. Toss lightly and chill for at least an hour.

Breadfruit Salad

This is still a favorite side dish throughout the Caribbean and better than any potato salad you've ever eaten. Canned beets and mixed vegetables are typical Caymanian additions to breadfruit and potato salad.

1 medium breadfruit
2 cloves garlic, minced
1/2 cup chopped onion
1 cup celery, diced
1/2 cup red onion, minced
2 hard-boiled eggs, chopped
2 teaspoons seasoned salt
2 teaspoons black pepper
8 ounce can mixed vegetables, well drained
 8 ounce can diced beets, well drained
2 teaspoons lime juice
1 teaspoon Tortuga Hell-Fire Hot Pepper sauce
Mayonnaise or Miracle Whip salad dressing (about 1-1-1/2 cups, to taste)

Peel the breadfruit and cut into slices. Boil in salted water with the minced garlic and 1/2 cup chopped onion until just turning soft –do not allow to become mushy. Drain and cool. Cut breadfruit into bite-sized cubes and place in a large bowl. Add the celery, onion and seasonings and mix well, then fold in the canned beets and mixed vegetables, lime juice and pepper sauce. Add enough mayonnaise or salad dressing to moisten the ingredients to your taste. Chill for at least an hour.

Rice and Peas (See Rice: The Caribbean's Common Grain)

Cayman-style Macaroni & Cheese

Oh come on, you're probably saying: that's American diner fare! But in Cayman and many other Caribbean islands, this popular side dish is more like a dense kugel, baked and sliced into squares – instead of the creamy pasta dish of blue plate specials in America. In Barbados, for example, it's called Macaroni Pie. For as long as I've been in the islands, boxes of inexpensive elbow macaroni, tins of evaporated milk and cans of cheese were always available when shelves were bare of perishables. When and why macaroni and cheese became such an enduring favorite on Caymanian plates isn't clear.

2-1/2 cups shredded sharp cheddar cheese (10 ounces)
12 ounces Mueller's elbow macaroni, (3/4 of a 1 pound box), cooked al dente (6 minutes) and drained well
4 tablespoons butter
1/4 cup flour
3 cups milk
4 eggs, separated
1 teaspoon black pepper
1 teaspoon seasoned salt
1 teaspoon Coleman's dry mustard

Preheat oven to 350. Lightly grease or spray with vegetable spray a 3-quart baking dish or 9 inch square pan. Separate the eggs and beat the egg whites until soft peaks form, and in separate bowl, beat yolks lightly. Make the white sauce: in a large saucepan, melt the butter and slowly stir in the flour, squashing any lumps. Cook over medium-low heat, stirring constantly, for about 2 minutes – do not brown. Slowly add the milk to the flour mixture, stirring constantly until smooth, and cook another 4 minutes until thickened. Remove from heat and whisk in the egg yolks quickly, then add the mustard, salt and pepper and stir in the cheese and blend well, then stir in the macaroni. Finally, fold in the egg whites just until mixed. Sprinkle top with additional cheese and bake at 350F for 40- 45 minutes or until knife inserted in center comes out clean and casserole is lightly browned on top. Remove from oven and cool 15 minutes before serving.

Oxtail

3-1/2 pounds oxtail, cut up
2 tablespoons vegetable oil
4 cloves garlic, mashed
3 medium onions, chopped
2 carrots, sliced
2 cups beef broth
1/2 cup Tortuga Dark Rum
1/2 teaspoon dried thyme
1 teaspoon browning
2 tablespoons Worcestershire
1 tablespoon Pickapeppa Sauce
1 teaspoon seasoned salt
1 teaspoon ground black pepper
1 teaspoon Tortuga Hell-Fire Hot Pepper Sauce
OR 1/16th teaspoon minced, seeded Scotch Bonnet pepper

In 5 quart Dutch oven, over medium heat, brown the oxtail in the olive oil on both sides. Add the onions, garlic, and thyme and cook until soft. Add the beef broth, rum, carrots, thyme, Worcestershire, Pickapeppa, browning, hot pepper sauce, salt, pepper and stir to blend. Bring to a boil, the cover and reduce heat to simmer. Cook for 2 hours or until meat is tender. Uncover and thicken gravy with flour or cornstarch as desired.

Stew Beef

2 pounds boneless chuck or beef stew meat, cut into 1-inch cubes
2/3 cup flour
1 tablespoon seasoned salt
2 teaspoons garlic powder
2 teaspoons ground black pepper
1/4 cup vegetable oil
3 large cloves garlic, chopped
2 large onions, coarsely chopped (about 4 cups)
1 medium green pepper, cored, seeded and diced
6 scallions, chopped
1 bay leaf
1 teaspoon dried thyme or 2 sprigs fresh
2 tablespoons Pickapeppa Sauce
1 teaspoon Tortuga Hell-Fire Hot Pepper Sauce or 1/16th teaspoon minced Scotch Bonnet
2 tablespoons Worcestershire sauce
2 teaspoons Browning
3 tablespoons tomato paste
3 cups beef broth
1 tablespoon sugar
1/2 cup Pimento Liqueur
1/2 cup Tortuga Gold Rum
2 cups peeled, sliced carrots
1 cup peeled, cubed potatoes
1/4 cup Tortuga Gold Rum

Combine the flour, garlic powder, seasoned salt and black pepper in a gallon-size zip-top plastic bag. Shake well to blend, then add the beef cubes and shake until meat is evenly coated all over.

Heat the oil in a large cooking pot or Dutch oven over medium heat and brown the beef on all sides. When browned, remove beef cubes to a container and cover with foil to keep warm. To the same pot, add the onions, green pepper and garlic and cook over medium heat, stirring frequently, until onions are soft. Add the chopped scallions, bay leaf, thyme, Pickappeppa, Worcestershire sauce and pepper sauce and stir well. Reduce heat to simmer. Blend the tomato paste with the broth and sugar and add to the stew. Stir the mixture well, scraping off any bits stuck to the bottom of the pan. Return the beef to the pot and add the Pimento Liqueur and 1/2 cup rum. Stir stew well, then cover and simmer over low heat, stirring occasionally, for 2 hours, or until beef is tender. Add the remaining 1/4 cup rum and sliced carrots and potatoes and simmer 20 minutes longer. If necessary, add thickener to gravy at this time. Serve with white rice or rice and beans.

Tortuga Rum Fever & Caribbean Party Cookbook

Fricasseed Chicken

Another favorite Sunday dish on many island tables. Unlike American style fricassee, this is boldly seasoned.

1 3-1/2 –4 pound frying chicken, cut into 12 pieces
1 large fresh lime

Seasoned Rub:
4 cloves fresh garlic, minced fine
1 teaspoon paprika
1 teaspoon ground ginger
1 teaspoon seasoned salt
1 teaspoon black pepper
1 large onion, sliced thin

Sauce:
2 large yellow onions, chopped
3 large ripe tomatoes, diced
4 scallions, chopped
1 teaspoon thyme
1 teaspoon Tortuga Hell-Fire Hot Pepper Sauce or 1/16th teaspoon minced Scotch Bonnet
1 teaspoon seasoned salt
1 teaspoon black pepper
1 cup chicken broth plus 1-1/2 cups if needed
3 tablespoons Tortuga Dark Rum
1/4 cup vegetable oil

Wash the chicken parts with cold water and lime juice and pat dry. Combine the first five ingredients for the seasoned rub in a small bowl and mix well. Rub each chicken piece well and place with onion slices in a large zip-top freezer bag. Refrigerate for 12 hours or longer, turning several times.

Remove chicken from bag and scrape off the seasonings and reserve. Heat the vegetable oil in large skillet. Brown chicken on all sides over medium-high heat, about 15 minutes. Reduce heat to simmer and add chopped onions, reserved rub seasonings, scallions, thyme, tomatoes, pepper sauce or whole pepper, seasoned salt, pepper, 1 cup chicken broth and 3 tablespoons Tortuga Dark Rum. Stir to distribute seasonings and make sure chicken does not scorch. Cover and simmer over low heat, stirring occasionally, adding chicken stock from time to time if needed, for an hour or until chicken is fork tender. Do not add too much broth – gravy should cook down and not be watery. Add more salt and pepper if needed.

Fish Cayman-Style

I've never learned the origin of this recipe, whose Creole-style seasoning always seemed curious in Caymanian culture. You can use any fish, but snapper, dolphin (mahi-mahi) or wahoo are best. This recipe is from West Bay, where I first learned how to cook fish, Cayman style.

4- 6 ounce fish steaks or fillets, bloodline removed
3 fresh key limes
1/2 cup water

2 teaspoons seasoned salt
2 teaspoons ground black pepper
1/4 cup olive or canola oil
1 large yellow onion, sliced thin (about 1-1/2 cup)
1 large green pepper, seeded and cored, sliced thin
1 14.5-ounce can stewed tomatoes, undrained
1/2 cup ketchup
2 tablespoons Tortuga Gold Rum
2 tablespoons Worcestershire sauce
1-2 tablespoons Pickapeppa Sauce
1 teaspoon dried thyme
2 teaspoons garlic salt
2 teaspoons ground black pepper
1 teaspoon Tortuga Hell-Fire Hot Pepper Sauce
OR 1/16th teaspoon minced, seeded Scotch Bonnet pepper

Place the fish fillets in a glass or ceramic dish and sprinkle with fresh key lime juice, then the water. Turn once or twice to be sure the lime water covers both surfaces of each filet. Let stand about 15 minutes while you prepare the vegetables.

Remove the fish filets from the marinade, pat dry and season with seasoned salt and pepper. In a large skillet with a cover, heat the olive oil or vegetable oil over medium heat until hot. Cook about 3 minutes on each side or until fish is opaque and just beginning to flake, then remove from pan and transfer to plate. Cover with foil to keep warm. Add the sliced onion and green pepper and cook over medium heat until soft. Stir in the undrained stewed tomatoes, ketchup, rum, and remaining seasonings. Stir well and bring to a simmer then reduce heat to low. Cover and cook 20 minutes. Return fish and any accumulated juices to pan and spoon sauce over fish and cover. Cook 4-5 minutes longer, until fish is hot. Serve immediately.

Brown Stew Fish

Brown stew fish is a popular dish in Jamaican and Cayman, but there are as many recipes as there are cooks in these islands. Two things are essential: the fish must first be lightly pan fried, and the gravy must be rich and well-seasoned.

4 –6 ounce snapper fillets
1 whole lime, cut in half for squeezing
2 tablespoons fresh lime juice
2 tablespoons orange juice
1/4 cup Tortuga Dark Rum
1 tablespoon finely chopped fresh gingerroot
3 cloves garlic, minced
1 teaspoon Tortuga Hell-Fire Hot Pepper Sauce
OR 1/16th teaspoon minced, seeded Scotch Bonnet pepper
2 teaspoons garlic pepper
2 teaspoons seasoned salt
2 tablespoons vegetable oil
1 large yellow onion, sliced into rings
2 tablespoons flour
1 medium green pepper, cored, seeded and diced
1-1/2 cups water
2 medium ripe tomatoes, chopped

1 tablespoon Pickapeppa Sauce
1 tablespoon Worcestershire sauce
1 medium ripe mango, peeled and cut into 1-inch chunks

Rinse the fish fillets in cold water and juice of whole lime and place in a shallow dish. Combine the remaining lime juice, orange juice, rum, ginger and garlic and mix well, then pour over the fish. Turn each filet over to be sure all are coated with the marinade. Cover with plastic wrap and refrigerate for an hour.

When ready to prepare the fish, drain off and reserve the marinade. Heat the oil over medium heat in a large skillet and sprinkle each piece of fish with the seasoned salt and garlic pepper. Cook the fish until light brown on each side, about two minutes per side, then remove and place on a serving plate and cover loosely with foil to keep warm. Add the onions and green pepper and cook until soft, about five minutes. Sprinkle the flour into the pan, stir to blend with vegetables and cook until flour is lightly browned. Pour in the reserved marinade, water, Pickapeppa Sauce, pepper sauce and Worcestershire sauce and stir well. Bring to a boil, then reduce heat to medium low and simmer until sauce thickens, about 20 minutes. Reduce heat to low, stir in the mango chunks, then carefully place the fish back in the pan and spoon the gravy over. Cook over low heat 4-5 minutes, just until fish has reheated. Serves 4.

Lobster Cayman Style

4-8 ounce lobster tails, uncooked
2 tablespoons fresh lime juice
1/4 pound bacon
1/2 cup olive oil
1 cup chopped onion
1/2 cup chopped celery
1/2 cup chopped green pepper
2 cloves garlic, minced
2 large tomatoes, peeled and diced
2 tablespoons tomato paste
1/2 teaspoon thyme
1 teaspoon ground black pepper
1 teaspoon seasoned salt
1 tablespoon Pickapeppa Sauce
1 tablespoon Worcestershire sauce
1 teaspoon Tortuga Hell-Fire Hot Pepper Sauce
OR 1/16th teaspoon minced, seeded Scotch Bonnet pepper finely chopped

Remove raw lobster meat from shells and cut into 1-inch pieces. Sprinkle with lime juice and set aside. In frying pan, cook bacon until almost crisp. Remove and drain on paper towels and chop into small pieces. Drain off all but 1 tablespoon bacon fat from pan and add 1/2 cup olive oil and heat over medium-high heat. Add onion, celery, garlic, green pepper and sauté until soft. Add lobster meat, stirring to mix well with vegetables. Cook 2 minutes. Add tomatoes, tomato paste, thyme, black pepper, Pickapeppa, Worcestershire sauce, pepper sauce and stir well. Cover and simmer 5-7 minutes longer. Serve with white rice or rice n peas.

Cayman-Style Stew Conch

This is another Caymanian traditional favorite. Mine never comes out as good as Mrs. Cleo Connolly and other cooks of Grand Cayman's East End. There is a secret to this dish that I hope to discover someday by planting myself alongside their pressure cookers and aluminum pots and watching the three-hour process. But for now, this comes close. This dish really should be made with freshly prepared coconut milk rather than canned.

3 pounds (about 12 large) conch, cleaned and well-tenderized
Juice of four key limes
1/2 pound salt pork
3 tablespoons butter or margarine
6 medium yellow onions, diced (about 6 cups)
1 medium green pepper, seeded and cored
3 cloves garlic, minced
2 quarts freshly made coconut milk or 4-1/2, -14 ounce cans coconut milk
2 teaspoons salt
1 teaspoon ground black pepper
1 teaspoon Tortuga Hell-Fire Hot Pepper Sauce
OR 1/16th teaspoon minced, seeded Scotch Bonnet pepper
Sea pie dough (recipe below)

Make the sea pie dough and set aside. Be sure the conch is well tenderized and all muscle broken. Conchs should resemble flattened cube steaks before slicing. Slice into one-inch pieces across the grain. Put the conch into large saucepan and add enough water to cover by two inches. Add the juice of three limes and bring to a boil. Reduce heat and simmer, covered, for 45 minutes, skimming off foam so it doesn't boil over. Remove from heat.

Remove rind from salt pork and dice into small pieces. Cook over medium heat, stirring often, in 5-6 qt. Dutch over or large pot until almost crisp and remove, drain on paper towels. Leave 1 tablespoon of fat in pot and add butter or margarine, onions, green pepper and garlic. Cook while stirring, until vegetables start to become soft but do NOT allow mixture to brown or scorch. Add the conch with remaining liquid and coconut milk, pork pieces, salt, black pepper and Hellfire Sauce or Scotch Bonnet and bring to boil for two minutes, then reduce heat and simmer, partially covered, over low heat for two hours, stirring occasionally to be sure nothing sticks to bottom of pot. Liquid should be reduced by about a third. Add sea pie dough and cook, covered, another 20 minutes. Can be stored in refrigerator – is actually best the next day! Have Tortuga Hell Sauce or other hot pepper sauce handy. Serves 10.

To make Sea pie:

Mix together 2 cups flour, 1 teaspoon salt and enough water to make a stiff dough. Knead until elastic and pull several times. Lay on wax paper and roll out, cut into 1-1/2 inch pieces. Drop pieces on top of simmering stew, cover and continue cooking about 20 minutes.

Curry Goat

Another favorite dish, preferred by many over curry chicken, and usually pronounced as one word.

3 pounds goat meat, cut into 1-inch cubes
1 tablespoon ground black pepper
2 teaspoons seasoned salt
1 teaspoon ground allspice
3 tablespoons **Chief** or other West Indian curry powder
2 large onions, peeled and chopped
3 scallions, white and green parts, chopped
1 teaspoon Tortuga Hell-Fire Hot Pepper Sauce
OR 1/16th teaspoon minced, seeded Scotch Bonnet pepper
1/4 cup vegetable oil (or even better, coconut oil if you can find it)
3 tablespoons curry powder
1 clove garlic, minced
1 cup diced potato
3 cup water
3 tablespoons Tortuga Gold Rum** (Optional but it makes a subtle sweet difference!)

Wash the meat and pat dry. Combine the goat meat with the pepper, salt, allspice, curry powder, chopped onions, scallions and hot pepper. Use your hands (those disposable vinyl gloves are handy here!) to mix the meat and seasonings and rub them into the meat. Let the meat marinate for 8 hours or overnight in the refrigerator.

In a large skillet or 6 quart pot, heat the oil over medium heat. Add the remaining curry powder and cook, stirring, one minute to remove the earthy taste, then add the garlic and cook another minute. Remove the meat from marinade and scrape off seasoning. Add meat to pan and stir well, browning all pieces. When all meat is browned, add the reserved marinade and seasonings,water and rum and stir again. Reduce heat to low and simmer for about 2-1/2 to 3 hours – goat is tough and takes a long time to become tender. Add more water as the meat cooks down, if necessary. When meat is tender, add the potatoes and cook another 15 minutes until potatoes are soft. Add more salt to taste if needed. Serve with white rice.

Curry Chicken

Another favorite, and the recipe is similar except for cooking time. West Indians like their meat chopped into small pieces so the bones flavor the dish. A whole 3 pound chicken (leaving out the back and neck) must be cut into at least 24 pieces to do this dish properly.

1 –3 pound fryer chicken, cut into small pieces
1 tablespoon ground black pepper
2 teaspoons salt
1 teaspoon ground allspice
3 tablespoons **Chief** or other West Indian curry powder
2 large onions, peeled and chopped
3 scallions, white and green parts, chopped
1 teaspoon Tortuga Hell-Fire Hot Pepper Sauce
OR 1/16th teaspoon minced, seeded Scotch Bonnet pepper
1/4 cup vegetable oil (or even better, coconut oil if you can find it)

3 tablespoons curry powder
1 clove garlic, minced
1 cup diced potato or breadfruit
1 cup water
1 can coconut milk
2 tablespoons Tortuga Gold Rum

Wash the chicken in water and fresh lime. Pat dry. Combine the chicken with the pepper, salt, allspice, 3 tablespoons curry powder, chopped onions, scallions and hot pepper. Use your hands (those disposable vinyl gloves are handy here!) to mix the meat and seasonings and rub them into the meat. Let the meat marinate for 8 hours or overnight in the refrigerator.

In a large skillet or 6 quart pot, heat the oil over medium heat. Add the remaining curry powder and cook, stirring, one minute to remove the earthy taste, then add the garlic and cook another minute. Remove chicken from marinade and scrape off seasonings – reserve. Add chicken to pan and brown all pieces. When all meat is browned, add the reserved seasonings, water, coconut milk and rum and stir again. Reduce heat to low and simmer for about 45 minutes, until chicken is almost cooked – cook for an hour if you like it falling off the bone, in shreds. Add potatoes or breadfruit during last 15 minutes, and more salt to taste if needed. Serve with white rice.

Traditional Desserts

Matrimony

This unique dessert is an old time favorite from Jamaica. Star apples (*Chrysophyllum cainito*), are another exotic tropical fruit often hard to find outside the Caribbean. Don't be confused: Star apples are not the same as mild, citrusy star fruit (carambolas) and other apples won't do. There really is no substitute for the sweet white flesh of these tropical purple fruit. Serves 4-5

4 large ripe star apples
3 oranges
1 can sweetened condensed milk
1 tablespoon Tortuga Dark Rum (optional)
1/2 teaspoon grated nutmeg (fresh if possible)

Peel the oranges and remove the seeds and any tough membranes from each section. Cut the star apples in half and scoop out the soft pulp inside, discarding the seeds and any membranes. Combine the fruits with nutmeg in a glass or plastic bowl. Mix the condensed milk with the rum and stir gently into the fruit, just to blend. Add a little more rum to taste if desired. Refrigerate several hours until thoroughly chilled. Garnish with grated nutmeg before serving.

Pineapple Upside Down Cake

Native to Brazil – not Hawaii – pineapples were introduced to the Caribbean by the Arawaks and cultivated long before Europeans arrived. Columbus saw his first one in Guadeloupe in 1493. This recipe has been a Caribbean favorite since "before time" and became popular in the USA by the early 1900's. Even today, no party or local food sale is complete without it. There are many recipes for this cake, but this is my favorite.

12-inch ovenproof skillet (cast iron is best) or heavy 10-inch cake pan

Topping:
9 canned pineapple rings, drained
9 maraschino cherries, drained
3 tablespoons butter
1/4 cup light brown sugar, packed

Cake:
1-1/4 cups flour
1 teaspoon ground coriander
1-1/2 teaspoon baking powder
1/4 teaspoon salt
3/4 cup sugar
1/4 cup unsalted butter, softened
1/2 cup milk
2 large eggs, beaten
1 teaspoon vanilla
2 tablespoons Tortuga Dark Rum
3 tablespoons Tortuga Dark Rum for top

Preheat oven to 350 F. Make the topping first. Melt the 3 tablespoons butter in the skillet or cake pan over medium heat and use a pastry brush to brush some of the butter up the sides. Sprinkle the brown sugar evenly over the melted butter on the bottom and reduce heat to low, to allow sugar to just melt, about 2 minutes. Remove skillet from heat and arrange pineapple slices in concentric circles, overlapping slightly, over the bottom, placing a cherry in center of each.

Make the cake batter: Sift together the flour, coriander, baking powder and salt in medium bowl. In large mixing bowl, cream the butter until light, then blend in the sugar until smooth. Add the eggs, mixing well, then blend in the vanilla and 2 tablespoons rum. Add the flour mixture alternately with the milk, blending well after each addition. Spoon the batter over the topping in the pan and bake in center of oven at 350 for 30-35 minutes or until toothpick inserted in center comes out clean. Remove from oven and allow to cool five minutes, then invert a plate over the skillet, using oven mitts to hold it firmly in place. Turn the skillet upside down to turn the cake onto the plate. Replace any pineapple pieces stuck to the skillet. Move the cake plate to a wire rack and brush remaining 3 tablespoons rum over the top. Cool until warm before serving.

Heavy Cakes and Pones

These traditional very dense sweets may have been adapted from what the English called pudding and were early West Indian desserts. Since sugar was not introduced to the Caribbean until the late 15th century, pones were not a Carib or Arawak creation, as some have suggested. Sweet potato and cassava pones are a dessert highlight of Caribbean fêtes, especially during the holidays, from Guyana to Grand Cayman. In Cayman, the dish is called heavy cake and the favorite is made from grated cassava. Different districts compete during festival times for the reputation of creating the best heavy cake – West Bay and East End are the most famous.

These recipes are a good example of West Indian resourcefulness, creating delicacies from what was available. While these recipes are "simple," meaning they have uncomplicated ingredients, they are time consuming to make – beginning with the task of making coconut milk. Each of these is delicious when served at room temperature (not chilled!) with **Rummy Whipped Cream** or rum raisin ice cream. (see **Rum Sauces and Uncommon Condiments**)

Cayman Cassava Heavy Cake

1 pound grated cassava (4 cups)
1 cup water
1 pound light brown sugar, plus 1/4 cup (2-1/2 cups)
1/2 cup cornstarch
1 cup water
4 cups coconut milk, (fresh if possible, made from 2 coconuts, grated)
1 teaspoon ground allspice
1 teaspoon cinnamon
1 teaspoon nutmeg
1 teaspoon salt

Grease a 10-inch springform pan and wrap bottom and sides with aluminum foil. In a 5 quart Dutch oven or large pot, over medium high heat, bring the coconut milk to a boil and cook at a low boil until oil appears on the top. Reduce heat to medium and add the sugar and cook, stirring constantly until dissolved. Set aside 1/2 cup of this mixture for glaze. Dissolve the cornstarch in 1 cup water and stir well until smooth. Add the grated cassava, 1 cup water, cornstarch mixture, spices and salt to the coconut milk-sugar mixture. Stir until thoroughly mixed. Pour mixture into prepared pan (batter should not go above last half inch of the pan) and bake at 350F for 1-1/2 hours. Every 20 minutes generously brush the top of the cake with the reserved glaze.

Sweet Potato Pone or Pudding

Another dish similar to Cayman heavy cake, delicious hot or cold. When do you serve it? Breakfast, lunch, dinner – or anytime in between.

2 pounds West Indian sweet potatoes (about 4 large or 6 medium) peeled and grated or chopped fine in processor
1/2 cup fine ground yellow cornmeal
1/2 cup flour
1 teaspoon baking powder
1 cup raisins
3/4 teaspoon nutmeg
1/2 teaspoon cinnamon
1/2 teaspoon salt
3/4 cup evaporated milk
5 cups coconut milk
1 cup light brown sugar, packed
1 tablespoon vanilla extract
1/2 cup Tortuga Dark Rum
2 tablespoons butter, melted

Preheat oven to 350. Pre heat oven to 350F. Grease a 9-inch springform pan and cover the bottom and sides with aluminum foil. In large mixing bowl, combine the grated or finely chopped sweet potato, cornmeal, flour, salt, nutmeg, cinnamon and raisins and stir to mix. In separate bowl, beat together the evaporated milk, coconut milk, brown sugar, vanilla, rum and butter until smooth. Gradually add milk mixture to potato mixture, blend well and pour into pan. Bake the pone in center of oven for an hour to 90 minutes, or until center is set. Cool pone in pan at least 30 minutes before removing sides and slicing.

Old Time Caribbean Sweets

See this heading in the **Carnival of Sweets** chapter

Holiday Fête Fare

Many holiday recipes for food and drink enjoyed in the Caribbean are similar to traditional favorites in the UK and North America. Roast turkey, glazed baked ham; roast beef and pork are as popular in the West Indies as they are in those countries. But there are distinctly West Indian traditions, like sorrel drink, Christmas Cake, Fruitcake and heavy cakes.

Christmas Beef

Unlike the English, Caymanians and Jamaicans like their roasts highly seasoned and many prefer local beef to USDA imports, claiming it has a more robust flavor. Roast beef means a boneless rump roast, bottom round, top sirloin or similar cut that is rubbed with a rich blend of spices and allowed to "age" in the refrigerator for at least 12 hours or better, for several days. The meat is then braised or slow roasted, covered, at 350 F until very tender. Beef roasted this way makes delicious hot or cold sandwiches if there are any leftovers. This is my adaptation of traditional Sunday roast beef.

A 3-1/2 - 4 pound boneless rump roast

Seasoning rub:
1-1/2 tablespoons coarse Kosher salt
1 tablespoon garlic pepper
2 teaspoons Garlic & Herb Mrs. Dash seasoning blend
1 teaspoon dried thyme or 2 large sprigs fresh thyme
8 cloves fresh garlic
4 large scallions, white and green parts
1 teaspoon ground allspice
2 tablespoons Pickapeppa Sauce **(see note below)
1 tablespoon soy sauce
1 teaspoon Tortuga Hell-Fire Hot Pepper Sauce
OR 1/8th teaspoon minced, seeded Scotch Bonnet pepper
1 tablespoon olive oil
2 tablespoons olive or canola oil

2 teaspoons browning or Kitchen Bouquet
1/2 cup beef broth
1 cup Tortuga Dark Rum
1 large onion, diced

Rinse the beef in cold water and pat dry. Trim off excess fat, but do not remove all. Pierce with a sharp knife all over, making shallow cuts deep enough to hold some seasoning. Combine the garlic, scallions and Scotch Bonnet or pepper sauce in a food processor and process into a paste. Use a rubber spatula to scrape this into a small bowl. Add the remaining rub seasonings through olive oil and mix well. Before you begin seasoning the meat, put on disposable vinyl gloves – the hot pepper in the seasoning will irritate your skin.

Put the meat on a platter and slather the paste all over one side. Use your fingertips to rub the blend into the surface, pushing it into the small cuts. Do not scrape off excess. Turn meat over and repeat on the other side and ends until covered with rub. Place in a gallon-size freezer zip-top bag and press out any air. Refrigerate for 12 hours, or even better, a day or two days, turning occasionally.

When ready to cook the meat, heat the remaining oil in a large covered ovenproof dish or Dutch oven and scrape off the rub, but save it. Brown the beef on all sides and then add broth, rum and, onion to the pot. Spread any reserved rub on the meat and sprinkle with 2 teaspoons browning or Kitchen Bouquet. Bring liquid to a boil then reduce heat to low and simmer beef, covered, for about 2-1/2 hours, adding more broth as necessary to keep the level about a half inch. When the roast is done, a fork should pierce the meat easily-it should not be too firm. Remove from heat and transfer the roast to a serving platter. Cover with aluminum foil and let stand for at least 10 minutes before carving. Make gravy if desired, from the remaining liquid. (** For a spicier roast, use 2 tablespoons **Pickapeppa Meat Seasoning**, a very piquant and spicy seasoning concentrate, instead of Pickapeppa Sauce.)

Caribbean Roast Turkey

Roast turkey is a Western Caribbean favorite any time of year, but always at Christmas. Begin preparing this bird at least a day ahead of time. Three days is the best marinating time.

1 – 12-15 pound turkey (fresh if possible)
3 tablespoons coarse Kosher salt
3 tablespoons olive oil
2 tablespoons Tortuga Dark Rum
1 teaspoon black pepper
1 teaspoon ground allspice
1 teaspoon dried thyme or 1 large sprig fresh thyme
6 cloves fresh garlic
4 large scallions, white and green parts
3 tablespoons melted butter (when ready to roast)

Remove neck and giblets and wash turkey inside and out with cold water and lime juice. Pat dry. Combine remaining ingredients except butter in a food processor or blender and grind into a paste, about 30 seconds.

Left the skin near the neck bone and push a few teaspoons of rub inside and replace skin. Rub with fingertips to distribute. Use remaining rub and rub bird thoroughly, inside both body and back cavity and all over skin. Cover tightly with plastic wrap and refrigerate for 24 –72 hours. When ready to roast the turkey, preheat oven to 350 F. Use the stuffing recipe below or your favorite. Stuff the turkey and close cavity with skewers or cover tightly with foil. Place the turkey on a rack in a large roasting pan. Drizzle the melted butter over the skin (leave the marinade on) and cover lightly with tent of foil. Roast for 20 minutes per pound, basting with juices several times, and removing foil for last 30 minutes of cooking time. To test for doneness, pierce the thickest part of the thigh with a sharp knife. If juices run clear, bird is done. If red, roast for another 10 minutes.

Honey Rum Glazed Turkey

1 -12 –15 pound turkey (fresh if possible)
2 tablespoons butter
1 large Granny Smith apple
8 whole cloves
3 tablespoons Tortuga Dark Rum
6 cloves garlic, peeled and crushed
1 medium onion, quartered
1 tablespoon Garlic Mrs. Dash
1 teaspoon Kosher salt
1 tablespoon plus 1 teaspoon garlic pepper

Glaze:
1/2 cup Tortuga Dark Rum
1/2 cup butter
1/2 cup honey
2 tablespoons orange juice
2 teaspoons grated orange zest
1 teaspoon Grace Jamaican All Purpose Seasoning *
2 teaspoons Grace Jamaican All Purpose Seasoning
1 tablespoon garlic pepper

Preheat oven to 450 degrees. Core and quarter apple and place 2 cloves in each quarter. Place on small dish and sprinkle apple slices with rum and set aside.

Make glaze: in small saucepan, melt butter over medium heat – do not allow to brown. When melted, add rum, honey, orange zest and orange juice and 1 teaspoon All Purpose seasoning, stirring well. Heat just until mixture begins to bubble and remove from heat. Cool slightly while preparing turkey.

Remove giblets from turkey cavities and rinse turkey in cold water. Pat dry with paper towel. Place turkey in roasting pan. Rub the 2 tablespoons butter into skin over turkey breast and thighs. Sprinkle the body cavity with the salt, Mrs. Dash and 1 teaspoon garlic pepper. Insert rum-soaked apple pieces, garlic, and onion. Seal cavity with piece of aluminum foil shaped to fit or secure with skewers.

Spoon half of glaze evenly over turkey, coating breast, wings, legs and thighs well. Use baster to reach all surface skin areas, tucks and all. Sprinkle remaining 2 teaspoons All purpose seasoning and 1 tablespoon garlic pepper evenly over skin. Cover with a tent of aluminum foil. Place turkey in very hot oven (450 degrees) for 30 minutes. Reduce heat to 350 and roast for 2 hours, or according to directions for weight of bird, basting with remaining glaze two or three times. Remove aluminum foil during last 30 minutes to brown skin.

Remove turkey from oven and allow to cool, covered loosely with foil, for 20 minutes before carving. Pour off remaining juices and glaze from pan into 1 quart measuring cup. You can use the drippings and juices to make gravy, or skim off fat as it rises to the surface and serve this delicious sauce as is. (Discard stuffing vegetables.)

Rum and Fruit Stuffing

You've never had turkey stuffing like this. Don't wait for the holidays – you can also stuff acorn squash or pork chops with it.

8 slices dry white or egg bread, cubed
1/4 cup butter or margarine
2 cups chopped yellow onion
2 cups apples, cored and diced (2 medium)
1/2 cup dried apricots, diced
1/2 cup currants or golden raisins
1/2 cup slivered almonds
1 cup chicken broth
1/2 cup Tortuga Dark Rum
1/2 teaspoon dried thyme
1 teaspoon poultry seasoning
1 tablespoon West Indian curry powder
1 teaspoon garlic salt
1 teaspoon ground black pepper

If the bread is still very moist, dry out the slices by spreading on a baking sheet and baking at 350 degrees for 10 minutes, When cool, cut into cubes. Combine the chicken broth, apricots, currants or raisins and rum in a small saucepan and bring to a boil. Remove from heat, cover, and let sit for 30 minutes while fruits absorb the liquid.

In large saucepan or skillet, melt the butter and over medium heat, sauté the apples, onions, almonds, thyme, poultry seasoning and curry powder for five minutes, stirring constantly. Stir in the rum fruit mixture, and then add the bread cubes and mix well. Add the salt and pepper and cool 15 minutes before using. This will stuff a 10-12 pound turkey.

Variations: Bake the stuffing separately as a side dish for any meal. Place in buttered 2 or 3 quart baking dish and bake at 350 for 30 minutes.

Sausage stuffing for pumpkin or acorn squash: Cook 1 pound seasoned pork sausage (Jimmy Dean Sage is good for this) a skillet until browned. Remove from heat and drain well on paper towels. Add to the stuffing recipe above before the bread cubes.

Baked Rum-Spice Glazed Ham

1 –12 pound precooked ham, unglazed
1 cup Tortuga Dark Rum
2 tablespoons Grace Jamaican All Purpose Seasoning

Glaze:
1/2 cup Tortuga Dark Rum

1/2 cup pineapple juice, from canned pineapple slices
1-3/4 cups dark brown sugar
2 teaspoons ground ginger
1 teaspoon ground allspice
24 whole cloves
1-8 ounce can pineapple slices, drained

Preheat oven to 325F. Place the ham fat side up on a rack in a shallow roasting pan lined with aluminum foil. Use a pastry brush to brush 1/2 cup rum over the surface of the ham and sprinkle with Grace Jamaican All Purpose Seasoning. Bake in the center of the oven uncovered for 2 hours – if using a meat thermometer, it should register between 130 F and 140 F when ham is done. Remove ham from oven and cool until you can handle it comfortably, then transfer the ham to a serving platter to finish glazing.

Using a sharp knife, score the top of the ham by cutting through the fat to the meat, making long cuts 1/2 inch apart the length and width of the ham in a criss-cross pattern. Preheat oven to 450F. Place the ham back in the rack and pan.

Make the glaze: Combine remaining 1/2 cup rum, pineapple juice, brown sugar and spices and blend into a syrupy paste. Brush the glaze evenly over the surface of the ham and pat firmly into the scored fat. Push a whole clove into the center of every other diamond. Arrange the pineapple slices over the top, using toothpicks to hold in place if necessary. Baste with any accumulated juices in the pan and then bake at 450F for 15 to 20 minutes, or until sugar has melted and formed a glaze. Remove from oven and cool 10 minutes before slicing. Spoon out remaining pan juices and serve as sauce.

Desserts and Drinks

West Indian fruitcakes are not just a holiday tradition, but a popular finale to many parties. In many islands, including Cayman and Jamaica, dark, rich fruitcake is still the favorite traditional wedding cake. Our fruitcakes are very different from the North American variety, in ingredients, flavor and texture.

First, the preferred fruits include raisins, currants, prunes, figs – and less candied peel and cherries. These are soaked for months in rum, sweet red wine, or both. Sometimes the fruit is ground into a thick paste before soaking. Good cooks keep a crock of rum-soaked fruits in the refrigerator year-round, replacing the stock as used, to insure there is always a supply of properly aged fruit cake starter. In Jamaica, the Christmas dish is often prepared from the same ingredients, but steamed for several hours instead of baked, and called Christmas Pudding, served cold with rum hard sauce.

Heavenly West Indian Rum Pot

This is *real* "stewed fruit," a centuries-old tradition in the West Indies and many other parts of the world. Originally, the fruits were marinated in stoneware crocks for months in the coolest place possible. Fresh cherries and/ or strawberries (frozen can be used) are essential to this recipe. The mixture is the secret ingredient in what many West Indians know is the best holiday punch in the world. But these delicious "stewed fruits" are also a wonderful topping for ice cream, tapioca pudding and cakes. (Not recommended with your breakfast cereal or yogurt.) This is not to be confused with the drunken soaked fruits used in Christmas puddings and cakes.

2 pounds (about 8 cups) fresh fruit (mangos, papaya, carambolas, cherries, strawberries, guava, pineapple – any kind except citrus) peeled, seeded and sliced or chunked.
2 cups white sugar
1-1/2 cups fruit juice (guava, mango or other non-citrus)
1/2 cup sugar
6 whole cloves
6 allspice berries
1 teaspoon ground ginger or 2 tablespoons grated fresh gingerroot
1 quart Tortuga Dark Rum or Tortuga 151 Rum

Prepare the fruit – cherries obviously do not have to be peeled and chunked, only pitted. Combine fruits with 1-1/2-cups sugar and stir until the sugar is dissolved. Pour the fruit into a clay crock jar or ceramic container with a cover. Combine the fruit juice with the remaining sugar, cloves, allspice berries and ginger in a small saucepan and bring to a boil. When mixture reaches rolling boil remove from heat and cool slightly. Pour over the fruit in the crock jar and stir well to distribute spices. Now add enough rum to cover the mixture by a half-inch and stir again. Cover and refrigerate for at least six weeks, stirring occasionally, until the flavors have mingled and aged. Some West Indian cooks insist the Rum Pot should be started six months in advance.

Some cooks say you can keep the Rum Pot going: for every cup of fruit salad you remove, add another cup of fruit, 1/4 cup sugar and 1/2 cup rum and stir to mix. Others say this dilutes the rum pot, and you should keep at least TWO in reserve so there is always enough stewed fruit to enjoy!

** If fresh tropical fruit is not available, then substitute 4 - 15-oz. cans of peaches, pears, pineapple chunks or fruit cocktail, drained. Use the syrup from the canned fruits for the fruit juice.

Rum Soaked Fruits

If you're not reading this in January, it's too late, any West Indian cook will warn. Traditionally, soaking the fruit for Christmas cakes and puddings begins in January. But if you're running late, you can get away with doing this as late as a month ahead and still get good results. After that...

1 pound raisins
1 pound pitted prunes, cut into pieces
1 pound candied cherries, cut into pieces
1 pound mixed candied citrus peel
1 pound currants
5 teaspoons ground allspice
3 teaspoons ground nutmeg
1 liter plus one pint Tortuga Dark Rum

Combine all fruits and spices in a large bowl and mix well. Pack firmly into a large crock or glass container and pour the rum over. Rum should completely cover fruit mixture – add more if necessary. Cover and keep in a cool place for months, adding rum if it goes below the level of the fruit. Never use metal spoons or utensils when mixing the fruit.

Christmas Cake

Variations of this dense, intensely flavored holiday fruitcake are an important part of Christmas season throughout the Caribbean. Each island has its own, slightly different recipe, sometimes called rum cake – probably because there is more rum than cake. In Barbados, this would be called Great Cake, and the cook would grind the prunes, raisins and currants into a paste before soaking. Don't wait until the last minute to make this holiday cake – it requires at least a week to age before serving.

1-1/4 cups pitted prunes
1-1/4 cups raisins
1-1/4 cups golden raisins
1-1/4 cups currants
1-1/4 cups glace (candied) cherries
4 cups Tortuga Dark Rum
2 cups port wine
1 cup butter
1-3/4 cups firmly packed dark brown sugar
6 eggs
2 cups flour
1 teaspoon baking powder
1/2 teaspoon ground cloves
1/2 teaspoon ground nutmeg
1/2 teaspoon allspice
1 teaspoon cinnamon
1 teaspoon ground coriander
1/4 cup molasses
1-1/2 cups chopped walnuts or pecans

Mix all the fruit together in a large jar or glass container and pour in the rum and wine. Refrigerate and let the fruit soak at least two months, stirring occasionally – most Caribbean cooks begin marinating their fruit at least six months ahead of baking time. Preheat oven to 300F. Line a 10-inch springform pan with brown paper and then wax paper. Lightly butter the wax paper using a pastry brush. Wrap the pan with heavy-duty aluminum foil around the outside bottom and sides.

Drain the soaked fruits well, reserving the rum and wine marinade. Add the chopped nuts to the fruit mix and stir well. In large mixing bowl, cream together the butter and brown sugar until light. Beat in the eggs, one at a time. In another bowl, using wire whisk, mix together the flour, baking powder, and spices. Gradually add the flour to the butter mixture. Stir in the molasses, then stir in the drained soaked fruit and nut mix, and 1-1/2 cups of reserved rum. Mix until all ingredients are well blended and batter should be soft – if too stiff, add a few more tablespoons of rum.

Pour into the prepared pan and bake at 300 F for 2-2 1/2 hours or until center appears set and cooked, but toothpick inserted in the center comes with a few particles clinging to it – it will be overcooked if the toothpick comes out clean! Remove the cake from the oven but leave it in the pan, and pour remaining rum over the top. The cake will sizzle when you do this. When it stops, cover and let cool. Store the cake wrapped in rum-soaked cheesecloth in a sealed container for at least a week. Many prefer to top this kind of fruitcake with marzipan (almond paste) and rich buttercream sugar icing.

Marzipan

This is an old recipe, created when packaged marzipan was not readily available. You can find it today along with other baking ingredients at most supermarkets.

1 pound almonds, ground
1 pound box confectioner's sugar
4 egg whites
2 teaspoons almond extract

Beat the egg whites with the almond extract until stiff. Combine the almonds and sugar and mix well. Fold in the egg whites and mix until it forms a stiff paste – add more sugar if necessary to be able to knead the mixture into a dough. Roll this out between pieces of wax paper to form circles large enough to cover the top of each cake layer. Use the rest of the marzipan to ice the sides of the cake.

West Indian Plum Pudding or Christmas Pudding

Baked or steamed, West Indian fruitcake resembles English plum pudding more than it does American fruitcake. Traditional Caribbean Christmas Pudding is almost identical. **Tortuga Rum Company's Cayman Rum Plum Pudding** is a rich, rum-infused confection and better than any recipe I have. It comes in two convenient sizes, 12. 8 ounces and 20 ounces and you can order it year-round from www.tortugarums.com.

Sorrel Drink

This unusual "nectar" is a Christmastime tradition throughout the Caribbean, especially in Jamaica and Cayman. Many like to enjoy it year round and keep a bottle hidden away for special occasions. Not to be confused with bitter European wild sorrel, West Indian sorrel is actually a variety of red hibiscus, *Hibiscus sabdariffa*.

4 cups dried sorrel sepals (flowers)
12 whole cloves
2 pieces cinnamon stick or 4 teaspoons ground cinnamon
Grated peel of one large orange
2 tablespoons grated fresh ginger
2 quarts boiling water
2-1/2 cups sugar
6 ounces Tortuga Light or Spiced Rum (or more as desired)

Place sorrel, cinnamon, orange peel, cloves, ginger and sugar in a large pot and cover with boiling water. Cool, and let stand, loosely covered for two or three days at room temperature. Strain the liquid into another container and the add rum and let sit, covered, for another two days. Makes about 2 quarts. Store in refrigerator and serve chilled or over ice.

Old Fashioned Eggnog

Originally a variation of a 17th century English drink called *posset*, egg nog in the West Indies and early American colonies and was made with ale – "nog" was British slang for ale. This concoction wasn't originally a holiday punch, but considered a nourishing health drink prescribed for "debilitated persons and consumptives." Once again, the

the caveat about consuming raw eggs today.

14 eggs, separated
1 cup sugar
1 whole nutmeg, freshly grated
2 cups Tortuga Dark Rum
1 cup brandy
3 quarts light cream or half and half

In a large bowl, beat the egg yolks until thickened, then gradually beat in the sugar until mixture is smooth. Blend in the grated nutmeg, rum and brandy. Beat the egg whites until stiff peaks form, and fold into the yolk mixture. Stir in the half and half and pour into a large chilled punch bowl.

** Variation: I came across an actual 19th century variation of this recipe that increases the amount of rum to *2 bottles*. I don't recommend this. Perhaps the recipe was written the morning after a party, when memories were wastelands.

Going Coconuts

Coconut *(Cocos nucifera)*

Since it first washed ashore, the coconut palm has been one of the Caribbean's most important resources, sometimes called the "tree of life" for its extraordinary versatility – the ultimate "no waste" product. During the last 400 years, islanders have learned how to use every part of the tree and nut. Coconut palms mature within two years after planting and bear year-round. A single tree can bear up to 100 coconuts at time, in varying stages of ripeness. Along with water and meat, the coconut tree provides everything from coconut oil for cooking, cosmetics and soaps to wood and thatching as building and roofing materials. Fresh coconut water in the shell is perfectly sterile, and can be used in medical emergencies. Many islanders swear by coconut water to keep their kidneys healthy and cure infections.

How the coconut migrated from Malaysia is one of the mysteries of Caribbean history. Coconut was not part of the Arawak culture and there were no recorded accounts of it by Columbus or other early Spanish explorers. Coconuts didn't appear in Europe until the early 1500's, and may have been carried to the New World by later European explorers. However, the nuts themselves are airtight, waterproof and can float at sea for months and still germinate after 100 days. That's about the time the ocean's currents could carry them 3000 miles to the Caribbean. The coconut most likely arrived as a gift of nature.

According to the Cholesterol Police, coconut is bad for you, loaded with saturated fat. But it's also one of nature's purest ingredients. Coconut has been a staple of Caribbean diets for centuries and many of our senior citizens are as vigorous as people half their age. There are 90 year old great-great grandmothers in Grand Cayman who still cook with coconut and would toss you out of their kitchens if you tried to change that.

Coconut facts:

● Be sure you pick a fresh coconut. Shake it – it should be full of liquid called coconut water – not coconut milk. The fresher the coconut, the more water it has.

● 1 medium brown coconut weighs about 1-1/2 pounds and yields about 1/2 -1 cup coconut water and 3 –3/12 cups grated meat. This will make about 2 cups coconut milk.

● Fresh coconut water should be refrigerated and used within 24 hours or frozen.

● To substitute fresh grated or finely chopped coconut for processed shredded or flaked coconut, use 1 cup fresh grated to 1-1/3 cups firmly packed shredded or flaked.

● To toast coconut, spread in a single layer on a baking sheet and bake at 325 degrees for 8-10 minutes, until just light golden brown.

● Coconut meat is sensitive to high heat. Add at the last minute to hot sauces or sprinkle over dishes, like curry.

● Fresh grated or finely chopped coconut meat can be covered with milk and soaked for 6 hours in refrigerator, then drained. This will give it a moisture content similar to commercial shredded or flaked coconut.

Coconut Milk

Canned coconut milk from Jamaica and Thailand is now available in many supermarkets, and simplifies many island recipes in today's too-busy world. My favorites are Grace, Goya and Jamaican Country Style (JCS) brand, because of their rich creamy texture. But even they can't compare with the flavor of the real thing, if you have the time and patience. One 14-ounce can of coconut milk contains 1-3/4 cups. **Here is the recipe for the real thing.**

1 fresh brown coconut (about 1-1/2 pounds)
1 nail
1 hammer
Boiling water

Hold coconut upright and drive a nail through two of the "eyes." Turn upside down and drain the coconut water into a measuring cup. You should get about a half-cup to a cup per medium coconut. Then place the coconut on a hard surface and whack with the hammer to crack in halves or several pieces. Using a knife, carefully pry the white coconut meat from the shell. If you are making coconut milk, you don't have to remove the thin brown skin. Cut into large chunks. **There are two ways to make coconut milk:**

1) Grate the peeled coconut chunks using a hand grater (tedious) or cut into smaller pieces and grind in food processor, a small amount at a time. Put the grated or finely ground coconut in a medium bowl. Add enough water to the drained coconut water to make 2 cups and heat this until boiling. Pour liquid over the grated coconut, stir well and allow to cool. Put two layers of cheesecloth over the top of another container, like a 1-quart Pyrex measuring cup, and slowly pour the coconut mixture onto it to strain. Squeeze the meat left in the cheesecloth to drain off as much liquid as possible. Let the liquid sit for a few hours. The heavier liquid that rises to the top is the cream and when

refrigerated, becomes a solid piece of butter.

2) Cut the coconut meat into small (one inch) chunks and grind in food processor. Measure and return coconut to food processor bowl. For every cup of coconut meat, measure a cup of water and include the coconut water in this amount. Heat liquid until boiling, add to coconut meat, then process on high speed about one minute. Stop and scrape down sides with rubber spatula, and resume processing until the mixture is a smooth puree, about two minutes longer. Let the mixture cool five minutes. Line a fine sieve with two layers of damp cheesecloth and place over a bowl. Pour the pureed coconut into it and press down with back of large spoon to squeeze out the coconut milk. Bring the edges of the cloth together over the bowl and wring out remaining liquid. Discard the coconut meat.

Generally, one cup of grated coconut meat combined with 1 cup of water will give you 1 cup of coconut milk.

Cream of Coconut

Don't mistake this for coconut milk – it's a sweet, thick blend of coconut, sugar, citric acid and other ingredients sold in 8 ounce and 15 ounce cans and used in pina coladas and other rum drinks and in cooking. The most popular brand is Coco Lopez and it's usually stocked in the drink mixer section of supermarkets and liquor stores.

Fresh Coconut Pieces

Hold coconut upright and drive a nail through two of the "eyes." Turn upside down and drain the liquid into a measuring cup. Then place the coconut on a hard surface and whack with a machete or hammer to crack in halves or several pieces. Using a knife, carefully pry the white coconut meat from the shell. Eat it sliced *au naturale* – you don't need to peel off the brown skin. Take sips of the fresh coconut water in between – coconut is dry.

Fresh Grated Coconut

One medium brown coconut makes about 3 cups fresh grated coconut. If you want pure white coconut meat, you have to peel the thin brown skin from the coconut pieces. The easiest way to do this is to take large chunks and use a sturdy vegetable peeler to peel away the brown skin. Then hand grate it or grind it in a food processor until very finely ground. I have used the large blade of my **Black & Decker Power Pro** processor to fine chop the meat of a whole coconut for 2 minutes, which works as well as hand grating a coconut.

Do you have to peel it?

There are several opinions about peeling off the brown skin. Purists say you must. I say, if the skin is thin and light enough, don't bother. Some say it's not necessary at all, peeling is purely aesthetic, and the skin actually gives a nuttier flavor. But if it's too coarse, you should at least scrape away some of it with a paring knife.

Coconut Trivia

It's too bad Tom Hanks' corporate character in the hit movie *Cast Away* didn't have a West Indian friend along instead of "Wilson". Caribbean folk know lots of uses for the coconut tree, like making thatch roofs, hats and mats to sleep on—even coconut "moonshine." Life would have been easier while marooned on that tropical island. Coconuts are the tropic's survival kit. When Captain William Bligh was cast adrift in 1789 by his mutinous crew from the *Bounty*, he and his 18 comrades survived their incredible 4000-mile voyage from Tahiti to Timor on coconuts. Just in case you ever find yourself in either predicament, here's some coconut trivia to remember:

- Coconut palms are fast growing trees that know no seasons. They mature as early as six years, produce as many as 60 coconuts a year and will keep bearing for up to 100 years, year-round.

- Coconut palms flower year-round and each mature tree has a dozen or more bunches of three to six nuts at various stages of development. Good news: coconuts develop quickly.

- Thirsty? Coconuts contain their maximum amount of coconut water, about 4 cups, at only 4 months old! No matter how hot the surrounding climate, the water inside a coconut right from the tree is always cool and delicious.

- After about 160 days, nuts reach full size and meat begins to form around the inside of the shell as a thin, sweet jelly-like layer. At this stage, they are the popular "jelly coconut" enjoyed throughout the Caribbean. You drink the cool, sweet coconut water and spoon the meat right out of the shell.

- Nuts are fully mature after a year—that's when they are harvested for the hard brown-skinned meat most people know as coconut. Lazy souls can wait 14 months for nuts to fall from the tree.

- Almost every part of the coconut palm has some reputed medical use. After only 120 days, the shell is already filled with clear, sweet coconut water, a sugar and mineral-rich liquid so pure and sterile it can be used in place of sterile glucose solution for medical emergencies. During World War II in the Pacific, surgeons used coconut water in IV drips directly into patients' veins when sterile glucose was unavailable. Islanders have long drunk coconut water to ease urinary tract infections and know coconut oil heals cuts and burns, including sunburn. Coconut milk is prescribed in Hindu medicine to soothe sore throats and alleviate stomach ulcers.

- One obvious coconut fact: this is not a dairy product! Neither coconut water nor coconut milk is a substitute for cow's or goat milk in nutritional value or in cooking. However, it's a great source of instant energy—consider it nature's sport drink.

Coconut Temptations

Damn The Arteries Fresh Coconut Pound Cake

Thanks to the Coconut Crab, this recipe has become a signature gift from my Cayman kitchen. Julia Child would applaud its shameless use of butter; cardiologists might faint at the combination of ingredients. This is a special occasion cake – don't feel guilty making it part of your next party menu.

2- 1/2 cups grated or finely chopped (in food processor) fresh coconut
1/4 cup Tortuga Dark Rum
1 cup butter, softened
3 cups sugar
1 14 ounce can coconut milk
2 tablespoons vanilla extract
3 large eggs
3 cups flour
2 teaspoons baking powder
1/2 teaspoon salt

In a small bowl, pour the rum over the coconut and stir well to mix. Let it sit while you prepare the batter. Preheat oven to 350 degrees. Spray a 12-inch bundt pan with Baker's Joy, or grease and lightly flour.

Cream the butter and sugar until light. Beat in the eggs, one at a time, blending well after each, then add the coconut milk and vanilla and mix well. Combine flour, baking powder and salt in a separate bowl and mix with wire whisk to blend. Add dry ingredients gradually to butter mixture and blend well. Stir in the rum-soaked coconut until blended. Pour batter into prepared pan and bake at 350 for an hour or until a toothpick inserted in center comes out clean. Remove from oven and cool in pan on wire rack for 15 minutes, then invert pan over serving platter and remove cake. Cool completely before slicing. For best flavor, refrigerate several hours before serving. This will keep in the refrigerator for a week or more.

Serve slices at room temperature or warm cake in microwave 10-15 seconds. Serve with fresh mangos or berries and Rummy Whipped Cream or Rum Chantilly (See **Rum Sauces and Uncommon Condiments**)

Variations: This rich pound cake is delicious by itself, but you can also try these variations:

Coconut-Rum: Increase Dark Rum to 1/2 cup for a bolder rum flavor
Coconut-Orange: Add 1 tablespoon grated orange zest when you stir in the coconut.
Nutty Coconut: Add 1 cup chopped toasted cashews, almonds or pecans

Coconut Pies for the Timid

Coconut cream pie – the mere mention of this makes many people sigh with memories of a mile-high confection. Yet this dessert confounds most of us would-be be pastry chefs. For one thing, it must have a rich, flaky crust, which is an art in itself. Here are the recipes I have tried and found work best – fresh grated coconut makes a big difference in any recipe.

Flaky Pie Crust for Cream Pies

Makes one single 9-inch pie crust. Use a glass pie plate, not a metal one, for best results.

1-1/2 cups flour
2 tablespoons confectioner's sugar
1/8 teaspoon salt
1/2 cup unsalted butter, well chilled
1 tablespoon Crisco or other vegetable shortening, chilled
1 large egg yolk, beaten
1/4 cup ice water

Combine the flour, sugar and salt in a large mixing bowl and whisk with a wire whisk to blend. Cut the chilled butter into small pieces and add this and the chilled shortening to the flour. Using a pastry blender, two knives, or your fingertips, cut or rub the butter and shortening into the flour mixture until it resembles coarse meal. Use a fork to blend in the egg yolk and water, mixing just until the dough holds it shape when you press it. Turn the dough out onto a surface covered with lightly floured wax paper and flatten into a half-inch thick circle. Cover with plastic wrap and place on a plate – refrigerate for at least two hours.

Preheat oven to 350 F. Remove dough from refrigerator and place on a lightly floured surface and dust the top very lightly with flour. You must also lightly flour the rolling pin and then roll the dough out into an 11-inch circle. Carefully transfer the rolled dough to a 9-inch glass pie plate and press gently into it. Trim the crust edge, leaving a half-inch margin all around, Fold this over and crimp edge into scalloped design with fingers, or use fork tines to flatten. Lightly prick the bottom and sides of the crust all over with a fork and line the shell with waxed paper and fill with a layer of dried beans (I'm not kidding – this old method works). Bake for about 18 minutes, until crust is just beginning to turn pale brown. Carefully lift out the wax paper and beans and bake another 5 minutes or until light golden brown. Remove from oven and cool on wire rack. The crust must be completely cooled before adding the filling.

Rum Coconut Cream Pie

1 baked 9-inch flaky pie crust from recipe above

Filling:
3/4 cup sugar
1/4 cup cornstarch
1/4 teaspoon salt
2-3/4 cups milk
1/4 cup Coco Lopez or other coconut cream
4 large egg yolks, lightly beaten
2 teaspoons Rum Vanilla or 1 tablespoon Tortuga Dark Rum
2 tablespoons unsalted butter
2/3 cup grated or finely chopped fresh coconut or 1 cup shredded sweetened coconut, toasted lightly

In top of double boiler, mix the cornstarch, sugar and salt and stir well. In separate bowl, beat together the egg yolks, milk and coconut cream until well blended. Use a wire whisk for the rest of this recipe. Gradually whisk the egg mixture into the sugar until smooth and the cornstarch is dissolved. Over medium heat, cook stirring constantly in a figure 8 motion, until the custard thickens and begins to boil. Continue boiling for one minute, stirring constantly. Remove from heat immediately and stir in butter, rum vanilla or rum and coconut. Stir mixture well and pour into a medium bowl and cover with wax paper pressed onto the surface. Cool for 20 minutes, then spoon into the prepared pastry crust, then refrigerate for at least four hours until firm. When ready to serve, prepare the following topping:

Rum Whipped Cream Topping
1 cup heavy cream
3 tablespoons confectioner's sugar
1 teaspoon Rum Vanilla or 2 tablespoons Tortuga Dark Rum
1/4 cup shredded coconut, toasted lightly

Beat the heavy cream until soft peaks just begin to appear, then gradually add the confectioner's sugar and rum, beating until soft peaks form. Mound the whipped cream on top of the filling. Sprinkle with the remaining toasted coconut.

Coconut Rum Custard Pie with Coconut Crumb Crust

This is a coconut pie lover's dream

Crust:
1 cup shredded sweetened coconut
1/2 cup gingersnap crumbs
1/2 cup graham cracker crumbs
1/4 cup melted butter or margarine
1/2 teaspoon nutmeg

Preheat oven to 350. Combine all ingredients and blend well. Press evenly over bottom and up sides of 9-inch pie pan. Bake at 350 for about 5 minutes. Remove from oven and chill.

Filling:
1-1/4 cups milk
1 cup coconut milk
2/3 cup sugar
4 large eggs
2 teaspoons Rum Vanilla or 1 tablespoon Tortuga Light Rum
1/2 teaspoon ground nutmeg
1/4 teaspoon salt
1/3 cup grated or finely chopped fresh coconut, toasted lightly

Preheat oven to 400. In medium mixing bowl, beat the eggs slightly with electric mixer or rotary hand mixer. On low speed, add the sugar, salt, Rum Vanilla or rum and mix well. Gradually stir in the milk and coconut milk and blend well, scraping bowl with rubber spatula. Pour into the baked shell and bake for 15 minutes, then reduce heat to 325 and bake an additional 30 minutes, or until knife inserted in custard center comes out clean. Cool to room temperature and sprinkle with toasted coconut.

Ice Cold Jelly

One of the most refreshing treats on a hot tropical day is an ice-cold jelly. In many Caribbean islands (except Cayman) street vendors selling "ice jelly" are still a common sight. It's cheap and healthy island fast food. What is it? A young coconut, often called a "jelly coconut," about five months old, pale green to greenish yellow in color. Inside is a generous gulp of pure, cool coconut water and meat that's just beginning to form with a soft, jelly-like texture. You don't even have to remove the entire husk. Just whack off enough to expose the nut, then cut a hole in the shell wide enough so you can drink the water and then scoop out the meat. A spoon makes it easy, but you can also use the shard of shell you removed. Then find a shady spot, relax and enjoy the tropic's best ready- made snack. In Cayman, you'll have to hunt for this treat—there are plenty of jelly coconuts around, but not in public places. And you'll have to chill it yourself.

Rice: The Caribbean's Common Grain

O n the Caribbean table, a main meal isn't complete without rice of some kind. It's the culinary bond that links the islands. Like sugar, rice was an import to the islands. It made its way from Asia to Spain after the Crusades and then to the West Indies with Spanish explorers. It did not come from Africa, as some believe – probably due to its reputation as "slave food" in the 17th and 18th century European colonies. Haiti, Cuba, Puerto Rico, the Dominican Republic, Trinidad and Honduras grow rice today, but not enough to supply the regions' insatiable appetite for it. Consequently, rice remains one of the Caribbean's top imports.

Caribbean White Rice

West Indians like white rice "soft and fluffy" not firm or sticky, and island cooks always seem to make perfect rice. Their secret is using long grain white rice and washing it in cold water first. To do this properly, you have to put the rice in a bowl, not a colander, and cover with cold water, swish it around gently until the water becomes cloudy, then pour it off. Repeat this until the water runs clear – then the rice is ready to cook. The other secret is to add the water to the rice in the pan and bring to a boil – not add the rice to boiling water. Since West Indians like lots of rice, here is a basic recipe to serve 4 foreigners or one West Indian.

1 cup long grain rice, well rinsed
2 cups water, approximately
1/2 teaspoon salt
1 tablespoon butter

Place the well-washed rice in a 2-quart saucepan or pot and add enough water to cover the rice by about 3/4 inch. Add the salt and butter and stir, then bring the rice to a boil. Do not stir again, cover the pot tightly and reduce heat to low. Cook for 15 minutes, then check rice and add a little more water if it looks too dry. Cover again and cook another

5-8 minutes, until rice is soft and water is absorbed. Remove from heat and let the rice stand, covered, for five minutes, then fluff with a fork.

Rice N Peas, Cayman Style

In the Western Caribbean, including Cayman, Jamaica and the Bay Islands of Honduras, the ultimate comfort food is Rice 'n Peas (or Rice N Beans) made with coconut milk and red beans. There is an art to making proper rice 'n peas, and recipes and techniques vary from cook to cook. Some add onion, garlic and green pepper, others use salt pork or ham hocks. And, like many other "simple" Caribbean dishes, it takes practice and patience to get your own recipe right. Here, my secret is a hint of dark rum.

1 cup dried red kidney beans
2 cups coconut milk (preferably freshly made)
2 cups white long grain rice
2 large scallions, chopped (green and white parts)
1 clove garlic, minced fine
1/2 teaspoon black pepper
1/2 teaspoon dried thyme or 1 sprig of fresh thyme
2 teaspoons salt
1 whole Scotch Bonnet pepper or 1 teaspoon Tortuga Hell-Fire Hot Pepper Sauce.
2 tablespoons Tortuga Dark Rum

Place the beans in a 3-quart or larger saucepan or aluminum pot and add enough water to cover. Soak overnight. (Or use the quick soak method: bring beans to a full boil and boil for two minutes, then remove from heat and let soak for an hour. Then proceed as follows) When ready to prepare the recipe, bring the beans to a boil and cover, then reduce heat to simmer. Cook the beans for an hour or until tender, adding water if necessary to cover. Never add salt to bean water before or during cooking or it will toughen them. Once the beans are tender, drain and reserve 2-3/4 cups of the bean broth, adding more water to make up that amount if necessary.

Return the beans and the 2-3/4 cups bean broth to the pot. Pour in the coconut milk, rum, scallion, garlic, thyme, whole Scotch Bonnet or pepper sauce, salt and pepper. Bring to a boil and simmer five minutes, then add the rice, stirring while adding. Be careful not to pierce the Scotch Bonnet. After rice has been added, there should be about 1/2 inch of liquid covering the mixture – add water if necessary. When the pot returns to a boil, reduce heat to low and cover tightly. Do not stir again until rice is done. Check after 15 minutes and if rice appears too firm and liquid has been absorbed, add about 1/3 cup more water and cover again. Repeat if necessary until the rice has absorbed all the liquid and is light and fluffy – about 25 –35 minutes. Remove from heat, keep covered and let steam for 10 minutes.

Rice and Beans, Honduran style

There are many Hondurans in Cayman, and I love the way they make this dish, which requires small dried red beans from Honduras and fresh coconut milk. They also add cumin, not thyme, and sauté the rice before adding to the beans.

2 cups dried Honduran red beans (small red beans or black beans can be used)
Water

2 cups fresh coconut milk
2 cups white long grain rice
2 tablespoons oil
2 cloves garlic, minced fine
1 teaspoon black pepper
2 teaspoons ground cumin
2 teaspoons salt
1 whole Scotch Bonnet pepper or 1 teaspoon Tortuga Hell-Fire Hot Pepper sauce.

Place the beans in a 5-quart or larger saucepan or aluminum pot and add enough water to cover. Soak overnight. (Or use the quick soak method: bring beans to a full boil and boil for two minutes, then remove from heat and let soak for an hour. Then proceed as follows) When ready to prepare the recipe, add the garlic, cumin, and black pepper and bring the beans to a boil and cover, then reduce heat to simmer. Cook the beans for an hour or until tender, adding more water if necessary to keep beans covered. Once the beans are tender, check water and if necessary, add enough to reach the level of the beans, then add the coconut milk and bring to a boil. In a large skillet over medium heat, saute the rice in the oil, stirring constantly to coat the grains, for about two minutes – do not brown. Add the rice to the bean mixture along with the whole Scotch Bonnet or pepper sauce – be careful not to pierce the whole Scotch Bonnet. When the pot returns to a boil, reduce heat to low and cover tightly. Do not stir again until rice is done. Check after 15 minutes and if rice appears too firm and liquid has been absorbed, add about 1/3 cup more water and cover again. Repeat if necessary until the rice has absorbed all the liquid and is light and fluffy – about 25 –35 minutes. Remove from heat, keep covered and let steam for 10 minutes. Add fine chopped onion or sweet pepper to taste, only as much as for the amount to be eaten right away.

Rice and Pigeon Peas

From the Bahamas to Jamaica, this equally delicious dish is what you might be served as Peas and Rice or Rice and Beans. In Cayman and Jamaican they're called gungo peas and used more often in soup than in rice and peas.

1 14-ounce can pigeon peas (gandules) or 1 cup cooked pigeon peas
3 cloves fresh garlic, minced
1 medium onion, chopped
1 small green pepper, chopped
1 large tomato, peeled and chopped
1/4 pound bacon, cut into small pieces
1/2 teaspoon thyme or 1 sprig fresh thyme
1 teaspoon seasoned salt
1 teaspoon ground black pepper
1 teaspoon Tortuga Hell-Fire Hot Pepper Sauce
OR 1/16th teaspoon minced, seeded Scotch Bonnet pepper
1 tablespoon Worcestershire sauce
2 tablespoons Tortuga Gold Rum
2-1/4 cups water
1 cup rice

In Dutch oven or large skillet over medium heat, fry the bacon pieces until almost crisp, then add, garlic, onion, pepper, tomato and seasonings until vegetables are soft and translucent, about five minutes. Stir in the pigeon peas and mix well, then add hot sauce, Worcestershire sauce, rum and seasonings. Add the water and rice and bring to a boil, stir, then reduce heat to low and cover tightly. Simmer about 25 minutes or until rice is cooked and all water is absorbed. Remove from heat and let steam for 10 minutes, covered.

Yellow Rice

There is no magic to making yellow rice – I buy the cellophane packaged yellow rice mixes available at supermarkets today. Vigo and Mahatma are my favorites, but I always add more seasonings: 1/2 teaspoon dried thyme, 1 clove minced garlic and 1/2 teaspoon ground black pepper. To make fluffy yellow rice, you may need to add more water than the package calls for. Check the rice after about 15 minutes and add a few tablespoons more water if necessary and stir. Cover again and cook until rice is fluffy and tender.

Saffron is one of the most expensive spices on earth. If the yellow color and not the delicate saffron flavor, is what you want, simply add 1 teaspoon turmeric or 2 teaspoons annatto oil when stirring in white rice and you'll have yellow rice. Both are popular seasonings throughout the Caribbean.

Coconut Rice

This old recipe really requires coconut oil and freshly made coconut milk for best flavor, but it's also delicious with canned coconut milk. Serve with curry or seafood dishes – or as the base of a vegetarian meal. The rum gives a hint of added sweetness

2 tablespoons coconut oil or butter
1 clove garlic, minced
2 teaspoons minced fresh gingerroot
1-1/4 cups long grain rice
1-1/2 cups water
2 tablespoons Tortuga Light Rum
1/2 teaspoon salt
1 cup coconut milk

Heat the oil in a large saucepan over medium heat and saute the, garlic and ginger until soft, about 2 minutes. Stir in the rice and saute for another minute, stirring frequently. Pour in the water, salt and rum and stir well, then add the coconut milk and stir again. Bring to a boil, stirring once, then reduce heat to simmer and cover pot. Cook for about 20-25 minutes until rice is fluffy and all liquid is absorbed.

The Sea's Bounty

Along with sipping exotic rum drinks, feasting on fresh local seafood is everyone's dream of Caribbean life. Once upon a time, that was true. The Arawaks and Caribs were the western world's first seafood gourmets, enjoying unlimited supplies of spiny lobster, green turtle and conch, once plentiful throughout the Caribbean. They may have been the first and last to fully appreciate the sea's bounty. Ironically, colonial European settlers ignored the Caribbean riches surrounding them and preferred to feast on imported foods, like salted cod from Canada and New England. Plantation masters fed their slaves as cheaply as possible and worked them long hours – there was no time for them to fish. Besides, seafood spoiled quickly in the tropic heat. Before ice and refrigeration, islanders preserved fish and conch by salting or drying in the sun – you never want to be downwind of a line of drying conch.

Today, lobster, conch and even fresh fish is an elusive and often expensive luxury for many Caribbean residents. Most catches are sold whole to restaurants and resorts: that's the reality of living in paradise. If you're lucky enough to have a regular source of seafood at home, you should know how to savor every bite. That means knowing how to select and prepare it properly. You'll find more Caribbean seafood lore and recipes in **Comfort Food, Western Caribbean Style** and the individual chapters on Conch and Turtle, important traditional Western Caribbean *fruits du mer*.

How to Buy and Prepare Seafood

Whether you are "lookin' fish" in the islands or seafood shopping back home, these tips for buying and preparing fish and shellfish are important.

● If you can't catch it yourself, buy seafood as fresh as possible. Most seafood, regardless of how it is labeled, has been frozen soon after it hits the boat, or it would spoil before it reaches the seafood counter. Seafood should be kept on ice, not just chilled, as ice keeps fish and shellfish much fresher.

● Never buy any fish, large or small, which has not been properly iced, whether fresh from a boat or a seafood counter. Improperly stored (i.e. not iced the moment it's caught) fish can make you very sick. If you are buying at a dock or pier, ask if the fish was put on ice as soon as it was caught. If you see it sitting, suntanned, in the bottom of the boat, walk away. Don't let the Robinson Crusoe impulse tempt you into buying it as part of the "island experience."

● Buy seafood the day you plan to cook it – if not, never store fish or shellfish longer than two days in the refrigerator and cover it with ice. You would be surprised how quickly "fresh" fish goes off.

● Remove the fish or seafood from its original wrapping when you get it home. Rinse it in cold water, and then rewrap tightly in plastic wrap or a zip-top plastic bag and store on the bottom shelf of refrigerator until you are ready to cook it

● All fish and shellfish will have a faint scent – but it should smell like the ocean, salty and sweet, not strong and fishy – or worse, a nose-stunning ammonia smell. If you can get away with it, ask to smell the seafood before you buy it – within 12 inches of your nose is fine. If you can smell it that close, forget it. If you get it home and find it is limp, slimy or sticky, return it immediately.

● On whole fish, the eyes should be clear – not cloudy or dull. The redder the gills, the better – they should be at least pink and definitely not slimy or smelly.

Fish flesh, whether steaks or fillets, skin on or off, should be firm to the touch, not mushy or slimy.

● If the fish has been cleaned (gutted), the stomach cavity should be clean, and if on, fins should not be ragged.

● If you are buying oily fish fillets, like salmon, king mackerel or tuna, try to buy skinless portions. Not only does the fatty skin retain any toxins, it taints the taste of the fish and adds a lot of weight –meaning higher cost for less edible fish.

● Shrimp should also be sold well-iced and the shells should be shiny, moist and firm, not soft or limp. Again, the smell –i.e. lack of a strong one – is important. Since 98 per cent of all shrimp sold has already been frozen, it's best to buy only as much as you plan to cook – it won't refreeze well – if at all. Even shrimp fresh off the trawler starts to go bad within two days unless frozen or eaten.

● For shrimp or lobster bisque or soup, buy whole shellfish – use the heads and shells to make the bisque stock, not the meat!

● Lobster tails should also be firm and exposed tail meat should be white or have a very pale orange cast – not brownish grey. A tail should be at least 6 inches long. In the Caribbean, the closed season for spiny lobster is Feb. 1- Aug. 1 when the crustaceans spawn. You should NOT buy any "fresh local lobster" during that period.

● Conch you buy outside the Caribbean has been frozen and should not be refrozen. It should be cream-colored, moist and smooth and have a faintly sweet smell. It should be cleaned of all mantle (orange and black flesh) and not have a greyish cast.

● Scallops, live clams, mussels and oysters (with the exception of local mangrove oysters) are an imported luxury in the Western Caribbean today, and not something you'd find in local markets. Live clams, mussels and oysters should be tightly closed –never buy open ones. At home, shopping for scallops requires some savvy to know the real thing from shark or stingray punches.   Whether large sea scallops or small bay scallops, they should be firm, shiny and moist and sweet smelling.

● **Do not** buy barracuda, period. Yes, it is delicious, but I don't care who swears small ones under 3 feet, or ones caught on the leeward coast or after a full moon are safe, or any other excuses. It is not worth risking ten seconds of taste for **ciguatera** (fish poisoning) a horrible illness. Barracuda, rockfish (large deepwater grouper) and certain kinds of large jacks (horseye and crevasse) have been known to carry ciguatera toxin in the Caribbean, and you never know.

● Shark, on the other hand, is not only safe to eat – but delicious. However, if not properly cleaned and iced right after it's caught, shark will develop a strong ammonia smell and taste. Shark should smell "salty sea sweet" when you buy it. The best kinds to buy are small mako, black tip and lemon.

Cooking Seafood – Silly Myths and Surprising Facts

● The two most important things in seafood cooking are buying a fresh product and not overcooking it.

● Caribbean cooks "wash" fish in cold water and lime juice right before cooking, but do not marinate seafood in lime for long periods unless trying make ceviche. Lime juice or any acid will "cook" raw fish or shellfish if allowed to marinate for several hours. Put the fish in a shallow bowl and pour cold water over, then squeeze one lime per 2 pounds of fish into the water. Use your hands to gently turn the fish so all parts are rinsed. Let sit for a minute, then rinse again in cold water and pat dry before seasoning. For whole fish, rinse the stomach cavity and head thoroughly.

● "Fish is done when it just begins to flake" – that's not accurate. You should be able to stick a fork into the thickest part of the fish and pry it slightly to reveal opaque flesh. It should not flake away easily – if it does, it's overdone.

● People overcook shrimp and lobster too easily. Both should be opaque and moist, not dried and rubbery. Shrimp should **just** turn pink, not red – *usually 3 minutes* in slow boiling water or simmering sauce. An 8-ounce lobster tail split in the shell should take about 5-6 minutes to cook if steamed or broiled.

● You don't need to devein most shrimp, unless you are using jumbo or large shrimp in which the black vein is pronounced and ugly looking.

● Never use salt when making ceviche, conch salad or marinating raw seafood – add it later, to taste, as salt will toughen the fish.

● For the best tasting fish, remove the skin, bloodline (brown area around bones) and the bellyflap. These are the parts that can give an offensive, fishy taste even to fresh delicate fish like dolphin and ocean yellowtail. The exception is when grilling fish –

leave the skin on to keep the fish moist and prevent it from charring.

● If buying fish steaks, you should still remove the triangle of dark brown bloodline at the top center of the steak. This will eliminate extra fishy flavor.

● Caribbean cooks like to "roast" fish so the seasoning permeates the fish. This means most baked fish recipes use a moderate oven (350F). A good rule is to bake at this temperature for about 15 minutes per pound of whole fish—25-30 minutes total time for 1-inch filets or steaks. The same applies when baking fish in sealed foil packets with vegetables and seasonings.

● If broiling fish, preheat the broiler and always brush the fish on both sides with olive or peanut oil to prevent it from drying out. You should place the pan 5-8 inches from the heat and broil for about 6-7 minutes per inch of thickness – less if you like rare fish.

Grilling:

Seafood, whether fish or shellfish, *requires very little time* on the grill –sometimes only a few minutes on each side. It should not be left cooking while you fix another rum punch or check your e-mail.

● Fish absorbs the flavor of marinade faster than meat or poultry – and breaks down from acidic ingredients like lime much faster. Don't marinate fish in the refrigerator for more than two hours. You will get more flavor and preserve the texture if you marinate less time and baste with a seasoned oil mixture before and during grilling.

● Have the seafood at room temperature when ready to grill – but do not remove it from the refrigerator more than 30 minutes before cooking.

● Use a greased grill basket for delicate fish like snapper and dolphin to prevent fillets from falling apart when turning over.

● Leave shells on shrimp or lobster when grilling, to protect the meat.

● Whether or not you marinate the fish, oil it lightly before grilling to prevent it from drying out.

● The seafood-loving Arawaks may have known how to grill conch, but most modern islanders don't. You could easily ruin this mollusk by cooking it this way and end up with smoky rubber. There are many delicious recipes for conch—why experiment?

Yellowfin Tuna with Tortuga Rum Pepper Rub

You can double the rub recipe and keep it in a tightly sealed jar in the refrigerator for up to a month, for a fast, easy and impressive seafood dish. Use about 1/2- 1 teaspoon of rub per side of a 6-ounce fish filet or steak, or to taste on grilled shrimp or scallops. Salmon, wahoo and kingfish are great substitutions for tuna in this recipe.

Rum Pepper Rub:

1/4 cup Tortuga Dark Rum or Rum Liqueur
1/3 cup cracked or coarse ground black pepper
1 teaspoon green or mixed fancy peppercorns, ground
2 teaspoons minced garlic
2 teaspoons minced shallot

1 tablespoon coarse kosher salt
2 tablespoons olive oil

Combine all ingredients in a food processor and grind until the mixture forms a paste, about 45 seconds.

Tuna:
4 –6 ounce yellowfin tuna steaks or filets, about 3/4 inches thick each
4 tablespoons fresh lime juice
Rum Pepper Rub

Make the rub first according to directions above. Rinse the fish in cold water and pat dry. Sprinkle each piece with fresh lime juice on both sides and then pat evenly with 1/2- 1 teaspoon rub per side, depending on how highly seasoned you like your fish. Let the fish marinate for 30 minutes, refrigerated, to absorb the flavors. Prepare the grill.

Spray a grill grid with vegetable oil spray and arrange the fish evenly on it. When the fire reaches medium-hot, put the fish on and grill about 3 minutes per side. Test for doneness – fish should just flake when prodded with a fork. Leftovers (if there are any!) make excellent fish salad or reheated and served with hot grits for breakfast.

Rum and Pepper-Stewed Shark

Shark is not a fish you should fear –at least in the kitchen. Its firm, white, sweet flesh is delicious, especially with bold seasoning and a hint of rum. Look for cuts from small mako sharks whenever possible.

2 pounds skinless shark filets, cut into 1-1/2 inch cubes
2 tablespoons fresh key lime juice
1/4 cup Tortuga Gold Rum
4 slices bacon
3 tablespoons canola or olive oil
1 teaspoon ground allspice
2 teaspoons seasoned salt
1 tablespoon garlic pepper
4 cloves garlic, minced
2 large yellow onions, chopped
2 large scallions, chopped
1 medium green pepper, seeded and diced
1 medium sweet red pepper, seeded and diced
4 ripe plum tomatoes, chopped (2 cups)
1 cup white wine or fish stock
1 teaspoon dried thyme
1 teaspoon Tortuga Hell-Fire Hot Pepper Sauce
OR 1/16th teaspoon minced, seeded Scotch Bonnet pepper
2 teaspoons Pickapeppa Sauce

Rinse the shark in cold water and remove any remaining bloodline or skin. Rub with lime juice and rinse again. Place fillets flat in a shallow glass dish or casserole. Pour the rum over the fish and stir to coat all pieces. Refrigerate and marinate fish for 2 hours.

In a large skillet or Dutch oven, cook the bacon over medium heat until crisp, then remove and drain on paper towels. Drain all but 1 tablespoon bacon fat, then add the oil to the skillet. Add the onions and sauté until soft, then add the scallions, garlic and peppers and cook for 5 minutes, stirring frequently. Remove the shark from marinade, saving all liquid. Add fish to the skillet and cook 3 minutes, stirring frequently. Pour in the reserved rum marinade and add the tomatoes, wine or stock, and remaining seasonings. Stir gently to loosen any ingredients stuck on bottom and blend flavors, and when mixture begins to bubble, reduce heat to low. Cover and simmer for 15 minutes, until fish just yields when touched with a fork.

Spicy Rum Battered Fish

1 pound dolphin or grouper fillets, cut into 2-inch fingers
1 tablespoon fresh lime juice
2 teaspoons Jamaican All Purpose Seasoning (see **Island Pantry**)
1 teaspoon ground ginger
1 cup flour
1/2 teaspoon salt
1/2 teaspoon baking powder
1/2 cup evaporated milk
1/2 cup water
2 tablespoons Tortuga Spiced Rum
1 large egg, beaten
1 cup flour (for dredging fish)

Add enough oil to a large deep skillet or Dutch oven to be able to deep-fry the fish, about 2 inches. Rinse the fish in cold water and lime juice, then pat dry and sprinkle with the all-purpose seasoning and ginger. Refrigerate and make the batter. In medium bowl, combine 1 cup flour, salt, baking powder, milk, water, rum and blend until smooth. Heat the oil to 375 F. Pour the remaining flour in a shallow dish and dredge each fish finger until coated, then dip into batter and fry until golden brown. Don't crowd the pot – fry the fish fingers in batches, so they cook evenly. Serves 2, in your household perhaps.

Garlic Lover's Fish

Have hot crusty bread on hand to capture the last drops of this garlic lover's sauce.

4- 6-ounce dolphin or snapper filets
1 large lime or 2 key limes
1 teaspoon fresh ground black pepper
1 teaspoon salt
1/4 cup butter
1/3 cup olive oil
8 large cloves fresh garlic, minced
1/2 cup minced shallots
1 small onion, chopped
1/2 cup Tortuga Gold Rum
1/2 cup chicken broth
1 tablespoon fresh parsley, chopped

Rinse the fish fillets in cold water and lime juice, pat dry and sprinkle with black pepper and salt. In large skillet over medium heat, combine butter and olive oil, stirring until margarine is melted and bubbling. Add onion, shallots and garlic and cook, stirring frequently for 3 minutes. Add chicken broth and rum and reduce heat to low, stirring well. Add fish and spoon sauce over, cover and simmer for 8-10 minutes or until fish is opaque when knife is inserted. Do not overcook this dish!

Serve with hot fettucini tossed with olive oil and pinch of garlic salt. Sprinkle each portion with chopped fresh parsley and serve at once.

Jump Up Fish Filets

This sweet & spicy dish will make your tastebuds "jump up".

6 dolphin filets, skin removed (about 6 ounces each)
3 tablespoons fresh lime juice
4 tablespoons Tortuga Citrus or Wildflower honey
3 tablespoon peanut oil
2 tablespoons Tortuga Dark Rum
1 teaspoon Tortuga Hell-Fire Hot Pepper Sauce
OR 1/16th teaspoon minced, seeded Scotch Bonnet pepper
 2 teaspoons garlic pepper
2 teaspoons Old Bay Seasoning

Spray bottom of 9 x 13" baking dish lightly with vegetable spray. Place fish fillets in dish. Combine lime juice, honey, rum, peanut oil and hot sauce and mix well. Drizzle evenly over filets or using basting brush to insure even coating. Cover with plastic wrap and marinate in refrigerator for 30 minutes. Preheat oven to 425F. Remove plastic wrap and turn fish over and sprinkle with garlic pepper and Old Bay seasoning. Bake fish for 10-12 minutes, or until fish just beings to flake with fork. Serve warm – or refrigerate and serve chilled on Caesar salad.

Caribbean Spiced Tilapia and Yellow Rice Casserole

There is a trendy mystique about this little perch-like fish I have never understood. Native to the Middle East and Africa, tilapia has been farm raised in warm water climates for centuries. The darling of restaurant menus and seafood counters today, tilapia was   first called St. Peter's Fish in Jamaica, where it became one of the Caribbean's first successful aquaculture ventures than 20 years ago. Hybrid varieties are now commercially farm raised in many places, including Costa Rica. It has a delicate, almost sweet taste and is easy to filet, with a texture like snapper or cod. You can substitute it for those fish, as well as flounder and orange roughy.

6 Tilapia fillets, 6 ounces each

Marinade:
3 tablespoons fresh lime juice
2 tablespoons Tortuga Gold Rum
1 tablespoon olive oil
1 teaspoon fresh minced garlic
2 tablespoons fresh cilantro, chopped
1 teaspoon sugar

Rice:
1-4 ounce package yellow rice mix

Sauce:
2 tablespoons olive oil

1 large onion, chopped (about 1-1/2 cups)
1 tablespoons minced garlic
2 tablespoons cilantro
2 oranges, peeled, seeded and chopped coarsely
1-28 ounce can diced tomatoes (undrained)
1 15-ounce can black beans, drained
1 tablespoon Worcestershire sauce
1/3 teaspoon ground allspice
1 teaspoon oregano
1 teaspoon Tortuga Hell-Fire Hot Pepper Sauce
1-1/2 teaspoons Kosher salt
1 teaspoon black pepper
2 tablespoons Tortuga Gold Rum
1 teaspoon seasoned salt
1 teaspoon black pepper

Marinate the tilapia: combine all the marinade ingredients and mix well. Place the tilapia in a shallow dish and pour the marinade evenly over fillets. Turn the fish to be sure marinade covers all surfaces. Refrigerate for 30 minutes to an hour. While fish is marinating, prepare the yellow rice according to directions.

In a large skillet, heat the olive oil over medium heat and add the onion and garlic. Sauté until soft, about five minutes. Add the remaining ingredients except rum and stir well. Cook over medium heat for 8-10 minutes, stirring occasionally. Add the rum last and remove from heat.

Preheat oven to 425 F. Spoon the prepared rice into a 3 quart casserole dish or 13x9x2 inch baking dish (not metal) and top with the sauce, blending both slightly. Turn fish once more in marinade to coat and arrange on top of the rice mixture. Season with remaining pepper and seasoned salt. Bake uncovered until the fish just beings to flake when pricked with a fork – about 10-15 minutes.

Shrimp in Shallot Rum Cream

Easy and delicious, you'll impress any seafood lover with this rum-spiced taste of the islands. Serve with pasta and a fresh salad garnished with carambola slices.

2 pounds large shrimp, peeled
1/2 cup Tortuga Gold Rum
2 tablespoons butter
1/4 cup olive oil
8 large cloves garlic, minced
3/4 cup minced shallots
1 cup chicken broth
1 tablespoon Kikkoman Teriyaki sauce
1 cup half and half

Combine the rum and shrimp in a large zip-top plastic bag and seal; turn several times so rum coats all the shrimp. Refrigerate at least three hours, turning occasionally, so rum marinates the shrimp thoroughly. When ready to prepare, drain shrimp, reserving the rum. Heat the butter and olive oil in a large skillet over medium heat, stirring until butter is melted. Add the minced shallots and garlic and sauté, stirring occasionally, until vegetables are soft. Do not allow them to brown. Stir in the chicken broth, reserved rum, Teriyaki sauce and half-and-half and cook over low heat for 10-12 minutes, stirring frequently, until sauce is reduced. Stir in the shrimp and cook 3 minutes longer, until shrimp just turn pink. Remove from heat and serve with angel hair or other pasta.

Jamaica Pepper Janga

There is really nothing to compare with fresh fiery peppered *janga*, freshwater crayfish caught in Jamaica's rivers – sometimes called "swimps" locally. If you substitute large or jumbo shrimp, you'll come close to duplicating the recipe. The authentic recipe calls for 2-3 Scotch bonnet peppers, seeded and coarsely chopped. Try it if you dare.

2 pounds large or jumbo raw shrimp
3 cups water
2 teaspoons allspice berries
1 tablespoon salt
2 tablespoons white vinegar

Marinade:
3 cups water
1 tablespoon Tortuga Hell-Fire Hot Pepper Sauce
OR 1/4th teaspoon minced, seeded Scotch Bonnet pepper
4 cloves garlic, minced
8 scallions, chopped
1 teaspoon ground allspice
2 teaspoons seasoned salt
1 tablespoon fresh ground black pepper
1/2 cup Tortuga Spiced Rum

Make the marinade first. In saucepan, combine 3 cups water and remaining ingredients except the rum and cook over medium heat until the mixture boils. Boil two minutes, then remove from heat and add the rum. Cool while you cook the shrimp.

Shrimp: Combine water, allspice berries and vinegar and bring to a boil for five minutes. Add shrimp and stir, then turn off heat. Steam the shrimp, stirring several times, about three minutes, until they just barely turn pink. Do not overcook! Remove shrimp immediately from water and place in 2 quart glass bowl or heat-proof plastic container with cover. Peel shrimp when cool enough to handle and pour marinade over. Stir well. Refrigerate 12 hours or longer before eating. Serve with cold Red Stripe.

Spicy Rum Shrimp Boil

Warm or cold, these are good enough to peel and eat by themselves – but especially good chilled with **Mango Colada Dip** (see **Rum Sauces, Salsas and Uncommon Condiments**) and avocado slices.

2 pounds large raw shrimp, unpeeled
2 cups water
2-1/2 cups orange juice
1/3 cup white vinegar
Peel and pulp of one orange
2 key limes, juiced
2 tablespoons whole allspice berries

8 whole black peppercorns
2 bay leaves, crumbled
8 garlic cloves, mashed
2 tablespoons garlic pepper
1 large onion, diced or 1/2 cup dried chopped onion
1 tablespoon Tortuga Hell-Fire Hot Pepper Sauce (Optional –for a touch of extra fire!)
12 whole cloves
1/3 cup Old Bay Seasoning
2 tablespoons salt
1/2 cup Tortuga Spiced Rum

In 5-quart pot or Dutch oven combine all ingredients except shrimp and rum and bring to a boil. Reduce heat and simmer 10 minutes, then return to a rolling boil and add the shrimp and stir. Remove pot from heat and cover, and let shrimp steam for 3-5 minutes, stirring a few times, until they have just turned pink.

Remove shrimp with a slotted spoon and place in glass or plastic container. Stir boil liquid and using slotted spoon, remove spices and solids and sprinkle over shrimp. Measure 1-1/2 cups of the hot boil liquid into a measuring cup and add rum. Stir and pour this over the shrimp and stir well. Allow shrimp to marinate for at least 20 minutes before serving. For the best flavor, refrigerate shrimp in this marinade for several hours or overnight, stirring occasionally. Peel shrimp and eat with Mango Colada Dip, Jerk Mayonnaise or nothing at all.

Caribbean Shrimp Souse

"Souse" is West Indian for spicy pickled seafood, chicken or meat – it does not refer to the neighborhood rumhead.

2 pounds raw medium pink or white shrimp, peeled
2 medium red onions, peeled
6 key limes or 2 Persian limes, cut into 1/8 inch slices
1-1/2 inch piece of fresh ginger root, peeled and cut into paper-thin slices
4 bay leaves
2 cups cider vinegar
2 tablespoons pickling spice
10 whole allspice berries
1/2 teaspoon nutmeg
2 teaspoons coarse or Kosher salt
2 teaspoons Tortuga Hell-Fire Hot Pepper Sauce
1/2 cup olive oil
1/2 cup canola oil
1 cup Tortuga Spiced Rum

Bring 1 quart of water to a boil in a large saucepan and add the shrimp. When water returns to a boil, remove pan from heat and let shrimp steam until they just turn pink – about 3 minutes. Drain the shrimp and pat dry with paper towels. Place shrimp in a deep non-metal bowl. Slice the onions into 1/4 inch slices and separate into rings. Add the onion, lime slices and ginger to shrimp and mix gently but thoroughly. Divide the shrimp mixture in half and place in two quart glass jars or ceramic containers (these must have tight covers) and push 2 bay leaves into each, covering with shrimp.

Refrigerate while making marinade.

In a medium saucepan, combine the vinegar, pickling spice, allspice, nutmeg and salt and bring to a boil, stirring until the salt dissolves completely. Remove from heat and add the rum and pepper sauce. Cool 10 minutes. Stir to mix ingredients and spoon the spiced vinegar mixture over the shrimp in each container, letting each spoonful drain to the bottom before adding more. Stir the liquid before each addition, to be sure the spices stay evenly mixed. Combine the olive oil and canola oil and divide in half. Pour each half very slowly on top of the soused shrimp mixture and cover containers tightly. Refrigerate for at least 48 hours before serving. The souse can keep in the refrigerator for up to a week.

Carambola Shrimp

An unusual, very tropical dish!

1 pound large shrimp (20-26), peeled
2 key limes
2 tablespoons olive oil
2 tablespoons butter
4 large cloves fresh garlic, minced
1 large sweet onion, chopped (1-1/2 cups)
2 tablespoons fresh gingerroot, minced
1 medium ripe carambola (starfruit)
1 teaspoon Garlic Mrs. Dash seasoning
1 teaspoon fresh ground black pepper
1 teaspoon Tortuga Hell-Fire Hot Pepper Sauce
OR 1/16th teaspoon minced, seeded Scotch Bonnet pepper
1/2 cup Tortuga Light Rum
1/2 cup chicken broth
Extra carambola slices for garnish

Put peeled shrimp in bowl and sprinkle with fresh lime juice, stirring to distribute juice. Trim off any brown edges from carambola and slice into thin stars, discarding seeds. In large skillet over medium heat, melt butter then stir in the olive oil. Add onion, ginger and garlic and cook , stirring frequently to prevent scorching, until vegetables are soft and garlic is cooked and fragrant but not browned. Add carambola slices, remaining seasonings, rum and chicken broth and stir well. Cook five minutes, stirring gently several times, then add shrimp and stir well, cover and simmer three minutes longer or until all shrimp have turned pink. Serve over jasmine rice with fresh ripe avocado slices on the side, and garnish with additional carambola slices.

Coconut Ginger Shrimp

Once you've made the spiced shrimp, this is a quick and easy recipe with a surprising, exotic blend of island flavors.

1 pound large shrimp, cooked 2 minutes in **Spicy Rum Shrimp Boil** (recipe above) peeled.
1/4 cup olive oil
2 tablespoons butter
8 cloves garlic, minced
6 scallions, chopped (green and white parts)

2 tablespoons grated fresh ginger
2 tablespoons Tortuga Dark Rum
2 tablespoons Kikkoman Terikayi Marinade
1 tablespoon fresh lime juice
1 cup coconut milk
1 teaspoon Tortuga Hell-Fire Hot Pepper sauce
1 teaspoon garlic pepper
1 tablespoon cornstarch
2 tablespoons water

Precook the shrimp following the Spicy Rum Boil recipe, but be sure to cook just until shrimp turn *barely* pink. These can be made ahead and refrigerated, so flavor intensifies, but shrimp should be at room temperature when preparing this dish.

In large skillet, combine the butter and olive oil and heat until butter is melted. Stir in the garlic, scallion, and ginger and stir well. Sauté over medium low heat until garlic and ginger are soft but not turning brown. Stir in the rum, Teriyaki marinade and lime juice, cook one minute, then add pepper sauce, garlic pepper and coconut milk, stirring well. Cook two minutes longer, then combine cornstarch and water to make a thick paste. Add the shrimp to the sauce and stir well, then add the cornstarch mixture. Cook another minute or until sauce thickens slightly. Serve immediately over white rice.

Mojito Garlic Scallops

Make a Mojito for yourself, then set aside ingredients for another for this recipe.

1/4 cup butter
6 cloves garlic, minced
4 large scallions, chopped
20 large sea scallops
1/4 cup Tortuga Light Rum
1/4 cup finely chopped fresh mint leaves
3 tablespoons fresh key lime juice
1 teaspoon sugar
1 teaspoon seasoned salt
1 teaspoon ground black pepper
Dash of Tortuga Hell-Fire Hot Pepper Sauce or more to taste (* optional)

In a large skillet, melt the butter over medium heat. Add the garlic and scallions and saute for two minutes, then add the scallops and sauté until tender, about 3 minutes on each side. Transfer the scallops to a platter and cover with foil while finishing sauce. Stir in the, rum, mint, lime juice, sugar, salt and pepper and bring the mixture to a boil. Cook over medium-high heat, stirring frequently, until the sauce is thick, about 3 minutes. Gently stir in scallops and pepper sauce and remove from heat. Serve over jasmine rice or angelhair pasta.

Drunken Orange Scallops

This unusual combination of orange and chili-style Creole seasoning is a surprising new taste for most. You can substitute fresh shark, grouper or dolphin fillets cut into 1-1/2 inch chunks.

20 large sea scallops
1/4 cup Tortuga Dark Rum
1/4 cup butter, divided
1/3 cup fresh orange juice
1/4 cup white wine
10 fresh garlic cloves, minced
3 tablespoons finely chopped scallions
4 tablespoons finely minced shallots
2 teaspoons Creole Seasoning (Tony Cachere's is good)
1 teaspoon Tortuga Hell-Fire Hot Pepper Sauce

In a large skillet, melt 2 tablespoons butter over medium heat. Add the garlic and scallops and sauté until scallops are tender, about 3 minutes on each side. Transfer the scallops to a platter and cover with foil while finishing sauce. Stir in the rum and orange juice and bring to a boil and cook for about 3 minutes, stirring frequently, until sauce has thickened. Add the wine, shallots and 2 tablespoons scallions, and Creole Seasoning, and pepper sauce, and stir well. Bring the mixture back to a boil. Cook, stirring frequently, over medium-high heat until the sauce is thick, about 4 minutes, then quickly stir in remaining butter. Remove from heat, adjust seasonings. Pour the sauce over the scallops and sprinkle with remaining chopped scallions.

Rum Steamed Lobster Tail with Rum Garlic Butter

I never broil lobster tails – it dries out the sweet, succulent meat. Steaming this way keeps the meat moist and infuses the flavor of seasonings. This *may* serve two.

2 8-ounce lobster tails, split lengthwise
Juice of two key limes
2 tablespoons minced onion
2 garlic cloves, minced
1/4 cup Tortuga Gold Rum
1-1/2 cups water

In a 10-inch skillet, place a small rack (a round cake cooling rack is good) and spray with non-stick vegetable spray. Add the water, rum, lime juice, onion and garlic. Bring the water to a boil and place the lobster tails, meat side down, on the rack. Reduce the heat to low and cover. Simmer about 4-5 minutes or until lobster meat is opaque and just separates when prodded with a knife, but is still moist. The meat should not separate from shell or it is overdone. Serve immediately with a small cup of Rum Garlic Butter.

Rum Garlic Butter
1/2 cup plus 2 tablespoons butter, at room temperature
1 tablespoon fresh minced garlic
1 shallot, chopped fine
1 tablespoon Tortuga Light Rum
1/4 teaspoon ground white pepper

In a small saucepan, melt 2 tablespoons butter over low heat and add the garlic and shallot, cooking until soft. Add the remaining 1/2 cup butter and when melted, whisk in the rum and pepper and heat another minute Do not let butter become too hot or it will break down.

Butter Rum Lobster

This slow sauté may be the best way of all to serve Caribbean lobster tail.

2- 8-ounce lobster tails
1/2 cup butter
1/4 cup Vidalia or other sweet onion, chopped fine
3 large cloves garlic, minced fine
2 tablespoons Tortuga Gold Rum

Using kitchen shears, cut the lobster shells lengthwise on top and bottom and remove the tails in one piece. Rinse with cold water and lime juice, then place on a cutting board and using a sharp knife, slice the tails into 1/2 inch medallions, cutting crosswise. In a large skillet melt the butter over medium heat and add the onion and garlic and cook 1 minute, then add the lobster and stir gently so you don't break apart the pieces. Add the rum and reduce heat to low and sauté, turning lobster pieces as they turn white on the outside, so that each piece cooks evenly, and stirring frequently so butter sauce does not brown or vegetables scorch. When lobster loses its translucence and is just opaque, about 6-7 minutes, remove from heat and using a slotted spoon, transfer the pieces to two serving plates. Spoon the butter sauce into individual serving cups for dipping. This should serve two.

Green Turtle Tales

Turtle Stew: Cayman's Enduring National Dish

Nothing draws a crowd in the Cayman Islands like turtle stew, the country's national dish, on the menu. Caribbean people have savored turtle dating to Arawak times, but nowhere has it played a greater cultural and culinary role than in the Cayman Islands. In fact, this Western Caribbean island trio was originally named "Las Tortugas" by Columbus. When he discovered them in 1503, during his third voyage to the New World, he saw an extraordinary number of green sea turtles along Little Cayman's coast. Later, Cayman became a popular rest and refueling stop for passing 17th and 18th century explorers and pirates. Cayman's first tourists took onboard supplies of fresh water and live green turtles – the Caribbean's first take away food, sustaining entire ships during long voyages home to Europe.

Turtling was critical to the Cayman economy until the mid-20th century and these islands produced some of the Caribbean's finest turtle fishermen. Our intrepid seamen sailed hundreds of miles in small boats, as far away as Nicaragua and Cuba, in search of green turtles. Today Cayman is one of the few places you can still find turtle on both local chalkboards and four-star restaurant menus. That's because green turtle is farmed locally at the **Cayman Turtle Farm Ltd.**, the world's only commercial green turtle farm. The turtle served in local restaurants comes only from the Cayman Turtle Farm and, turtle meat is available to the community in limited quantities year-round at the Farmers Market Cooperative in George Town.

Steak or Stew?

Some turtle meat is as tender as choice beef. The prime cuts are the steaks, called the mongershares, and come from the shoulder. The "filet" or light steak meat is as tender as beef tenderloin and as delicate and delicious as fine veal. Sliced against the grain, this steak needs no tenderizing before cooking. Other cuts of steak need to be pounded with a meat mallet and braised to make them tender. Many Caymanians prefer cheaper cuts for a good turtle stew. Turtle meat for stew is strong tasting and includes a mix of parts and fat.

Turtle Stew, Cayman Style

Turtle stew is made from a variety of meat and fat – but not turtle steak, which is cooked separately.

2 pounds turtle meat, including fat, cut into 1 inch cubes
3 cups water
2 bay leaves
1 teaspoon dried thyme or 2 sprigs fresh
3 large scallions, chopped
3 cloves garlic, minced
3 medium yellow onions, chopped
1 tablespoon Worcestershire sauce
1 tablespoon fresh lime juice
1/2 cup Tortuga Dark Rum or sweet sherry
1 teaspoon ground allspice
1/2 teaspoon ground cloves
2 teaspoons seasoned salt
2 teaspoons ground black pepper
3 tablespoons coconut or vegetable oil
2 tablespoons butter
1 tablespoon light brown sugar
2 cups water
2 teaspoons Tortuga Hell-Fire Hot Pepper Sauce
OR 1 whole Scotch bonnet pepper, unbroken
1 14.5 oz. can peeled or stewed tomatoes
2 teaspoons browning or Kitchen Bouquet

Put the turtle meat in a large bowl. In a small saucepan, combine the water and bay leaves and bring to a boil. Remove from heat and pour over the turtle meat and let stand for 10 minutes, stirring to "wash" the turtle meat well. Drain the turtle and add the lime juice, salt, pepper, scallions, garlic, onions, spices, rum and Worcestershire sauce. Stir so meat and seasoning are well blended, then refrigerate for 8 hours or overnight. Remove the meat from the marinade and scrape off the seasonings, but save both marinade and seasoning mixture.

In a large pot or Dutch oven, heat the oil and butter over medium heat until butter is melted. Add the sugar, stirring constantly, until it begins to caramelize, then add the meat without seasonings and stir quickly, browning all surfaces. Reduce heat to simmer and add the water, tomatoes, browning, reserved marinade and seasonings and whole hot pepper (be careful not to pierce or break) Simmer, covered, for an hour, stirring occasionally, and then check stew to see if it needs more water. Add another half to whole cup if necessary and return stew to a simmer. Cook an hour longer or until turtle is very tender. Remove hot pepper before serving. Serve hot stew with individual shots of rum or sherry for guests to add, and lime wedges.

Turtle Steak

I learned how to cook turtle steak from Mrs. Rita Scott in Cayman Brac 25 years ago in the kitchen of the old Buccaneer's Inn. There, she and fellow cook Mrs. Eloise Scott created delicious Caymanian dishes that fed hoards of voracious divers. But it was their Turtle Steak that was the Buccaneer's Inn's signature dish, served on Sundays after the Saturday turtle was available. Many guests ate and relished this wonderful meat (which tastes like veal) before they knew what it was – and after tasting it, couldn't resist. Except for the prime cuts of "filet," turtle steak must be well tenderized before cooking. Use the toothed side of a meat mallet and pound both sides, breaking all sinews, until each piece is only about 1/4 inch thick.

Buccaneer's Turtle Steak, Cayman Brac Style

2 pounds turtle steak
3 tablespoons fresh lime juice
1 teaspoon garlic powder
1 tablespoon ground black pepper
3 tablespoons coconut or vegetable oil
1 large or 2 medium yellow onions, sliced
1 large sweet green pepper, sliced
1 teaspoon garlic powder or 2 cloves fresh garlic
1 teaspoon dried thyme or 1 large sprig fresh thyme
2-14.5 ounce cans stewed tomatoes
2 teaspoons SeasonAll or seasoning salt
2 tablespoons Worcestershire sauce
2 tablespoons Pickapeppa Sauce
2 tablespoons Tortuga Gold Rum

Tenderize the turtle steak, pounding both sides with a meat mallet, until pieces are only about 1/4 inch thick. Sprinkle with lime juice, garlic powder and black pepper and refrigerate for an hour. Heat oil over medium high heat in a large heavy skillet or Dutch oven and brown the turtle steak on each side. Add remaining ingredients and stir well, reduce heat to simmer and cover. Cook for 45 minutes or until turtle is fork tender and sauce is reduced and thickened. Serve with hot white rice or rice and peas.

Jim Dailey's Turtle Steak, Cayman Style

My husband Jim was one of the founders of the Cayman Turtle Farm. In our household, I relinquish control of the range to the Turtle Ranger himself for this dish, who insists his recipe is the *only* way to make turtle steak. Coconut oil is a must and you will need two heavy skillets for this recipe.

4- 6-ounce turtle steaks, cut 1/2 inch thick from the shoulder (must be sliced against the grain)
Juice of two limes
3 medium yellow onions, cut into 1/4 inch slices lengthwise
5 tablespoons coconut oil, divided
3/4 cup flour
2 tablespoons yellow cornmeal
2 teaspoons ground black pepper
2 teaspoons seasoned salt
1/2 teaspoon ground allspice
3 tablespoons coconut oil, divided
1 medium green pepper, seeded and sliced into rings

3 medium ripe tomatoes, coarsely chopped
2 large cloves garlic, minced
1 West Indian seasoning pepper, minced
OR 1 teaspoon Tortuga Hell-Fire Hot Pepper Sauce
2 tablespoons Tortuga Dark Rum
Pickapeppa Sauce

If you have prime turtle steak filets, you don't need to tenderize the steaks. Otherwise, place the steaks on a cutting board covered with plastic wrap and cover with additional plastic wrap. Using the toothed side of a meat mallet, pound on both sides until steaks are only 1/4 inch thick. Sprinkle with lime juice and set aside.

In one medium skillet, heat 1 tablespoon coconut oil over medium heat and add **half** the sliced onions. Cook, stirring frequently, until onions are dark brown and caramelized, about 10 minutes. Remove from heat and transfer onions to a small bowl and cover with aluminum foil. Add another tablespoon of coconut oil to the skillet and heat over medium-low heat. Add the remaining onion, garlic, green peppers, seasoning or hot pepper and cook until onions are turning soft. Add the chopped tomatoes and rum and stir to blend all ingredients. Reduce heat to low, and let simmer while preparing turtle.

In a large zip-top plastic bag or bowl combine the flour, cornmeal, pepper, salt and allspice and mix well. Dredge or lightly toss each turtle steak in the seasoned flour mixture and shake off excess. Heat the remaining 3 tablespoons coconut oil in a large skillet over medium-high heat. When oil is hot but not smoking, quickly brown the turtle steaks, about 2 minutes on each side. Transfer to individual plates and spoon a generous amount of hot onion-tomato mixture over each steak and top with caramelized onions. Serve with hot white rice and Pickapeppa Sauce to use as desired.

Tatiana's Turtle Soup

Mrs. Tatiana Hamaty, who is still busy in the kitchen at age 81, is Robert Hamaty's mother. She shared this recipe from her native Jamaica, which was a household favorite when turtle meat was available. The secret is well-seasoning and marinating the turtle meat for several days. The seasoning blend also works well with turtle steak and any kind of meat or fish. This recipe should serve 6, but in her house, it seldom stretched that far.

2 pounds turtle meat, cut into one-inch pieces (stew meat, not steak)
Cold water
Juice of 2-3 fresh limes
1 cup Tortuga Rum Liqueur or dry sherry
3 large scallions, chopped
3 cloves garlic, minced
1 large yellow onion, chopped
1-1/2 teaspoons ground allspice
1 sprig fresh thyme or 1 teaspoon dried thyme
2 teaspoons salt
2 teaspoons ground black pepper
8 cups water
1 whole Scotch bonnet pepper, unbroken
2 large onions, chopped
1 tablespoon salt

1 tablespoon browning or Kitchen Bouquet
2 cups peeled diced cho-cho
1 cup sliced carrots
1 cup peeled diced white potatoes
Additional Rum Liqueur or sherry

Wash the turtle meat thoroughly with cold water and lime juice – use a generous amount of lime. Place the turtle meat in a large bowl and pour over the rum, turning meat so rum covers each piece. In a food processor, combine the scallions, garlic, 1 large onion, allspice, thyme, salt and pepper and grind to form a smooth paste, about 30 seconds. Using your fingertips, spread the seasonings all over the turtle meat and rub in well. Transfer the rubbed meat and rum marinade to a large freezer zip-top bag, seal and turn several times, "massaging" the meat to better rub in seasonings. Refrigerate for 2-3 days, turning several times.

Place the seasoned turtle and marinade in a large heavy pot or Dutch oven and add water. Add one whole Scotch Bonnet pepper, pierced once, remaining chopped onion and browning. Bring the water to a full boil, then reduce heat to low and simmer for three hours. Add more water if necessary so turtle cooks evenly. When turtle is falling apart tender, add diced chocho, carrots, and potatoes and cook another 15 minutes, stirring occasionally. Carefully remove hot pepper and adjust seasonings to taste, adding more salt and pepper as desired. Serve each portion with a shot of rum or sherry for guests to add.

The Cayman Turtle Farm Ltd.

Tucked away on the Caribbean Sea in West Bay at Grand Cayman's Northwest Point, the Cayman Turtle Farm Ltd. is home to more than 15,000 green sea turtles. The first venture of its kind in the world, the Turtle Farm was established as Mariculture Ltd., in 1968 and became a government owned-operation in 1983. Today it is the only commercial green sea turtle farm in the world. Year round, hundreds of thousands of visitors come to see green turtles in every stage of development, from tiny hatchlings to mature adult breeding stock weighing several hundred pounds.

A group of turtles is called a flap-and Cayman's attempts to replenish this important natural resource and preserve part of its culture have caused a flap of a different kind internationally. The outside world can't seem to understand the importance of the Cayman Turtle Farm's research and conservation work in repopulating Caribbean waters with this species, while preserving an important part of Caymanian culture. The Cayman Turtle Farm does not gather wild sea turtles to grow as captive stock. The Farm has its own herd of mature breeder turtles and raises hundreds of green turtles from eggs laid here every year. Furthermore, the Farm has a unique year-round release program. Since 1980, more than 30,000 young green turtles have been tagged and released into the Caribbean Sea off Cayman's coastline.

On 4 November 2001 the Cayman Turtle Farm suffered extensive damage to its seaside facilities when Hurricane Michelle, a Category 4 Storm packing 145 mph. winds, passed 140 miles northwest of Grand Cayman. Although the monstrous storm seemed far away, it battered the island's west coast with the worst storm surge Caymanians had seen in 50 years. Northwest Point was among the areas hardest hit. As giant waves crashed over the Turtle Farm, Manager Kenneth Hydes and his staff, assisted by volunteers from the island, worked around the clock to rescue turtles swept from their tanks. Thanks to their heroic efforts, most of Cayman's treasured turtles were saved. And the next day, the Farm staff started to clean up and rebuild.

The Farm is open daily except Christmas Day from 8:30 a.m. until 5:00 p.m. Admission for adults is US$6.00; for children 6-12, US$3.00 and children under 6 are admitted free of charge. For the latest information on developments at the Farm, contact: P.O. Box 645 GT, Grand Cayman, BWI; Ph: (345) 949-3894; Fax: (345) 949-1387 or E-mail: CTFL@candw.ky To learn more, visit their website, http://www.turtle.ky

Please note: Under the Convention on International Trade in Endangered Species (CITES) law enacted in 1978, visitors from many countries including the US, Canada and UK are prohibited from taking home any sea turtle products. Although a variety of farmed turtle products are available in Cayman, they are intended for local use or consumption and not for export.

Conch Pearls

What a curious creature the conch is. How Neolithic man ever got beyond appearances to discover this animal was edible remains an enigma of Western anthropology. From the Bahamas to Venezuela, Lucayan, Carib and Arawak Indians were feasting on conch, the original New World cuisine, long before Columbus arrived. He described his "discovery" of the mollusk's sweet edible meat within shells "as large as a calf's head" off the south coast of Cuba during his second voyage to the New World.

Queen conch, *Strombus gigas*, whose other Caribbean names are **caricol**, **lambi** and **sea snail**, was once a dietary staple in the Cayman Islands – and 17 other Caribbean countries. Along with green turtle, there seemed to be an endless supply of this mollusk, a plentiful resource which when dried, was a durable source of sustenance. Conch stewed in coconut is a traditional Caymanian dish –today nothing draws attention like a chalkboard menu advertising "stew conch." Unfortunately, like much of the region, Cayman's conch population has dwindled to the point of being endangered. Along with spiny lobster, harvesting conch from local waters is strictly limited by our Marine Conservation Act and most conch eaten in Cayman is imported from Honduras and Jamaica.

This single sea creature has inspired innovative dishes ranging from nouvelle appetizers to New World fusion entrees. But here in the Caribbean, traditional, simple dishes remain our favorites.

Conchology for Beginners

Let's begin with pronunciation: it's KONK, not Kawnch and it was once common in the turquoise shallows from Bermuda to Brazil. You may already recognize conch as that beautiful pink spiral shell, nature's original Art Deco home, ingeniously sculpted from layers of calcium carbonate. Its lustrous, protruding lip wears a polish of nacre ranging from sunrise pastel yellow to vivid deep rose. Properly cleaned, it makes the perfect island souvenir. Hold it to your ear and you'll hear the gentle swells of the Caribbean Sea, calling like a siren long after you're home.

If you've never eaten conch, stop right now. You must sample this delectable shellfish before you go any further. It's succulent flesh is considered the ultimate West Indian aphrodisiac –what are you waiting for?

The meat of the Queen conch has an incomparable, distinctive and delicately sweet seafood flavor many compare to pink abalone, with a "crunchier" texture. It's not fishy like clams or mussels, closer in taste to calamari (young squid) than to either. It's also the perfect protein-rich, low fat food for today's heart-smart diet. A four-ounce serving has only 100 calories, and 0.5 grams of fat, none of it saturated.

From gestation to gastronomy, this creature is a compact bundle of curiosities as mysterious as the ocean itself. A complete herbivore, conchs eat only algae which thrive in turtle grass flats. Conch don't crawl, they hop. At the end of the meaty muscular foot is a horny claw called the operculum. It's a dual-purpose survival tool that seals out predators like spiny lobster and stingrays and provides mobility. The conch plants this claw into the sand and punts along by snail-sized leaps and bounds, feeding, mating, whatever. You have to see it to believe it.

Conch is also the sea's natural Swiss Army knife. Pre-Columbian Indians made tools from its shell, ranging from crude hammers and blades to heavy fishhooks. They carved dug out canoes with conch shell scrapers, and made horns and ornaments which served both religious and practical purposes. Inedible conch guts made excellent fishing bait.

West Indian folklore fashioned it into an aphrodisiac allegedly empowering man with paranormal potency. Meanwhile, prim mid 19th century England missed the point entirely, fashioning it instead into fine porcelain, importing hundreds of thousands of shells a year. Until early this century, conch was recognized, like the coconut, as one of nature's versatile, no-waste commodities. If marooned on a palm-lined isle, with a little ingenuity, you could easily survive if a supply of conch was within reach.

We'll skip the queasy details of conch anatomy and simply confirm there are males and females and each has two eyestalks, a snout and mouth and the usual animal things adapted to allow this enormous snail to squash all of itself neatly inside a spiral. This makes for a bizarre creature whose big tough foot is the only part you eat.

When wrestled from its shell, cleaned and peeled (a challenge best left to experienced pros), a large adult conch produces about a quarter pound of white steak. When cleaned, it resembles a firm boneless chicken breast.

Firm meaning relentlessly rubbery. You have to tenderize the meat with conviction before eating it in any form. Savvy chefs have secret techniques and clever devices for this. We Islanders simply whack this mollusk into mushy submission with the toothed side of a meat mallet. In a pinch, the bottom of a soda or beer bottle will do. For chowders and fritters, conch sliced and splashed with lime and spun around the grind blade of the Cuisinart is ideal. A pressure cooker is fast and handy too. Have plenty of fresh lime juice handy – nature's citrus Teflon for any surfaces within conch contact.

There's one rare, romantic quirk of conch: the **conch pearl**. This splendid gem, whose natural luster ranges from pale opalescent peach to deep passionate pink, appears in only in one of every 100,000 shells. At prices spiraling upward from about $500 for a tiny pearl to thousands for perfectly round carats of deep rose, the most desirable of all, this is truly a treasure fit for a Queen – just as it was in 19th century Europe.

How to conquer a conch

If you really want to go native and learn how to clean a conch, you'll have to take a North Sound snorkeling trip on Grand Cayman with one of our Caymanian captains. Otherwise, it would take an entire illustrated chapter to cover this complicated and messy process and it would leave you bewildered, discouraged and probably unwilling to try conch at all.

Use the freshest cleaned conch possible and tenderize it properly. Whether fresh or frozen and thawed, it should have a slightly salty, sweet sea smell, and not a strong fishy or rancid odor. It should not be dry, grey or brown, but creamy white in color. In these recipes, there is no substitute for conch, so I am not going to even suggest one. The nutty, sweet flavor of Queen conch is unique and nothing like its fishier mollusk cousins.

To tenderize conch: For cracked conch or stewed conch, and other dishes requiring conch steaks or large pieces, use the toothed side of a heavy meat mallet. Before pounding, score the conch across the surface grain first (do not cut all the way through) and place on heavy cutting board or other strong surface, covered with plastic wrap, plastic bag or other material to contain the conch slime.

It's best to do your whacking outside, as conch splatters when hammered. Nothing attracts ants faster than conch splat on your counters and walls. Cover conch with a plastic grocery bag – most plastic wrap is too thin and disintegrates. Or place inside a jumbo or gallon-size zip-top plastic bag. Pound repeatedly on BOTH sides, turning as necessary, until all muscle is broken and conch resembles a lacy, flattened white mass. Slice across the grain into strips and cut strips in half for one-inch pieces. Use whole conch steak for cracked conch, or slice into pieces for recipes like stew or gumbo.

For ground conch, use a meat grinder or a heavy food processor (not a mini-chopper) with the large blade. If you buy conch very fresh, the horny operculum may be still on. Remove it and slice conch into half-inch pieces that can be easily processed. If the end of the conch close to the operculum is too thick and tough, discard that half-inch or so. Rub the bowl and blade with lime or lemon before using, and sprinkle the conch with more lime juice in the bowl before processing. Repeat this for each batch of conch. Many island cooks still use a traditional hand turning meat grinder, which also works very well.

Conch Quantities and Measurements

How much should I buy? The edible part of an adult conch can range in size from 4 inches to almost 8 inches from operculum to mantle. Recipes that call for "a pound of something" will drive you crazy, which is how many old conch recipes are written. **Here is a handy guide for buying conch:**

Tortuga Rum Fever & Caribbean Party Cookbook

- 7-8 average conch or 4 large ones will make up a pound. Conchs vary in size, and measurements by pound or number are not exact. A pound of conch should give you about 2-2-1/4 cups of ground conch.

- There is no predetermined standard for sizing a conch. However, a general rule is a cleaned average conch sold in seafood shops weighs about 2 to 2-1/2 ounces and large ones weigh about 4 ounces

- Only buy conch that are moist and creamy colored –never buy conch that are dried and grey. They should have a slightly sweet, salty smell – NOT a strong odor.

- Plan on four ounces of conch per serving, or 2 average or 1 large conch

- Use Peanut Oil: This is the best oil for deep-frying because it does not smoke at high temperatures

Still curious about conch? Consider a trip to the **Caicos Conch Farm Ltd.** on Providenciales in the Turks & Caicos Islands. There, at the world's only commercial conch mariculture facility you'll see more than 3 million conchs, from microscopic eggs to mature adults. The farm is the world's only source of tiny 1-1/2 inches long, year-old conch, an exotic nouvelle delicacy being exported as live **Ocean Escargot** to international gourmet seafood markets and restaurants from San Francisco to Miami's South Beach. **For information, contact Chuck Hesse, Caicos Conch Farm Ltd., Ph: (649) 946-5849 or e-mail: concfarm@tciway.tc**

Conched-Out Recipes

Cracked Conch

Marinating the conch in rum makes its flavor even sweeter.

4 large conch, cleaned and pounded until lacy
1/4 cup fresh lime juice
4 tablespoons Tortuga Gold Rum
1/2 teaspoon Tortuga Hell-Fire Hot Pepper Sauce
1 cup flour
2 large eggs, beaten
2 tablespoons evaporated milk or half-and-half
1 cup fine cracker meal or dried unseasoned bread crumbs

Combine the conch, lime juice, rum and pepper sauce in a large zip-top bag; seal and turn conch to coat with marinade. Refrigerate for two hours, turning a few times. Drain the conch and pat dry. Beat the egg with the milk in a shallow bowl. In a heavy skillet, add enough oil to cover the bottom generously and heat to 375 (hot but not smoking). Put the flour on a plate and dredge each conch in flour, then dip in the egg mixture to coat well, holding to let excess drip off. Dredge in the cracker meal or breadcrumbs and fry in hot oil until light golden brown, about 2 or 3 minutes on each side. Serve immediately with tartar sauce, Jerk Mayonnaise (see **Rum Sauces & Uncommon Condiments**) or additional lime and hot pepper sauce.

Steamed Conch

This is a favorite Bahamian breakfast dish, served with grits.

4 large conch, cleaned and well-pounded
1 teaspoon white vinegar
2 tablespoons butter
2 tablespoons canola oil
1 medium onion, chopped
1 medium green pepper, seeded and diced
4 slices bacon, cooked until firm but not crisp, cut into small pieces
1- 14.5 ounce can stewed tomatoes
1/4 cup catsup
1 tablespoon Worcestershire sauce
2 cups water
1 teaspoon dried thyme
1 teaspoon salt
1 teaspoon ground black pepper
1/4 Scotch bonnet pepper, seeded, deveined and chopped fine
2 tablespoons Tortuga Gold Rum or sweet sherry
1 teaspoon fresh lime juice

In a 3-quart saucepan or Dutch oven, add the vinegar to 2 quarts water and boil the tenderized conch for 30 –40 minutes, skimming off foam and adding water as necessary, until conch is fork tender. Remove from heat, drain the conch, and cut into I-inch pieces. In a large skillet, heat the butter and oil over medium heat and sauté the onion, green pepper, conch and bacon until the vegetables are soft. Add the tomatoes and remaining ingredients and stir well, and when mixture just starts to boil, reduce heat to low, cover and let steam for 15 minutes. Serve with hot grits or white rice.

Conch Salad

4 medium conch
1 medium red or sweet onion, diced
1 small green pepper, diced
1/2 cup chopped celery
1 large tomato, chopped
1/2 cup fresh lime or sour orange juice
Seasoned salt and ground black pepper to taste
Tortuga Hell-Fire Hot Pepper Sauce

Pound the conch until thoroughly tenderized and then cut into thumbnail size pieces. Or, carefully use a very sharp knife and slice each conch in razor thin strips across the grain. Combine conch in a plastic or glass bowl with all other ingredients and mix well. Marinate in refrigerator for at least four hours. Add hot pepper sauce to individual taste.

Cayman Style Marinated Conch

4 medium conch, cleaned and pounded until well tenderized (1/2 pound)
1 medium red or sweet onion, diced
1 small green pepper, diced
2 stalks celery, diced
1/4 cup fresh lime juice
1 tablespoon Worcestershire sauce

2 tablespoons Pickapeppa sauce
1/3 cup chili sauce
2 teaspoons garlic pepper
1 teaspoon Tortuga Hell-Fire Hot Pepper Sauce
1 teaspoon seasoned salt (or to taste)

Be sure each conch has been well tenderized and all membranes broken! Slice in very thin strips across the grain. Put in a sealable container and add all other ingredients. Stir well and cover tightly. Marinate in refrigerator for at least four hours or overnight. Pass more pepper sauce to suit individual tastes.

Conch Cakes

These are a conch-lovers delight.

2 large cleaned conch (1/2 pound)
Juice of two key limes
1 peeled clove fresh garlic
1 small red onion, chopped fine
1/2 medium green pepper, chopped fine
2 tablespoons chopped sweet red pepper
1-1/2 teaspoons Old Bay seasoning
1 teaspoon black pepper
1/2 teaspoon or few dashes Tortuga Hell Fire sauce
1/4 cup flour (approximately.)
1/2 teaspoon thyme
Peanut oil for pan-frying.

Rub the food processor bowl and blade with lime. Place cut up conch in processor bowl and squeeze remaining lime over it. Grind the conch with the garlic clove using large blade of food processor until it forms a chunky paste. Use rubber spatula to scrape conch into mixing bowl. Using same food processor bowl, add onion and green pepper and chop fine but do not puree. Add the chopped vegetables to the conch and mix well. Add Old Bay seasoning, black pepper, thyme and hot sauce and blend ingredients well. Add flour and mix well – if batter is very sticky, add a little more flour to make it stiffer. For best flavor, refrigerate batter for an hour or two.

Heat enough oil to cover bottom of large frying pan. Drop enough batter by large spoonfuls into hot oil to make two-inch cakes and cook 3 minutes. Turn over with spatula or pancake turner and flatten, cook 3 minutes more. Both sides should be golden. Keep turning if more cooking is needed. Remove from pan and drain on paper towels. Serve immediately with tartar sauce, red sauce or even better, Jerk Mayonnaise.

Conchburgers

4 large conch, cleaned and cut into half inch chunks
1 tablespoon fresh lime juice
1 medium onion, chopped
1/2 medium green pepper, chopped
2 large cloves garlic
1 large egg, beaten
2 teaspoons Old Bay Seasoning
1 teaspoon Tortuga Hell-Fire Hot Pepper Sauce

1 teaspoon ground black pepper
1/2 teaspoon ground allspice
1/2 teaspoon dried thyme
1 cup fresh bread crumbs or crushed Ritz crackers
Peanut oil for frying

Rub the inside of a food processor bowl and blade with lime. Combine the conch, lime juice, onion, garlic and green pepper in the processor and pulse until the conch is thoroughly ground and blended with the other ingredients. Add remaining ingredients except breadcrumbs and pulse until blended. Use a rubber spatula to scrape the conch mixture into another bowl. Stir in the bread crumbs or cracker crumbs and mix well. Shape conch mixture into 4-inch patties. In a large skillet, heat enough oil to cover the bottom to 375 or very hot and fry conchburgers until golden brown on both sides, using a spatula or pancake turner to turn carefully. Serve with tartar sauce, jerk mayonnaise or the sauce of your choice.

The Ultimate Conch Fritters

8 large conch, cleaned and cut into chunks (about 4 cups ground)
3 key limes, cut in half
2 medium yellow onions, sliced
1 medium tomato
1 medium green pepper, seeded and sliced
3 cloves garlic, minced
2 small stalks celery with leaves
1 teaspoon Worcestershire sauce
1 teaspoon Tortuga Hell-Fire Hot Pepper sauce
OR 1/16th tsp. minced seeded and deveined Scotch Bonnet
2 large eggs, lightly beaten
2 cups flour
3 teaspoons baking powder
1-1/2 teaspoons seasoned salt
1 teaspoon ground black pepper
1 teaspoon garlic powder
1/2 teaspoon thyme

Rub food processor bowl sides and blade with lime juice and place conch in bowl. Sprinkle with remaining juice and grind into coarse paste, in batches if necessary, using lime juice on bowl and blade before each batch. Place ground conch in large mixing bowl. Using same processor bowl and large blade of food processor, chop in individual batches the onion, celery, green pepper, and tomato. Do NOT puree! Mix chopped vegetables and garlic with ground conch until well blended. To this paste add the Worcestershire, pepper sauce or minced scotch bonnet and eggs and stir until well blended. Mix together flour and baking powder and remaining seasonings and add to conch and blend well. If batter is too thick, add 2 tablespoons to 1/4 cup water.

Drop by tablespoonfuls into deep peanut oil (375 degrees) and fry until golden brown and floating. Serve with red sauce.

Fiery Jerk Conch Fritters

4 large conch, cleaned and ground

1/2 cup chopped red onion
1/4 cup sweet red bell pepper, diced fine
2 teaspoons Walkerswood Jamaican Jerk seasoning concentrate
2 large eggs, lightly beaten
1/2 cup milk
1 tablespoon Tortuga Gold Rum
1 teaspoon seasoning salt
1 teaspoon garlic pepper
Dash Tortuga Hell-Fire Hot Pepper sauce
2 cups self-rising flour

Mix together conch, onion and red pepper. In large bowl, mix together eggs, milk, seasoned salt, jerk seasoning, garlic pepper, pepper sauce and rum. Stir in the conch mixture. Add flour and mix well. Refrigerate the batter for an hour. Heat at least 2 inches of oil to 375 (very hot) in a heavy saucepan or skillet. Drop batter by tablespoons into deep hot oil and fry until deep golden brown, turning fritters to cook thoroughly. Drain on paper towels and serve hot.

Tradewinds Conch Stew

I created this recipe for my friend John Lucas, CEO of Tradewinds Nursery in Pembroke Park, FL, one of the world's experts on bougainvillea and exotic succulents. He is also a conch connoisseur. The sweetness of the coconut milk, a hint of ginger and lots of conch make this a rich stew-like chowder a meal in itself. The vegetables create enough liquid – don't add more water.

2-1/2 pounds conch (about 10 large conch, cleaned and ground – 5 cups)
1/2 pound lean salt pork, diced into small pieces or 1/2 pound lean bacon, cut in small pieces
3 tablespoons butter or margarine
6 medium yellow onions, diced
2 medium green pepper, seeded, cored and coarsely chopped
4 stalks celery, sliced in crescents
4 medium carrots, diced
6 cloves garlic, minced
1 tablespoon fresh gingerroot, minced
2 cups coconut milk, divided
1 tablespoon Old Bay seasoning
1-1/2 teaspoons dried thyme
1/2 cup Tortuga Dark Rum
2 tablespoons garlic pepper
2 medium Yukon Gold potatoes peeled and diced or 2 cups diced breadfruit
1 teaspoon Tortuga Hell-Fire Hot Pepper sauce
Salt to taste

Remove rind from salt pork and dice into small pieces. Cook pork or bacon in 5-6 quart Dutch oven or large pot over medium heat, stirring frequently until almost crisp then remove and drain on paper towels. Leave 2 tablespoons of fat in pot and add butter or margarine, 1 tablespoon garlic pepper, onions, green pepper, garlic, ginger, celery and carrots. Cook over medium heat , stirring frequently, until vegetables start to turn soft – do NOT allow mixture to brown or scorch.

Add half the ground conch and stir gently – do not break up all the clumps. At least half the conch should be left this way. Cook another 3 minutes. Add 1 cup coconut milk, Old Bay seasoning, pork pieces, thyme, remaining black pepper and pepper sauce and stir gently. Bring to boil for two minutes, then stir in remaining conch and rum. Reduce heat and simmer, slightly covered, over low heat for about 30 minutes, stirring occasionally to be sure nothing sticks to bottom of pot. Liquid should be reduced by about a third. Add the remaining coconut milk and potatoes and simmer another 15 minutes, uncovered, until potatoes are tender. Stir in the pepper sauce (add more to taste if desired). Stew can be stored in refrigerator – it's actually better the next day! Have additional Tortuga Hell-Fire Hot Pepper Sauce or other hot pepper sauce handy.

Curry Conch with Pasta

6 large conch, cleaned and ground
1/4 cup Tortuga Coconut Rum
1/4 cup butter
2 large yellow onions, coarsely chopped
1 medium green pepper, seeded and coarsely chopped
3 cloves garlic, minced
1 tablespoon grated fresh gingerroot
1/4 cup Jamaican or Trinidadian curry powder (Chief, for example)
1 teaspoon Grace Jamaican All Purpose Seasoning (see **Island Pantry**)
2 teaspoons ground black pepper
1 teaspoon Tortuga Hell-Fire Hot Pepper Sauce
1 teaspoon chicken bouillon granules
1 cup coconut milk
Cooked fettuccini or angelhair pasta

In a medium bowl, combine the ground conch and rum and stir gently to make sure rum seeps through to bottom. Refrigerate for an hour or more then drain, reserving rum. In a 5-quart Dutch oven or large pot, melt the butter over medium heat and add the onions, green pepper, garlic and ginger. Saute, stirring frequently, until vegetables just begin to soften, about four minutes, then add the curry powder, Grace seasoning and black pepper, stirring until blended. Cook two minutes longer, then add the conch and stir in gently, leaving some clumps instead of breaking all into fine pieces. Cover and cook for 10 minutes, stirring several times so nothing sticks to the pot bottom. Stir in the rum, coconut milk and chicken bouillon and bring just to a simmer for 2 minutes. Serve over hot pasta and garnish with thin slices of ripe banana and mango on the side.

Cayman Red Conch Chowder with Rum

This is the traditional recipe most people think of when they ask for conch chowder – rum is the surprise lagniappe. Serve each bowl with a half-shot of dark rum on the side to add right before eating.

8 large cleaned conch, ground (about 2 pounds)
1/3 cup fresh lime juice
1/4 pound lean salt pork
2 cups chopped yellow onion
1 cup chopped green pepper
3 cloves fresh garlic, chopped

1 cup diced carrots
3/4 cup diced celery
2 15- ounce cans stewed tomatoes, undrained
4 cups clam juice
2 tablespoons tomato paste
1 bay leaf
1/2 teaspoon ground allspice
1 teaspoon dried thyme
1 teaspoon oregano
2 teaspoons Old Bay Seasoning
2 teaspoons ground black pepper to taste
1 teaspoon garlic salt
3 tablespoons Worcestershire sauce
2 teaspoons Tortuga Hell-Fire Hot Pepper Sauce
OR 1 whole Scotch Bonnet
1-1/2 cups peeled diced potatoes
Tortuga Dark Rum

Sprinkle the ground conch with the lime juice and marinate in the refrigerator for an hour or two. Dice salt pork very fine and cook over medium heat in a Dutch oven or heavy pot, stirring often, until the fat has almost cooked away and pork is browned but not crisp. Drain off all but 2 tablespoons of fat and add onions, garlic green pepper, carrots and celery. Cook until vegetables are just beginning to soften, about 3 minutes.

Add the tomatoes, clam juice, tomato paste and remaining seasonings. (Be careful not to pierce the whole scotch bonnet or your chowder will be incredibly hot.) Bring to a boil and add the conch and stir well. Reduce heat to medium low and simmer, stirring often, skimming off any foam that forms, for about 45 minutes. Add the potatoes and cook until tender, about 15 minutes longer. Taste the chowder and add salt if necessary. Remove bay leaf and serve hot. Have a bottle of Rum Peppers (see **Caribbean Heat**) or additional hot pepper sauce on the table. Pass the rum bottle and a shot glass so each guest can add a measure of rum to the chowder before eating.

White Conch Chowder Cayman Brac Style with Sea Pie

2 1/2 cups ground conch (about 5 large)
8 slices bacon, cut in pieces or 1/2 pound salt pork, diced fine
2 large or 4 medium yellow onions, diced
1 medium green pepper, diced
2 cloves garlic, peeled and minced
2 ribs celery
1 quart water
1 teaspoon dried thyme or 1 large sprig of fresh thyme
1 tablespoon Pickapeppa Sauce
1 teaspoon fresh ground black pepper
1 teaspoon seasoned salt
2 cups peeled, diced breadfruit
1 8-ounce can mixed vegetables
1 14- ounce can evaporated milk
2 tablespoons cornstarch
Cold water
Sea pie

Make the sea pie dough first (see recipe below) and set aside. Brown bacon or salt pork over medium heat in large pot or Dutch oven until almost crisp. Remove pork pieces and drain on paper towels; set aside. Drain off all but 2 tablespoons fat and cook the onion, green pepper, celery and garlic until turning soft. Add the conch, stir well and cook another two minutes, stirring frequently – do not allow vegetables to scorch. Add bacon or pork pieces, water, seasonings and simmer for and hour over low heat, stirring occasionally. Add breadfruit, evaporated milk and mixed vegetables, stir well. Mix the cornstarch with just enough water to form a paste and stir into the chowder. Return to a simmer and add sea pie dough: drop pieces on top of simmering chowder and continue cooking for about 20 minutes until breadfruit is tender and sea pie is done. Serve with additional Pickapeppa sauce.

To make Sea pie:

Mix together 2 cups flour, 1 teaspoon salt and enough water to make a stiff dough. Knead until elastic and pull several times. Lay on wax paper and roll out, cut into 1-1/2 inch pieces. Drop pieces on top of simmering stew, cover and continue cooking about 20 minutes.

Curried Conch and Pumpkin Chowder

1 pound (2-1/4 cups) ground conch
2 tablespoons butter
3 tablespoons curry powder
4 tablespoons butter
2 cups diced onion
4 cloves garlic, minced
2 tablespoons curry powder
2 tablespoons minced peeled fresh gingerroot
1/2 teaspoon ground coriander
5 cups peeled pumpkin (calabaza) diced in 1/2 inch pieces (about 2 pounds)
3 cups chicken broth or clam juice
1-14 ounce can coconut milk
1/3 cup Tortuga Dark Rum
1 teaspoon Tortuga Hell-Fire Hot Pepper Sauce
2 teaspoons seasoned salt
1 teaspoon ground black pepper

Melt 2 tablespoons butter in 5-quart Dutch oven over medium high heat and stir in ground conch, sprinkled with 3 tablespoons curry powder. Sauté for five minutes, stirring frequently, then remove conch from the pot to a bowl and cover with foil. Melt the remaining butter and add the onion, garlic, gingerroot, coriander and 2 tablespoons curry powder. Cook, stirring often, until vegetables are soft, about five minutes. Stir in the chicken broth or clam juice and pumpkin and bring to a boil. Reduce heat to medium-low, cover and simmer until pumpkin is very soft, about 20 minutes. Allow to cool 15 minutes, then puree half the soup in food processor or blender. Return it to the pot and bring to a simmer and add the conch, rum, coconut milk, hot pepper sauce, seasoned salt and pepper. Simmer uncovered about five minutes. Adjust seasonings to taste and serve hot.

Conch Bisque

This rich, easy and delicious recipe can be made in a hurry.

2 cups ground conch (about 4 large conch)
1/4 cup butter
1 cup chopped Vidalia or sweet onions
1 cup chopped celery
2 cloves fresh garlic, minced
2 –10.5 ounce cans cream of potato soup
1/2 cup water
2 cups half and half
1/2 teaspoon white pepper
1/4 teaspoon paprika
2 teaspoons Beau Monde seasoning (more to taste)
2 tablespoons Tortuga Dark Rum

In large saucepan sauté onion, garlic and celery and ground conch in butter over medium-low heat about five minutes, until vegetables are soft but not brown or scorched. Remove from heat. Stir in condensed soup, water, half-and-half, pepper, paprika and 2 teaspoons Beau Monde and rum and mix well. Return to heat and bring just to a simmer (do not boil), stirring frequently, for about 10 minutes or until thoroughly heated. Taste and adjust seasonings. Serve with Tortuga Hell-Fire Hot Pepper sauce on the side.

Conch and Shrimp Gumbo

This beats the bayou version of Gumbo!

6 slices bacon
1/4 cup plus 1 tablespoon flour
5 cups chicken broth
2- 14.5 ounce cans stewed tomatoes, undrained
1 pound fresh okra, sliced or 1- 10 ounce package frozen sliced okra
1 large yellow onion, chopped
2 cloves garlic, minced
1 bunch scallions, chopped
2 stalks celery, sliced
1 large green pepper, diced
1 teaspoon Tortuga Hell-Fire Hot Pepper Sauce
2 cups diced ham
3 teaspoons seasoned. Salt
1 teaspoon ground black pepper
2 bay leaves
1-1/2 teaspoon dried whole thyme
4 large or 8 small conch, cleaned, well tenderized and sliced into 1-inch pieces
1 pound large shrimp, peeled and deveined
1 tablespoon fresh parsley
Hot white rice

In 5 quart Dutch oven or large pot, cook bacon until crisp. Remove bacon, crumble and set aside. Add flour to bacon drippings and cook over medium heat, stirring constantly, to make a roux, cooking until roux is the color of a copper penny (10-15 minutes).

Gradually stir in water and mix well, stirring constantly. Add tomatoes and all remaining ingredients except conch, shrimp and parsley to roux mixture and stir well. Simmer covered over low heat for 1 hour, stirring occasionally. Stir in conch and cook another hour, stirring occasionally and skimming off any surface foam. Add shrimp and cook until shrimp just turn pink, about 3 minutes – do not overcook. Stir in crumbled bacon pieces and serve over hot white rice. Sprinkle with fresh parsley.

Conch Creole

A hint of rum makes this spicy dish even better.

6 large conch, well tenderized (1-1/2 pounds)
2 tablespoons fresh lime juice
1/4 cup butter
1 tablespoon olive oil
6 tablespoons flour
6 cloves garlic, minced
1 cup diced celery
1-1/2 cups diced yellow onion
1 medium green pepper, seeded and diced
1- 28 ounce can stewed tomatoes, undrained
2 bay leaves
1/2 teaspoon dried thyme
1 teaspoon Creole seasoning (such as Tony's)
1 teaspoon sugar
2 tablespoons tomato paste
3/4 cup clam juice or chicken broth
1/4 cup Tortuga Gold Rum
1 tablespoon Worcestershire Sauce
1 teaspoon Tortuga Hell-Fire Hot Pepper Sauce
1 teaspoon salt
1 teaspoon ground black pepper
4 scallions, chopped

Be sure the conchs are very well tenderized and almost "lacy." Slice each conch into bite size pieces (about an inch) and sprinkle with lime juice. Marinate while preparing the sauce. In a large heavy skillet or Dutch oven, melt the butter over medium heat and add the oil. Sprinkle the flour over the mixture, stirring to blend evenly. Cook, stirring frequently, until flour turns light brown, then add the onions, celery, green pepper and garlic. Sauté until soft, stirring frequently, about 5 –6 minutes. Add the canned tomatoes with liquid, clam juice or broth, tomato paste, bay leaves, thyme, Creole seasoning and sugar. Stir well, then add the conch. Bring mixture to a boil, then reduce heat to simmer and cook for an hour, stirring occasionally. Add the rum, Worcestershire sauce, hot pepper sauce, salt and black pepper and stir well. Cook another 15 minutes. Remove bay leaves and taste – add more salt and pepper if desired. Serve over white rice and garnish with chopped scallions.

Conch Scampi

4 medium conch, well tenderized and cut into one-inch, bite-sized pieces
1 tablespoon chopped onion
1 clove garlic, minced
1/2 cup large shallots, minced
1/4 cup butter
2 tablespoons olive oil
2 tablespoons fresh lemon juice
1 tablespoon Tortuga Light Rum
2 tablespoons chopped fresh parsley
1 teaspoon salt
1 teaspoon black pepper

In large saucepan, combine 6 cups water, 1 tablespoon lemon juice, 1 clove minced garlic, 1 tablespoon chopped onion and conch. Bring to a boil and skim off foam, reduce heat to medium and continue simmering for 15 minutes. Drain conch and set aside. In frying pan or large skillet, over medium heat, melt butter and add the olive oil, parsley, salt, remaining garlic, shallots, lemon juice and rum cook for two minutes Add drained conch and stir well until all conch pieces are coated with sauce. Add the salt and pepper. Cook for another five minutes, stirring occasionally. Sprinkle with additional fresh parsley and serve over angel hair pasta or fettucini.

Conquering Giant Crabs

Blue crabs in the Caribbean are not seafood – they're big, formidable terrestrial crustaceans with an attitude and enormous claws. These crabs have "backs" that can stretch four inches across with a claw span of two and a half feet. They have one big claw called a "biter" that can remove a finger. You have to *really* want to eat one to tackle this recipe. Once abundant in Cayman and Jamaica after the start of the rainy season, *Cardisoma guanhumi*, the big blue land crabs islanders consider a delicacy, have become increasingly scarce. Gardeners are happy about this, as one crab can devour a kitchen garden as a late night snack.

The "little thing" omitted in every "easy" recipe for crab backs I've come across is this: you have to catch the crabs first, then boil them alive. And survive with your fingers intact.

"Crabbin" used to be a popular adventure, especially for Caymanian youngsters. The thrill of the hunt still lures many out after dark into swampy areas, armed with a flashlight, long stick with a sharp end, a thick croaker sack – and a partner to help. Once you spot the crab, shine the light right in its eyes to stun it, then you have to act fast. Pin the creature in the center of the back with the stick and use the other hand to grab the crab back at the point where the small legs join the back and the claws can't reach. Once you've got a good grip there, pick the crab up and HOLD ON, scream at your partner to get ready and toss the crab into the sack *fast* and close tightly.

Once caught, crabs are "purged," kept for a week or more in a cool, shaded tightly enclosed pen or large clean garbage can too tall to crawl out of. They are fed lettuce, mango scraps, vegetables and fruits to clean out or purge" their systems before they go into the pot. When getting ready to cook the crabs, remember: these are not like sluggish Maine lobsters. These critters can move – even leap out of a pot boiling water, causing chaos in the kitchen for novice cooks. If you're planning to serve crab to guests, prepare the meat a day ahead. Trust me. You've never seen anything like people running for cover with rabid land crabs on the loose in the dining room.

This actually happened at the Southern Cross Club resort in Little Cayman in 1981. Hoping to impress a fam trip of visiting New York travel agents with a truly native experience, the cooks had gathered a 40-gallon garbage can filled with land crabs and were planning a native feast. While the agents were getting soaked with rum punches, the cook was sampling the rum too and knocked over the garbage can. Twenty *really* mad crabs surged in a Tsunami of legs and claws out the kitchen door and into the party, catapulting 20 hysterical agents onto tabletops.

Crab Backs (Stuffed Crab)

6 live land crabs (3 to 4 inch backs)
One huge 12 quart or larger pot half full of boiling water
3 tablespoons fresh lime juice
1/2 cup white vinegar
3 tablespoons butter
2 cups fresh bread crumbs
1 teaspoon Tortuga Hell-Fire Hot Pepper Sauce
OR 1/8th teaspoon minced, seeded Scotch Bonnet pepper
3 scallions, chopped fine
1 medium yellow onion, chopped fine
3 large cloves garlic, minced
3 tablespoons fresh parsley, chopped
1 tablespoon Worcestershire sauce
1/4 teaspoon ground allspice
1 teaspoon seasoned salt
1 teaspoon ground black pepper
2 tablespoons Tortuga Dark Rum
3 teaspoons butter, softened, divided
Paprika

The tricky part is cooking the crabs and picking and preparing the backs. Maybe you can get someone to do that for you. After that, this recipe is a piece of crab cake, comparatively speaking.

First, be sure the pot has a tight-fitting lid. Fill half way with water and add 1/2 cup vinegar. Bring the water to a rolling boil. Carefully plunge one or two crabs at a time, or as many as pot will hold, into the boiling water and put the lid on immediately and hold down tight with an oven mitt. The crabs are going to be boiling mad and you may have crabs flying out of the pot if not careful. Reduce heat to medium and boil for 8-10 minutes until crabs turn bright red. Now you can safely remove them with tongs and cool. Repeat until all crabs are cooked. Break off the legs and claws and crack open the claws and pick out the meat, removing any shards of shell. Carefully split open the bottom side of the crab backs, so you don't crack the top shell, and remove the meat and fat. Throw away the gills and white intestines. Carefully pick over the meat again to remove any shell and cartilage, sprinkle with lime juice and set aside. Scrub the crab shells or "backs" and pat dry.

Preheat oven to 350 F. In a large skillet, melt the butter over medium heat and stir in the onion, garlic, hot pepper and scallions and cook until soft – do not let the mixture brown. Remove from heat and stir in the flaked crab, Worcestershire sauce and remaining seasonings and rum and mix well. Stir in the breadcrumbs until well blended.

Stuff each crab back and place on a foil-lined baking sheet. Place 1/2 teaspoon of butter on each crab back and sprinkle with paprika. Bake at 350 F for 15-20 minutes, or until lightly browned. You can also place crab backs under a preheated broiler for 3-5 minutes. This recipe should serve 6, but that's unlikely.

The Great Caribbean Cook-Out: Jerk & Barbecue

Forget Texas. Move over Memphis. Barbecue was born in the Caribbean and no island party is complete without a taste of the *real* thing. The Arawak and Carib Indians made the first pit barbecues, roasting wild pig and game over fires in sand pits. They also grilled on a *barbacoa*, a wooden grate over an open fire. Early Spanish settlers called this kind of cooking *boucan* and ruthless 17th century "buccaneers" were named after it. Those seafaring rogues took boucan to extremes by sailing into port and barbecuing entire towns, burning them the ground and grilling local livestock – their idea of partying between plundering the European trade fleet.

Jerk is a Jamaican creation. This technique of slowly smoking highly seasoned meats in pits lined with allspice wood was created by Jamaica's 17th century Maroons— slaves freed by Spanish settlers who fled Jamaica during the English conquest of 1655. Hiding in Jamaicaa's remote rugged mountainous interior, they escaped renewed slavery and harrassed the English settlers with continual raids until 1739. Jerking created survival food by preserving the meat of wild pigs for months—the word "jerky" comes from this. Maroons still live in that remote 1,500 acre area called the Cockpit Country and their fiery, jerk- style barbecue and spice blends have become a culinary rage far beyond Jamaica's coast.

Today Jerk seasoning is one of the world's most provocative blends; the combination of spices and slow smoking over allspice (pimento) wood creates unforgettable flavors. Jerk centers and makeshift roadside "pits" (converted oil-drum smokers) are common sights throughout Jamaica but Boston Beach near Port Antonio on Jamaica's northeast coast still reigns as Jamaica's jerk capital. Grand Cayman has a few roadside vendors on weekends, but pimento wood is not readily available here and genuine Boston-style jerk is hard to find.

Caribbean Barbecue Tips

There are some easy secrets to good jerk – or any Caribbean barbecue. We're not talking about simply firing up the grill and throwing on a few steaks. There is an art to this kind of cooking.

Begin with a spicy rub or marinade and let meat or chicken marinade for several hours – even overnight. Slow, covered cooking is the next step. For the best flavor, you need to build a fire that gives low, even heat and let the smoke help flavors develop slowly. Use hard wood or a combination of soaked hardwood chips and charcoal instead of charcoal briquettes alone whenever possible. I don't recommend mesquite – the flavor clashes with jerk and other Caribbean spice blends. If you are using sugar or tomato-based barbecue sauce, never drench the meat from the start and put it on the grill – it can burn into a carbon crust. Baste meat with sauce during the last half of cooking and serve a generous amount on the side to guests. Finally, meat straight from the fire, especially a whole roast, does not carve easily. Let it sit covered with foil for a few minutes (up to 15 minutes for a 6-10 pound roast) to let the juices drawn to the surface during grilling seep back into the meat.

Jerk Seasoning

Every jerk chef has his own secret seasoning blend, but the basic combination of ingredients includes garlic, allspice, thyme, Scotch Bonnet peppers, salt, black pepper, nutmeg, cinnamon, scallions and a pinch of sugar. True jerk seasoning is a very spicy and you should experiment to find the degree of heat and spice right for your palate.

With so many excellent varieties of jerk seasoning and sauces now available, making your own almost seems unnecessary. My favorite "wet" jerk seasoning concentrate, hands down, is **Walkerswood Traditional Jamaican Jerk Seasoning**, sold in 10-ounce jars. You can find out where to buy it near you by calling 1-800-827-0769. For a shake-on dry seasoning, to give a hint of jerk flavor, I use **Walkerswood Jerk Seasoning** or **Jamaica's Island Spice Jerk Seasoning**.

If jerk flavor is a sudden impulse or afterthought, I use **Tortuga Jerk Sauce** Unfortunately this piquant sauce is sold only in 5 ounce bottles, which I can consume in a sitting. Next choice is **Grace Island Style Jerk Sauce** which is a blend of basic jerk spices and mango, cane vinegar, cho-cho and tomato paste. Both are mild.

If you can't find any of these, or are determined to make your own, try these recipes for jerk rub and jerk marinade.

Jerk Rub

2 tablespoons ground allspice
6 cloves garlic
2 tablespoons fresh gingerroot, peeled and chopped
1 teaspoon ground nutmeg
1 teaspoon cinnamon
1 teaspoon salt
1 teaspoon sugar
3 Scotch bonnet peppers, seeded and deveined **(see note)

10 large scallions (enough to make 2 cups chopped)
1 medium onion, chopped
3 teaspoons dried thyme or 1/3 cup fresh sprigs, chopped
1 tablespoon black pepper
4 tablespoons vegetable oil
2 tablespoons fresh lime juice

Combine all ingredients in a food processor or blender and puree until it forms paste, about a minute. Store in a sealed glass jar in refrigerator. (**For very hot seasoning, do not remove the seeds – but use with caution! For milder jerk seasoning, use one Scotch bonnet – even milder, remove the pepper seeds and membrane.) Makes about 2-1/2 cups.

Jerk Marinade

Prepare the recipe for Jerk Rub and add 3/4 cup soy sauce and 1/4 cup Tortuga Dark Rum and increase lime juice to 1/2 cup. Blend well and pour in a glass bottle; seal and store in refrigerator.

Jerk Sauce

2-3 tablespoons Jerk Rub (recipe above)
1/2 cup soy sauce
2 tablespoons Tortuga Dark Rum (*Optional)
1/4 cup Worcestershire Sauce
1 teaspoon brown sugar

Combine all ingredients in a jar and shake well until blended. Use this when you want a milder jerk flavor, or keep a bottle on the table as a condiment –it adds zest to soups too.

The Jerk Fire

Regardless of the authenticity of the seasoning blend, unless you have access to a supply of allspice (pimento) wood and leaves, you won't be able duplicate the rich, musky flavor of true Jamaican jerk dishes. The cooking process itself is as important as the seasoning: very slow smoking, often 12 hours or longer, over pimento (allspice) wood and leaves – materials you're not likely to find outside of Jamaica. The next best thing is to use a smoker or prepare a slow fire in a kettle grill using a combination of charcoal and soaked hardwood chips – NOT mesquite. Pouring a jar of allspice berries into the fire is not the answer either.

Jerk Pork or Chicken

For jerk pork, use a whole 4-5 pound boned pork shoulder or boneless pork loin. For chicken, use split 3-pound chicken or 3 pounds chicken pieces. Dark meat chicken pieces, thighs especially, are best for jerk because they have more fat and won't dry out as much as breasts and wings. Rub meat generously all over with jerk rub mixture and place in a covered bowl or sealed zip-top bag for at least 8 hours – 24 hours is better, turning several times to marinate evenly.

Prepare the barbecue, using enough coals to make a slow fire for the amount of meat to be cooked (refer to the directions on your grill or smoker.) After coals are lit, soak hardwood chips in water. When coals are gray and covered with ash, add the soaked chips to the fire and place the meat on the grill. Cover, leaving ventilation holes open and cook slowly, about 2 hours, turning meat every 20-30 minutes and basting with additional jerk marinade. Add more coals or soaked chips after the first 30 minutes as necessary after that to keep the fire going slowly, but do not let coals flare up or flame. When meat is cooked, chop pork or chicken into 1-1/2 inch pieces with a meat cleaver or heavy knife, splintering any bones. Serve with more hot sauce or jerk sauce on the side.

Jerk Turkey Breast

Never heard of Jerk Turkey? You may never want turkey any other way after this. You can do a whole turkey this way too. For a mild jerk flavor with a little kick, decrease the jerk concentrate to 1-1/2 tablespoons.

1 –6 pound turkey breast
3 tablespoons Jerk Rub or Walkerswood Traditional Jamaican Jerk seasoning concentrate
1/4 cup Tortuga Gold Rum
1 tablespoon Worcestershire Sauce
1/2 cup soy sauce or Kikkoman Teriyaki marinade
3 tablespoons finely minced onion
1 tablespoon Pickapeppa sauce
1 teaspoon ground black pepper

Combine all ingredients except turkey breast in a medium bowl and blend well with wire whisk.

Lift the skin on the breast and place a few teaspoons of marinade on each side and use fingers to rub in. Place breast in jumbo zip-top bag and pour remaining marinade over it and seal bag. Turn and massage the breast (do not open bag, do this from the outside carefully) several times to rub in the marinade. Allow to marinate for 1-2 days, turning and massaging several times. Remove turkey from marinade, reserving to use as baste.

Build a medium hot fire and when ready, place turkey on a rack on grill in center of grill grate using indirect heat method – coals should be divided and pushed to two sides of the grill when covered with ash and glowing. Cover with grill lid and cook about an hour, basting frequently with remaining marinade, until all juices run clear when breast is pierced with small sharp knife. (If you want to cook a whole turkey, cook an estimated 10 minutes per pound.) Remove from grill and transfer turkey to large serving platter. Cover with aluminum foil and let sit for 10-15 minutes before carving.

The next two recipes will give you plenty of jerk flavor, but don't require slow-cooking.

Jerk Chicken Tenders

Easy preparation and bold jerk flavor make this recipe a party favorite and leftovers are great for Jerk Chicken Caesar Salad. For extra punch, serve with Mango Colada Dip or Tamarind Tango Dip (see **Rum Sauces & Uncommon Condiments**.)

2 pounds chicken breast tenders or boneless chicken breast strips

1 cup Kikkoman Teriyaki marinade
1/4 cup Tortuga Gold Rum
2 tablespoons canola or vegetable oil
2 tablespoons Jerk Rub or Walkerswood Traditional Jamaican Jerk Seasoning concentrate
2 tablespoons dried chopped onion or 3 tablespoons chopped scallions
1 medium red or yellow onion, sliced

Combine all ingredients except the sliced onion in a large zip-top bag and seal tight. Turn bag several times to blend and distribute ingredients over chicken. Refrigerate 8 hours or longer, up to 48 hours. Prepare grill for medium heat Spray two pieces of aluminum foil with vegetable oil spray and divide the sliced onion between them. Remove chicken from marinade and divide between the two foil pieces. Drizzle marinade over each then fold edges over and seal tight to make packets. Cook 20 minutes in foil, then remove chicken and place directly on grill to brown, reserving onions and juice from foil. Cook chicken another 2-3 minutes. Serve warm with the onions and reserved juice, or chill for salads.

Jerk Burgers

Another easy party choice. For sensitive palates, use only 1-1/2 teaspoons jerk rub or seasoning.

1-1/2 pounds ground chuck or round
1-1/2 tablespoons Jerk Rub or Walkerswood Traditional Jamaican Jerk Seasoning concentrate
2 tablespoons soy sauce
2 tablespoons Tortuga Gold Rum
1/4 cup finely diced red onion
2 teaspoons ground black pepper
1 teaspoon salt

Combine all ingredients in a medium bowl and blend with a fork. Divide meat and shape into 4 patties. Chill 6 hours or longer. Prepare grill for a medium hot fire and when ready, grill burgers until they reach desired degree of doneness.

Barbecued Ribs

The Caribbean-wide craving for spicy grilled *pork* spareribs dates back to the Carib's passion for wild pig roasts. If you follow these few tips from Tortuga's Managing Director Robert Hamaty, it's easier to create tender, delicious ribs than it is to render them inedible, like carbon-crusted pork jerky – which unfortunately is what too many people do.

Know your ribs

There are three cuts of ribs: spareribs, the outer ends of pork ribs, which have the least amount of meat; country-style ribs, from the pork shoulder, are thick and meat, more like pork chops, and require longer cooking. Finally, my choice, baby back ribs, short rib sections which are the tenderest of all. Plan on 1 pound of ribs per serving.

Remove the tough membrane

Remove the thin but tough membrane on the bottom of each rack of ribs. This simple step makes ribs much more tender but is one most people ignore. Do this before you dip, rub or marinate your ribs.

Parboil or pre-bake?

Some barbecue purists are insulted by this idea, but unless you have perfected the art of slow wood cooking, this step insures tender ribs. **Parboil ribs** –add seasonings to water if you like – about 20-30 minutes and then cool in the liquid for 20 minutes. **Or bake** them at 350F for 45 minutes to an hour and cool. Then marinate or rub the ribs and refrigerate, covered, at least four hours – overnight is better. If you skip this step, then you must plan on slow-grilling for about 90 minutes to two hours for spareribs and 2-2-1/2 hours for country-style ribs, depending on the amount of meat being cooked, over a medium to low fire.

Leave the Sauce until Last

To finish, baste with barbecue sauce and grill the meat for about 10 minutes, covered, over medium-hot coals. Don't brush on sugar or tomato-based barbecue sauce at the start if you are slow grilling meats. Wait until meat is at least half-cooked or the sauce will turn into a charred crust from over-cooking.

Use wood if possible

Today's cooks don't usually have the luxury of a real wood fire, but you can use a combination of wood chips and charcoal for a better flavor during slow cooking. Soak hickory or other hardwood chips for 30 minutes. When fire is ready, place the chips directly on the coals. You may have to add more coals and chips during the cooking process to maintain the low fire, so keep some soaked chips ready.

Café Tortuga's Famous Ribs

Café Tortuga, the company's first restaurant on Grand Cayman, is no longer around, but Captain Robert Hamaty shared the restaurant's famous rib recipe for the first time. While it doesn't require slow cooking the flavor and texture will be similar. The secret was not only in the cooking, but also in Tortuga's special sauce, now sold as one of its private label items. This recipe works with chicken too.

4 pounds baby back ribs (more or less to suit)
1 tablespoon Liquid Smoke
1 gallon water
1 bottle **Tortuga Rum Bar-B-Que Sauce®**

Preheat oven to 350F. Have a deep roasting pan with a flat or broiler rack ready large enough to hold the amount of meat you're cooking. Remove rack from pan and spray lightly with non-stick vegetable oil spray. Mix the Liquid Smoke and water and place in a large pot or Dutch oven. Dip each section of ribs into the mixture until completely coated and dripping and arrange on the rack. When all ribs have been dipped, pour a half-inch of the Liquid Smoke mixture into the roasting pan and place the rack of ribs on top. Cover pan with aluminum foil and seal edges and bake for 50-60 minutes, or longer if necessary until ribs are tender. Check and if necessary, add more water after 30 minutes. Reduce baking time for smaller quantities.

Remove ribs from oven and chill for several hours until ready to grill. Prepare a medium fire and baste ribs with **Tortuga Rum Bar-B-Que Sauce** or other favorite sauce (see other recipes in this chapter.) Place ribs directly over medium coals, about 8 inches from the heat. Cover the grill and open vent holes, and cook about 4-5 minutes on each side, basting generously with additional sauce.

If you want crusty ribs: After the first four minutes, move ribs to the side so they are not directly over the main heat of the fire. Turn and brush with sauce or marinade and cover again, and continue cooking, turning several times, about 15 minutes longer, basting every five minutes until ribs are browned and crusty to suit your taste.

From the Sea

Barbecued Fish with Rum Ginger Sauce

4-6 ounce yellowfin tuna or wahoo steaks or fillets, cut 3/4-1 inch thick
1/2 teaspoon ground allspice
1 teaspoon white pepper
2 teaspoons Kosher salt

Marinade:
Juice and grated peel of one large orange (1/3 cup juice, 2 teaspoons grated peel)
2 tablespoons olive oil
2 tablespoons soy sauce
1 tablespoons cider vinegar
1 tablespoon sugar
1 tablespoon minced fresh ginger
2 tablespoons Tortuga Dark Rum
Rum Ginger Sauce (recipe follows)

Rinse the fish in cold water and lime juice. Combine the ingredients for the marinade in a zip-top bag and mix well. Add the fish, press out air and seal bag. Turn bag over several times, to be sure marinade coats all surfaces. Cover and refrigerate for an hour.

Prepare the grill and when coals are hot, oil or spray a barbecue fish basket or grid with non-stick vegetable oil spray. Remove fish from marinade saving marinade, sprinkle with salt, allspice and pepper and place in the basket or grid. Grill the fish for about 5 minutes on each side, basting generously with the reserved marinade. Serve with **Rum Ginger Sauce**.

Rum Ginger Sauce
1/2 cup butter
1 tablespoon orange juice
1 tablespoon minced fresh ginger
2 tablespoons Tortuga Dark Rum
1 tablespoon light brown sugar

Combine all ingredients in a small saucepan and heat over medium heat, stirring constantly, until butter melts, sugar is dissolved, and all ingredients are blended.

Maple Rum Glazed Fish Steaks

If you prefer, you can substitute four chicken breast halves for the fish and adjust grilling time accordingly.

2 teaspoons fresh or 1 teaspoon dried thyme
1/2 cup maple syrup
1/4 cup Tortuga Dark or Gold Rum
1 tablespoon canola or safflower oil
4 – 6 ounce salmon, yellowfin tuna, wahoo or other firm fish steaks, about 3/4 inch thick
1 teaspoon seasoned salt
2 teaspoons garlic pepper (about 1/2 teaspoon per steak)

Wash the fish steaks in lime and cold water and pat dry. Combine the first four ingredients in a small bowl and whisk until blended. Place the fish steaks in a large zip-top plastic bag and pour in the marinade. Seal bag and turn several times until fish is evenly coated. Refrigerate for an hour, then prepare a medium hot fire. Remove fish from marinade, saving marinade. Spray a grilling grid with vegetable oil spray. Place the fish on the grid, sprinkle with salt and pepper and baste with reserved marinade. Cook about five minutes on each side, basting a few times with the marinade. Glaze can scorch, so use carefully.

Sauces:

Tortuga Rum Bar-B-Que Sauce®

Sorry, this is another secret family recipe, sold under the Tortuga Rum Company private gourmet label. A robust, spicy barbecue sauce, it's especially good with ribs. You can buy it in 12 ounce bottles direct from Tortuga Rum Company retail outlets in Grand Cayman and our local supermarkets. See **Party, Island Style with Tortuga Products** for information about ordering overseas.

Hot N Tangy Rum Barbecue Sauce

This will add fire and island flavor to your meat or chicken.

1/3 cup Tortuga Dark Rum
1/2 cup light molasses
2 cups catsup
1/4 cup Tortuga steak sauce
1 tablespoon Tortuga Hell-Fire Hot Pepper Sauce
2 tablespoons Worcestershire sauce
1/2 teaspoon ground allspice
1/2 teaspoon ground cinnamon
1 teaspoon garlic powder
1 tablespoon grated fresh gingerroot

Combine all ingredients in a large heavy saucepan and bring to a boil over medium heat, stirring frequently. Reduce heat to medium-low and simmer, uncovered, stirring frequently until sauce reduces and thickens slightly, about 15 minutes. Remove from heat and pour into a container with a cover. Refrigerate if you don't plan to use immediately.

Three Fingers Tortuga Poultry or Pork Glaze

Three fingers of rum is what you get in a rum shop, without asking. This easy barbecue glaze makes a delicious sauce – be sure to make extra to pass at the table.

3 tablespoons Tortuga Wildflower honey
1/3 cup soy sauce
1/3 cup Tortuga Dark Rum
1 tablespoon salt
2 tablespoons sugar
1/2 teaspoon coriander

Combine all ingredients in a small bowl and stir well until thoroughly blended. Brush desired cut of pork or chicken pieces lightly with olive oil then generously brush with glaze. Grill, basting several times with glaze until meat is cooked. Refrigerate remaining glaze or heat and serve at table.

Piquant Rum Citrus Marinade

This is delicious with chicken or fish, especially salmon. It will marinate 4-6 ounce fish steaks or boneless chicken breasts.

1/4 cup fresh orange juice
2 tablespoons fresh lime juice
1/4 cup Tortuga Dark Rum
1/4 cup soy sauce
1/3 cup scallions, chopped
3 large garlic cloves, chopped
1/4 cup dark brown sugar, packed

Combine all ingredients in a food processor or blender and blend until smooth. Combine with chicken or fish in a large zip-top and seal, turning several times to coat evenly. Marinate fish no longer than an hour, chicken for 4 hours or longer. Prepare grill and remove fish or chicken from marinade. Cook on a grill rack or grid over medium-hot coals, about 5-6 minutes on each side, basting frequently with reserved marinade.

Drunken Meats & Tipsy Birds

There are two things Caribbean folks expect of any meat or chicken dish. It must be well seasoned and when appropriate (which is almost always), accompanied by lots of equally well-seasoned gravy – or at the very least a bottle of Tortuga Steak Sauce, Pickapeppa or other spicy sauce on the side. Remember this if you are thinking of serving plain old filet mignon or grilled porterhouse steaks to island guests. And always have Tortuga Hell-Fire Hot Pepper Sauce or another fiery West Indian pepper sauce within reach. No sissy foreign imports, please. (For another recipe, see **Comfort Food; Western Caribbean Style.**)

West Indian Roast Beef

Anything less spicy just won't do. The original 200-year old recipe instructed cooks to rub and marinate the beef for two weeks before roasting. I advise against such mummification for obvious health reasons.

1-4-1/2 pound top round roast
1 cup dark brown sugar
1/2 cup Kosher Salt
1 tablespoon ground allspice
1 tablespoon freshly ground black pepper
2 teaspoons ground ginger
1 teaspoon ground cinnamon
1 teaspoon nutmeg
3 teaspoons Tortuga Hell-Fire Hot Pepper Sauce or 1 teaspoon cayenne pepper
1/2 cup Tortuga Gold Rum
1/2 cup water

Trim excess fat from the roast and rinse in cold water. Pat dry and cut small slits all over surface of beef. Place the roast in a large bowl while you make the rub. In a medium mixing bowl, combine the brown sugar, salt, spices and pepper sauce or cayenne and blend well. Using your fingertips, rub the spice mixture into the whole roast, turning to cover all surfaces, and rubbing as much into the small slits as you can. (Wash your hands well after this to get rid of the hot pepper!) Cover the bowl tightly and marinate the roast for 2-3 days, turning several times and basting with the marinade that will accumulate.

When ready to cook the roast, preheat the oven to 275 F. Remove beef from marinade, saving marinade. Place the beef on a rack in large pot or ovenproof Dutch oven. Combine the rum, water and 1/2 cup of the marinade and pour into the cooking pan. Place roast in the center of the oven, cover and braise for 3-1/2 hours or until the beef is fork tender. Remove from the roasting pan and transfer to a serving platter. Use pan juices to make gravy. Cool for 20 minutes before slicing. For the best flavor, cover with plastic wrap, wrap with aluminum foil and refrigerate for 8 hours or overnight. Slice and reheat or serve cold: slice in very thin slices and serve with hard-dough bread or other heavy bread and jerk mayonnaise.

Tortuga Pepper Steak

Marinade:
1/2 cup Tortuga Dark Rum
2 tablespoons dark brown sugar
1 tablespoon ground black pepper
3 tablespoons soy sauce
1 teaspoon seasoning salt
6 cloves garlic, crushed
1/4 cup diced onion
1 teaspoon Tortuga Hell-Fire Hot Pepper
1-1/2 pounds top round or sirloin, cut into 1/2 inch strips
2 tablespoons olive oil
2 large onions, sliced
1 medium green pepper, seeded and sliced
1 red sweet pepper, seeded and sliced
1 teaspoon browning or Kitchen Bouquet

Combine rum, sugar, pepper, salt, garlic, soy, hot sauce and 1/4 cup diced onion in gallon-size zip-top bag and add meat; seal and turn bag several times to coat all pieces. Marinate in refrigerator 6 hours or overnight (longer if you want) turning bag occasionally. Remove meat from bag and save marinade.

Heat oil in skillet until hot and add meat. Stir and brown for three minutes and then add sliced onion and pepper slices. Cook two minutes. Then add browning and reserved marinade and stir well. Reduce heat to low and simmer about 20 minutes or until meat is fork tender. Additional salt to taste. Note: If you like your peppers al dente, add them during the last five minutes instead of with onion. Serve over rice and beans or white rice and bottle of Tortuga Hell sauce on the side to season.

Steak with Rum Butter

Many Caribbean folk think plain grilled steak is a waste of meat. They would rather cut it up for pepper steak, stew or any other dish with seasonings and GRAVY. However, "sophisticated cuisine" is not new to the Caribbean. This recipe from Jamaica was "old" when I first jotted it down 20 years ago.

4 –12 ounce rib eye steaks, 1-1/2 inches thick
2 teaspoons Beau Monde seasoning mixed with 1/2 teaspoon ground allspice
4 teaspoons Worcestershire sauce
4 tablespoons Tortuga Gold Rum
1-1/2 tablespoon chopped shallots
1/2 teaspoon salt
1 teaspoon ground black pepper
6 tablespoons unsalted butter, room temperature
2 teaspoons fresh lime juice
1 tablespoon plus 1 teaspoon fresh chopped parsley

Combine the rum, shallots, salt and pepper in a small saucepan and simmer until the mixture is reduced by half. Cool until lukewarm, then blend in the butter, lime juice and parsley and mix well. Divide the butter mixture into four round portions and place on wax paper in a plastic container with a cover. Refrigerate, covered, until firm.

Sprinkle each steak all over with 1 teaspoon Worcestershire and seasoning. Heat a heavy non-stick skillet over medium high heat and add the steaks. Cook five minutes on each side for medium-rare, longer if you desire more well-done meat.   Serve immediately with a portion of the rum butter on top.

Rumhead Pot Roast

The ultimate American comfort food is greatly improved by adding rum and island spice. This spicier version of my mom's recipe, handed down from generations of Southerners, confirms that Rum Fever was in my genes.

3 pounds boneless chuck roast
1-1/2 cups Tortuga Gold Rum, plus 4 ounces for cook's drinks
2 tablespoons Worcestershire sauce
2 teaspoons garlic pepper
1 teaspoon seasoned salt
1 teaspoon Grace All Purpose Seasoning
2 tablespoons oil
2 large onions, coarsely chopped
1 large green pepper, cored, seeded and sliced
10 cloves garlic, crushed and chopped
1 tablespoon Worcestershire sauce
2 tablespoons soy sauce
2 teaspoons Tortuga Hellfire Hot Pepper Sauce
2 large carrots, sliced in rounds
1 envelope onion soup mix
3 cups water
1 teaspoon dried thyme
1/2 teaspoon whole allspice berries
1 teaspoon ground black pepper
2 teaspoons Tortuga Hellfire Hot Pepper Sauce
3 tablespoons cornstarch
2 tablespoons water

Trim chuck roast of excess fat and pierce with knife all over and place in a heavy zip-top bag with the rum. Seal and turn to coat meat evenly with rum, then refrigerate for 24 hours. Remove meat from bag and save the rum and juices. Combine the 2 tablespoons

Worcestershire sauce, All Purpose Seasoning, garlic pepper, and seasoned salt and blend well. Rub mixture over the meat and let sit for five minutes. Heat oil over medium heat in 5-6 quart Dutch oven and brown meat on all sides. Add chopped onion, garlic, green pepper and carrots and stir. Add dried onion soup mix, soy sauce, 1 tablespoon Worcestershire, reserved rum marinade and enough water to almost cover meat and stir well. Stir in allspice berries, thyme, black pepper, and pepper sauce. Return to a slow simmer and cook for two hours, covered, or until beef is very tender. To thicken gravy when beef is done, combine cornstarch and water and mix until it forms a smooth paste. Gradually stir into stock and simmer over low heat until sauce thickens.

Wild West Indian Meatloaf

I swore I was not going to include meatloaf (or macaroni and cheese) recipes in this cookbook, as they seem to be last resort filler in too many local cookbooks. But I was wrong. I forgot that Meat Loaf, two words, is a popular snack in Jamaica and Cayman. It's patty meat baked inside a small turnover-shaped loaf of bread. I created this moist, highly seasoned recipe after I realized how many of my Caribbean friends enjoy this classic American blue plate special. I've adapted it for the West Indian palate with much bolder seasonings. Like a big meat patty without the dough crust.

1-1/2 pounds ground chuck
1 pound ground pork
1 envelope onion-mushroom soup mix
3 tablespoons Tortuga Dark Rum
1 teaspoon Tortuga Hell-Fire Hot Pepper Sauce or 1/16th teaspoon minced Scotch Bonnet
1tablespoon garlic powder
1 tablespoon garlic pepper
1 teaspoon thyme
1 teaspoon ground allspice
1 teaspoon seasoned salt
1 tablespoon regular Mrs. Dash seasoning
1 tablespoon Walkerswood Traditional Jamaican Jerk Seasoning® concentrate
1/2 cup chili sauce
1/4 cup Worcestershire sauce
1/2 cup milk
2 cups soft white breadcrumbs (ground in food processor)
2 large eggs, lightly beaten
1 cup finely diced red onion
1/4 cup finely diced sweet red pepper
2 tablespoons browning or Kitchen bouquet
2 teaspoons coarse ground black pepper

Preheat oven to 375. Spray a foil-lined roasting pan with vegetable spray. Combine all ingredients except meat, browning and 2 teaspoons black pepper in large bowl and stir to mix. Crumble in the beef and pork and use your hands to mix, just until all ingredients are blended. – do not over mix or the meatloaf will be too firm.

Form mixture into two oval loaves and place in the roasting pan. Drizzle each with 1 tablespoon browning or Kitchen bouquet, then sprinkle with the coarse ground black pepper. Cover loosely with aluminum foil to avoid splattering in oven. Bake at 375 for 45 minutes, then drain off fat and continue baking, uncovered another 15-20 minutes until meatloaf is browned on top. Meatloaf should be firm but still ooze some juices. Remove from oven, cover with foil and let stand for 10 minutes before slicing. (Variation: For spicier meatloaf, increase the jerk seasoning to 2 tablespoons.)

Plantation Pork Chops

You don't have to hunt wild pig anymore to enjoy this old recipe.

4-6 ounce boneless pork loin chops
1/4 cup olive oil
2 tablespoons dried minced onion
1/2 cup pineapple juice
1/ 4 cup Tortuga Dark Rum
1 tablespoon plus 1 teaspoon lime juice
1 tablespoon plus 1 teaspoon brown sugar
4 cloves garlic, minced
1/4 teaspoon ground ginger
1/8 teaspoon ground nutmeg
1 teaspoon ground allspice
1/2 teaspoon Tortuga Hell-Fire Hot Pepper sauce

Combine pork chops and all ingredients in a heavy zip-top plastic bag. Seal bag and marinate for at least 8 hours, turning bag several times. Prepare grill for indirect heat cooking (coals on both sides rather than piled in center). Remove chops from marinade. Pour leftover marinade into saucepan and cook over medium heat until boiling. Reduce heat to low and simmer 10 minutes while pork chops cook. Grill chops about 5 minutes on each side minutes over indirect heat in covered grill, turning once to brown both sides. Serve with cooked marinade as sauce.

Cuban Roast Pork

Nothing is more delicious than boldly seasoned *lechon asado*, or roast suckling pig, the highlight of the traditional Cuban Nochebuena (Christmas Eve) celebration and many other Caribbean fêtes.. But if roasting a whole 40-pound pig isn't convenient, try this scaled down recipe for a delicious island-style pork feast.

1 8-pound fresh ham or boneless pork loin roast
12 large cloves garlic, peeled and mashed
1 tablespoon salt
1 bay leaf, ground
2 teaspoons dried oregano
2 sprigs fresh thyme (or 1 teaspoon dried)
1 teaspoon ground cumin
2 teaspoons fresh ground black pepper
1/3 cup olive oil
1/2 cup Tortuga Dark Rum
1 cup sour orange juice, or 1/2 cup orange juice and 1/2 cup lime juice
2 medium yellow onions, sliced into thin rings

Trim off excess fat from pork and make shallow cuts all over meat. Combine garlic, salt, bay leaf, oregano, thyme and pepper in food processor and grind into paste. Place the pork on a plate to catch any seasoning drips. Rub seasoning mix into the pork, making sure it goes into the cuts in the surface. Put the roast in a large bowl or jumbo zip-top bag . Combine onions, olive oil, and rum and bitter orange juice and blend well and pour over roast, turning so roast is covered with marinade. Cover bowl with plastic wrap or seal bag tightly and refrigerate 24 hours, turning roast occasionally to marinate all surfaces.

Preheat oven to 350F degrees. Remove roast from marinade (save marinade) and pat dry. Place in roasting pan lightly oiled with olive oil. There are two suggestions from Cuban friends about how to cook this.

The first one: roast pork for an hour at 350F, turning during cooking so all sides are browned. Remove roast and pour reserved marinade and onions over roast and tent with aluminum foil, and reduce heat to 300. Roast for 2-1/2 hours longer, basting often with pan juices and marinade, or until roast is well done. **The other method** is to heat the oven to very low heat, 225 and cook the roast slowly, about 8-hours or overnight – basting frequently with marinade. Islanders like their pork very well done, falling apart tender. The internal temperature should read at 180 degrees on a meat thermometer. Let stand 20 minutes, covered, before serving.

Roast Pork Port Royale

Legendary Port Royale off Kingston's coast was once called the Wickedest City on Earth. The outpost of some of history's boldest pirates literally disappeared beneath the sea in 1692. This equally bold, spiced pork roast will disappear just as dramatically from your table.

1-6-7 pound center cut pork loin
2 cups chicken broth
6 cloves garlic, minced
1 tablespoon fresh grated gingerroot
1 teaspoon Tortuga Hell-Fire Hot Pepper Sauce or 1/16th teaspoon minced Scotch Bonnet
1/4 cup Tortuga Dark Rum
1 cup light brown sugar
1 teaspoon ground allspice
1/2 teaspoon mace
1 bay leaf
2 teaspoons salt
2 teaspoons ground black pepper
1/4 cup Tortuga Spiced Rum
3 tablespoon lime juice
1 tablespoon cornstarch, dissolved in 1 tablespoon water

Preheat oven to 325. Trim the roast of most excess fat, but leave a thin layer on one side. Lightly score the fat side of the roast with diagonal cuts (no deeper than 1/4 inch) at 1-inch intervals. Place roast fat side up in roasting pan and roast uncovered for 1 hour. Remove from oven and skim off as much fat from pan juices as possible. Discard fat and pour the chicken broth into remaining pan juices. Combine garlic, ginger, hot pepper sauce, 1/4 cup rum, brown sugar, allspice, mace, bay leaf, salt and pepper in a food processor and blend into a smooth paste. Spread evenly over the top and sides of the roast and return roast to oven for 1-1/2 -2 hours or until meat thermometer reaches

160-165. Top should have a brown crust but not be charred.

Place roast on a platter and let sit for 15 minutes. Pour the pan juices into a separate saucepan and stir in the remaining 1/4 cup rum and lime juice. Bring to a boil over high heat. Add the cornstarch mixture and reduce heat to medium, stirring constantly until mixture thickens. Adjust salt and other seasonings to taste and pour sauce into bowl to serve with roast.

Pork Chops In Green Mango Chutney

If you like apples with your pork, try this delicious and spicy Caribbean alternative.

6 – 6 ounce boneless pork loin chops, about 1 inch thick
6 teaspoons Island Spice dry jerk seasoning (or other dry jerk seasoning blend)
4 large cloves garlic, sliced thin
1/3 cup Tortuga Gold Rum
6 teaspoons Grace All Purpose Seasoning
6 teaspoons garlic pepper
2 tablespoons olive oil
3 medium yellow onions, quartered
2 tablespoons grated fresh gingerroot
2 medium (1 pound each) green mangos, peeled and diced into 1-inch pieces
1 teaspoon Tortuga Hell-Fire Hot Pepper Sauce or 1/16th teaspoon minced Scotch Bonnet
2 teaspoons chicken bouillon granules
2/3 cup orange juice with pulp
1/2 cup light brown sugar
2 tablespoons Tortuga Gold Rum

Rub each pork chop on both sides with 1 teaspoon dry jerk seasoning. Combine the pork chops, garlic and 1/3 cup rum in a large zip-top plastic bag and refrigerate for 4 hours or longer, turning bag several times so meat marinates evenly. Remove chops from bag and save marinade. Sprinkle each chop with 1 teaspoon all purpose seasoning and 1 teaspoon garlic pepper.

In a large heavy skillet or Dutch oven, heat the olive oil over medium heat until hot, then add the pork chops. Brown chops on both sides, about two minutes per side. Add the onions, reserved marinade with garlic, and remaining ingredients except 2 tablespoons rum and stir well. Bring to a boil, then reduce heat to low and cover. Simmer covered for 30 minutes, then remove cover and continue cooking for 10 minutes or until pork is fork tender. Add the remaining rum and stir well. Cook 2-3 minutes longer.

Fiery Lamb Curry

This traditional spicy curry recipe is delicious with mutton, beef or pork too.

1/2 cup golden raisins
1/3 cup Tortuga Gold Rum
2 tablespoons coconut or vegetable oil
4 medium onions, coarsely chopped
4 large cloves garlic, minced
1/3 cup Chief or other good West Indian curry powder
1 teaspoon ground cumin
1 teaspoon ground allspice

1 teaspoon ground coriander
2 pounds lean lamb stew meat, cut into 1-1/2 inch cubes, excess fat removed
2 cups chicken broth
2 tablespoons fresh grated gingerroot
1 teaspoon Tortuga Hell-Fire Hot Pepper Sauce
1 medium (1 pound) green mango peeled and sliced thin (about 1 cup)
1/2 cup fresh grated coconut (or finely chopped in food processor)

Combine the raisins and rum and mix well. Let the raisins soak for two hours to absorb rum.

Heat the oil in a large heavy skillet or Dutch oven over medium heat and cook the onions and garlic, stirring frequently, until they just begin to soften, about four minutes – do not brown. Stir in the curry powder, cumin, allspice and coriander, blending thoroughly with the onion mixture. Cook one minute, stirring frequently, then add the lamb and stir again to mix ingredients well. Add the chicken broth, ginger and hot pepper sauce and stir well. Cover pan and reduce heat to low and simmer slowly for an hour. Stir occasionally and add more broth if necessary to keep curry from becoming too dry. After an hour, add the raisins and rum, stirring to blend well, cover and cook 45 minutes longer, until lamb is tender, then add the green mango stirring gently, and cook 15 minutes longer. Serve with hot white rice and sprinkle each serving with coconut.

Tipsy Birds

These recipes have come a long way since Arawak days. The Amerindians feasted on gamebirds seasoned with annatto and chile peppers –then sealed in a thick mud crust and sand-pit roasted. This left the meat delicate and savory – once you peeled off the feathers and skin. The Indians' mud-roasting method never caught on with the early colonists, but their taste for birds endured. From Barbados to Connecticut, plantation cooks and colonial wives shied away from mud and discovered spice and rum instead. Recipes for poultry and wild game basted and baked with rum date back to 17th century kitchens.

Since then, chicken, turkey and duck cooked with bold seasoning blends, marinades and sauces, often combining tropical fruits with a hint of rum, have become trademarks of Caribbean cuisine. Here's a surprise: some of the world's best fried chicken comes from the skillets of Caribbean cooks – whose secret is often a long soak in a marinade made with rum.

Rum Honey Baked Chicken

This is adapted from an 18th century plantation recipe.

3-1/2 pound chicken, cut in quarters (remove neck and back for other recipes)
Juice of two key limes
2 tablespoons butter, softened
2 teaspoon seasoned salt
2 teaspoons ground black pepper
1/4 cup plus 2 tablespoons Tortuga Dark Rum
1/4 cup chicken broth
1/4 cup Tortuga Wildflower Honey

Preheat oven to 425F. Line a 9 x 12 x 2 shallow baking dish or pan with aluminum foil and spray lightly with vegetable spray. Rinse the chicken in cold water and lime juice and pat dry. Rub each piece with butter and sprinkle with salt and pepper. Arrange the pieces, skin side down, in the prepared pan and bake in the center of the oven for 20 minutes. Reduce heat to 400F and turn pieces over, then bake another 10 minutes. Combine 1/4 cup rum, chicken broth and honey and blend well, and remove pan briefly, baste chicken generously with marinade and continue baking another 15 minutes. During this time, baste chicken two more times with rum honey sauce. Remove the chicken from the pan and cover with foil to keep warm. Pour the remaining rum glaze and any pieces stuck on the pan bottom into a small saucepan and cook over medium heat another two minutes. You can either add the remaining 2 tablespoons rum to the sauce for a stronger flavor and spoon over the chicken on individual plates. Or, for a more dramatic presentation, flambé the dish. Place the chicken back in the pan, bring it to the table, spoon the original sauce over and pour on the remaining 2 tablespoons rum. Ignite with a long handled match and when flames die down, serve.

Roast Chicken Tropicale

Banana-stuffed chicken is an old Caribbean recipe that varies from island to island. Some contemporary chefs have gone overboard and turned the simple, delicious stuffing into a fruit compost, and added incongruous elements like tarragon and goat cheese. Less is more, and this is still a true chicken feast for any table.

1 4-1/2- 5 pound roasting chicken
Cold water
2 tablespoons fresh lime juice
2 tablespoons butter, softened
2 teaspoons coarse or Kosher salt

Sauce:
2 tablespoons Tortuga Wildflower Honey
1/2 cup fresh orange juice
1 teaspoon grated orange zest
1/4 teaspoon ground allspice
2 tablespoons Tortuga Dark Rum
1 teaspoon ground black pepper

Stuffing:
3 medium ripe bananas, peeled and chopped into 1/2 inch pieces.
1-3/4 cups cooked white rice, cooled
1/2 cup shredded sweetened coconut
1/2 teaspoon garlic powder
1/4 cup fresh orange juice
1 teaspoon grated orange zest
1 teaspoon dark brown sugar
3 tablespoons Tortuga Dark Rum
1/2 teaspoon Tortuga Hell-Fire Hot Pepper Sauce
2 tablespoons golden raisins
1/2 teaspoon ground ginger or 2 teaspoons fresh grated ginger
1/4 teaspoon nutmeg
1 teaspoon salt

Preheat oven to 350F. Spray a roasting rack with nonstick vegetable spray and place in a foil-lined roasting pan. Remove giblets from chicken and save for another recipe. Rinse the chicken inside and out with cold water and lime juice and pat dry. Rub in the 2 tablespoons butter and salt all over the chicken with fingertips.

Make the stuffing: Combine the bananas, rice, coconut, rum, garlic powder and orange juice and mix gently until blended. Stir in the remaining ingredients. Spoon all but 1/2 cup of the stuffing mixture into the body cavity, and use the rest in the smaller neck cavity. Close both cavities with skewers or cover tightly with aluminum foil. Place the chicken on the roasting rack and make the sauce.

For sauce: In a small bowl, whisk together all ingredients except pepper until well blended, using a wire whisk. Slowly drizzle half the sauce over the chicken, coating the whole chicken. Sprinkle chicken with ground black pepper.

Roast the chicken, uncovered, at 350F for 1 hour and 45 minutes to 2 hours, basting several times with the sauce and adding remaining sauce during last hour. To test for doneness, pierce the thickest part of the thigh near the bone with a sharp knife – juices should run clear, and leg should move easily at the joint from the body. If using a meat thermometer, it should read 180F. Remove from oven and transfer the chicken to a warm serving platter and cover with foil. Let sit for 10 minutes before carving. Remove stuffing from both cavities and place in a serving bowl before carving chicken and refrigerate leftovers immediately. Pour off the remaining sauce and juices from the roasting pan into a 1 quart glass measuring cup and chill 10 minutes, then skim off fat. Serve warm sauce (microwave on high, covered, for 20 seconds to reheat) on the side in a gravy boat.

Garlic Fever Roast Bird

5-6 pound turkey breast or a 5-pound whole roasting chicken
Juice of 2 key limes
8 whole fresh garlic cloves, sliced very thin
2 teaspoons dried rosemary
1 cup BADIA Mojo Marinade
1/4 cup olive oil
3 tablespoons soy sauce
1/2 cup Tortuga Spiced Rum
1/2 cup orange juice
1 teaspoon thyme
1 teaspoon kosher salt
2 teaspoons garlic pepper
1 teaspoon Garlic & Herb Mrs. Dash
1 medium onion, quartered
3 whole garlic cloves

Wash poultry in cold water and lime juice and pat dry with paper towel. Trim away excess fat. Rub the outside of turkey breast or chicken with 2 tablespoons olive oil or enough to coat the skin. Lift breast skin and place some slices of fresh garlic and rosemary underneath. Combine remaining garlic and rosemary with other ingredients except onion and whole garlic in a jumbo zip-top and add the bird, turning several times to distribute marinade evenly. Marinate, turning several times, for 24 –48 hours.

Preheat oven to 400F. Remove bird from marinade and reserve marinade. Place the meat, breast side up, on a rack in a foil-lined roasting pan or heavy foil pan. Place the onion and whole garlic in the body cavity of the chicken or neck cavity of the turkey breast and cover area with a piece of aluminum foil to seal it. Baste meat generously with marinade and cover loosely with a tent of aluminum foil. Roast for 45 minutes, basting several times, then remove foil and cook another 25-30 minutes, until juices run clear when the meat is pierced close to the breastbone with a sharp knife. If using a meat thermometer, it should read 180 F inserted in the thickest part of the thigh of chicken.

Remove the bird from oven, cover with foil again and cool on rack for 15 minutes, then transfer carefully to serving platter. Spoon any drippings into a glass measuring cup to use for gravy or sauce if desired.

Citrus-Rum Roast Chicken

Leftovers, if there are any, make wonderful chicken salad.

1 4 to 4-1/2 pound roasting chicken
1 tablespoon butter
1/2 cup peeled and chopped green mango or apple
2 tablespoons Tortuga Dark Rum
1/2 cup chopped onion
3 cloves garlic, mashed
1 stalk celery, cut into 2-inch pieces
1 peeled carrot, cut into 2-inch pieces
1-1/2 teaspoons ground thyme
1/2 teaspoon salt
1/2 teaspoon ground black pepper
1 tablespoon Grace Jamaica All-Purpose Seasoning

Sauce:
2 tablespoons butter
1/4 cup drippings from roast
2 tablespoons chopped scallions
1 tablespoon grated orange zest
Pulp of 1/2 orange, seeded and pureed
1/3 cup Seville orange marmalade
1/4 cup firmly packed light brown sugar
1/4 cup Tortuga Dark Rum

Remove the giblets from the chicken and rinse thoroughly with cold water. Pat dry and rub with butter. Preheat oven to 375 F. Combine the thyme, salt and black pepper and rub inside body cavity (of the chicken.) Combine the mango or apple, 2 tablespoons rum, garlic, carrot, celery and onion and stir well to blend. Spoon mixture into the cavity. Seal the cavity of the chicken with skewers so it stays securely closed. Place chicken, breast side up, on a rack in a shallow roasting pan and rub the butter into the breast areas, then sprinkle with the All-Purpose Seasoning. Cover (use a tent of aluminum foil) and roast for 2 hours or until juice runs clear when chicken is pierced. Remove from oven and measure out 2 tablespoons of drippings from the pan. Cover again with foil and let cool 20 minutes. Remove vegetables from cavity and discard.

Sauce: While chicken is cooling, in a medium skillet, melt the butter with drippings sauté the scallions, orange zest and orange pulp until soft. Stir in the marmalade and brown sugar and bring to a boil, Cook for five minutes, stirring constantly, then stir in the rum. Rum may bubble up, so stir rapidly. Blend well and remove from heat. Spoon sauce over the chicken.

Chicken with Coconut & Cashews

4 boneless chicken breast halves, cut into 1- inch pieces
1/2 cup Tortuga Dark Rum
2 teaspoons Jamaica All Purpose Seasoning
2 tablespoons butter
3 cloves garlic, mashed and chopped
1 medium onion, chopped
1 tablespoon grated fresh gingerroot
1 teaspoon chicken bouillon granules
2 cups coconut milk
1 tablespoon fresh minced cilantro
1 teaspoon sugar
1/4 cup toasted coconut
1/2 cup cashew halves

Place the chicken in a heavy zip-top bag and sprinkle with the rum, seal bag, and turn several times to coat all surfaces. Cover and refrigerate for four hours. Remove chicken from marinade, reserving leftover rum. Sprinkle chicken with All-Purpose Seasoning. In a large skillet, melt the butter over medium heat and add the garlic, sautéing for one minute, then stir in the chicken. Cook for five minutes, stirring several times until chicken turns white on all sides. Remove the chicken from the pan using a slotted spoon and place in a bowl, covered with foil. Add ginger and onion to the skillet and cook for five minutes, then stir in the reserved rum marinade and chicken bouillon. Stir well to blend and loosen any bits stuck to the bottom of pan. Cook until onions are soft, about five minutes. Add the coconut milk, sugar and cilantro and stir well, then return the chicken to skillet. Stir, bring to a boil then reduce heat and simmer slowly for 15 minutes, stirring several times. Remove from heat, sprinkle with toasted coconut and cashews and serve over hot white rice.

Chicken with Rum and Pineapple

Another favorite West Indian dish that changes from island to island.

1 whole frying chicken (3-1/2 pounds) cut into quarters
1/4 cup fresh lime juice
1/4 cup Tortuga Dark Rum
2 tablespoons olive oil
3 cloves garlic, minced
2 teaspoons salt
2 teaspoons ground black pepper
1 cup flour
1/4 cup butter
1 large onion, chopped
3 tablespoons currants or raisins
2 tablespoons Tortuga Dark Rum

1 teaspoon grated lime zest
1 tablespoon light brown sugar
2 large tomatoes, peeled and chopped
Pineapple Rum Sauce (recipe follows)

Wash the chicken parts in cold water and drain, then place in a large zip-top plastic bag. Combine the olive oil, lime juice, rum and garlic and mix well. Pour over the chicken and turn pieces to be sure marinade coats all surfaces. Seal bag and refrigerate for three hours or longer, turning occasionally.

Remove the chicken from the marinade. Pat dry and save the marinade. Pour the flour into a shallow bowl. Season the chicken with salt and pepper, and roll in the flour, shaking off excess. In a large skillet, heat the butter over medium heat and brown the chicken on all sides. Reduce heat to low and add the reserved marinade and stir to loosen any bits stuck to the bottom of the pan. Cover and cook the chicken for 15 minutes. Add the onion, currants, lime zest, brown sugar and tomatoes and stir well. Cover and cook another 30 minutes while making the pineapple sauce.

Pineapple rum sauce:
1-12 ounce can crushed pineapple, undrained
3 tablespoons Tortuga Dark Rum

Pour the crushed pineapple into a medium saucepan and cook over medium heat, stirring occasionally, for 15 minutes until reduced by 3/4, then stir in the rum. Spoon sauce over each portion of chicken.

Rum Marinated Fried Chicken

A late night plane ride on Cayman Airways from Kingston 20 years ago led to a new friendship in flight. My Jamaican seatmate gave me this unusual recipe, claiming it made the chicken taste better than anything in the world. She's right.

1/2 cup Tortuga Dark Rum
1/4 cup soy sauce
1/4 cup fresh lime juice
1 3-1/2 pound fryer chicken
Cold water
2 tablespoons fresh lime juice
1 tablespoon Grace All Purpose Jamaican Seasoning
1 tablespoon freshly ground black pepper
1-1/2 cups flour

In a small bowl, combine the rum, soy sauce and 1/4 cup lime juice and stir well. Remove the neck, back and gizzards from chicken. Wash chicken thoroughly in cold water and remaining lime juice and pat dry. Chop the chicken into 16 pieces, by cutting in half each breast, thigh, wing and drumstick. Place all chicken pieces in a zip-top plastic freezer bag and pour in the rum marinade. Seal tight and turn bag over several times to coat all pieces with marinade. Refrigerate and marinate for at least 12 hours, turning several times.

When ready to cook, turn the oven to 200 or low heat and line a baking sheet with aluminum foil and two layers of paper towels. Remove chicken from marinade and pat each piece dry. Discard the marinade unless you want to boil it with other ingredients to make a sauce. Pour flour into a clean heavy zip-top plastic bag. Season each chicken piece well with the all-purpose seasoning and black pepper and drop in bag. Shake a few pieces at a time until all are floured and shake off any excess. Pour 2 inches of peanut or vegetable oil into a large heavy skillet and heat over medium high until very hot but not smoking. Fry chicken in batches so you don't crowd the pan, turning each piece to fry evenly and not burn, about 7 minutes on each side, until rich golden brown. Remove chicken from pan and place on the baking dish in the oven to keep warm while you fry the rest of the chicken. Serve immediately with rice n peas.

Pina Colada Chicken Breasts

Chilled leftovers make a delicious chicken salad.

1/2 cup Tortuga Dark Rum
6 boneless breast halves
1 teaspoon nutmeg
1 teaspoon ground cinnamon
1 teaspoon salt
1 teaspoon ground white pepper
3 tablespoons butter
1 cup Coco Lopez or other cream of coconut
1/4 cup fresh lime juice
Reserved rum marinade
1 tablespoon soy sauce
1 cup diced green pepper
1 cup pineapple chunks, well drained
1 medium onion, chopped

Combine the chicken breasts and rum in a heavy zip-top plastic bag and seal, turning bag several times to coat chicken evenly. Refrigerate for four hours or longer. Remove chicken from marinade and reserve rum. Pat chicken dry. Combine dry spices, salt and pepper and sprinkle each breast on both sides with mixture. Preheat oven to 350 F. Spray a 13 x 9 inch baking dish or casserole with vegetable oil spray.

In a medium skillet melt the butter over medium heat and brown the chicken about 1 minute on each side then transfer to prepared baking dish. Scrape the bottom of the skillet and remove any browned or scorched bits but leave butter and juices. Add the coconut cream, reserved rum, lime juice, soy sauce, and bring to a boil. Add the pepper, pineapple and onion and stir well. Pour the sauce over the chicken and bake for 30-35 minutes or until chicken is fork tender.

The Soup Pot

Throughout the Caribbean, hot soup remains a favorite food – including at breakfast! West Indian soups are among the best in the world, often a meal in themselves. Rum and other Caribbean ingredients have inspired many interesting recipes, including cold fruit soups. This unusual group of Caribbean soups rounds out the recipe collection offered in **Comfort Foods, Western Caribbean Style**.

Avocado Rum Cream Soup

Incredibly easy, this soup is delicious warm or chilled.

1 tablespoon butter
3 cloves garlic, minced
4 large scallions, chopped
2 large ripe avocados, peeled and chopped and pureed in food processor
3 cups chicken broth
3 tablespoons Tortuga Light Rum
1 teaspoon Beau Monde seasoning
1/2 teaspoon white pepper
1 cup half and half
Salt to taste
6 tablespoons diced ripe avocado

In a large saucepan or Dutch Oven, melt the butter over medium heat and saute the garlic and scallions until soft, about five minutes – do not allow vegetables to brown. Add the chicken broth and stir well, then stir in the pureed avocado, rum and seasonings. Bring to a boil, stirring frequently, then reduce heat to low and stir in the half and half. Cook another two minutes, until soup is heated through, but do not boil again. Add more salt if desired. Garnish each serving with a tablespoon of diced ripe avocado on top.

Coconut Chicken Curry Soup

For a mild curry flavor, use only 2 tablespoons curry powder.

2 tablespoons vegetable oil
1/4 cup **Chief** or other good quality Caribbean curry powder
1 large onion, chopped
6 scallions, chopped
1 stalk celery, diced
1 large carrot, diced
3 cups chicken broth
2 green bananas, peeled and sliced into 1/2 inch chunks
1 cup grated fresh coconut or frozen unsweetened flaked coconut
1 teaspoon ground coriander
1 teaspoon ground white pepper
1/2 cup Tortuga Gold Rum
1/4 cup uncooked long grain rice
3 cups cooked, boned chicken
2 cups coconut milk

In a large pot or Dutch oven, heat the oil over medium heat and saute the onion, scallions, celery and carrot for two minutes, then sprinkle with the curry powder and stir well to mix. Cook three minutes longer, until vegetables are softened. Add the chicken broth, green banana, cooked chicken, coriander, coconut, pepper and rum and stir well. Bring to a boil and add the rice; stir well, reduce heat to medium-low and cook 25 minutes or until rice is tender. Stir in the coconut milk and cook another five minutes. Adjust seasonings and add more salt and pepper to taste. You can serve this soup hot or chilled.

Day's Catch Chowder

As long as it's not barracuda, any good fish filets will work in this old standard white chowder recipe. Snapper and grouper are favorite choices.

4 slices bacon, cut into small pieces
2 pounds grouper filets, skin and bloodline removed
2 cups chopped celery
2 medium white potatoes, peeled and diced
3 medium onions, chopped
1 medium green sweet pepper, cored, seeded and chopped
1 teaspoon Tortuga Hellfire Pepper Sauce (more to taste)
4 cloves garlic, minced
5 cups fish stock
1 tablespoon seasoned salt
1 large spring fresh thyme or 1 teaspoon dried thyme
1 tablespoon ground black pepper
1/2 cup butter
1/2 cup flour
4 cups evaporated milk
1/4 cup Tortuga Dark rum or sherry (if desired)

In 5-quart Dutch Oven or large pot, cook the bacon over medium heat until just turning brown and limp. Add the onion, celery and green pepper and saute until bacon is crisp and vegetables are tender. Stir in the garlic and cook, stirring frequently, another minute. Add the fish stock, fish filets, potato, seasonings and stir well. Bring to a boil and reduce heat and simmer, covered, 15-20 minutes until potatoes are tender.

In a heavy saucepan, melt butter over low heat, then sprinkle the flour evenly over it and stir until smooth. Cook one minute, stirring constantly. Gradually stir in the evaporated milk, stirring constantly and cook over medium heat until sauce is thickened. Gradually stir the white sauce into the fish chowder and cook, stirring constantly until chowder is thoroughly heated. Stir in the rum or sherry last, if desired. If not, pour over ice and enjoy.

Groundnut Soup

Groundnut is the old English-speaking Caribbean name for peanut, a legume originally from Brazil, not Africa as many people think. Columbus discovered peanuts when he arrived in Haiti and they became another New World treasure carried back to Europe. Roasted peanuts are a favorite universal snack throughout the Caribbean, but ground peanuts are also used as a seasoning in soups and stews. This soup was a favorite recipe of the late Sandys "Sandy" Sherwood, Cayman's Police Chief in the late 1960's who retired to open the legendary Cayman Arms pub in George Town. The original recipe was made with roasted peanuts instead of peanut butter.

2 tablespoons butter or coconut oil
2 medium onions, diced
1 tablespoon fresh minced gingerroot
3 cloves garlic, minced
4 cups chicken broth
2 cups chunky peanut butter
2 cups evaporated milk
1 teaspoon ground black pepper
1 teaspoon Tortuga Hellfire Pepper Sauce
1 tablespoon Pickapeppa Sauce
1 tablespoon Angostura Bitters
6 tablespoons Tortuga Rum Liqueur or dry sherry (Optional)
6 teaspoons chopped scallions or chives

In large pot or Dutch Oven, melt the butter over medium heat. Add the onions, ginger and garlic and saute until soft, about 3 minutes. Add the chicken broth and stir well, then bring to a boil. Stir in the peanut butter and black pepper and whisk to blend. Reduce heat to medium low and simmer 15 minutes. Add the milk, pepper sauce, Pickapeppa sauce, pepper and bitters and stir well. Adjust seasonings if necessary. Cook another 5 minutes over low heat, until soup is hot. Add one tablespoon rum liqueur or sherry to each serving if desired and stir, then top with 1 tablespoon chopped scallions or chives.

Rum-spiked Coconut Black-Eyed Pea Soup

2-1/2 cups dried black-eyed peas
Cold water
3 large ham hocks or 1-1/2 pounds ham on the bone
2 bay leaves
4 medium onions, diced
4 cloves
1 teaspoon nutmeg
2 teaspoon sugar
2 tablespoon peanut oil
4 medium tomatoes, peeled and chopped
5 cups coconut milk
3 sprigs fresh thyme
2 tablespoons chicken bouillon
2 teaspoons ground black pepper
2 teaspoons Tortuga Hellfire Pepper Sauce
1/2 cup Tortuga Dark Rum

Soak the peas overnight in enough water to cover by an inch. Drain and rinse under cold water and place in a 5-6 quart pot with the ham hocks or smoked ham and add enough water to cover. Add the bay leaves, half the onions, cloves, nutmeg and sugar and bring to a boil over medium heat. Boil for 10 minutes, skimming of any foam on the surface. Lower heat, cover and simmer for about an hour, or until the peas are soft and meat is falling off bone tender. Remove from heat and remove the meat, cloves and bay leaves.

Cut the meat off bones, trim off fat and dice. Set aside. Heat the oil in a large frying pan or skillet and sauté the remaining onion over medium heat until soft. Add the tomatoes and cook for about four minutes, stirring constantly. Add this mixture to the soup pot, and then add the coconut milk, thyme, chicken bouillon, black pepper and Tortuga Hellfire Sauce. Bring to a boil, then lower heat to low and cover. Simmer for about 20 minutes. Remove from heat and let cool.

Puree half of the soup in a food processor or blender and return to the soup kettle. Add the diced meat and rum and cook over low heat for about 10 minutes, until thoroughly heated. Taste and add any seasonings desired. Serve warm with cornbread.

** If you prefer a smooth soup rather than one with substance, puree the entire soup stock and finish by adding the diced ham and rum.

Lime Coconut Soup

1-1/2 cups fresh grated coconut
1/2 teaspoon mace or grated nutmeg
1/4 teaspoon cinnamon
1 teaspoon salt
1 teaspoon ground black pepper
3 cups chicken broth or stock
2 large egg yolks, beaten
1/4 cup fresh lime juice
1/4 cup flour
1 teaspoon Tortuga Hellfire Pepper Sauce
1/4 cup Tortuga Coconut Rum

In a 3-quart or larger saucepan, combine the coconut, spices, salt, pepper and chicken broth. Bring to a boil, then reduce heat and simmer for 30 minutes. Pour mixture through a fine strainer to remove coconut, then return strained broth to saucepan. Combine egg yolks, lime juice and flour and blend into a smooth paste. Mix 2 tablespoons of the hot broth into the egg mixture and blend, then add slowly to the soup, stirring constantly to mix well. Add pepper sauce. Cook for another 10 minutes or until soup thickens slightly. Adjust salt and pepper and pepper sauce. Add rum just before serving.

Cold Soups

Conch Gazpacho

Why not? It's just a juicier, gourmet variation of marinated conch and the perfect summer lunch. This is a picnic-sized recipe that serves about 10. Reduce by half if you wish.

2 pounds conch , cleaned and ground (4 cups)
1/4 cup fresh lime juice
6 cloves garlic, minced
6 cups water
4 cups Clamato juice
4 cups V-8 Juice
1/2 cup fresh key lime juice
1 medium green pepper, diced
1 large red onion, diced fine
2 medium cucumbers, peeled and diced
2 stalks celery, diced fine
2 teaspoons Tortuga Hellfire Pepper sauce
2 tablespoons Pickapeppa Sauce
1 tablespoon coarse Kosher salt
1 tablespoon ground black pepper
Tortuga Gold Rum or Tortuga Rum Liqueur

In a large saucepan, combine the conch, lime juice, garlic and water – add more water if necessary to cover conch. Bring to a boil, skimming off foam and stirring, and then reduce heat and simmer for 30 minutes. Keep stirring and skimming as necessary. Drain the conch and garlic through a strainer and set aside to cool.

Combine remaining ingredients in a large bowl. Stir in the conch and mix well until all ingredients are blended and adjust seasonings to taste. Refrigerate for four hours or longer – until well chilled. Add a teaspoon to shot of Tortuga Gold Rum or Rum Liqueur to each serving as desired.

Hell's Rum Consommé

Hell, of course, is a town in West Bay, Grand Cayman. This combination of hot and cold would be even better if it were turtle consomme instead of beef.

1/4 cup Tortuga Dark Rum
2 –10 ounce cans beef consommé
2 tablespoons Worcestershire sauce
2 teaspoons Tortuga Hell-Fire Hot Pepper Sauce
2 fresh green scallions, chopped
Fresh lime slices

Combine the rum, consommé, Worcestershire sauce and pepper sauce and stir well. Chill 12 hours until the mixture thickens slightly. Serve in chilled soup cups, sprinkled with scallion and garnished with a thin slice of lime.

Rum and Ginger-Spiked Consomme

Hot, this is ideal flu-food – cold, it makes a nice hot weather lunch.

1/3 cup Tortuga Dark Rum
1 tablespoon grated fresh gingerroot
3 –10 ounce cans beef consommé or beef broth
2 tablespoons fresh lime juice

Combine the rum, ginger and consommé or broth in a 2 quart saucepan and heat over high heat until very hot, but not boiling. Remove from heat and add the lime juice. Let the mixture steep for 20-30 minutes before serving warm. Do not strain out the ginger. If you want to serve chilled, pour into a glass or plastic container and refrigerate for an hour or more. Will keep 2 –3 days in the refrigerator.

Breadfruit Vichyssoise

1/4 cup butter
4 medium onions, diced
4 cloves garlic, minced
4 large scallions, chopped
1 tablespoon fresh grated gingerroot
3 cups peeled, cored and diced breadfruit
2 teaspoons salt
2 cups chicken broth
2 cups coconut milk
1 cup heavy cream
1/4 cup Tortuga Gold Rum
Finely chopped scallions

In a 5-quart Dutch oven or heavy pot, melt the butter and add the onion, garlic, scallions and ginger. Cook over medium heat, stirring frequently, until vegetables are just turning soft, about four minutes. Do not brown! Add the breadfruit, chicken broth and salt and stir well. Bring to a boil and boil for one minute, then reduce heat to low and simmer, covered for 45 minutes, stirring occasionally. Remove from heat and cool 30 minutes. Using a food processor or large blender, puree the mixture in batches until smooth, returning soup to original pot. Stir in the coconut milk and heavy cream and refrigerate, covered for four hours until well chilled. Stir in the rum just before serving and garnish with additional finely chopped scallions.

Cold Papaya Rum Soup

2 cups vanilla lowfat yogurt
2 tablespoons Tortuga Wildflower or Citrus Honey
4 cups ripe papaya, peeled and cut into small cubes
2 tablespoons fresh key lime juice
1/4 cup Tortuga Dark Rum
1 teaspoon nutmeg

Put the papaya in a food processor in batches and puree for 30 seconds or until smooth. Pour into a large bowl and using an electric mixer on low speed, blend in the yogurt until smooth, then add the lime juice, honey, nutmeg and rum and stir well, until blended. Refrigerate for four hours or longer. Serve garnished with small chunks of fresh papaya on top of each bowl. Add more rum to taste, if desired.

Mango Fever!

Mango fever! That's the madness that spreads throughout the Caribbean every summer. Mango Season unleashes a craving so strong it turns honest men into thieves. Nothing tempts a Caribbean soul like the sight of ripe mangos hanging from a tree. Suddenly property boundaries, fences, mad dogs and surly owners are no obstacles to tasting that luscious fruit.

Native to the Himalayas, the mango is an evergreen that traveled a long way from Hindustan to reach the West Indies. But exactly how mangos arrived in the Caribbean remains unclear. Portuguese explorers discovered them in the East Indies and carried plants to West Africa and later, Brazil, where they flourished. From there, mangos migrated north—they were first reported in Barbados in 1742—and Jamaica, around 1782.

The mango's botanical name, *Mangifera indica*, sounds like "magnificent." And that's the way Caribbean people feel about mangos, the Queen of all tropical fruits. One of nature's most sensuous edibles, the mango's fragrance and flavor are almost impossible to describe – it has hints of so many tantalizing tastes. Mangos are the world's finest peach with a touch of lime, pineapple or grape. Sometimes you'll taste a dash of vanilla, cinnamon or coriander. No wonder Caribbean residents, native and transplanted, go crazy over them. Consider this Jamaican explanation of mango magic, translated from the vernacular: "Mango is the breast-shaped fruit grown men nip greedily in public without shame. It God's way of making West Indian man outgrow his mother."

The tough, hairy reputation of West Indian mango is no longer true. There are now more than 200 varieties of mango throughout the Caribbean, many with smooth, voluptuous, fiber-free flesh. These are much different from the messy balls of syrupy dental floss that turned many people – like me – off this fruit initially. Jamaicans are fortunate enough to have mangos of some kind ripening almost year-round, but in Cayman, mango season is usually late May through August, with some varieties straggling into September. In both countries Julie and Carrie mangos are the most popular.

Springfels. For that reason, in these recipes a "medium mango" means one weighing about a pound, and provides 1-1/2 cups diced fruit or 1 cup of pureed pulp.

When selecting ripe mangos, choose fruits that yield slightly to pressure but are not completely soft. Don't rely on the color. Some varieties, like Martin, remain green even when fully ripe. The test: ripe mangos are very fragrant and will give slightly to gentle finger pressure. If you buy unripe mangos and don't plan to use them green, place them in sealed paper bag at room temperature and they will ripen in three or four days.

Green mangoes used in chutneys and pickles must be very firm and at least a week away from fully ripe. They are the ideal Caribbean substitute for apples in desserts and chicken or pork dishes. In Cayman, they are also the favorite snack of the endangered Cayman parrot, feathered fiends who infuriate farmers and tree owners by nibbling away just enough of the unripe fruits to ruin them.

International Mango Festival: The Ultimate Mango Fête

Want to learn more about the tropics' most desirable fruit? Then don't miss the ultimate mango fête! Every July **Fairchild Tropical Garden in Miami, Florida** hosts the **International Mango Festival**, a celebration of all things mango. The fascinating three-day festival features exhibits and events ranging from sales of the newest Fairchild-selected cultivars to mango tasting. Highlights include Mangoville mango market, café and music; a Mango Art Exhibit, Mango Auction and Mango Brunch with a menu comprising the latest mango creations by top South Florida chefs. **For information visit their website at www.ftg.org or contact (305) 667-1651.**

A Mini Mango Festival

How to Eat a Mango

The sea bath is a summer tradition in Cayman and Jamaica and the very best way–I say, the *only* way – way to eat a ripe mango. Grab some ripe mangos, jump into your swimsuit and head to the sea. Plunge in, cool off in the Caribbean and cut the mango in half across the middle, and peel away the skin of the top half. Push your face right into the fruit, sucking the juice and chomping on the pulp, and make as big a mess as you want. Then grab the pit and do the same with the other half. The sea salt enhances the mango flavor – and when you're done, just duck under and splash yourself off. Make sure you pick up the skins and pits and don't leave your debris behind in the sea. That's not fish food – it's pollution.

Rum Mango

This is just what it says and is perfect for a beach party or picnic. Adults only, please!

1 medium to large ripe mango (must be stringless variety) per person

Tortuga Gold Rum (or any kind desired)
1 sharp knife

Cut the mango in half across the width, not the length, and remove the pit. Bite or scoop out a few spoonfuls of flesh from each half to make the hole large enough to hold a shot of rum. Use a knife to punch several slits in each mango half. Pour rum to fill the center of each half and let the rum soak in a little. Sip the rum. Eat the mango by pushing your face right into it so you don't miss any rum. Go for a sea bath to clean up and then find a hammock for the rest of the afternoon.

Mango Fever

1 cup ripe mango chunks
1-1/2 ounces Tortuga Light Rum
2 ounces Tortuga Rum Cream Liqueur
1 ounce Galliano
1 tablespoon fresh key lime juice
2 ounces fresh orange juice
2 ounces whole milk
1 cup cracked ice

Combine all ingredients in a blender and blend until smooth, about 40 seconds. Pour into a Hurricane glass and garnish with a skewer of two 1-inch mango chunks. Serve with a straw.

Mango Rum Pepper Salsa

Try this with seafood or chicken-hot or cold – or spoon it on top of salad greens for different side dish.

2 medium ripe but firm mangos, peeled and diced (about 4 cups)
1 medium red onion, diced
1 small red sweet pepper, diced (about 3/4 cup)
1 medium cucumber, peeled and diced
2 teaspoons Tortuga Hell-Fire Hot Pepper sauce
OR 1/4 fresh minced Scotch bonnet, seeded and deveined and minced fine
1 teaspoon seasoned salt
1 teaspoon fresh ground black pepper
2 tablespoons lime juice
2 tablespoons Tortuga Gold Rum
2 tablespoons fresh cilantro, chopped

Combine all ingredients in a large bowl with a cover and stir well. Refrigerate for several hours to let flavors blend. Will keep, covered, for 3-four days.

Mango Colada Dressing or Dip

This unusual recipe is so good, you'll have to stop guests from eating it by the spoonful.

Serve as a dip or even better, as a dressing for fruit, chicken or shrimp salad. It's also great on waffles, puddings and pound cakes.

1-8 ounce package cream cheese (reduced fat can be substituted), at room temperature
6 tablespoons Coco Lopez or other coconut cream
2 tablespoons Tortuga Dark Rum
1-1/2 cups ripe mango puree
2 teaspoons fresh key lime juice

In a medium bowl, use an electric mixer to beat the cream cheese until light, then blend in the coconut cream until smooth. Add the rum, lime juice and mango puree, beating on low speed until blended. This makes a sweet sauce or dip – for a sweet/tangy sauce with a little fire, add pepper sauce. Store in refrigerator but serve at room temperature. For a bolder rum flavor, add another tablespoon or two. To use as a salad dressing, increase lime juice to 2 or 3 tablespoons or more to desired taste and consistency.

Paradise Chicken Mango

This is fantasy island cuisine! Start the chicken marinating a day ahead of time. Chilled leftovers, if they exist, make a delicious chicken salad.

6 large boneless chicken breast halves
1/2 cup Tortuga Gold Rum
2 teaspoons Grace Jamaican All-Purpose Seasoning (See **Island Pantry**)
2 tablespoons canola or peanut oil
2 tablespoons butter
3 large cloves fresh garlic, minced
1 medium Vidalia or other sweet onion, chopped
1 tablespoon fresh grated gingerroot
1 teaspoon Tortuga Hell-Fire Hot Pepper Sauce or 1/16th teaspoon minced Scotch Bonnet
1 cup Coco Lopez or other cream of coconut
1/4 cup fresh orange juice
1 teaspoon fresh grated orange zest
1 cup coconut milk
1 tablespoon soy sauce
1 cup diced ripe but firm papaya
2 cups diced ripe but firm mango
1/2 cup shredded coconut, toasted

Combine the chicken and rum in a gallon-size zip-top bag, seal and turn several times to coat all areas. Refrigerate for 24 hours. Remove chicken from marinade and reserve the rum. Sprinkle each breast half on both sides with All-Purpose seasoning. In a large deep skillet or Dutch oven, heat the oil over medium heat and brown the chicken on both sides. Remove the chicken to a platter and cover with foil to keep warm. Wipe the pan clean of any oil or browned bits and add the butter. Melt the butter over medium heat and add the onion, garlic and ginger and sauté, stirring frequently, until vegetables just begin to turn soft but not brown, about 3 minutes.

Return the chicken to the pan and add the Coco Lopez, rum reserved from marinade, orange juice, coconut milk, orange zest, soy sauce and hot pepper sauce. Stir well to mix evenly. Simmer uncovered over medium- low heat until chicken is tender, about 30 minutes. Stir in the papaya and mango last, and continue cooking another 3 minutes until all ingredients are heated. Sprinkle each serving with toasted coconut.

Cayman Mango Bread

This is one of my most requested Cayman creations. I freeze as many bags of mango chunks as possible once mango season starts and make this recipe at Christmas – an unseasonal surprise for special friends. Fill one quart-size zip top plastic bag, packed tight, with 1-inch chunks of ripe but firm mango and freeze immediately. It will keep until December and provides enough for one cake.

1 cup margarine
2 cups white sugar
3/4 cup light brown sugar (packed)
4 large eggs
1 cup lowfat vanilla or peach yogurt
3 tablespoons Tortuga Dark Rum
3 cups flour
1-1/2 teaspoons baking powder
1-1/2 teaspoons baking soda
1/2 teaspoon salt
1 teaspoon ground coriander
1 teaspoon nutmeg
1/2 teaspoon cinnamon
2 cups mango pulp (puree which includes some 1/2 inch chunks of mango)
1 cup sweetened shredded coconut
1 tablespoon grated orange zest
2 cups chopped pecans

Preheat oven to 350 degrees. Spray 12 inch bundt pan with Baker's Joy or lightly grease and flour. Combine flour, soda, baking powder, salt and dry spices in medium bowl and use fork or whisk to blend.

In large bowl using electric mixer, cream margarine and sugars until smooth. Add eggs, one at a time, blending on medium speed. Blend in yogurt and rum. Add flour mixture, blending on low mixer speed until well mixed. Add mango pulp and orange zest, mixing well. Stir in coconut and nuts until just mixed. Pour batter into prepared pan and bake approximately 1 hour until toothpick in center comes out clean. Remove from oven and cool in pan for 10 minutes, then invert onto wire rack and cool completely. Wrap leftover bread tightly in plastic wrap or aluminum foil and refrigerate – it will keep for two weeks.

Green Mango Pie

Many Caribbean islanders consider this old-time recipe far superior to apple pie.

Pastry for 9-inch two crust pie

5 cups peeled green mangoes, sliced thin
2 cups water
2 teaspoons key lime juice
1 cup plus 2 tablespoons sugar

1/2 teaspoon grated nutmeg
1 teaspoon cinnamon
1/8 teaspoon salt
2 tablespoons Tortuga Dark Rum
1 tablespoon cornstarch
2 tablespoons butter or margarine, cut into small pieces

Preheat oven to 425F degrees. Make pastry and line 9-inch pie pan with crust – do not bake. In a large saucepan, combine the mango slices and water and bring to a boil, then remove from heat – you just want to blanch the mangos, not stew them. Drain mangoes well and pat dry with paper towels. Combine the mango slices and lime juice and stir well. Add the sugar and spices and stir again. Spread the mangos evenly in the unbaked pie crust. Combine the salt, cornstarch and rum and mix, spread over the mangos. Dot the top of fruit with the butter or margarine. Cover with remaining pastry and seal edges well. Make small cuts in top crust to vent steam and bake pie for 15 minutes, then lower oven temperature to 375 F and bake for about 45 minutes longer until crust is golden and mangos are tender.

Mango Madness Cheesecake

Another one of my original mango creations, this is a creamy cheesecake that also makes a nice cool breakfast on a hot summer morning. For a firmer cheesecake, store in freezer.

Crust:
1-1/2 cups gingersnap crumbs, finely ground
1/4 cup shredded sweetened coconut
1/4 cup almonds, finely chopped
2 tablespoons light brown sugar, firmly packed
3 tablespoons unsalted butter, melted

Filling:
1-1/4 cups mango pulp (it should resemble chunky puree)
1/4 cup Tortuga Dark Rum
2 teaspoons Rum Vanilla (see Island Pantry) or 2 teaspoons vanilla extract
4 – 8 ounce packages cream cheese, softened to room temperature
2 tablespoons flour
1-3/4 cups sugar
4 large eggs
1 tablespoon fresh grated gingerroot
1/2 teaspoon ground coriander

Topping:
2 cups diced ripe but firm mango
2 tablespoons Tortuga Dark Rum

Preheat oven to 350F. Lightly butter the inside bottom and sides of a 9-inch springform pan and wrap the outside with aluminum foil. **Make the crust**: In a medium bowl, combine the gingersnap crumbs, almonds, coconut and sugar and stir well to blend. Gradually add the melted butter and blend well. Press crust mixture firmly and evenly over the bottom of the prepared pan making sure where bottom joins side is not too thin. Bake crust for about 10-minutes. Remove from oven and cool on wire rack.

Make the filling: Keep oven set at 350 F. Combine the mango pulp, ginger, rum and coriander in a small bowl and stir to blend. In a large mixing bowl using an electric mixer beat the cream cheese until light. Gradually beat in the sugar until smooth. Add the eggs, one at a time, beating just until blended after each, then beat in the vanilla and flour. Add the mango-rum mixture and blend until mixed.

Place an 8-inch square pan filled 2/3 with hot water in center of bottom oven rack and close oven door. Let oven heat another five minutes before opening again. Pour cheesecake batter into prepared crust and position pan on upper rack, above the water pan. Bake for an hour and 10 minutes or until top is just pale brown, edges are slightly puffed and center is set. Cake will jiggle slightly, but center area should not be watery. Remove from oven and cool on wire rack for 10 minutes, then refrigerate uncovered until thoroughly chilled, about 4 hours, then cover lightly with plastic wrap. Chill 24 hours before serving for best flavor. When ready to serve, run a sharp knife all the way around the inside rim and remove pan sides.

Make the topping: Put the diced mango in a small bowl and sprinkle with the rum. Toss lightly and chill for an hour. Garnish each slice of cheesecake with a spoonful of the spiked mangos and whipped cream if desired.

Mango Fool

3 cups diced ripe mango
3 tablespoons Tortuga Dark Rum
1 tablespoon fresh lime juice
1/4 teaspoon cinnamon
1 tablespoon confectioners sugar
1-1/4 cups heavy cream
1 teaspoon vanilla extract
Grated nutmeg

Puree 1-1/2 cups mango in a food processor with rum, cinnamon and lime juice until smooth. Pour into a bowl and stir in the remaining diced mango, cover and refrigerate until well-chilled, about four hours. Whip the heavy cream with the sugar and vanilla until stiff peaks form and chill for an hour. When ready to serve, fold whipped cream into the mango mixture leaving streaks of mango and cream – do not try to blend evenly. Garnish with nutmeg and a slice of ripe mango. This should be eaten the same day it's prepared.

Mango Daiquiri Pie

Ripe mangoes and key limes are such a natural flavor combination, you may never eat plain old key lime pie again.

2-8 inch prepared graham cracker crusts
1 cup mango puree (1 medium mango)
2 ounces Tortuga Dark Rum
3/4 cup fresh key lime juice
1 teaspoon grated lime zest
2- 14-ounce cans sweetened condensed milk

6 egg yolks, beaten
2 egg whites
Rummy Whipped Cream (see **Rum Sauces & Uncommon Condiments**)

Preheat oven to 350 F. In a small deep bowl, beat the eggs whites until soft peaks form. In a large mixing bowl, beat the egg yolks until slightly thickened, then gradually add the condensed milk and rum and mix just until blended. Gently stir in the mango puree, lime zest and lime juice and mix just until blended. Fold the egg whites into the mixture, just until blended. Divide the filling evenly between the two pie crusts. Bake the pies for 15 minutes. Remove from oven and cool on a wire rack for 15 minutes, then refrigerate uncovered for four hours or more. For longer storage, cover the surface with wax paper, or cover tightly with plastic wrap and freeze.

When ready to serve, arrange 6 thin slices of mango on top of the pie, one for each serving, and garnish with a generous dollop of Rummy Whipped Cream.

Mango-Berry Cobbler

Any recipe you make with fresh peaches is better with ripe mangoes.

3 cups sliced peeled ripe mangos
2 cups fresh raspberries or blueberries
2 teaspoons fresh key lime juice
2 tablespoons flour
1/3 cup sugar
1 teaspoon ground cinnamon
2 tablespoons Tortuga Gold Rum

Topping:
3/4 cup flour
1 tablespoon sugar
1-1/2 teaspoons baking powder
1/4 teaspoon salt
2 tablespoons butter, chilled and cut into small pieces
1/2 cup heavy cream
2 teaspoons sugar

Preheat oven to 400 F. Spray a 2-quart baking dish or casserole lightly with butter-flavored nonstick vegetable spray. In a small bowl, mix 1/3-cup sugar, 2 tablespoons flour and cinnamon and blend well. In a medium bowl, combine the mangoes and berries and sprinkle with lime juice and rum and stir well. Sprinkle the flour mixture over the fruit and toss to combine. Pour the fruit mixture into the baking dish.

In a medium bowl, combine the remaining 3/4 cup flour, sugar, baking powder and salt and stir to mix. Using a pastry blender or two knives cut in the chilled butter until the mixture resembles small peas. Slowly add the heavy cream, stirring just until moistened. Using a large spoon, drop the dough in small mounds over the filling and sprinkle with the remaining 2 teaspoons sugar. Bake at 400 F. for 20-25 minutes or until a toothpick insert into topping comes out clean. Serve with Rummy Whipped Cream or vanilla ice cream.

A Carnival of Sweets

aribbean people love sweets and I would never think of inviting friends around without having a special confection to offer. Columbus brought the cane, but historians blame the 17th century English for infecting the West Indies with that indelible craving for sugary things. The colonial era culinary exchange between the West Indies, Africa, America and Europe was blurry. It's not certain where some recipes originated and who borrowed what from whom. But the similarity between traditional favorite sweets of the Caribbean and those of New England, the Southern states and England is unmistakable. Along with sugar, rum was the common ingredient. Sneaky or deliberate, slipping rum into recipes was as popular on plantations in the Indies as it was in prim Puritan kitchens up north. It wasn't always subtle –as in rum-soaked trifles, fruitcakes and steamed puddings, the traditional grand dames of Caribbean sweets. Today every island has its own signature recipes for these, some appearing only around the Christmas holidays.

Pastry chefs all over the world are rediscovering what a difference a hint of rum makes. Cayman's **Tortuga Rum Cake** has earned a worldwide reputation as one of the Caribbean's great rum desserts of all times, and that recipe deserves a chapter of its own (see **Exclusive:Tortuga Rum Cake Recipes.**)

Rum Vanilla (see **The Island Pantry** for recipe)

The marriage of rum and sweets dates to Colonial kitchens long before vanilla extract existed. Any recipe can be improved by replacing vanilla extract with dark rum or better, Rum Vanilla. Vanilla extract is actually 35% alcohol, the infusion of vanilla beans soaked in grain alcohol. Centuries before vanilla extract was created commercially, brandy and cognac were used in baking cakes and other confections – not only for flavor, but also for its unique leavening ability, creating a lighter baked product.

Little Sweets

Although West Indians are notorious snackers and have created some of the world's best street food, cookies were not common in the Caribbean's culinary landscape. This puzzled me for years, since the region offers such a rich pantry of ingredients – sugar, molasses, coconut, exotic fruits and spices and of course, rum.

I finally asked Caribbean friends knowledgeable on the region's culinary history why this was so. Their reply: for centuries, little sweets were considered an English extravagance. Shortbread and similar confections were luxuries served during afternoon Tea, something not customary to a native West Indian lifestyle. Furthermore, ingredients including New Zealand butter were imported and expensive. Cookie fever never gripped the region as it has in the US – until satellite TV and tourism exported the craving en mass to the region.

There are some old-time sweets like spicy bullas and coconut gizzadas still popular in Cayman and Jamaica. These are the cookies of the Western Caribbean – and they are big, fat, satisfying sweets, not dainty tea wafers. I have combined traditional and contemporary treats in this section, including original recipes I created during attacks of Rum Fever.

Old Time Caribbean Sweets

Totoes

This is a very old recipe from Jamaica. You can make these little cake squares without coconut, but this recipe is by far the best.

1 cup light brown sugar, firmly packed
1/2 cup butter, softened
1 egg beaten
2 tablespoons Tortuga Dark Rum (or 1 tablespoon vanilla extract)
1/2 cup milk
2 cups self-rising flour
1/2 teaspoon cinnamon
1/2 teaspoon nutmeg or mace
1/8 teaspoon ground allspice
1-3/4 cups fresh coconut, grated or finely chopped

Preheat oven to 400F. Lightly grease a 9-inch square baking pan. In a large mixing bowl, cream together the butter and sugar until light. Add the egg, milk and rum and blend well. In a separate bowl, combine the flour and spices and whisk with wire whisk to blend well. On low speed of electric mixture, gradually blend flour mixture into butter mixture, then stir in the coconut and mix well. Spread the dough in the prepared pan and bake at 400 for 30 minutes or until toothpick inserted in center comes out clean. Cool and cut into 12 squares. Store in airtight container. These will keep for a week or longer in the refrigerator.

West Indian Gingerbread

Whether the English introduced this to the Colonies, or Jamaica's abundant pungent ginger inspired the first recipe centuries ago....no one remembers. In any event, gingerbread remains a popular sweet in the Western Caribbean today. Fresh ginger, coconut and dark rum make the difference here.

1/2 cup butter, melted
2-1/2 cups flour
1/2 teaspoon salt
2 teaspoons baking powder
1 teaspoon baking soda
2 teaspoons ground ginger
1/2 teaspoon grated nutmeg
2 tablespoons Tortuga Dark Rum (** Optional)
1/2 cup dark molasses
2/3 cup dark brown sugar, packed firmly
1 cup coconut milk
2 eggs, beaten
1/2 cup sweetened shredded coconut
1 tablespoon grated fresh gingerroot

Preheat oven to 325. Lightly grease and flour a 9 x 5" loaf pan or a 6-cup bundt pan. Combine the flour, baking powder, baking soda, salt and dry spices in a large mixing bowl and mix with wire whisk until blended. In a small saucepan, combine the molasses, rum, sugar and butter and heat over low heat until ingredients are melted; stir until smooth and well blended. Remove from heat and cool 10 minutes. Add the coconut milk and eggs, mixing well. Pour the egg and milk mixture into the flour and blend thoroughly. Stir in the fresh grated gingerroot and coconut. Pour batter into bundt or loaf pan and bake for 50 minutes or until toothpick inserted in center comes out clean. Remove from oven and cool in pan 10 minutes, and then invert onto a plate. Serve with rum raisin ice cream, Rummy Whipped Cream or lemon sauce.

Rock Buns

1 tablespoon Tortuga Dark Rum
3 tablespoons raisins or currants
2 cups flour
1/2 cup dark brown sugar, firmly packed
1/4 cup margarine
2 tablespoons fresh coconut, grated or chopped fine
1 teaspoon baking powder
1/2 teaspoon grated nutmeg
3-4 tablespoons milk
1 egg

Preheat oven to 400 F. Lightly grease baking sheet or spray with nonstick vegetable spray. Combine the currants or raisins and rum and stir. Set aside. Combine the flour, sugar, baking powder and nutmeg and blend with wire whisk until well mixed. Using a pastry blender cut in the butter until mixture resembles coarse crumbs. Add the coconut and currants or raisins and any unabsorbed rum, egg and enough milk to make a stiff dough – use more if necessary. Drop by tablespoonfuls onto prepared baking sheet and bake for 12-15 minutes, until edges are brown. Remove from oven and cool on wire racks.

Bullas

These soft fat spice cookies are a popular snack found throughout Cayman and Jamaica.

3 cups flour
1 teaspoon baking powder
1/2 teaspoon baking soda
1/4 teaspoon salt
1 teaspoon cinnamon
1/2 teaspoon nutmeg
1/2 teaspoon ground ginger
1/2 teaspoon allspice
1-1/4 cups dark brown sugar, firmly packed
1/4 cup water
2 tablespoons Tortuga Dark Rum
2 tablespoons butter or margarine, melted

Preheat oven to 350. Grease and flour a large baking sheet or spray with Bakers Joy. Combine all dry ingredients except the brown sugar in a large mixing bowl and whisk with wire whisk until well blended. Combine the sugar, water and rum and stir until a thick syrup forms, adding more water if needed. Stir in the butter until smooth. Make a well in the center of the dry ingredients and pour in the sugar syrup and melted butter and stir until all ingredients are blended. Place the dough on a lightly floured surface and pat or roll with floured rolling pin to 1/4 inch thickness. Use a 2-1/2 inch round cookie cutter or drinking glass with floured rim to cut out circles. Transfer the bullas with a floured spatula to the baking sheet and bake for about 20 minutes or until done.

Gizzadas

These sunflower-shaped coconut tarts are a favorite sweet snack, sold at gas stations, corner stores and supermarkets in Jamaica and Cayman. (Also called Pinch Me Rounds.)

Pastry:
2 cups flour
1/3 cup shortening
1/4 teaspoon salt
1/4 teaspoon nutmeg
3 tablespoons or more water

Coconut filling:
4 cups fresh coconut meat, grated or chopped fine in processor
1/2 teaspoon nutmeg
3 tablespoons water
1/2 cup water
1 tablespoon Tortuga Dark Rum
1-1/4 cups light brown sugar
1 teaspoon rose water

Make the crust: Combine the flour, nutmeg and salt and cut in the shortening using pastry blender or two knives. Add just enough water to make a stiff dough that can be easily handled. Form into a ball and chill for two hours. Roll out on floured surface about 1/2 inch thick and cut out 4-inch circles. Shaped each circle so edges rise about 1/2 inch high around a pocket to hold the filling. Crimp edges between fingers all around, giving a sunflower shape with "petals". Place on greased cookie sheet.

Filling: Preheat oven to 350F. Combine the coconut, nutmeg, sugar and water in a medium saucepan and cook over low heat, stirring constantly, until sugar is dissolved, about 10 minutes. Stir in the rum and rose water and blend well. Drop by spoonfuls into center of prepared pastries and bake for about 15-20 minutes or until edges are golden brown.

Coconut Drops

This simple candy recipe has been a Western Caribbean favorite for over 100 years.

2 cups fresh coconut, sliced into thin half inch chunks
2 cups water
2 tablespoons Tortuga Dark Rum
2 cups dark brown sugar, packed firmly
1 tablespoon fresh grated gingerroot

Line a baking sheet with wax paper and butter lightly. The coconut should be sliced almost like you were making coconut chips, only smaller – it should not be grated or chopped fine, but can be coarsely chopped. In a large saucepan, bring the water to a boil over medium high heat and stir in the coconut and ginger. Reduce the heat to medium and cook uncovered, stirring occasionally, for 15 minutes. Gradually stir in the brown sugar and rum and continue stirring until sugar dissolves. Increase the heat to medium-high and cook, stirring frequently, until mixture is thick, about 20-30 minutes (if using a candy thermometer, it should reach 236 F). To test, drop a tiny amount into a dish of cold water and if it forms a ball, the candy is ready. Remove from heat and drop mixture by tablespoonfuls onto the prepared baking sheet. Let candies cool, then store in plastic sandwich bags or airtight container.

Coconut Lace

These delicate crispy cookies are another old favorite, but must be stored in an airtight container or they will go limp.

1/2 cup sugar
1/2 cup light molasses
1/2 cup butter
1/4 cup Tortuga Gold Rum
1 cup unsifted cake flour
1/2 teaspoon baking powder
1/4 teaspoon baking soda
1/4 teaspoon ground mace
3/4 cup fresh grated or finely chopped coconut

Preheat oven to 350 F. Lightly grease a baking sheet. In a mixing bowl, combine the flour, baking powder, baking soda and mace. Set aside. In a medium saucepan, combine the sugar, butter and molasses and stir well. Over medium heat, bring the mixture to a slow boil, stirring constantly and boil for one minute. Remove from heat and stir in the rum, blending well. Add the flour mixture, mixing well and stir in the coconut. Drop batter by teaspoonfuls onto the prepared baking sheet, leaving two inches between each for batter to spread. Bake at 350 for 5-8 minutes until golden and set. Remove from oven and cool slightly, then carefully transfer cookies with a spatula on a wire rack to cool. Store in an airtight container, with wax paper separating stacked layers.

Rum Balls!

But there is an odd exception to the Caribbean cookie shortage: Rum Balls! From Barbados to Jamaica, Caribbean folks love these things , but recipes vary dramatically in the amount of rum added.

The Official *Rum Fever* Rum Ball Technique
Rum ball recipes never warn you how messy these things are to make properly. Here are some tips to prevent that. First, use a food processor, not rolling pin, to crush and grind both the cookies and nuts – it's fast and easy. Second, you absolutely must use your hands. The stiff dough is hard to mix with a spoon or hand mixer, and using your hands to "knead" the mixture blends the ingredients more uniformly. This is messy and unsanitary, but you simply can't form rum balls with a melon baller or tablespoon. You need to roll them around in the palms of your hands. Solution: buy a supply of inexpensive disposable vinyl or latex gloves. It's a handy kitchen aid you probably didn't know exists. The dough won't stick to them and your hands stay clean. You can find them in the cleaning supply aisle of any supermarket.

Traditional Rum Balls

2-1/4 cups finely crushed vanilla or chocolate wafer crumbs (grind in food processor)
1 cup finely chopped pecans or walnuts
3 tablespoons unsweetened cocoa
1 cup powdered sugar
3 tablespoons light corn syrup
1/3 cup Tortuga Dark Rum
1 cup powdered sugar or chocolate sprinkles

Sift together the cocoa and 1 cup powdered sugar into a small mixing bowl. In a large mixing bowl, combine the cocoa mixture, nuts and cookie crumbs. Combine the corn syrup and rum and stir into the dry ingredients. Use your hands to knead and blend the mixture to a smooth consistency. Shape dough into 1-inch balls and roll in the remaining powdered sugar or chocolate sprinkles. Store in airtight container at least overnight to ripen. Will keep for two weeks in refrigerator, but you may want to freshen the sugar coating before serving. Makes about 3 dozen one inch balls.

Medicine Balls

Starve a cold and feed a fever? Island "bush medicine" says rum cures almost everything. These incredibly rich and rummy balls will definitely feed Rum Fever cravings – more like a drunken fudge brownie than a cookie.

1-1 pound box Nabisco gingersnaps (makes about 3-1/2 cups crumbs)
1 cup finely crushed vanilla wafer crumbs (grind in food processor)
2 cups finely chopped walnuts (grind in food processor)
1-1/2 cups powdered sugar
1/2 cup Hershey's Dutch Processed unsweetened cocoa
3/4 cup sweetened shredded coconut
1-11 ounce bag Ghirardelli Double Chocolate morsels or semi-sweet chocolate chips
1/2 cup light corn syrup
2/3 cup Tortuga Dark Rum
2 cups sifted powdered sugar

Use the processor to grind the gingersnaps into fine crumbs. After removing cookie crumbs, do not clean bowl, but add the package of chocolate morsels and chop for about a minute until chips are well broken – do not grind into a paste, just make sure the chips are finely chopped. Use a rubber spatula to remove.

In a 6-quart mixing bowl, combine gingersnaps and vanilla wafer crumbs, walnut pieces, 1-1/2 cups powdered sugar, cocoa, coconut, chopped chocolate morsels and stir until well mixed. Combine corn syrup and rum and stir well to blend. Using a heavy spoon, stir the mixture into the dry ingredients and mix well. Now use your hands to "knead" the sticky dough to blend ingredients into a smooth dough. This recipe is best if you refrigerate the dough overnight to let the rum permeate all the ingredients.

When ready to make the balls, pour the remaining powdered sugar into a small bowl. Use your hands to roll dough into 1-inch balls, the roll in the powdered sugar. You can store the balls in an airtight plastic container in refrigerator for two weeks. It's not very likely they will last anywhere near that long. You may want to refresh the rum balls before serving by rolling in powdered sugar one more time. Makes about 4 dozen balls.

Tortuga Date Coconut Sugarplums

Originally a Christmas treat, you'll crave these year round.

8-ounce package chopped pitted dates
1/4 cup butter or margarine
1/2 cup light brown sugar
1 egg, beaten
2-1/4 cups Cocoa Rice Crispies cereal
1/2 cup sweetened shredded coconut
1 cup finely chopped pecans
1/4 cup Tortuga Dark Rum
Additional shredded coconut for rolling balls

Melt butter in 1-quart saucepan over medium heat, then reduce heat to low and stir in dates and brown sugar and mix well. Add half the rum and cook three minutes or until mixture is well blended and dates have softened and partially dissolved. Remove from heat and rapidly stir in egg so it mixes thoroughly and does not curdle. Return to heat, cooking over medium heat, stirring constantly, for another minute. Remove from heat and stir in the remaining rum and blend well. Then add cereal, 1/2 cup coconut and nuts. Allow to cool to touch. Shape into 1-inch balls and roll in remaining coconut. Store in airtight container in refrigerator for a few days to age before serving. Makes about 2-1/2 dozen.

Reggae Bars

A rich, spirited Caribbean variation of the popular Conga Bars.

3/4 cup unsalted butter or margarine, softened
1 pound box (2-1/4 cups) light brown sugar
1 teaspoon vanilla extract
1/4 cup Tortuga Dark Rum
3 large eggs
2-1/2 cups flour
3 teaspoons baking powder
1/2 teaspoon salt
1 teaspoon cinnamon
1 teaspoon nutmeg
1 semisweet chocolate morsels
1 cup white chocolate morsels
1 cup chopped mixed nuts
1 cup fresh grated or 1-1/3 cups sweetened shredded coconut

Preheat oven to 350 F. Lightly grease and flour or spray with Baker's Joy a 13 x 9 x 2" baking pan. Cream together butter or margarine and sugar with electric mixer until smooth. Add eggs, one at a time, beating well after each, then mix in vanilla and rum until well blended. In a separate bowl, combine flour, baking powder, cinnamon, nutmeg and salt and stir with wire whisk to blend. Add to butter mixture and blend well. Stir in chocolate pieces, coconut and mixed nuts and spoon evenly into the prepared pan. Bake for 45 minutes or until toothpick inserted in center comes out clean. Cool in pan for at least two hours or chill in refrigerator until completely cooled. Cut into squares.

Cayman Kruggerands

These chewy golden butterscotch bars are so rich they earn their name – and should be cut into small nuggets about that size. Leftovers are unlikely, but are best stored in the refrigerator.

2 tablespoons Tortuga Dark Rum
1/2 cup fresh coconut, chopped fine, or 2/3 cup shredded sweetened coconut
3/4 cup butter or margarine, softened
1 cup light brown sugar, packed
2 large eggs
2 tablespoons coconut milk
1 teaspoon vanilla
1-1/2 cups flour
1 teaspoon baking powder
1/2 teaspoon baking soda
1/4 teaspoon salt
1 cup chopped macadamia nuts or hazelnuts (you can substitute cashews or almonds)
1-11 ounce package butterscotch morsels

Preheat oven to 350. Lightly grease a 9" x 13" baking pan. Combine the rum and coconut and stir well. Set aside. In large bowl, cream butter and brown sugar until light and fluffy. Add eggs, one a time, then coconut milk and vanilla. Blend well. In separate bowl, combine the flour, baking powder, baking soda and salt and stir well with wire whisk to blend. Gradually add to the butter mixture and beat until well blended. By hand, stir in the nuts, coconut and butterscotch chips. Spread evenly in prepared pan. Bake 30-35 minutes or until golden brown. Remove from oven and cool completely on wire rack then chill several hours to let flavors blend before cutting.

Sinful Rum Fudge Nut Brownies

This recipe could almost double for fudge. Store these in the refrigerator and they will improve with age – if they last long enough!

1/2 cup butter
1 cup sugar
1/4 cup Dutch Process cocoa
1/2 cup water
1/2 cup Tortuga Dark Rum
1-1/4 cups flour
1/2 teaspoon baking powder
1 egg, beaten
1 cup chopped mixed nuts without peanuts

In a small bowl, combine the sugar and cocoa and mix with a wire whisk until well blended. In a medium saucepan, melt the butter over medium heat and stir in the sugar-cocoa mix and water and stir well. Cook stirring constantly, over medium heat for five minutes until thickened. Remove from heat and stir in the rum, stirring until it stops foaming. Set aside to cool for 30 minutes. Preheat oven to 350F. Spray a 9-inch square baking pan with Baker's Joy or lightly grease and flour. In a small bowl, combine the flour and baking powder and stir well. Stir the egg into the chocolate mixture, then gradually add the flour and blend thoroughly. Stir in the chopped nuts. Pour into the prepared pan and bake for 25 minutes or until toothpick inserted in center comes out with only a few crumbs attached, but no liquid. Remove and cool completely before cutting. Store in refrigerator.

Chocolate Rum Fudge

1/4 cup Tortuga Dark Rum
3 cups semi-sweet chocolate chips
1 14-ounce can sweetened condensed milk
Pinch of salt
1 teaspoon vanilla extract
1/2 cup chopped walnuts or pecans

Melt chocolate in top of a double boiler over hot water, stirring occasionally. When completely melted and smooth, remove from heat. Add the rum, condensed milk, salt, vanilla and nuts. Stir until smooth. Spoon into an 8-inch square pan lined with waxed paper and spread evenly, smoothing the surface with a spatula. Chill two hours or more, until firm. Cut into small squares and store in airtight container or refrigerator.

White Chocolate Rum Fudge: Substitute 3 cups white chocolate morsels.

Island Lime Coconut Crumble Bars

For the crust and topping:
2/3 cup butter or margarine, softened
1 cup light brown sugar, packed firm
1-1/2 cups flour
1/2 teaspoon nutmeg
1/2 teaspoon salt
1 teaspoon baking powder
3/4 cup grated fresh or fine chopped coconut
1 cup old-fashioned oats

Filling:
1/2 cup fresh key lime juice
3 egg yolks, lightly beaten
1 teaspoon grated lime peel
1-14 ounce can sweetened condensed milk
1 tablespoon Tortuga Dark Rum

Make the crust: Preheat oven to 350. Grease or spray a 13 x 9 x 2 inch baking pan. In a small bowl, combine the flour, nutmeg, salt, baking powder, coconut and oats. Stir with wire whisk to mix. In large mixing bowl, cream the butter or margarine and sugar until light. Blend in the flour mixture and blend well. Spread half of the mixture over the bottom of the prepared pan and press down firmly, so that crust is evenly distributed over pan. Do not leave thin edges – work from center out.

Make the filling: Combine the condensed milk, lime peel, lime juice, rum and egg yolks and beat with rotary or electric mixer until blended, about one minute. Let stand for another minute to thicken. Pour this evenly over the crust and crumble the remaining crust mixture over the top, avoiding large clumps. Bake at 350 for about 25 minutes, or until center is set. Cool in pan for about 15 minutes then refrigerate until firm. Cut into 2-inch squares. Keeps in refrigerator, covered, several days if they last that long!

Lemon Curd Squares

Americans would know these as lemon squares – but they're called this in the British Caribbean islands. I've livened up the recipe with the Caribbean flavors of rum and coconut. For more island flavor, substitute fresh Key Lime juice and peel.

Crust:
1-1/4 cups flour
1/2 cup confectioners' sugar
1/2 teaspoon nutmeg
3/4 cup shredded sweetened coconut
3/4 cup almonds, toasted and finely ground in food processor
1 cup margarine or butter, softened

Filling:
1/3 cup fresh lemon juice
1 teaspoon grated lemon peel
2 cups granulated sugar

4 large eggs, beaten
1 tablespoon Tortuga Dark Rum
1/4 cup flour
1/2 teaspoon baking powder
2/3 cup shredded sweetened coconut, toasted for topping

Make the crust. Preheat oven to 350. Grease a 9 x 13" baking pan. In a food processor bowl fitted with large blade, combine the nuts, flour, nutmeg, confectioner's sugar and coconut. Process until well blended. Add the butter and continue processing until mixture forms soft dough. Press dough evenly over the bottom of prepared pan. Press down firmly, so that crust is evenly distributed but thicker along the edges – do not leave thin edges or crust may become too brown – work from center out. Bake crust at 350 for about 115 minutes or until just turning pale golden brown. Remove from oven and cool while preparing filling.

Make the filling: In medium bowl, combine sugar, eggs, lemon juice, lemon peel and rum. Beat with whisk or electric mixer on medium speed until well-blended, about two minutes. In separate bowl, combine flour and baking powder and stir well. Add to the lemon mixture and beat until well blended. Pour the topping over the warm crust and bake at 350 for about 25 minutes, or until filling is set and firm to the touch. Remove from oven and sprinkle toasted coconut over the top. Cool pan on wire rack for 30 minutes, then chill for a few hours until firm, but bring back to room temperature to serve.

Coconut Macaroons

This classic and easy recipe has been around for at least 20 years. It is popular in the Caribbean where condensed milk is a pantry staple and starter for many sweets. I use Rum Vanilla for a hint of rum flavor.

1 -14 ounce package. sweetened shredded coconut, like Bakers (about 5-1/3 cups)
1-14 ounce can sweetened condensed milk
2 teaspoons Rum Vanilla or Tortuga Dark Rum
1 teaspoon almond extract
3 egg whites
1/8 teaspoon salt
Candied (not maraschino) cherries

Preheat oven to 350. Line a baking sheet with aluminum foil and grease generously. In small deep bowl, beat the egg whites with the salt until stiff peaks form. Set aside. In large mixing bowl, combine the condensed milk, coconut, Rum Vanilla or rum and almond extract. Stir with a heavy spoon until well blended, using a rubber spatula to scrape bowl sides. Fold in the beaten egg whites, blending evenly. Drop by rounded spoonfuls onto baking sheet and use back of spoon to flatten any coconut shreds sticking out so they don't scorch. Bake 8-10 minutes or until just lightly golden brown around edges. Remove from oven and remove immediately from baking sheet and cool on wax paper covered plate or wire rack. While still warm, press a candied cherry in the center of each macaroon. Store in plastic container, covered loosely, at room temperature.

Cayman Millionaire Macaroons

With the price of macadamia nuts, this is a shameful indulgence. But in Grand Cayman, such luxuries are always available in local supermarkets if you can afford them.

1 14-ounce can sweetened condensed milk
2 cups unsalted macadamia nuts, chopped
5 cups shredded coconut
2 teaspoons vanilla extract
1 tablespoon Tortuga Dark Rum
4 egg whites
1/8 teaspoon salt
12 ounce semisweet chocolate morsels, melted

Preheat oven to 350. Line baking sheets with aluminum foil and grease well. If macadamias are salted, rinse them off and dry completely, patting and rolling around, on paper towels. Place the coconut and macadamia nuts on a cookie sheet and toast lightly, stirring several times, at 350 for about 10 minutes. Let cool.

Combine condensed milk, vanilla and rum in large bowl. Stir in the macadamia nuts and coconut and blend well. Using electric mixer beat the egg whites with the salt until stiff peaks form and fold into the coconut mixture. Drop batter by tablespoonfuls onto prepared cookie sheets. Bake 10-12 minutes, or until macaroons are just turning light golden brown around the edges. Remove immediately to wax paper lined plates or wire rack and cool completely.

Melt the chocolate chips over low heat, stirring until smooth. Line cleaned and cooled baking sheets with wax paper. Dip the cooled macaroon bottoms just lightly into the melted chocolate and arrange, chocolate side down, on the prepared sheets. Refrigerate immediately until chocolate is firm, about 20 minutes. Store macaroons in covered container in refrigerator.

Post-Hurricane Season Peanut Cookies

West Indians love peanuts, but during hurricane season, we all seem to stock up on enough peanut butter and cornflakes to thwart global famine. In March, when I finally get around to cleaning out last year's hurricane pantry, I bake these.

1 cup Crisco solid shortening
1 cup granulated sugar
1 cup light brown sugar, packed
1 cup creamy peanut butter
2 eggs
1 tablespoon Rum Vanilla or Tortuga Dark Rum
2-1/4 cups flour
1-1/2 teaspoon baking soda
1 teaspoon baking powder
1/2 teaspoon salt
1 teaspoon cinnamon
1 cup salted peanuts (Spanish preferred)
1 cup cornflakes

Preheat oven to 375. In large mixing bowl, cream the shortening, margarine, peanut butter and sugars until creamy. Blend in the eggs and Rum vanilla. In separate small bowl, combine the flour, baking soda, baking powder, salt, and cinnamon and mix with wire whisk to blend. Gradually beat in the flour mixture to the creamed batter. Stir in the peanuts and cornflakes and blend evenly. Drop by tablespoonfuls onto lightly greased baking sheets and press down with fork to flatten. Bake for about 10 minutes or until edges are set but centers are soft. Remove from oven and let sit for 5 minutes, then cool on wire racks.

Lime Rum Drops

These simple cookies are a teatime treat recipe shared by a friend from Barbados. They would make a nice addition to a beach picnic basket.

1 cup Crisco or other vegetable shortening
1-1/2 cups granulated sugar
2 large eggs
1 tablespoon fresh key lime juice
2 teaspoons fresh grated lime peel
3 cups flour
1 teaspoon baking powder
1 teaspoon baking soda
1/2 teaspoon salt

Glaze:
6 tablespoons confectioners sugar
2 tablespoons water
2 tablespoons Tortuga Dark Rum

In large mixing bowl, cream together the shortening and sugar until light. Beat in the eggs, one at a time, until well blended. Blend in the lime juice and grated peel. In separate bowl, combine the flour, baking powder and salt and mix well. Gradually add to the sugar mixture until well blended. Chill dough several hours.

Preheat oven to 350. Shape dough into 1-inch balls and place 2-1/2 inches apart on ungreased baking sheet. Flatten each ball to 1/4 inch high using bottom of glass dipped in flour. Make the glaze by blending all ingredients until smooth. Using a fine pastry brush, brush a little glaze over each cookie. Bake for 8-10 minutes until light golden and slightly puffed. Remove from oven and cool on wire racks.

Guilty Pleasures

The kind of dream cookie you'd expect to find in Paradise.

3/4 cup butter, softened
1/4 cup shortening
1/2 cup sugar
1 cup light brown sugar, firmly packed
1 large egg
2 teaspoons Rum Vanilla or 2 teaspoons Tortuga Dark Rum
1 teaspoon baking soda
2-1/4 cups flour
1/4 teaspoon salt
1/2 teaspoon ground coriander
1 cup chopped cashews

1/2 cup Ghirardelli Milk Chocolate morsels
1/2 cup Ghirardelli Double Double Chocolate Chips
1 cup Ghirardelli White Chocolate Chips

Preheat oven to 350F. In a small bowl, combine the flour, baking soda, salt and cinnamon and mix with wire whisk or fork until well blended. In large mixing bowl, cream the butter and shortening until light. Add both sugars gradually and cream until smooth. Beat in the eggs, one at a time, blending well after each, and then blend in the Rum Vanilla or rum. Gradually blend in the flour mixture until smooth. Stir in the nuts and chocolate morsels. Drop dough by tablespoonfuls onto ungreased cookie sheets and bake at 375 for 9-11 minutes. Cool three minutes on cookie sheets and then transfer to wire racks and cool completely.

Gold Doubloons

These melt-in-your-mouth confections are "an embarrassment of riches" combining indulgences found in Cayman supermarkets – and expensive to make. Created during a Rum Fever attack.

3/4 cup butter, softened
1 cup granulated sugar
1/4 cup light brown sugar, packed firm
2 large eggs
1/2 cup coconut milk
1 tablespoon Tortuga Dark Rum
2-1/2 cups flour
1/2 teaspoon baking soda
2 cups shredded sweetened coconut
1 cup chopped unsalted macadamia nuts
1/2 cup chopped almonds
2 cups Ghirardelli white chocolate chips

In large mixing bowl, combine butter and sugars and cream until light. Beat in the eggs, one at a time, blending well after each. Add the coconut milk and rum and mix well. Combine the flour and baking soda and stir to mix. Add gradually to the butter mixture, until thoroughly blended and smooth. Stir in the coconut, then the nuts and white chocolate chips. Chill dough for 30 minutes.

Heat oven to 350. Drop dough by teaspoonfuls (walnut sized portions) onto lightly greased baking sheet, about 2 inches apart. Bake at 350 for 9-11 minutes, until edges are lightly browned and tops are set but not brown. Remove and cool 2 minutes, then use spatula to transfer to wire racks to cool. The flavor improves after storing overnight, so bake a day ahead.

Fudge Sins

One of the best chocolate cookies you'll ever taste.

3/4 cup shortening
1/2 cup butter, softened
1 cup sugar
3/4 cup light brown sugar, firmly packed
2 large eggs

1 teaspoon Rum Vanilla or Tortuga Dark Rum
2 tablespoons coconut milk
2-1/2 cups flour
1/2 cup Dutch processed cocoa
1 teaspoon baking soda
1/4 teaspoon salt
1 cup white chocolate chips
1 cup milk chocolate chips
1 cup chopped almonds
1 cup shredded sweetened coconut

Preheat oven to 350. Cream shortening and butter with sugars until light. Beat in the eggs, one at a time, then the rum and coconut milk. In separate bowl, combine the flour, cocoa, baking soda and salt and mix with wire whisk or fork until blended well. Gradually add to the sugar mixture, beating until smooth. Stir in the chocolate chips, nuts and coconut until blended.

Drop dough by rounded teaspoonfuls, about walnut-sized onto ungreased baking sheet, about two inches apart. Flatten any coconut shreds sticking out. Bake 10-12 minutes or until edges are set and tops are no longer wet looking, but not hard. Remove from oven and cool 2 minutes on baking sheet, then transfer to wire rack.

Coconut Calypso Cookies

These rich treats offer a sweet taste of the islands.

1/2 cup butter or margarine
1/2 cup sugar
1/2 cup light brown sugar, firmly packed
1 large egg
1 tablespoon Rum Vanilla or Tortuga Dark Rum
1 –8 ounce can crushed pineapple, well drained
2 cups flour
1 teaspoon baking powder
1/2 teaspoon baking soda
1/4 teaspoon salt
1 cup cashews or macadamia nuts, coarsely chopped
1 cup sweetened shredded coconut

Preheat oven to 375 F. Lightly grease a baking sheet. In a large mixing bowl, cream the butter and sugars until light, then add egg and Rum Vanilla or rum and beat until smooth. Stir in pineapple. In a small bowl, whisk together flour, baking powder, baking soda and salt. Gradually beat into butter mixture until well blended. Stir in the nuts and coconut. Drop by tablespoonfuls onto prepared sheet, about 2 inches apart. Bake 8-10 minutes or until edges are lightly brown. Remove from oven and transfer cookies to wire rack to cool. Store in airtight container.

Flambés, Fools and other Spirited Finales

Flambés and Flaming Rum Desserts

No dinner finale is as spectacular as a flambé or flaming coffee and it is best to do this before you start sampling the rum quality. The secret to both is to warm the rum first – warm, never boil! Flame only small amounts of spirits, 1/2 cup or less. And obviously, never try to ignite spirits when pouring directly from the bottle.

How to Flambé Desserts

To prepare flaming desserts, be sure to assemble everything ahead of time. Long- stem wooden fireplace matches, available at almost any supermarket, are the safest way to ignite alcohol. The secret: it's the fumes, not the alcohol itself, that flame.

Obviously, the point of this is showing off and dazzling your guests, so arrange the display to take place at the table or within full view – -don't play Caribbean fire dancer and carry a flaming pot across the room. Put the rum or liqueur in a small saucepan and warm quickly just until tiny bubbles appear or you smell fumes – do not overheat or allow it to boil or the alcohol will simply evaporate and not flame. Remove immediately from heat and take it to the serving area to ignite and pour over the waiting dish. Once you've ignited the alcohol, pour it quickly and evenly over the dessert – and wait until the flames die down to serve!

You don't have to use a separate pan and can flambé directly in the pan if there is little if any other liquid and the pan is still warm, not very hot. Gently pour the rum or liqueur evenly over the dish and the heat of the pan will fume the spirits. Simply ignite with a long match. When the flames die, the dish is ready to serve. Never try to flambé or ignite anything in a glass container unless it's Pyrex and fireproof

The higher the alcohol content, like Tortuga 151 Rum, the more easily it will ignite. And sweet liqueurs of more than 40 proof will flame; the higher the proof, the less warming required. Liqueurs have a higher sugar content and will produce a higher flame and burn slightly longer than liquor with less sugar but same alcohol content.

Remember, the alcohol burns off quickly and the dazzling display lasts only seconds, so wait until your guests are ready to attempt any grand *coup de theatre* finale.

Bananas Tortuga

1/4 cup (1/2 stick) butter or margarine
1/2 cup dark brown sugar, firmly packed
4 ripe but firm bananas
1 tablespoon banana liqueur
2 tablespoons Tortuga 151 Rum
2 tablespoons peach brandy
1/2 cup toasted sweetened coconut

Toast coconut by spreading on aluminum foil and baking at 350 for about 8 minutes or until golden brown. Slice bananas in half lengthwise, then in half crosswise. Combine butter and brown sugar in skillet and cook over medium heat until sugar melts and dissolved. Add bananas to skillet and cook until just tender, but not soft and mushy, a few minutes. Add banana liqueur and stir. In a small saucepan, heat rum and brandy until warm. Remove from heat and ignite with long-stemmed wooden match and pour flaming liquor over bananas in skillet. When flames die down, sprinkle coconut over bananas and sauce. Spoon over rich vanilla or coconut ice cream.

Mangoes Jubilee

1/4 cup butter or margarine
4 teaspoons sugar
1 inch slice orange peel
1 inch slice lemon peel
3/4 cup orange juice
2 tablespoons Kirsch
1/4 cup Grand Marnier
2 tablespoons Tortuga Dark Rum
2 cups ripe firm mangoes, cut into 1/2-inch chunks

Melt butter in a skillet or chafing dish just until bubbling. Add sugar and stir until it melts and blends with butter and begins to caramelize. Add the orange and lemon peel and heat over low heat for a minute to blend flavors. Add orange juice to deglaze pan and stir well until heated. Stir in mangoes and continue cooking over low until ingredients are thoroughly heated. Pour in Kirsch and Grand Marnier and stir gently. Heat the rum in a small saucepan with a pouring spout until warm. Ignite with long wooden match and pour over mango mixture and when flames die down, serve immediately over rich vanilla ice cream.

Tropical Rum Rice Pudding

Rice pudding, which most people know as American comfort food, is enjoyed throughout the Caribbean.

3 cups water
1 teaspoon salt
2 teaspoons cinnamon
8 whole cloves
1 tablespoon fresh grated ginger
1-14 ounce can coconut milk
1/2 cup Tortuga Dark Rum
1/2 cup water
1/2 cup sugar
1 cup short grain rice (Valencia or arborio)
1/3 cup golden raisins
1/2 cup shredded sweetened coconut
Ground cinnamon and additional for garnish

In a large saucepan, combine the water, salt, cinnamon, cloves and ginger. Bring to a boil and boil for 2 minutes. Remove from heat and strain water, discarding spices, and return spiced water to the saucepan. Add the coconut milk, rum and remaining 1/2 cup water and bring to a boil. Gradually stir in the sugar, then the rice, raisins and coconut. When mixture returns to a boil, reduce heat to low, cover and simmer for 20 minutes. Remove the cover after 20 minutes and stir. Add a little more water if necessary and cook for another 15 minutes or until the rice is tender and liquid is absorbed. Pour into a bowl and cool slightly but serve warm. Garnish each serving with a sprinkling of cinnamon and shredded coconut. Serve with whipped cream

Coconut Rum Mango Tapioca

3-3/4 cups milk
1 cup sugar
1/3 cup quick cooking tapioca
2 large eggs, beaten
1 cup fresh chopped coconut
1/4 teaspoon salt
1 teaspoon vanilla extract
2 tablespoons Tortuga Dark Rum
1-1/2 cups diced ripe mango plus 1/4 cup for garnish
Whipped cream
Grated nutmeg

In a medium saucepan, combine milk, sugar, tapioca, eggs, coconut and salt and stir well. Let stand five minutes. Cook tapioca over medium heat, stirring constantly, about 10 minutes or until mixture thickens and just begins to boil. Pour the tapioca into a large bowl and cover with plastic wrap. Cool to lukewarm and then stir in vanilla and rum. Cover again and refrigerate at least four hours.

Place 1/4 cup diced mango in each of six parfait glasses or bowls. Spoon tapioca over mango and divide remaining 1/4 cup mango among the dishes as garnish. Serve with whipped cream and sprinkle of nutmeg

Cassava Pudding

4 cups grated cassava
3-1/2 cups sugar
3/4 cup butter
6 eggs
3 cups whole milk
2 cans evaporated milk
1 teaspoon cinnamon
1 teaspoon nutmeg
2 cups coconut
1/3 cup Tortuga Dark Rum
1 teaspoon vanilla extract

You can buy frozen grated cassava at the Farmer's Market in Grand Cayman and in supermarkets in the US carrying Latin and Caribbean food items. Otherwise, forget this recipe unless you have a helper willing to peel, grate, rinse and drain the cassava!

Preheat oven to 350. Grease two 13 x 9 inch baking pans. Cream together the butter and sugar and beat in eggs, one at a time. Add whole milk and evaporated milk and mix well. Stir in the grated cassava, coconut, spices, rum and vanilla and mix well. Divide between the two pans and bake for 40 minutes. Remove from oven and allow to cool several hours before serving.

Fresh Coconut Pudding with Rum Liqueur Topping

3 cups fresh grated coconut
3/4 cup butter or margarine
3/4 cup sugar
1/2 teaspoon ground mace
1 large egg, beaten
3 large egg yolks
1-1/2 cups evaporated milk or half-and-half
1 teaspoon vanilla extract
2 tablespoons Tortuga Dark Rum

Preheat over to 350 degrees. Butter (or spray with butter-flavored Pam) eight 2-1/2 inch Pyrex glass custard cups. Cream the butter and sugar together until light and fluffy. Blend in the beaten egg and egg yolks and by hand, mixing well, then stir in the mace, coconut, milk or half and half, vanilla and rum. Divide the pudding among the 8 cups, filling each about 3/4 full. Place cups in a pan large enough to hold all and pour hot water to reach halfway up the cups. Bake at 350 for about 45 minutes or until set. Cool for 20 minutes, then serve with rum liqueur topping:

Rum Liqueur Topping:
1/2 cup heavy whipping cream
1 teaspoon confectioner's sugar
2 tablespoons Tortuga Rum Liqueur

Whip the cream and sugar until stiff peaks form, then fold in the Rum Liqueur. Makes about one cup of topping.

Rum Fudge Pudding

This old-time sponge pudding dessert separates to create a rich rum-spiked sauce on the bottom.

1/4 cup margarine
1/4 cup plus 2 tablespoons light brown sugar, packed firmly
2 eggs, beaten
3 tablespoons Tortuga Rum Liqueur or Dark Rum
1-1/4 cup milk
1/2 cup chopped almonds or pecans
1/4 cup flour
2 tablespoons Hershey's unsweetened cocoa
Confectioner's sugar

Preheat oven to 350F. Lightly grease a one-quart baking dish or 8-inch square pan. Cream together the margarine and sugar in a large mixing bowl until light and fluffy. Beat in the eggs until blended, then add the rum liqueur or dark rum. Gradually blend in the milk, then stir in the nuts. Sift together the flour and cocoa into the butter mixture and fold in gently, until just mixed. Spoon the mixture into the prepared dish and bake at 350F for 35-40 minutes or until the top layer is firm and puffed. Remove from oven and dust with confectioner's sugar. Serve while warm.

Grand Caribbean Charlotte Russe

An island variation on an old Southern US holiday tradition.

20-24 ladyfingers (see note below)
1/4 cup Tortuga Coffee Liqueur or Tia Maria
1-1/2 envelopes unflavored gelatin
1/3 cup cold water
1 cup sugar
Pinch salt
4 large egg yolks
2 cups milk
1 teaspoon Rum Vanilla (see Ingredients) or vanilla extract
1/2 teaspoon cinnamon
1/4 cup Tortuga Dark Rum
1 quart heavy cream
1 cup diced ripe firm mango

Split ladyfingers (see note below) in half lengthwise and brush cut sides lightly with coffee liqueur. Arrange with curved sides up along bottom and standing up along sides of 3-quart glass bowl or 10-in springform pan. Cover with plastic wrap to keep fresh while preparing filling.

In a small saucepan, sprinkle the gelatin into the cold water and let stand for 1 minute. In a small bowl, beat egg yolks until slightly thickened. In the top of a double boiler, heat the milk and stir in the sugar and gelatin and continue stirring until both are dissolved. Add a small amount of the hot milk mixture to the beaten egg yolks, cinnamon and salt and stir, then add this to the milk-sugar mixture. Keep the water at a simmer and cook, stirring constantly until the custard coats the back of a spoon. Stir in the rum vanilla or vanilla extract and set aside to cool.

When the custard has cooled and begun to thicken, combine the heavy cream and rum in a large deep bowl and beat with an electric or rotary mixer until stiff peaks form. Gently fold the whipped cream into the custard mixture and spoon into the prepared bowl or springform pan. Cover the surface with plastic wrap and refrigerate at least 8 hours.

Garnish each serving with a tablespoon or more of the diced mango. Serves 6-8. (**Note**: The ladyfingers used in this recipe are the 3-inch soft, finger-shaped sponge cakes, not the hard Cuban sweet biscuits by the same name.)

Pina Colada Bread Pudding with Rum Sauce

8 slices rich white or egg bread, cut into cubes
3 large eggs
1 cup Coco Lopez or other cream of coconut
2 cups milk
1-8 ounce can crushed pineapple, well drained
1 cup fresh grated coconut
1/2 cup Tortuga Dark Rum
1 teaspoon ground cinnamon
1 teaspoon ground nutmeg
1 tablespoon vanilla extract

Rum Sauce:
1 cup butter
1-1/2 cups sugar
2 large eggs, lightly beaten
1/4 cup Tortuga Dark Rum

Preheat oven to 325 degrees. Lightly butter and 8-inch square glass baking dish and arrange bread cubes over the bottom. In a large mixing bowl, beat the eggs until light, then add the cream of coconut and remaining ingredients. Mix until well blended, then pour over the bread cubes. Let the pudding stand for 10 minutes until bread has absorbed the milk mixture. Bake 45-50 minutes or until knife inserted in center comes out clean. Cool completely and serve with **Rum Sauce**.

Rum sauce: Combine butter and sugar in saucepan and cook over low heat, stirring constantly, until caramelized, about 20 minutes. Gradually add 1/2 cup of this mixture to beaten eggs, stirring quickly. Then add the egg mixture back into the sugar mixture, stirring constantly. Cook sauce over medium low heat until thickened. Remove from heat and cool 10 minutes, then stir in rum.

Tortuga Mango Trifle

This is a very elegant dessert.

2 cups whole milk
1/2 cup white sugar
6 egg yolks
2 tablespoons Tortuga Dark Rum
1 –16 ounce pound cake, cut into 1/2 inch slices
3 cups diced ripe but firm mangos
2 tablespoons light brown sugar
1/2 teaspoon nutmeg
1-16 ounce container mascarpone

First, make the custard. Whisk together sugar and egg yolks until light colored and well blended. Heat milk just until boiling in a heavy saucepan, then remove from heat. Beat a tablespoon of hot milk into egg-sugar mixture, then stir egg mixture into the hot milk and whisk slowly while cooking over medium heat for about 3 minutes until custard thickens. Do NOT stop stirring, or mixture will scorch, and do not boil! Remove from heat and let custard cool for 10 minutes, then stir in rum.

Put mangoes in a bowl and sprinkle with brown sugar and nutmeg. Empty mascarpone into another bowl and whisk (use clean whisk) until smooth. Add 1/3 of the custard to mascarpone and mix well.

To assemble the trifle, use a 2-quart glass bowl. Pour enough custard mix in to lightly cover the bottom and place a layer of pound cake on top. Spread with half the mascarpone mixture and place a third of the mangos on top. Make another layer of cake, custard, mangos and rest of mascarpone. Add the final layer of cake, custard and top with mangos. Cover with plastic wrap and refrigerate at least four hours before serving. Makes about 10 servings.

God Save the Queen's Trifle

This is a modern – and rummier version of the old trifle served in colonial England and her colonies. The recipe is based on serving a party of 12.

1 4 1/2 ounce package French vanilla pudding mix (not instant)
2 cups half and half
2 tablespoons Tortuga Dark Rum
2 1/4 cups heavy whipping cream
3 tablespoons confectioner's sugar
1/2 cup raspberry preserves or jam
1 pound loaf or 10-inch round golden pound cake
1/4 cup Tortuga Rum Liqueur
1/2 cup sweet sherry
1/2 teaspoon vanilla extract
1/2 cup sliced or slivered blanched almonds
Maraschino cherries, drained, for garnish

Make the pudding according to directions, using half-and-half instead of milk. When mixture is thick, add the 2 tablespoons dark rum, remove from heat, and chill for two hours. Whip 1-1/4 cups heavy cream with 1 tablespoon sugar until stiff peaks form; fold into chilled pudding.

Cut cake into 1-inch thick slices and coat with raspberry preserves. Arrange about a third of the cake slices in bottom of 10-inch glass bowl. Combine sherry and rum liqueur and stir well. Sprinkle the cake with 1/3 of sherry/rum mixture. Spread a third of pudding over this. Repeat entire procedure two more times. Whip remaining heavy cream, vanilla and remaining 2 tablespoons sugar until stiff. Spread over trifle and decorate with almonds and cherries. Chill at least four hours.

Fools

"Any fool can make it" or "West Indians are fool for sweets with fruit." One of these may be the origin of the name of this favorite Caribbean dessert imported from England. Here are two variations of this simple, popular West Indian dessert

Spiced Pineapple & Papaya Fool

You could serve a tiny square of gingerbread with this as a special treat.

1 cup fresh pineapple, diced into small pieces, drained of all juice
1 cup fresh ripe papaya, diced
2 tablespoons light brown sugar
1/2 teaspoon ground mace
2 tablespoons Tortuga Spiced Rum
1-1/4 cups heavy cream
1 tablespoon confectioner's sugar
1 teaspoon vanilla extract

In a small bowl, combine the well-drained pineapple, papaya, mace, rum and brown sugar and stir well. Chill for several hours. About an hour before serving, whip the heavy cream with the confectioner's sugar and vanilla extract and chill for an hour. When ready to serve, gently fold the whipped cream into the fruit mixture.

Grand Fool with Strawberries, Mangoes & Rum

Spoon this rich creamy confection over individual warm shortcakes or serve it in champagne glasses by itself – it should be served the same day it's made or it will separate. This recipe makes enough for a party – about 12 servings.

1 8-ounce package cream cheese
1-1/2 cups whole milk
2 packages white chocolate flavor instant pudding mix (4 serving size)
1/4 cup Tortuga Dark Rum
1 8 ounce container frozen whipped topping, thawed
1 cup lightly toasted sliced almonds
3 cups sliced fresh strawberries plus 1/2 cup for top garnish
2 tablespoons sugar
2 cups diced, peeled ripe mangos

Combine the sliced strawberries and sugar and stir well. Let stand 10 minutes then add the mangos and stir again. In large bowl, beat the cream cheese with electric mixer until light, and add 1/2 cup milk. Beat until very smooth. Add rum, remaining milk and both boxes of pudding mix and beat until smooth again. Fold in the mangos and sliced strawberries and then stir in the whipped topping mix and 1/2 cup toasted almonds. Spoon the mixture into a 3-quart bowl and top with remaining toasted almonds and sliced strawberries for garnish. Refrigerate at least six hours until set.

Tortuga Rum Flan

Throughout the Caribbean, this popular custard appears with variations from island to island. A hint of dark rum makes this recipe memorable.

1/2 cup sugar
1 tablespoon water
1 –14 ounce can sweetened condensed milk
2 cups milk
4 large eggs
1/4 teaspoon mace or nutmeg
1/8 teaspoon cinnamon
1 teaspoon vanilla extract
2 tablespoons Tortuga Dark Rum

Preheat oven to 350. Spray 8 custard cups (6 ounce) with regular nonstick vegetable oil spray. Arrange in a large baking pan. In a small saucepan, combine the sugar and water and cook over medium high heat, stirring constantly, until sugar dissolves and begins to caramelize. Remove from heat and divide evenly among the custard cups, making sure the caramel coats the bottom of each cup.

In food processor or blender, combine all remaining ingredients and process until very smooth. Divide evenly among the 8 cups in the baking pan and place in oven. Add enough hot water to pan to reach halfway up custard cups. Bake 30 minutes or until a knife inserted in the center of custard comes out clean. Remove cups from pan carefully and cool on wire rack, then refrigerate covered, overnight (or at least 8 hours).

When ready to serve, carefully run a rubber spatula around the edge of each custard to loosen and place the cup upside down on a dessert plate and remove. Scrape out any remaining caramel onto the flan.

Rum Almond Crème Brulee

3 tablespoons Tortuga Dark Rum
3/4 cup sugar
9 large egg yolks
1-1/2 teaspoon almond extract
2-1/2 cups heavy whipping cream
Hot water
6 tablespoons light brown sugar
1/2 cup sliced almonds, toasted

Preheat oven to 350 degrees. Place six 3/4 cup custard cups or soufflé dishes in a baking or roasting pan. Using wire whisk, in 2-quart bowl or larger beat together egg yolks, sugar, rum and almond extract until well blended and smooth. Set aside and in a medium non-stick saucepan bring the whipping cream to a slow boil, stirring to prevent scorching. Remove from heat and gradually whisk the hot cream into the egg/ sugar mixture, blending smoothly. Pour the custard into the six dishes in even amounts. Add hot water carefully to roasting pan to come halfway up sides of custard cups. Bake about 30 minutes, until just set in the center of each. Remove from oven and remove cups from hot water and cool completely, then cover with plastic wrap and refrigerate at least 6 hours. The custards can be prepared up to 2 days ahead if refrigerated.

When ready to serve, lightly toast almonds by placing in 350 oven for about 10 minutes. Do not allow to scorch. Remove and cool. Preheat oven broiler and place custards on baking sheet. Sprinkle each with 1 tablespoon of brown sugar and broil, rotating the baking sheet so custards brown evenly – about 2 minutes, until sugar melts and turns dark brown. Sprinkle each brulee with toasted almonds and cool slightly before serving.

Tortuga Tortoni

This simple but elegant dessert is based on a classic recipe –one you seldom see on menus today.

1/3 cup Tortuga Dark Rum
1-14 ounce can sweetened condensed milk
3 large egg yolks, beaten
1 tablespoon vanilla extract
2/3 cup coconut macaroon crumbs
3/4 cup shelled, chopped pistachios or toasted almonds, slivered or chopped
1/2 cup maraschino cherries, drained and chopped
2 cups heavy cream

Line a 12-cup regular muffin tin with foil liners. In small bowl, whip the heavy cream until medium soft peaks form. In large bowl, combine the rum, condensed milk, egg yolks, vanilla, macaroon crumbs, nuts and cherries and stir until well mixed. Fold in the whipped cream. Spoon the mixture into the individual foil-lined cups, filling 3/4 full. Use additional muffin tin if necessary. Cover tightly with plastic wrap and freeze at least 6 hours and let stand a few minutes at room temperature before serving. Store uneaten tortonis in freezer.

Cakes

How to Glaze a Cake

There are two ways to glaze a cake with rum glaze. Most recipes advise using a fork to prick the warm cake all over. I recommend using a wooden skewer or even an ice pick instead. Most fork tines are too dull to pierce the cake's surface cleanly and not cause cracks from the pressure. A skewer will pierce the cake much deeper – allowing better absorption of the glaze.

You can let the cake cook in the pan about 30 minutes, then prick the surface all over with an ice pick and gradually spoon the glaze over it. When you have used all the glaze, or the amount desired, let the cake sit in the pan for two hours before removing.

Or, you can remove the cake from the pan, invert it onto a round cooling rack and position it on top of a larger plate – not onto the final serving plate itself. Drizzle the glaze, spoonful by spoonful, slowly over the cake – don't just pour it from the pan. Then remove the cake and rack, and use a rubber spatula to scrape the collected glaze back into the cup and repeat until you have used as much glaze as desired. When you're done, gently lift the glazed cake onto a clean platter and let sit for an hour or more to let the glaze seep in.

Either way, the leftover glaze will not collect in a bug puddle on the serving plate and soak the flat bottom of the cake, creating a soggy mess and making it almost impossible to serve in neat slices.

Rum-Kissed Key Lime Coconut Cake

3/4 cup butter, softened
2 cups sugar
4 eggs
1 tablespoon grated lemon peel
1-1/3 cups lemon or key lime flavored lowfat yogurt
2 tablespoons fresh key lime juice
3 cups flour
3/4 teaspoon salt
1-1/4 teaspoons baking powder
3/4 teaspoon baking soda
2 teaspoons ground ginger
1/2 teaspoon ground coriander
1-1/2 cups fresh coconut, finely chopped in processor
2 tablespoons Tortuga Dark Rum
1 teaspoon lemon extract
1 cup chopped pistachios or pecans

Preheat oven to 325 F. Spray two –6 cup bundt pans or one 12-cup bundt pan with Baker's Joy. Combine the coconut with 2 tablespoons rum and stir to mix. Set aside. Sift together the flour, baking powder, baking soda, salt, coriander and ginger. In large mixing bowl, cream the butter and sugar until light. Beat in eggs, one at a time, mixing well after each, then add the lime peel and lime juice. Add the flour mixture alternately with the yogurt, blending well after each addition. Stir in the lemon extract, coconut and nuts. Spoon batter into prepared pans and bake for about 30 minutes or until toothpick inserted in center come out clean. Remove from oven and cool in pan 10 minutes, then invert onto serving plate and cool to room temperature. Frost or glaze with one of the following. Refrigerate several hours to let flavors blend.

Lime Cream Cheese Frosting

2 cups confectioner's sugar, sifted
1/4 cup butter or margarine, softened
3 tablespoons cream cheese, softened (half a 3-oz. package)
1-1/2 teaspoons grated key lime zest
1/2 tablespoon Tortuga Dark Rum
1 tablespoon fresh key lime juice

Combine all ingredients in medium deep bowl and beat until smooth. You can omit the rum and increase the lime juice to 2-1/2 tablespoons. When cake is cool to the touch, frost as desired.

Lime Rum Glaze

1/3 cup butter or margarine
2 cups confectioner's sugar
1/2 teaspoon grated key lime zest
2 tablespoons Tortuga Dark Rum
1-2 tablespoons key lime juice

In medium saucepan, melt the butter or margarine over medium low heat. Blend in the sugar and lime zest and stir to blend. Stir in the rum and add lime juice until the right thickness – do not let glaze become too watery. Heat for another minute, stirring until smooth. Let cool until lukewarm. Prick cake all over with a fork or ice pick. Spoon glaze over the top of cake and let it trickle down the sides.

Cayman Banana Colada Pound Cake

1 cup butter, softened
3 cups sugar
1/2 cup Tortuga Dark Rum
2- 1/2 cups grated or finely chopped (in food processor) fresh coconut
1 cup coconut milk
2 teaspoons vanilla extract
3 large eggs
3 cups flour
2 teaspoons baking powder
1/2 teaspoon salt
1/2 teaspoon ground mace
1 teaspoon ground coriander
1-3/4 cups pureed very ripe bananas (about 4 medium)

In a small bowl, pour the rum over the coconut and stir well to mix. Let sit while you prepare the batter. Preheat oven to 350 degrees. Spray a 12-inch bundt pan with Baker's Joy, or grease and flour it.

Cream the butter and sugar thoroughly. Blend in the eggs, one at a time, then coconut milk and vanilla. Combine flour, baking powder, spices and salt in a separate bowl and mix with wire whisk to blend. Add gradually to butter mixture and blend well. Add the pureed bananas and blend well, then stir in coconut until blended. Pour into prepared pan and bake at 350 for an hour or until cakes is light golden brown and toothpick inserted in center comes out clean. Cake may crack – you can also to the touch test and if the cracked area springs back and does not look soggy, cake is done. For best flavor, refrigerate several hours. For a very rich cake, top with Rum Glaze:

Rum Glaze:
1/4 cup butter
2 tablespoons water
1/2 cup sugar
1/4 cup Tortuga Dark Rum

In saucepan, melt butter over medium heat. Stir in water and sugar and bring to a boil, stirring constantly, and cook for five minutes. Remove from heat and stir in rum – mixture will foam up, so continue stirring. Allow to cool at least 30 minutes before using. With an ice pick or skewer, prick cake all over and spoon the glaze over until all is absorbed or you have used as much as desired. Refrigerate any leftover glaze.

Fantasy Island Rum Fudge Cake

This incredibly rich cake is a chocolate lover's fantasy and the subtle rum flavor intensifies the experience. Serve with whipped cream or vanilla ice cream.

1 cup unsalted butter or margarine
1 cup sugar
1 cup light brown sugar, packed firm
3 large eggs
2 teaspoons almond extract
1 teaspoon vanilla extract
1/2 cup Tortuga Dark Rum
1-1/2 cups vanilla yogurt
2-1/2 cups flour
3/4 cup Hershey's European Style Dutch Cocoa
1 teaspoon salt
2 teaspoons baking soda
1 cup sweetened shredded coconut
1 cup chopped pecans
1 cup white chocolate morsels
Chocolate Rum Glaze (See **Rum Sauces and Uncommon Condiments** for recipe)

Preheat oven to 350 degrees. Spray a 10-inch tube pan or 12-cup bundt pan with Baker's Joy. Cream together butter or margarine and sugars until light. Add eggs, one at a time, beating on low speed after each. Add almond and vanilla extracts and rum. In separate bowl, mix together flour, cocoa, salt, baking soda with wire whisk until blended. Add flour mixture alternately to batter with yogurt, blending after each addition. Stir in coconut, pecans and chocolate morsels until blended. Pour into prepared pan and bake for an hour or until top of cake springs back. It may crack in center and appear moist when done. Prepare glaze (see recipe). Allow cake to cool for 10 minutes then remove from pan and cool 10 minutes longer. Prick cake with fork all over and then spoon glaze over. Use all of the glaze. Refrigerate cake at least an hour before serving. Cake should be stored in refrigerator to maintain fudgy texture and moistness. Serve with whipped cream or vanilla ice cream.

Siesta Pina Colada Cake

I cheat in this delicious recipe and use a prepared cake mix. In theory, that shortcut leaves time for a quick tropical afternoon siesta before or after baking.

4 large eggs
1 package French Vanilla cake mix (18.5 ounce box) without pudding
1 3-3/4 ounce package toasted coconut or coconut cream instant pudding mix
1/2 cup unsweetened pineapple juice
1/2 cup Tortuga Dark Rum
1 teaspoon coconut extract
1/2 cup canola oil
1-1/2 cups shredded sweetened coconut
1/3 cup shredded sweetened coconut (for topping)

Preheat oven to 325. Spray a 12-cup bundt pan with Baker's Joy (or grease and flour pan). In large mixing bowl, beat the eggs until light and lemon colored. Add cake mix, pudding, pineapple juice, rum, coconut extract and oil and beat with electric mixer on medium speed for 2 minutes, scraping sides and bottom of bowl with rubber spatula to insure even blending. Add 1-1/2 cup coconut and beat on low just until blended, then scrape beaters to return any coconut to batter. Pour into prepared pan and bake for 50-55 minutes or until toothpick inserted in center comes out clean. Remove from oven and cool in pan on wire rack for 10 minutes, then invert onto serving platter. When still (but only) lukewarm, drizzle with one of these glazes, then sprinkle remaining coconut over top. Flavor improves if made a day ahead of time and rum glaze is allowed to permeate the cake.

Creamy Glaze:

1 tablespoon half and half
1 teaspoon butter
1 cup sifted confectioner's sugar
1-1/2 tablespoons Tortuga Coconut Rum

In small saucepan combine the milk and butter and heat until butter is melted. Add the sugar and rum and stir until smooth. Add a little more rum if you want thinner glaze. Use a spoon to drizzle evenly over cooled cake

Rum Glaze

1/2 cup (1 stick) butter or margarine
1/4 cup pineapple juice
1 cup sugar
1/2 cup Tortuga Dark Rum

Melt the butter in a small saucepan and stir in the pineapple juice and sugar. Stir well and bring to a low boil for five minutes, stirring constantly as mixture thickens. Remove from heat and stir in the rum, stirring constantly as glaze foams. When cake cools to lukewarm, prick all over with a fork and drizzle with glaze, allowing cake to absorb each spoonful before adding more. Repeat until all glaze is used or you have used as much as desired. Store any leftover glaze in refrigerator. Sprinkle remaining coconut over top. Let sit, covered, overnight for best flavor. Cake will keep in refrigerator for at least a week.

Cheesecakes in Paradise

When I first started islandhopping , I was surprised to find cheesecake among the sweets Caribbean people craved. Hardly what you would call a traditional Caribbean dish, this rich dessert has fans from Honduras to Guyana with variations as different as the countries themselves. West Indian spices and a sip of rum have turned this celebrated confection into an extraordinary one.

One of the best cheesecakes I have ever eaten was at a restaurant in Kingston, Jamaica 20-some years ago. That's a long way from Lindy's. It was rumored to be a favorite of the legendary late Prime Minister Michael Manley. I resurrected the recipe – which gave ingredients only – from a piece of notebook paper rediscovered decades later. I have tried to duplicate that memorable combination of flavors and texture.

Kingstonian Cheesecake

Unexpected additions to a traditional graham cracker crust are just the beginning. Start your Rum Pot now – a spoonful of that traditional West Indian treat is the perfect topping for this rich dessert.

Crust:
2-1/2 cups vanilla wafers, finely ground
1-1/4 cups sweetened flaked coconut
1/2 cup unsalted butter, melted
1 teaspoon grated lime or lemon zest
1/2 teaspoon grated nutmeg
1/4 teaspoon ground allspice

Filling:
5- 8 ounce packages cream cheese softened to room temperature
1-3/4 cups sugar
5 large eggs
2 large egg yolks
1/3 cup Coco Lopez or other cream of coconut
2 tablespoons Rum Vanilla (see Island Pantry)
1/8 teaspoon salt
3 tablespoons flour
2 teaspoons grated lime zest
1 tablespoon grated orange zest

Preheat oven to 350 degrees. Butter lightly the bottom and inside of a 10-inch springform pan. Wrap the outside with aluminum foil. Make crust by combining all ingredients in a mixing bowl and blending well. Press the crumbs evenly and firmly into the bottom and about 3/4 inch up sides of pan. Bake at 350 for 10 minutes, then cool on wire rack while preparing filling.

In a 6-quart or larger mixing bowl, cream the cream cheese with an electric mixer until very light. Beat in the sugar until smooth, then add the eggs and egg yolks, one at a time, beating well after each addition. Add the Coco Lopez and Rum Vanilla and blend well. Add salt, flour, lime and orange zests and mix thoroughly.

Place a 9 x 13" pan of hot water on the bottom shelf of the oven. Pour the cheesecake mixture into the prepared crust – the pan should not be more than three-quarters full. Place the springform pan on the top shelf above the hot water pan. Bake at 350 for 55-minutes to an hour or until top is just turning golden, edges are slightly puffed, and center area jiggles but is set. Remove from oven, cool five minutes and then refrigerate, uncovered, for at least 12 hours – 24 hours is better.

Decorate with fresh strawberries, mangoes or even better – top each slice with a generous spoonful of **Heavenly West Indian Rum Pot** (see **Comfort Food, Western Caribbean Style**)

Coconut Rum Cheesecake

Crust:
1-1/4 cups finely crushed chocolate graham cracker crumbs
1/2 cup finely chopped cashews or almonds
1/2 cup flaked coconut, toasted
2 tablespoons light brown sugar
1/4 cup unsalted butter, melted

Filling:
4-8 ounce packages cream cheese, softened to room temperature
1-1/2 cups sugar
4 large eggs
1 cup Coco Lopez or other cream of coconut
2 tablespoons flour
1 teaspoon grated key lime zest
1/4 teaspoon salt
1/4 cup Tortuga Coconut Rum
1-1/2 cups sweetened, shredded coconut, toasted
Fresh mango or pineapple chunks

Preheat oven to 350F. Lightly butter bottom and sides of 10-inch springform pan. Wrap the outside of the pan with aluminum foil. Prepare the crust by mixing all ingredients in a medium bowl until well blended. Press the crumb mixture evenly and firmly over the pan bottom only. Bake 10 minutes, then cool on a wire rack.

Make the filling: With an electric mixer, beat the cream cheese in a large mixing bowl until light. Gradually blend in the sugar until smooth. On low speed, add the eggs, one at a time, blending after each, then add the salt, flour, cream of coconut, rum and lime zest on low speed, mixing well.

Place an 8x8' pan of hot water on the bottom shelf of the oven and heat oven another five minutes. Pour filling into prepared crust and bake at 350 for 55 minutes to an hour or until edges are slightly puffed and golden and center is set. Cake will jiggle, but should not have a watery center. Remove from oven, cool 10 minutes on wire rack then refrigerate for at least 12 hours –after cake has chilled thoroughly, you can cover with foil or plastic wrap for remainder of chilling. When ready to serve, run a sharp knife inside the pan rim to loosen cake and remove the side band. Sprinkle cooled cake with coconut and garnish with fresh mango or pineapple chunks if desired.

Rasta Russian Cheesecake

A Rasta Russian (see recipe in **Rum Fête**) is a lethal variation of the classic White Russian. I make no apologies for the ingredients required, or for the rich, creamy, decadent results.

Crust:
1-1/2 cups shortbread cookie crumbs (about 24 finely crushed or processed)
1/2 cup chopped almonds
3 tablespoons unsalted butter, melted
2 tablespoons sugar
or
1-1/2 cups chocolate graham cracker crumbs
1/4 cup sugar
1/2 cup chopped almonds
1/4 cup unsalted butter, melted

Filling:
4- 8 ounce packages cream cheese, softened to room temperature
14 ounce can sweetened condensed milk
4 ounces (30 unwrapped) Hershey's Hugs without nuts, melted until smooth
4 large eggs
2 tablespoons flour
2 tablespoons vanilla extract
1/4 cup heavy cream
1/4 cup Tortuga Coffee Liqueur, Tia Maria or Kahlua
1/4 cup Tortuga Dark Rum

Topping: (Optional)
1 tablespoon Tortuga Coffee Liqueur
1 tablespoon Tortuga Dark Rum
2 tablespoons sugar
1 cup sour cream

Prepare crust: Preheat oven to 350. Grease a 9-inch springform pan lightly with butter and wrap bottom and outside with aluminum foil. Use a food processor to grind the graham crackers into fine crumbs and chop the nuts. Combine cookie crumbs, nuts and sugar in medium bowl and stir well with fork to blend. Add melted butter and mix until well blended. Press crust mix firmly and evenly on bottom of pan. Bake about 10 minutes, or until just golden brown. Remove from oven and cool.

Prepare filling: Reduce heat to 325. With electric mixer, beat cream cheese on medium speed until smooth. Gradually beat in the condensed milk, scraping sides with rubber spatula to be sure cheese and milk blend evenly. On low speed, add eggs, one at a time, blending well after each, then the flour. Blend in the heavy cream, then the melted Hugs. Add vanilla, Tortuga Rum and Coffee Liqueur and mix just until blended.

Place an 8-inch square pan filled 2/3 with hot water in center of bottom oven rack and close oven door. Let oven heat another five minutes before opening again. Pour cheesecake batter into prepared crust and position pan on upper rack, above the water pan. Bake for one hour and 10 minutes, or until top is just turning pale brown, edges are puffed and center is set. Cake may jiggle slightly, but center area should not be watery.

Remove from oven.

If using sour cream topping, increase heat to 400. Prepare topping recipe below and spread over top of cake. Bake another five minutes. Cool cake in pan five minutes on wire rack, and run a sharp knife around the edge, but do not remove from pan. Refrigerate for at least 12 hours uncovered on bottom shelf of refrigerator. If you don't use topping, serve with whipped cream and chopped almonds.

Topping:
Blend sour cream, sugar, rum and coffee liqueur and spread over baked cheesecake. Bake an additional 5 minutes at 400.

Guava Colada Cheesecake

Islanders love the combination of guava and cheese and this recipe is a rich blend of those favorite flavors.

Crust:
1-1/2 cups finely crushed lemon cookies
3 tablespoons butter, melted
1/2 cup shredded sweetened coconut
2 tablespoons sugar

Filling:
1 cup guava paste
1/3 cup Tortuga Dark Rum
4 – 8 ounce packages cream cheese, at room temperature
1-1/3 cups sugar
4 large eggs
1 tablespoon fresh key lime juice
1/2 cup Coco Lopez or other cream of Coconut)
1 teaspoon coconut extract
2 teaspoons grated lime zest

Topping:
Rum Chantilly
Shredded coconut

Preheat oven to 350. Butter bottom and inside of a 9 –inch springform pan and wrap the outside bottom and sides with aluminum foil to prevent leaks.

Make the crust: Mix all ingredients together until well blended, then press the dough evenly over the bottom of the prepared pan, and about 1/2 inch up the sides. Bake the crust for 10 minutes. Remove from oven and cool.

Make the filling: Combine the guava paste, rum and lime juice in a medium saucepan and heat over medium low heat, stirring constantly, until paste melts and mixture is blended. Remove from heat and cool. In a large mixing bowl, cream the cream cheese until smooth, then add the sugar and beat until light. Add the eggs, one at a time, beating well after each. Use a rubber spatula to scrape the sides of the bowl so that all ingredients are blended. Add the coconut extract, Coco Lopez, guava rum mixture and lime zest and blend until smooth. Pour the filling into the cooled crust. Bake the cheesecake at 350 for 60 –70 minutes, or until center is set. Remove and cool for 20 minutes on a wire rack, then cover with wax paper and chill in refrigerator overnight.

When ready to serve, prepare **Rum Chantilly** (see **Rum Sauces & Uncommon Condiments**) and top each slice with a dollop and a sprinkling of 1 teaspoon shredded coconut.

Pies

Tortuga Key Lime Pie

This is my variation of this popular tropical dessert. Please use only fresh key lime juice – or don't bother with this recipe. This makes a tart pie – if you like a very tart pie increase the lime juice to 2/3 cup. And never, ever add green food coloring. This pie is meant to be pale yellow!

Crust:
1-1/4 cups finely crushed graham cracker or crisp lemon cookie crumbs
3 tablespoons butter, melted
2 tablespoons light brown sugar, packed
1/2 teaspoon grated nutmeg
1/2 teaspoon grated lime zest

Filling:
4 large egg yolks
1 teaspoon grated lime zest
1 14- ounce can sweetened condensed milk
1/2 cup plus 2 tablespoons fresh key lime juice
1 tablespoon Tortuga Light Rum
2 dashes Angostura Bitters

Topping:
1 cup heavy cream
1 tablespoon confectioner's sugar
1 tablespoon Tortuga Light Rum

For crust: Preheat oven to 350 degrees. Combine ingredients and blend well. Press into 9-inch pie pan, covering bottom and sides to top. Bake for about 8 -10 minutes and then remove from oven and allow to cool at least 20 minutes. (If you're intimidated by making your own crust, use a 9-inch prepared graham cracker crust.)

For filling: Use an electric mixer to beat egg yolks and lime zest at high speed until slightly thickened, about 2 minutes. On low speed, gradually add condensed milk, blending well, then add lime juice, bitters and rum, mixing until just blended. Pour mixture into the cooled pie crust and bake at 350 about 12-15 minutes or until center is firm and set.

Allow pie to cool 20 minutes on rack, then refrigerate uncovered at least four hours, or store in freezer. When ready to serve, whip the heavy cream, sugar and rum until it forms stiff peaks. Mound onto the pie and spread evenly.

The Original Key Lime Pie

Old "conchs," Key West natives, are key lime pie purists look down their noses on cooks who use condensed milk. They swear this is the original, and still the best recipe, more like a lime curd.

1 baked 9-inch pastry pie crust, not graham cracker

Filling:
3 tablespoons cornstarch
1 cup sugar
1/4 teaspoon salt
2 cups milk
4 large yolks
1 teaspoon grated key lime zest
1/3 cup fresh key lime juice
2 tablespoons Tortuga Light Rum
2 tablespoons butter

Combine the first three ingredients in a large heavy saucepan and stir to blend. Gradually add the milk, stirring until blended. Over medium heat, cook the mixture, stirring constantly, until it thickens and comes to a full boil. Boil for one minute, stirring constantly, then remove from heat. In a small bowl, beat the egg yolks on high until thickened. Measure out 2/3 cup of the milk mixture and stir quickly into the egg yolks, until blended. Add the egg mixture to the custard in saucepan, stirring constantly. Return to stove and cook over medium heat, stirring constantly, for 3 minutes. Remove from heat again and stir in the lime zest, lime juice, rum and butter. Stir quickly to blend, then spoon into the baked pastry shell and chill the pie for least four hours. Top with **meringue** or serve each slice with a dollop of **Rummy Whipped Cream** or **Rum Chantilly**.

Meringue:
4 eggs whites
1/2 teaspoon cream of tartar
1/4 cup sugar plus 1 tablespoon
1 tablespoon Tortuga Light Rum

Preheat oven to 350 F. Beat the egg whites and cream of tart on high about 1 minutes. Gradually beat in the sugar, beating in one tablespoon at a time, then the rum and beat until stiff peaks form, about 3-4 minutes. Spread the meringue in swirls over the top of the lime filling, right to the edge, sealing the pie. Bake the pie for 12-15 minutes until meringue is lightly browned.

West Indian Banana Cream Pie

You've probably never tasted banana cream pie this wicked.

9 inch flaky pie crust, baked and cooled
1/4 cup plus 1 tablespoon flour
1/2 cup granulated sugar
1/4 teaspoon salt
1/2 teaspoon ground coriander
1/2 teaspoon ground mace or nutmeg
3 large egg yolks

2 cups milk
2 tablespoons butter, cut into two pieces
1/2 teaspoon almond extract
3 tablespoons Tortuga Dark Rum
1-1/2 cups heavy cream, divided
6 ripe applebananas (finger bananas) or 3 large ripe bananas, sliced into 1/4 inch rounds
1/2 cup shredded sweetened coconut, lightly toasted
1 tablespoon Tortuga Dark Rum
1 tablespoon confectioner's sugar

Sift together the flour, sugar, salt and spices into a large mixing bowl. Using electric mixer on low speed, beat in the egg yolks one at a time, blending well after each addition. In a small saucepan, combine the milk and butter and heat over medium heat, stirring several times, until butter melts and bubble begin to form around the edge of the saucepan. Remove from heat and slowly add the milk to the flour mixture, using a wire whisk to blend ingredients quickly and evenly. Add the almond extract and rum and blend well. Use a rubber spatula to return the mixture to the saucepan and bring almost to a boil, then reduce heat to low. Simmer, stirring constantly, until filling is smooth and thickened, like a heavy custard. Remove from heat and cool until lukewarm.

In small deep mixing bowl, beat 1/2 cup heavy cream until stiff peaks form. Use rubber spatula to fold whipped cream gently but thoroughly into custard. Spread 1/4 of the custard over the bottom of the pie crust, and then sprinkle with 2 tablespoons coconut and a layer of banana slices. Repeat until all ingredients are used, ending with a top layer of bananas. Beat the remaining 1 cup heavy cream with remaining 1 tablespoon rum and confectioner's sugar until stiff peaks form and spread over pie in swirls, using a clean spatula. Chill pie for four hours before serving.

Caribe Black Bottom Pie

I've given this Southern US dessert classic a Caribbean accent with coconut, nutmeg and dark rum.

Crust:
1-1/2 cups finely ground gingersnaps
3 tablespoons butter, melted
1 tablespoon sugar

Custard filling:
3/4 cup sugar
2 tablespoons cornstarch
1/4 teaspoon salt
2-1/2 cups milk
3 large egg yolks
6 ounces semisweet chocolate, chopped
1/2 cup sweetened shredded coconut, lightly toasted
2 tablespoons butter, softened
2 tablespoons Tortuga Dark Rum
1 teaspoon vanilla extract
1/4 teaspoon nutmeg

Topping:
3/4 cup heavy cream
2 tablespoons confectioner's sugar
1 tablespoons Tortuga Dark Rum
6 ounces sweet chocolate (any sweet kind) for shavings

Preheat oven to 350 degrees. In a small bowl, combine crumbs, sugar and melted butter. Stir until well blended and press mixture into bottom and sides of ungreased 9-inch pie pan. Bake for 8 minutes. Remove pie pan and cool on wire rack.

For custard, combine sugar, cornstarch and salt in heavy saucepan and stir to mix well. Add 1/2 cup milk and whisk with wire whisk (NOT spoon) until smooth. Add remaining milk and eggs yolks and whisk again until smooth. Over medium-high heat, cook custard while whisking constantly until it comes to a slow boil. Keep whisking and cook for 1 minute. Remove from heat.

In small bowl, mix 1 cup of custard and chopped chocolate and stir until chocolate melts and mixture is smooth. Pour into cooled pie crust and spread evenly. Add 2 tablespoons butter to remaining warm custard and stir until blended. Stir in the vanilla, rum, nutmeg and toasted coconut. Gently pour this mixture over the chocolate custard. Chill the pie for 8 hours or overnight.

An hour before serving, prepare topping: Using electric mixer, beat heavy cream and confectioner's sugar in small bowl until soft peaks form. Add rum and beat until stiff. Spread over chilled pie. Make chocolate shavings by using a sharp vegetable peeler to shave strips from chocolate pieces and sprinkle over topping. Chill pie in refrigerator until ready to serve.

Caribbean Rum Cashew Pie

Another sinful creation, using the Caribbean's native cashews instead of pecans.

Crust for 9-inch pie:
1-1/2 cups flour
1/2 teaspoon salt
1/4 cup vegetable shortening, chilled
1/4 cup butter, chilled
1 large egg, lightly beaten
2-3 tablespoons ice water

Filling:
2 tablespoons unsalted butter, melted and cooled
1 cup sugar
3 large eggs, lightly beaten
1 teaspoon almond extract
1 cup dark Karo corn syrup
1/4 cup Tortuga Dark Rum
1 cup roasted unsalted cashew halves

For Crust: Sift together flour and salt into medium bowl. Using a pastry cutter or two knives cut in the chilled shortening and butter into the flour until mixture resembles coarse crumbs. Add the beaten egg and blend with fork, then add just enough ice water, stirring with fork until the dough holds together. Form a ball with the dough, wrap in plastic wrap and chill for 2 hours. Remove from refrigerator and on a floured board, roll dough into a 12" circle. Carefully place rolled dough into 9-inch pie pan and pinch edges.

Preheat oven to 375F and **make the filling**. Beat together the melted butter, sugar, eggs, corn syrup, vanilla extract and rum in large bowl, mixing until smooth and well blended. Pour filling into the unbaked pie shell. Spread cashew halves evenly on top. Bake for 35-40 minutes or until knife inserted in center comes out clean. Cool completely for 30 minutes room temperature before slicing. Serves 6.

Ginger Rum Pumpkin Pecan Pie

Caribbean people have grown to love pumpkin pie and add their own spice accents to this traditional favorite. Surprise guests at your next holiday dinner with this recipe.

1-9 inch unbaked deep dish pie crust, (pastry, not graham cracker)

Filling:
2 large eggs
1- 15 ounce can pumpkin
1/2 cup light brown sugar, firmly packed
1/4 cup granulated sugar
1 tablespoon flour
1/2 teaspoon salt
1 tablespoon grated fresh gingerroot
1 teaspoon cinnamon
1/4 teaspoon nutmeg
1/4 teaspoon ground allspice
3 tablespoons Tortuga Dark Rum
1 –14 oz can evaporated milk

Preheat oven to 400 F. In a small bowl, combine the sugars, flour salt and spices and mix well. In a separate large bowl, beat the eggs, and then blend in the canned pumpkin, rum and the sugar and spice mixture. Mix well, then gradually beat in the evaporated milk on low speed. Pour pie mixture into prepared crust. Bake at 400 for 40 minutes then spread the Pecan Rum Glaze (recipe follows) over the top and bake another 15 minutes until pie is set. Remove from oven and cool on a wire rack until pie reaches room temperature (about 2 hours) then serve.

Rum-Pecan Glaze
1/2 cup chopped pecans
1/3 cup light brown sugar, firmly packed
2 teaspoons dark corn syrup
1 tablespoon Tortuga Dark Rum

Combine all ingredients in a small bowl and blend well.

Island Breads

Breads and flat cakes are among the Caribbean's and America's oldest and most important foods. The Carib Indians considered cassava bread sacred. Simple cornmeal cakes sustained the Arawaks and Mayans. Much later, the introduction of sugar to the New World opened up endless possibilities for island cooks. English plantation owners imported recipes for breads from home, as did immigrants to Colonial America. A tot of rum made its way into many spice buns and tea breads – often substituted for brandy, which was used as flavoring long before vanilla extract.

Jamaica's durable hard-dough bread, fried johnnycakes, dense coco bread, banana bread and corn breads are enduring Western Caribbean favorites. So is cornbread in its many forms, one of this hemisphere's oldest recipes. Simple corn cakes were eaten by the Amerindians and Native American Indians, who taught white Europeans what to do with corn. Today every island has its own favorite variations of this popular bread, some dense, moist and spicy, others flat and fried like American hoecakes.

Sweet Caribbean Cornbread

3/4 cups fine ground yellow corn meal
1 cup flour
1/4 cup dark brown sugar
2 teaspoons baking powder
1/2 teaspoon salt
1/2 teaspoon nutmeg
1/2 teaspoon cinnamon
1/4 cup butter, melted and cooled
1/2 cup milk
1/2 cup coconut milk
2 tablespoons Tortuga Rum Liqueur or Dark Rum
2 eggs, beaten
1/2 cup finely chopped fresh coconut

Preheat oven to 400F. Grease or lightly spray with vegetable oil spray a 9-inch square baking pan. Combine the flour, cornmeal, sugar, baking powder, baking soda, salt and spices in a large mixing bowl and mix well. Combine both kinds of milk, melted butter, rum and the eggs and blend well and gradually add to the cornmeal mixture. Stir in the coconut and mix well, then pour batter into prepared pan and bake at 400 for 25-30 minutes or until toothpick inserted in center comes out clean and top is light golden brown.

Peppered Cornbread

A tiny amount of Scotch bonnet pepper gives a surprising bite to this recipe – warn your guests who are pepper-sensitive.

1 cup flour
1 cup fine yellow cornmeal
1 tablespoon baking powder
3 tablespoons sugar
1/2 teaspoon garlic powder
1/2 teaspoon garlic pepper
1/2 teaspoon salt
1 large egg
1 cup milk
2 tablespoons sour cream
1/4 cup butter or margarine, melted
1/4 red Scotch bonnet pepper, seeded, deveined and minced fine or 2 teaspoons Tortuga Hell-Fire Hot Pepper Sauce
1 teaspoon grated orange zest

Preheat oven to 400. Lightly spray a 9 inch square pan with butter flavored vegetable oil spray. In medium mixing bowl, whisk together flour, cornmeal, baking powder, sugar, dry spices and salt. In another bowl , beat egg lightly, then stir in milk, sour cream, and melted butter. Stir in hot pepper or pepper sauce and orange zest. Add milk mix to flour mixture and stir just until ingredients are combined. Spoon batter in greased pan and bake 20 minutes until golden brown and toothpick inserted in center comes out clean. Makes 9 squares.

Pina Colada Bread

1 cup fresh coconut, chopped fine in food processor
2 tablespoons Tortuga Dark Rum
2-1/2 cups flour
2 teaspoons baking powder
1 teaspoon baking soda
1 teaspoon salt
3/4 cup sugar
1 large egg, lightly beaten
3/4 cup pineapple juice
1/4 cup coconut milk
2 teaspoons vanilla extract
1/4 cup canola or other vegetable oil

Preheat oven to 350 F. Grease a 9' x 5' inch loaf pan or 6-cup mini bundt pan. Combine the coconut and rum and stir to mix well. Let stand while preparing the batter. In a large mixing bowl, combine the flour, baking powder, baking soda, salt and sugar. Make a well in the center. In separate bowl, mix together the egg, oil, pineapple juice, coconut milk and vanilla. Stir in coconut and rum mixture. Pour this into the well in the flour mixture and stir just until combined. Pour batter into prepared pan and bake at 350 F for 45 minutes or until toothpick inserted in center comes out clean. Remove from oven and cool 10 minutes in the pan, then remove and place on wire rack to cool. For a richer bread, use the following glaze:

Glaze:
1/4 cup butter
2 tablespoons pineapple juice
1/2 cup sugar
1/4 cup Tortuga Dark Rum

In saucepan, melt butter over medium heat. Stir in pineapple juice and sugar and bring to a boil, stirring constantly, and boil for five minutes. Remove from heat and stir in rum – mixture will foam up, so continue stirring. Return to heat and cook another minute over medium heat, stirring constantly. Allow to cool at least 30 minutes before using. With a fork or ice pick, prick bread all over and spoon the glaze over until all is absorbed or you have used as much as desired. Refrigerate any leftover glaze.

Rum Raisin Banana Bread

1/2 cup raisins (golden are best)
3 tablespoons Tortuga Dark Rum
1-1/4 cups flour
1 teaspoon baking soda
1/2 teaspoon nutmeg
1/2 teaspoon salt
1 cup sugar
1/2 cup Crisco or other vegetable shortening
1 cup mashed very ripe bananas (about 3 medium)
2 eggs, lightly beaten

Combine the raisins and rum and let stand for at least an hour. Preheat oven to 350. Spray an 8-1/2 x 4-1/2 inch loaf pan with Baker's Joy or grease and flour. In small mixing bowl, combine the flour, baking soda, nutmeg and salt. In large mixing bowl, cream together sugar and shortening, then add eggs and bananas. Stir in raisins with remaining rum. Add the dry ingredients, and beat just until batter is blended. Spoon into the prepared pan and bake at 350 for 35- 40 minutes, or until toothpick inserted in center comes out clean. Cool bread in pan for 10 minutes, then remove and cool on wire rack. Flavor improves if refrigerated overnight to allow rum to permeate loaf.

Cayman Apple Banana Nut Bread

Apple bananas are small, sweet bananas with a taste that hints of ripe apple. They are hard to find outside of the Caribbean, and you can substitute very ripe "regular" bananas from your supermarket. This is my recipe which won a Blue Ribbon at the Cayman Islands Agricultural Show a few years ago.

3 cups flour
1-1/2 teaspoons baking powder
1-1/2 teaspoons baking soda
1 teaspoon salt
1 teaspoon ground coriander
1/2 teaspoon nutmeg
1 cup margarine
2 cups white sugar
3/4 cup light brown sugar (packed)
4 large eggs
1 cup lowfat vanilla yogurt
1 tablespoon vanilla extract
2 tablespoons Tortuga Dark Rum
2 cups mashed ripe apple bananas –about a dozen small (2-3 inch long).
1 cup sweetened shredded coconut
1/3 cup old fashioned oats
2 cups chopped walnuts

Preheat oven to 350 degrees. Spray 12-cup bundt pan or two 6-cup mini bundts with Baker's Joy or lightly grease and flour. Combine flour, baking soda, baking powder, salt and dry spices in small bowl and use wire whisk to blend. In large bowl, using electric mixer, cream margarine and sugars until light. Add eggs, one at a time, blending on medium speed. Blend in yogurt, vanilla and rum, then bananas. Gradually add flour mixture blending on low speed. Stir in oats, coconut and nuts until just blended. Pour batter into prepared pan and bake approximately 1 hour until toothpick inserted in center comes out clean, or bread springs back from touch. Remove from oven and cool in pan for 10 minutes, then invert onto serving plate and cool completely on wire rack.

Store bread tightly wrapped in refrigerator and it will keep for a two weeks. When completely cool, the bundt style allows you to cut thin slices easily for tea sandwiches— use flavored cream cheese filling.

Fresh Coconut Bread

3 cups flour
3 teaspoons baking powder
1 teaspoon salt
1 cup sugar
2 cups grated or finely chopped (in food processor) fresh coconut
2 eggs, beaten
1 cup evaporated milk
2 teaspoons Tortuga Dark Rum
1/2 cup butter, melted and cooled

Preheat oven to 350. Spray a 10-inch tube pan or two 8 x 4 " loaf pans with Baker's Joy or grease and flour. In large mixing bowl, combine the flour, baking powder and salt, then stir in the coconut and sugar. Make a well in the center. Combine the butter, milk, eggs and rum and stir. Pour into the well in the flour mixture and mix lightly, just until blended. Divide between the two loaf pans and bake at 350 for about 50 minutes, or until toothpick inserted in center comes out clean. Cool bread in pans for 10 minutes, then remove and cool on wire racks.

Coconut Johnny Cakes

Humble, simple Johnny cakes are a favorite throughout the Caribbean and each island's recipe varies slightly. This is my coconut version and delicious baked or fried.

2 cups self-rising flour
1 tablespoon sugar
1/4 cup solid vegetable shortening (like Crisco)
1/4 cup grated or shredded coconut
1/2 - 3/4 cup coconut milk

Combine flour and sugar in small bowl. Using pastry blender or two knives, cut the Crisco into the dry mixture until mixture resembles fine crumbs. Add the coconut and stir, then add enough coconut milk to make a stiff dough. Flour your hands and pinch off dough to shape into 2 inch cakes. Fry in hot oil in heavy skillet until puffed and brown on both sides. (You can also bake cakes on greased baking sheet at 425 for 10-12 minutes.) Serve hot. Serves 4 , maybe.

West Indian Pumpkin Bread

This delicious island pumpkin bread is made from our local pumpkin, or calabaza, which tastes similar to Hubbard squash. You can use canned "pie pumpkin" but the flavor will be different.

1/2 cup golden raisins (or chopped dates)
3 tablespoons Tortuga Dark Rum
1-2/3 cups flour
1 teaspoon baking soda
1/4 teaspoon baking powder
3/4 teaspoon salt
1/2 teaspoon cinnamon + 1/2 teaspoon ground allspice
1/3 cup Crisco or other solid vegetable shortening
2/3 cup sugar
2/3 cup light brown sugar, packed
2 eggs, lightly beaten
1/3 cup coconut milk
1 cup cooked, mashed West Indian pumpkin
1/2 cup chopped walnuts

Combine raisins and dark rum and let sit for several hours until raisins are plump. (For a richer bread, substitute 1/2 cup chopped dates for raisins.) Preheat oven to 350F. Grease and flour or spray with Baker's Joy a 9 x 5 x 3 inch loaf pan. In a medium mixing bowl, using a wire wisk or fork, whisk together flour, baking soda, baking powder, salt and dry spices. In a large mixing bowl cream together the shortening and sugars until light, then blend in eggs and coconut milk. Add pumpkin, then stir in walnuts and raisins. Add the flour mixture and stir with a large spoon just until batter is blended and lumps disappear. Spoon batter into prepared pan and bake for 45 minutes or until toothpick inserted in center comes out clean. Remove from oven and cool in pan for 10 minutes before turning out loaf onto wire rack to cool completely.

Rum for Breakfast?

Why not? In the Caribbean, the infectious spirit of *Carpe Diem* begins with breakfast and there are no rules for this meal. Islanders start the day with everything from spiced fish and goat soup to spirited breakfast creations that give chefs in the Brunch Capital of New Orleans a rum for their money. Have Caribbean Milk Punch or other refreshments from **Rum Fête** ready.

Caribbean Milk Punch

This is a classic breakfast or brunch drink for special occasions.

1 ounce Tortuga Dark Rum
1 ounce brandy
1 teaspoon sugar
1/2 teaspoon vanilla extract
4 ounces whole milk
Grated nutmeg

Combine all ingredients except nutmeg in a cocktail shaker with ice cubes and shake until foamy. Pour into a tall glass and garnish with grated nutmeg.

Rum Omelet (Omelette au Rhum)

A variation of this recipe was a specialty at Antoine's Restaurant in New Orleans' French Quarter for years, but this is a traditional Caribbean one. You might argue this belongs in the dessert chapter and is not breakfast and brunch fare. I say anyone who eats rum with their eggs – and sets it on fire – can eat it whenever they want!

1 tablespoon Tortuga Dark Rum
3 tablespoons butter
6 large eggs, separated
2 teaspoons sugar plus 1 tablespoon for topping
4 teaspoons half and half
pinch of salt

1/2 cup guava jelly, mango jam or Seville orange marmalade
1/4 cup Tortuga Dark Rum

Beat the egg yolks with 1 tablespoon rum, 2 teaspoons sugar, milk and salt until light, about 2 minutes. In a separate bowl, beat the egg whites until stiff peaks form, then fold into the yolk mixture.

Preheat oven to 400 F. Melt the butter over low heat in a large ovenproof or cast iron skillet. Pour the omelet mixture into the skillet and cook without stirring for 5-6 minutes until the omelet is puffy and slightly brown on the bottom – check this by using a spatula to lift up an edge.

Place the skillet in the oven and sprinkle with remaining 1 tablespoon sugar. Bake until the sugar begins to caramelize and top is light golden brown, about 8 minutes. Remove skillet from oven and using a spatula, carefully slide the whole omelet to a serving platter. While very hot, spread a thin layer of jelly on top or along the rim of the omelet. In a small saucepan, heat the remaining rum until warm (do not boil) then pour evenly over the omelet and ignite with long wooden match. When the flames die down, cut into four large wedges and serve. This is intended as a showy dish, flamed at the table in front of guests.

Banana Tortilla (Tortilla de amarillo)

This old recipe is an unusual breakfast or brunch dish, usually served with a side of spicy meat, such as chorizos or hot sausage. It originated in Cuba, where *tortilla* also means omelet. This should serve 4.

2 tablespoons Tortuga Dark Rum
4 tablespoons butter
4 medium ripe bananas, sliced into 1/4 inch rounds
6 large eggs, separated
6 tablespoons milk
1/2 teaspoon salt
Minced green scallions for garnish

Melt the butter in a large ovenproof or cast iron skillet over medium heat and sauté the banana slices, turning frequently until they are evenly browned. Remove the bananas with a slotted spoon and cover to keep warm.

Preheat oven to 325 F. Beat egg whites until stiff peaks form. In another medium mixing bowl, beat the egg yolks with the milk and salt until well blended. Fold in the egg whites. Heat the skillet again over medium heat and add 2 tablespoons more butter. When butter is bubbling, add the egg mixture and arrange the banana slices on top. Pour the rum evenly over the top and reduce heat to low. Cook until the tortilla is slightly puffed and set. Immediately place the skillet in oven and bake 4-5 minutes or until omelet is lightly browned on top. Sprinkle with scallion and serve, dividing the tortilla into 4 pie-shaped wedges.

RumFest Breakfast Pudding

Here's another delicious breakfast that could double as dessert. It's best served warm, but if you don't think you can handle that much work in the morning, make the pudding the night before, cover and refrigerate like a strata and bake at leisure.

1-16 ounce loaf egg bread or French bread
6 large eggs
1 cup shredded sweetened coconut
1 cup diced mango chunks
1-3/4 cups milk
2 cups half and half
1-1/2 cups sugar
1/4 cup Tortuga Dark Rum
2 tablespoons melted butter
1 teaspoon vanilla extract
1/3 cup slivered almonds or pecan pieces

Spray a 13 x 9 x 2 inch baking dish lightly with butter-flavored vegetable spray or butter lightly. Slice bread into 1-1/4 inch thick slices and place in a single layer in baking dish. Sprinkle the coconut and mango evenly over bread. In a large bowl, combine eggs and all remaining ingredients except nuts and beat until smooth and well blended. Pour egg mixture over the bread and let stand 30 minutes.

Heat oven to 350F. Sprinkle nuts over the pudding. Place baking dish inside a larger roasting pan and place on upper oven rack. Add hot water to the larger pan to a depth of 1 inch. Bake for 30 minutes and then place a sheet of aluminum foil lightly over the top of pudding so it doesn't over-brown. Bake another 15 minutes or until knife inserted in center comes out clean. Serve warm, plain or with Rummy Whipped Cream and a side of spicy sausage.

Tropical Breakfast Bread Pudding

6 slices day old cinnamon raisin bread
1/2 cup shredded sweetened coconut
1-11.5 ounce can evaporated milk
1 tablespoon Tortuga Dark Rum
1/4 teaspoon nutmeg
1/4 cup orange juice concentrate, thawed
3 eggs, beaten
2 tablespoons sugar

Orange Rum Sauce:
1/4 cup orange juice concentrate, thawed
2/3 cup water
1 tablespoon plus 1 teaspoon cornstarch
2 tablespoons Tortuga Gold Rum
1 tablespoon Tortuga Wildflower Honey
Ground nutmeg

If bread is still soft and moist, place in a single layer on a baking sheet and bake at 325F for 10 minutes. Cool, and cut into cubes and set aside.

Spray six –6 ounce glass custard cups with vegetable oil spray. Have a 13 x 9 x 2 inch baking pan handy. Divide the bread cubes evenly among the cups and sprinkle with coconut. In medium mixing bowl, combine the milk, rum, 1/4 cup of the thawed orange juice concentrate, eggs and sugar and beat until mixture is well blended. Pour mixture evenly over bread in each custard cup. Press cubes down lightly until coated with egg-milk mixture and let stand for 15 minutes until liquid is absorbed. Arrange custard cups in the baking pan and place in oven. Carefully pour hot water into the pan to a depth of 1 inch. Bake at 325 F for 35–40 minutes or until knife inserted in center of puddings comes out clean. Remove from oven and remove cups from pan. Cool 15 minutes.

Make the sauce: combine the orange juice concentrate, water, cornstarch, rum, honey and nutmeg in a small saucepan and cook over medium heat, stirring constantly, until mixture begins to boil and thicken. Cook for two minutes, stirring. Remove from heat.

Remove the bread puddings from the cups by running a knife around the edge of each and invert onto individual serving plates. Serve with the warm sauce. Fresh mango chunks are a nice garnish.

Cornmeal Pancakes

This was the first meal I ate in Grand Cayman 25 years ago at the original Beach Club Colony hotel. It was served with warm light molasses laced with rum and New Zealand butter. Breakfast was never the same for me after that.

1/2 cup plus 2 tablespoons flour
1/2 cup yellow cornmeal (3/4 cup for thicker pancakes)
1 teaspoon sugar
3/4 teaspoon salt
1/4 teaspoon cinnamon
1/4 teaspoon nutmeg
1 teaspoon baking powder
1 large egg, beaten
3/4 cup milk
3 tablespoons melted butter or margarine
1 tablespoon vegetable oil

Preheat a griddle or large skillet. In a medium mixing bowl, combine the flour, cornmeal, sugar, salt, nutmeg, cinnamon and baking powder and stir with wire whisk to blend. Add the egg, milk and melted butter all at once and stir until ingredients are blended.

Brush the hot griddle with the oil and drop 2 tablespoons of batter per pancake onto griddle. Cook until bubbles appear around the edges and bottom is lightly browned, then turn with spatula or pancake turn and brown other side lightly. Serve with warm Rum Molasses or Rum Maple Syrup (below).

Rum Molasses
2 tablespoons butter
1/2 cup light molasses
2 teaspoons Tortuga Dark Rum

Combine all ingredients in small saucepan and heat over low heat and stir until butter melts and mixture is blended. Serve warm with pancakes.

Rum Maple Syrup

Add 3 tablespoons Tortuga Dark Rum to a 16-ounce container of maple syrup or breakfast syrup. Seal tightly and turn upside down several times to mix. Mark the container clearly so it is not confused with plain syrup.

Tortuga Rum Raisin French Toast

This makes a rich, custardy recipe, much better if you can find whole loaf raisin bread, and slice 3/4-inch thick pieces. You can substitute thick white bread, egg bread or sourdough bread slices if you prefer.

8 slices cinnamon raisin bread
4 large eggs, beaten
1-1/2 cups half and half or evaporated milk
3 tablespoons Tortuga Dark Rum
1 teaspoon almond or vanilla extract
1 teaspoon grated nutmeg
1 tablespoon brown sugar
3 tablespoons butter or vegetable oil (for griddle)

In a large shallow mixing bowl, use a rotary beater to beat together eggs, half-and-half or milk, rum, extract, nutmeg, and sugar and beat until batter is frothy. Dip each slice of bread into batter long enough to soak completely to center – this will depend on the thickness of the bread, but could take about 5 minutes. Heat the butter or vegetable oil in a large non-stick skillet over medium-low heat. Transfer the bread slices to the pan with a pancake turner or spatula. Cook until golden brown on each side, about 3 minutes – do not crowd the skillet or slices will cook unevenly. Serve immediately with butter and rum maple syrup – or top with fresh diced mangos or bananas.

Banana Mango Fritters

2-1/2 cups flour
1/4 cup sugar
2 tablespoons baking powder
1/8 teaspoon salt
1/2 teaspoon nutmeg
1/2 teaspoon cinnamon
1 large egg
1-1/3 cups milk
2 tablespoons canola oil
2 tablespoons Tortuga Dark Rum
1 cup diced ripe but firm mangos
1 cup diced ripe bananas
Vegetable oil for deep frying
Confectioner's sugar

In a large mixing bowl, sift the flour, sugar, baking powder, salt and spices into a large bowl, In a separate bowl, beat the egg and milk together, then blend in the canola oil and rum. Gradually add the egg mixture to the flour mixture and mix well. Stir in the diced bananas and mangos and let the batter sit for 30 minutes.

In a deep heavy skillet or saucepan, heat 2 inches or more of vegetable oil to medium hot, about 350 F and drop batter by tablespoonfuls into the hot oil. Fry a few fritters at a time, turning until golden brown on all sides. Do not crowd the pan or fritters will not cook evenly inside. Remove from oil with a slotted spoon and drain on paper towels. Sprinkle with confectioners' sugar while still warm and serve.

Sweet Potato Fruit Fritters

When you have leftover sweet potatoes, try this delicious and unusual island creation instead of Johnny cakes with your breakfast.

2 tablespoons Tortuga Dark Rum
2 cups cooked mashed American sweet potatoes
1 cup mashed ripe banana
1 cup crushed pineapple, completely drained
1/4 cup butter, melted
1/2 teaspoon ground nutmeg
1 teaspoon cinnamon
1 cup flour
1 teaspoon baking powder
1/2 teaspoon salt
Confectioner's sugar or sweetened shredded coconut

In a large mixing bowl, beat together the rum, sweet potatoes, banana, pineapple and melted butter until well blended. In separate bowl, combine the flour, baking powder, salt, nutmeg and cinnamon. Gradually add this to the sweet potato mixture, blending well. In a deep saucepan or skillet, heat 2 inches of oil to 375 F. Drop batter by tablespoonfuls into the hot oil and cook until light golden brown. Drain on paper towels and sprinkle with confectioner's sugar or coconut. Serve hot.

Rum Grapefruit Eye-Opener

Grapefruit is another West Indian invention, believed to have originated in Jamaica – that's also where the Royal Navy's daily rum ration was introduced in 1655. "A "tot" or ration of rum was the Royal Navy's way to start the day until 1970. This would have been much healthier and the recipe has been around almost that long.

2 large grapefruit, cut in half
2 oranges or tangerines
2 tablespoons granulated sugar
1/4 cup Tortuga Gold Rum
4 tablespoons dark brown sugar

Line a baking sheet with aluminum foil. With a sharp knife remove the seeds and scoop out the individual grapefruit sections, remove membranes and cut into pieces. Place grapefruit pulp in a medium bowl. Peel the oranges or tangerines and separate into sections, removing seeds and pithy membranes. Coarsely chop the fruits and combine in a medium bowl. Sprinkle with the granulated sugar and rum and stir. (You can increase the rum to 1/2 cup if you want.) Let marinate for 2 hours, stirring occasionally, then spoon the fruit back into the four grapefruit shells and sprinkle each with 1 tablespoon of brown sugar. Place grapefruit on the prepared baking sheet and broil four inches from heat for about 4 minutes, until tops are lightly browned and bubbling. Remove from oven and serve.

Salads from Paradise

This festive selection of original salads is just a hint of the healthy fare you can create in an island Paradise. They are perfect additions to any party menu for guests who want lighter fare.

Jerk Chicken Caesar Salad

The Caribbean accents of spicy jerk chicken, Scotch bonnet pepper and a garnish of carambola make this an unusual and delicious main course.

3/4 cup olive oil
1/4 cup red wine vinegar
6 flat anchovy filets, minced
2 teaspoons fresh minced garlic
1 tablespoon fresh key lime or lemon juice
2 teaspoons Dijon mustard
1 teaspoon ground white pepper
1 teaspoon Tortuga Hell-Fire Hot Pepper sauce
1 cup freshly grated Parmesan cheese
Salt to taste
1 head Romaine lettuce, washed (for 6 servings)
1 ripe carambola (star fruit)
1-1/2 pounds cooked **Jerk Chicken Tenders** (See recipe in **Great Caribbean Cookout**)

Make the dressing: Combine all ingredients from olive oil to pepper sauce in blender or food processor and blend until very smooth. Add the Parmesan cheese and mix again until well blended. Season with additional salt to taste if necessary. Refrigerate several hours until well-chilled.

Chop the jerk chicken into 1/2 inch pieces. Tear romaine lettuce into bite-size pieces into a large salad bowl just before serving. Pour on desired amount of salad dressing and toss. Refrigerate any unused dressing for up to a week. Remove the brown ribs along the sides of the carambola and slice crosswise into thin stars. Divide the salad among six plates, and top with jerk chicken. Arrange carambola slices on top of salad. Have additional grated cheese available for guests.

Paradise Papaya Salad

6 cups mixed salad greens
1 medium ripe papaya, peeled and seeds removed (save for dressing)
Rum Papaya Seed Dressing
Make the dressing recipe below and chill thoroughly. Dice the papaya into half-inch cubes and combine with greens in a large bowl. Toss with the chilled dressing. This recipe should serve 4.

Rum Papaya Seed Dressing

A hint of rum wakes up this versatile recipe, good on fruit or mixed greens.

1/4 cup cider vinegar
1/4 cup key lime or lemon juice
2 tablespoons Tortuga Gold Rum
1/4 cup sugar
1 cup olive or canola oil
1 tablespoon chopped onion
1/2 teaspoon dry mustard
1/2 teaspoon salt
1/4 teaspoon ground allspice
1/2 cup papaya seeds

Combine all ingredients in a food processor or blender and process until papaya seeds resemble coarse black pepper. Cover and refrigerate until well-chilled. Serve over mixed greens topped with fresh fruit.

Tropical Spinach Mango Salad

2 blood or navel oranges or tangelos, peeled and sectioned, seeds removed
5 cups fresh spinach leaves, washed and stems removed
3 cups red leaf lettuce, torn into bite-size pieces
1 cup peeled, diced ripe mango
1 small red onion, sliced razon thin, separated into rings
1 cup toasted pecan halves

Balsamic Orange Spice Dressing:

1/3 cup balsamic vinegar
1 tablespoon Tortuga Light Rum (add more if desired, to taste)
1/3 cup orange juice (from salad oranges, adding more if necessary)
2/3 cup olive oil
1/4 teaspoon ground allspice
1 teaspoon Tortuga Hellfire Hot Pepper Sauce

Over a small bowl, carefully remove the white membrane and fiber from orange sections, saving any juice and pulp that drips for the dressing, and cut each section into bite size pieces. Chill until ready to use. **Make the dressing**: combine all ingredients in a jar or covered container and shake well. Refrigerate several hours, until well-chilled. In a large bowl, combine the spinach, lettuce, oranges, onion, mango and pecans. Add desired amount of dressing and toss lightly. Serves 4.

Coconut-Pineapple Slaw

There are still plenty of coconuts on Grand Cayman and Jamaica. This very Caribbean recipe only works with fresh coconut, and is best with fresh pineapple.

3 cups finely shredded green cabbage
2 large carrots, peeled and shredded
1 cup fresh chopped or grated coconut
1 cup finely diced fresh pineapple (or canned pineapple chunks, well drained)
1/2 cup unsweetened pineapple juice
1/4 cup condensed milk
1/4 cup canola oil
3 tablespoons lime juice
2 tablespoons Tortuga Light Rum
1 teaspoon salt

Combine all ingredients in bowl and toss lightly. Chill for at least two hours, covered and toss again before serving.

Pear, Grapefruit and Spinach Salad

In the Caribbean, avocados are called "pears," regardless of the variety – and there are many. Be sure the avocado is just ripe and still firm – if it is overripe it will make this dish green and mushy.

Spinach, for four salads (1 package) washed and patted dry and stems removed
1 large firm-ripe avocado
1 large ripe grapefruit (pink or red, preferably)

Dressing:
1/4 cup fresh grapefruit juice
1 teaspoon honey or Dijon mustard
1 teaspoon sugar
1/2 teaspoon minced garlic
1 tablespoon Tortuga Light Rum
1/3 cup olive oil
Salt and black pepper to taste

Peel the grapefruit and separate the sections, removing the seeds and the white membranes. Peel the avocado and cut into inch-inch chunks. Combine grapefruit and avocado in a bowl and chill. **Make the dressing**: Combine all remaining ingredients except olive oil in a small bowl and whisk until blended. Gradually whisk in the olive oil, then taste and add salt and pepper as desired. Pour desired amount of dressing over the grapefruit and avocado and stir gently to mix. Place the spinach on four plates and divide the salad among them. Serve immediately.

Caribbean Fruit and Curry Chicken Salad

West Indians love chicken so much, there are seldom leftovers for salads.

3 avocados, chilled and sliced in half
3 cups roasted chicken, diced
1 cup raw cho-cho (christophene), peeled and diced
1/2 cup fresh or unsweetened canned pineapple chunks (drained well)

1/4 cup almond slices, toasted

Dressing:
3/4 cup mayonnaise
2 tablespoons Coco Lopez or other coconut cream
1 tablespoon Tortuga Dark Rum
2 tablespoons Chief or other good West Indian curry powder
1 teaspoon garlic salt
1 teaspoon fresh ground black pepper

Spray a small saucepan lightly with nonstick vegetable oil spray. Over medium heat, cook the curry powder for about two minutes, stirring constantly, to remove the "raw" taste. Let cool. Combine the chicken, cho-cho, pineapple and almonds in large bowl. **Make the dressing**: Mix the mayonnaise, Coco Lopez, rum, curry powder, garlic salt and pepper and blend well. Add to the chicken mixture and blend well. Chill for at least an hour to allow flavors to blend. Remove pits from avocados and fill centers with salad. Serve with Tortuga Hell-Fire Hot Pepper sauce to pass around. This recipe is meant for six lunch servings.

Carrot and Rum Raisin Salad

An old Caribbean favorite, spiced with rum. You can soak the raisins in water or fruit juice instead, but the rum gives this a *je ne sais quoi* that will surprise your guests.

3 cups shredded carrots
1/2 cup golden raisins
3 tablespoons Tortuga Dark Rum
1/4 cup salted peanuts or cashews, chopped
1/2 cup salad dressing or mayonnaise
2 tablespoons fresh orange juice
1 teaspoon Grace Jamaican All Purpose Seasoning (see **The Island Pantry**)

Heat the rum in a small saucepan until warm and add raisins. Let soak for an hour until plump. In a medium bowl, combine carrots, raisins and peanuts. Combine salad dressing, orange juice and seasoning and mix well. Add to carrot mixture and blend well. Refrigerate several hours until well chilled. Stir again before serving.

Rum and Honeyed Tropical Fruit Salad

Some insist this easy dish is breakfast fare!

1/4 cup Tortuga Dark Rum
1/4 cup Tortuga Citrus or Wildflower Honey
1-1/4 teaspoons Angostura Bitters
2 tablespoons fresh lime juice
2 tangerines or tangelos
1 ripe carambola
4 ripe apple bananas, peeled and sliced into rounds
1 cup ripe papaya chunks
2 cups fresh pineapple, diced
2 cups ripe mango chunks
1/3 cup grated fresh coconut

In a large bowl, combine the rum, honey, bitters and lime juice and blend well with wire whisk. Peel the tangerines over the bowl, and divide into segments, removing membranes and seeds, and letting juice drip into bowl. Remove brown edges from carambola and slice into thin stars into the bowl. Add the remaining fruit (except coconut) and the rum lime mixture and stir, mixing all ingredients.

Cover bowl and chill for four hours or longer, stirring occasionally to be sure the fruit marinates evenly. When ready to serve, spoon fruit salad into small bowls or champagne glasses and garnish with coconut.

Caribbean Heat

The West Indies' Fiery Surprises: Tiny Powerful Peppers and Hot Sauces

West Indians love pepper with their food, a passion developed centuries ago. Here in the islands, if you ask for "pepper" it means hot pepper, or chiles, not black pepper, and it's an important seasoning in many recipes. The two most common types of hot peppers steaming up this region are bird peppers (*Capsicum annuum*), and varieties of *Capsicum chinense*, including habaneros and Scotch Bonnets, shaped like tiny colored Scottish tams.

Chiles were eaten liberally by the Arawak and Carib Indians, who seasoned almost everything with the Western world's first hot pepper sauce, called *coui*, a blend of cassava juice and hot peppers. They also invented the first fiery meat rub. Caribbean peppers were a New World discovery for Christopher Columbus. He launched a chile conquest of Europe when he returned with seeds gathered on his first Voyage in 1492. Since then, these little fruits have been both cursed and blessed for causing or curing a variety of ailments.

In Jamaica and Cayman, "country pepper" is a general term for hot pepper, and it includes Scotch Bonnets, mutton peppers and several other tamer varieties – but the Scotch bonnet is the most commonly used. It a smaller relative of the Habanero – one of the world's hottest peppers. In Scoville Units (the international scale which measures the intensity of *capsaicin*, the heat source of chiles) the Scotch Bonnet ranks 9 to 10 with 100,000 units – lots hotter than a jalapeno, which has only 2,500 –5,000 units. You'll find these peppers in a variety of colors, from pale green through orange and bright red.

Caribbean people eat pepper for its unique hot fruity flavor and not just heat. We use peppers sensibly – usually not a whole minced Scotch bonnet- or more – in a single dish. The exception: a whole pepper, unpierced, is used in soups and stews, but removed before it can burst. The Scotch bonnet is a key ingredient in Jamaican jerk seasoning, Bajan seasoning and more than 40 varieties of Caribbean hot sauces. Many, including **Tortuga Rum Company's Hell-Fire Hot Pepper Sauce**, are a blend of Scotch Bonnets, vinegar and spices. Others add mustard, papaya or mango puree for more exotic flavors.

Many recipes in this book call for Scotch Bonnet pepper and the amounts I suggest tend to be less than I would normally use. You can add more heat to taste later if desired – but it's very hard to reduce heat once it's already added. If you are not familiar with Caribbean peppers and hot sauce, I suggest you start out a few drops of Tortuga Hell-Fire Hot Pepper Sauce or another bottled crushed Scotch Bonnet pepper sauce until you determine your heat tolerance level. Tortuga's blend of Scotch Bonnets, vinegar and spices captures the wonderful flavor of these peppers and preserves just enough heat.

Pepper tips:

● A whole Scotch bonnet, minced, even without the membrane and seeds, is a lot of heat. When you are ready to experiment, start conservatively, using a very tiny amount, perhaps a few slivers – definitely not a whole minced pepper – in any recipe. You can always add more later. Or use a milder mutton pepper – or if you are lucky enough to find one, use what we call "seasoning peppers," including hybrid varieties of Scotch Bonnet, that have the bold Scotch bonnet flavor without the intense fire.

● Use disposable or rubber gloves when handling the peppers and never touch your eyes, nose or any mucous membranes until you have removed the gloves and washed your hands.

● To reduce the heat while retaining flavor, remove seeds and membranes or veins inside the pepper – these contain the most intense heat.

● If you want to taste a tiny piece of fresh pepper, put it in your mouth without touching your lips or you may be in pain.

● If you get a pepper overdose, put out the fire with milk, sour cream, ice cream or any dairy product. Bread, rice and starchy foods also help absorb the capsaicin.

● The heat intensity of chiles is not affected by cooking or freezing. The only thing that can reduce the fire is drawing out the oil containing capsaicin. Add several large pieces of potato to soups or stews and cook for 20 minutes, then remove and discard (or eat). Repeat if necessary. This will help reduce the heat of some dishes.

● Are these peppers worth so much work – and possible pain? Absolutely. Many islanders swear good health requires a dose of pepper every day.

● Consuming huge quantities of Red Stripe or rum will NOT cure pepper afterburn...you just won't care anymore.

Cayman Pepper Sauce

On my first visit to Cayman, this fiery but colorful concoction was my introduction to Caribbean peppers. I ate a spoonful of peppers instead of drops of the sauce. After they resuscitated me, I could never again settle for that sissy Louisiana red sauce. No

Caymanian table is complete without a jar of this.

1 dozen Scotch bonnet peppers, including red, yellow and green, sliced
1/2 medium onion, sliced very thin
2 cloves garlic, sliced very thin
1 medium carrot, peeled and sliced into very thin rounds
2 or 3 small slices of raw cho-cho, peeled and seeded
2 teaspoons salt
2 cups white vinegar

Take a very clean 16-ounce jar and add the peppers and other vegetables and salt. Heat the vinegar until very hot but not boiling. Pour over the peppers and vegetables to cover, then seal jar. Let stand at least a week for flavors to blend. Drops (or spoonfuls) of the peppery vinegar is the actual "sauce" but many of us cannot resist digging into the pickled veggies – including the peppers. (**Some add four or five whole allspice berries to this recipe.)

Sandys Sherwood's Bomb in a Bottle

The late Sandys "Sandy" Sherwood was Cayman's Chief of Police in the peaceful 1960's and retired to go into less stressful work: running his own English-style pub and restaurant, the legendary Cayman Arms in George Town. His incendiary pepper sauce was legendary among those who survived it.

24 whole Scotch Bonnet peppers, stems removed, cut in half
2 large onions, peeled and chopped
3/4 cup prepared mustard
4 large cloves garlic
2 tablespoons cayenne pepper
1/2 cup brown sugar
1/8 teaspoon ground cloves
1/4 cup Tortuga Gold Rum
2 tablespoons dry sherry
2 tablespoons gin

Combine all ingredients in a food processor or blender and process until mixture is pureed. Pour into glass bottles and seal. Store in refrigerator.

Spiced Rum Peppers

A delicious way to wake up soups, marinades and Bloody Mary's. Use both the pepper-infused rum and rum-infused pepper slices. But be careful of the Scoville units in this!

1 750 ml bottle Tortuga Dark or Light Rum
6 whole cloves
24 whole small red Scotch Bonnet peppers or bird peppers, seeded and cut into thin rings
1 stick cinnamon, broken into four pieces

Decant the rum into a clean glass container. Add the cloves and cinnamon, then the pepper slices and stir well. Seal and let stand for two weeks at room temperature to age.

Pepper Wine or Pepper Rum

This old recipe uses rum, but is still called "wine" in many islands. It's a nice accent to many dishes, especially soups. You've heard of Bermuda's famous sherry peppers. This is the Western Caribbean's answer to that, and it gives a flavor kick to chowders, Bloody Mary's and many other things.

10 whole fresh Scotch Bonnet peppers or other hot Caribbean peppers
1 pint Tortuga Dark Rum

Put the whole peppers in a sterilized glass jar or bottle and pour the rum over. Stir gently so you don't crush the peppers. Some cooks like to pierce one pepper, or slice it in half, to intensify the heat per drop. Seal the container and let it stand in a cool place for at least week, preferably longer. Use a few drops in soups, chowders, Bloody Mary's and other recipes. When the pepper rum starts to run low, add more rum and let it stand, sealed, several days.

Crushed Scotch Bonnet Pepper Sauce

20 Scotch Bonnet peppers
1 cup chopped yellow onion
6 cloves garlic, minced
2 tablespoons canola oil
1 cup chopped carrots
1/2 cup water
1/2 cup lime juice
1 cup white vinegar
2 teaspoons salt

Sterilize the bottles or jars you plan to store the sauce in. Remove the stems from the peppers. In a medium saucepan, sauté the onions and garlic in the oil until soft. Add the carrots and water and simmer until carrots are crisp-tender. Remove from heat and cool 10 minutes. Combine the peppers and the vegetable mixture in a food processor and puree until smooth. Pour the puree back into the saucepan and add the salt, lime juice and vinegar and stir well. Heat the mixture over medium heat until it begins to boil, then reduce heat and simmer for 3 minutes so flavors blend. Cool slightly, then pour pepper sauce into prepared containers and seal. Store in refrigerator. Use a few drops at a time!

Rum Sauces & Uncommon Condiments

Rubs, Marinades and Sauces for Meat & Seafood

Jump Up Meat Rub & Marinade

This will make about 3 pounds of meat or poultry "jump up," Caribbean style.

1 medium yellow onion, chopped
6 large cloves garlic
2 large scallions, chopped
1 sprig fresh thyme or 1 teaspoon dried
1 teaspoon ground allspice
1/4 cup Tortuga Gold Rum
2 tablespoons soy sauce
1 teaspoon Tortuga Hell-Fire Hot Pepper Sauce
2 tablespoons fresh lime juice or cider vinegar
1 tablespoon coarse or Kosher Salt
1 tablespoon ground black pepper

Combine all ingredients in a food processor or blender and process into a paste. **For beef or pork**: make shallow cuts all over meat surface. Use your fingertips to rub the marinade into the meat, pushing small amounts into the cuts. **For poultry**: left small sections of skin and rub marinade over meat, then replace skin, and using fingertips, rub rest of skin thoroughly. Refrigerate rubbed meat for 12 hours or longer, covered or sealed in a zip-top plastic bag. If you are browning the meat to braise or stew, carefully scrape off and reserve the marinade and add it into the cooking liquid later. This isn't necessary if you're roasting or grilling the meat.

Taste of Many Islands Meat Marinade

This is a lively marinade for almost any meat, poultry or seafood, infusing a variety of Caribbean flavors. Use it as a base to create your own more exotic marinades and sauces. Don't discard the marinade when you remove the meat – but *don't eat* it uncooked. Bring to a boil and simmer for 10 minutes, or use it as a base for gravy or sauce. This seasons about 3 pounds of meat, poultry or seafood:

Basic marinade:
1/2 cup Tortuga Gold or Dark Rum
1/3 cup olive or peanut oil
1-1/4 cups fresh orange juice
1/4 cup soy sauce
2 teaspoons light brown sugar
3 garlic cloves, minced
1 tablespoon fresh grated gingerroot
1 tablespoon grated orange zest
1 teaspoon ground allspice
1/2 cup finely chopped fresh red onion
2 large scallions, chopped
1 tablespoon Garlic Mrs. Dash seasoning
1 teaspoon garlic pepper
1 tablespoon fresh lime

Additional suggestions: Add one or more of the following to create a spicy marinade to suit your taste:

2 teaspoon s Tortuga Hell-Fire Hot Pepper Sauce
1 tablespoon Grace Jamaican All Purpose Seasoning
2 tablespoons Pickapeppa Meat Seasoning
2 tablespoons Worcestershire sauce
1/2 cup Badia Mojo Marinade or Kirby's Criolla

Combine all ingredients in a food processor and puree until almost smooth, about 30 seconds. Place the meat or seafood to be marinated in a heavy zip-top bag and pour in the marinade. Squeeze out the air and seal. Now roll the bag around and "massage" the marinade throughout so the meat is coated well.. Marinate meat or poultry for at least four hours and up to 2 days – longer is better, turning the bag several times to insure even marinating. Marinate seafood for an hour or two only.

Rum Glaze for Ham

2 cups fresh orange juice
2 teaspoons grated orange zest
1/2 cup Tortuga Dark Rum
1 cup dark brown sugar
2 tablespoons ground ginger
12 whole cloves
1 teaspoon ground allspice

Combine all ingredients in a medium saucepan and stir well. Bring to a boil over medium-high heat, stirring frequently, and reduce heat to low. Simmer for 25-30 minutes, until sauce has thickened to light syrup. Brush glaze generously over ham during the last hour of baking, basting several times. Reserve unused glaze and keep warm to serve as a sauce.

Tortuga Rum Raisin Sauce

This is different and delicious with baked ham, pork – or for something completely different, serve with roast chicken.

1/2 cup raisins
1 –10.5 ounce can beef consommé
1 teaspoon browning
2 tablespoons Tortuga Steak Sauce
2 tablespoons minced red onion
3 tablespoons red currant or cherry jelly
1 teaspoon ground black pepper
3 tablespoons Tortuga Dark Rum

Combine all ingredients except rum in a medium saucepan and stir well. Bring to a simmer and cook for 10 minutes. Stir in the rum and cook two minutes longer. Serve warm over sliced meat. Store leftover sauce in refrigerator.

Tortuga Spiced Orange Ginger Rum Sauce

This is good with roasted or baked chicken or pork and can also be used as a dipping sauce for shrimp.

2 tablespoons butter
1 tablespoon fresh grated gingerroot
2 medium onions, minced
2 cups orange juice
12- ounce jar orange marmalade
1/2 cup + 1 tablespoon Tortuga Gold Rum
1 teaspoon Grace Jamaican All Purpose Seasoning
1 tablespoon Tortuga Hell-Fire Hot Pepper Sauce

In 2-quart saucepan, melt butter over medium high heat and add onions and ginger, sautéing until onions are translucent. Combine marmalade, orange juice, All Purpose Seasoning, pepper sauce and 1/2 cup rum and add to onions, stirring well. Bring to a boil again, reduce heat to medium-low and simmer, stirring occasionally, until sauce is reduced by half and thickened, about 30 minutes. Remove from heat and stir in remaining 1 tablespoon rum. Allow to cool 15 minutes before serving. Brush generously on chicken or other poultry before roasting. If using as a dip, serve warm.

Ginger Lime Rum Sauce

This is a light, very Caribbean sauce and delicious on shrimp, fish or chicken

1 cup butter or margarine
1/4 cup Tortuga Dark Rum
2 tablespoons fresh key lime juice
1 teaspoon key lime zest
2 tablespoons minced fresh ginger
1 tablespoon dark brown sugar

Combine all ingredients in a small saucepan and cook, stirring frequently, over medium heat until the butter melts and sugar is dissolved. Remove from heat and pour into a heat-proof glass measuring cup until ready to use. Baste fish or chicken with sauce before and while grilling and serve remaining sauce on the side.

Seafood Dips

Tamarind Dip

Try this unusual, tangy blend of Caribbean flavors with warm spiced boiled shrimp, chicken kebabs or any kind of fritters.

1-8 ounce package cream cheese (reduced fat can be substituted), at room temperature
1/2 cup sour cream (reduced fat can be substituted)
2 tablespoons Tortuga Gold Rum
1 –5 ounce bottle Pickapeppa sauce
1-2 tablespoons confectioner's sugar (to taste)

In a medium bowl, use an electric mixer to beat the cream cheese until light, then blend in the sour cream. Add the rum and Pickapeppa sauce and blend until smooth. Taste the dip and see if it needs sugar to suit your taste and if desired, add sugar and blend well. Store in refrigerator until ready to use, but it is best at room temperature.

Jerk Mayonnaise

Try this with conch fritters or instead of plain mayonnaise with sandwiches.

1 cup mayonnaise or Miracle Whip (you can substitute light or fat free of either)
1 teaspoon fresh lime juice
1-1/2 teaspoons Walkerswood Traditional Jamaican Jerk seasoning (or more to taste)
1 teaspoon soy sauce
1/2 teaspoon ground pepper

Mix all ingredients together and blend well. Let stand for 15 minutes before serving, to allow flavors to blend. Store leftover sauce in covered container in refrigerator.

Caribbean Red Sauce

A spicy sauce for conch fritters, shrimp or any seafood.

1 cup ketchup
1 tablespoon Worcestershire sauce
1 tablespoon lime juice
1/2 teaspoon seasoned salt
1/2 teaspoon ground pepper
1 teaspoon Tortuga Hell-fire Hot Pepper sauce (more to taste)

Mix all ingredients together in a small bowl and serve at room temperature. Store leftovers in refrigerator.

Dessert and Fruit Sauces

Tortuga Rum Glaze

This is the standard glaze for cakes and sweet breads.

1/2 cup butter
1/4 cup water or fruit juice
1 cup sugar
1/2 cup Tortuga Dark or Gold Rum

In saucepan, melt butter over medium heat. Stir in water or fruit juice and sugar and bring to a boil, stirring constantly, and cook for five minutes. Remove from heat and stir in rum. Mixture will foam up, so continue stirring. Return to heat and cook another minute over medium heat, stirring constantly. Remove from heat and cool at least 30 minutes before using. With a sharp wooden or metal skewer or ice pick, prick cake all over and spoon the glaze over slowly, until all is absorbed or you have used as much as desired. Refrigerate any leftover glaze and warm in microwave or bring to room temperature before using.

Quick Rum Glaze

This is an easy glaze for cookies and small cakes.

2 cups sifted confectioners' sugar
2 tablespoons melted butter
3 tablespoons Tortuga Rum Liqueur or Tortuga Coffee Liqueur

Combine all ingredients in a small bowl and mix well. Spread on cookies or cake when cooled.

Chocolate Rum Glaze

This glaze will have a glossy look when cool.

3 tablespoons unsweetened Hershey's cocoa (Dutch process is best)
1 cup sugar
1/2 cup butter
1/4 cup water
1/2 cup Tortuga Dark Rum

Combine the sugar and cocoa in a small bowl and stir until completely blended. In a medium saucepan melt the butter and stir in the water and sugar-cocoa mixture. Bring to a boil over medium heat, stirring constantly. Reduce heat and keep at a low boil for five minutes, until mixture has thickened to syrup. Stir in the rum and remove from heat – mixture will bubble up immediately, so keep stirring. Cool for 10 minutes, then drizzle over cake or other dessert.

Traditional Hard Sauce

Recipes for this old colonial topping for cake and pudding meander all over the culinary map. The amount of butter varies from 2 tablespoons to a cup, and the rum, from a teaspoon to 1/4 cup. You can experiment until you reach your desired taste and texture.

2 cups confectioner's sugar
1/2 cup butter, softened
1/4 cup Tortuga Dark Rum

Cream the butter until light and then blend in the sugar until very smooth. Gradually add the rum and beat until smooth. Chill until firm and serve with Christmas fruitcake, gingerbread and other desserts. Store leftover sauce in covered container in refrigerator.

Caribbean Hard Sauce

An old recipe served with steamed puddings, fruitcake and heavy cakes.

1/2 cup butter
1 cup light brown sugar
3 tablespoons Tortuga Dark Rum

Cream the butter until smooth and then beat in the sugar until very smooth. Gradually add the rum and beat until smooth. Chill until firm and store leftover sauce in covered container in refrigerator.

Traditional Creamy Rum Sauce

Serve warm over ice cream, tapioca, puddings, fresh fruit –even waffles.

1 cup brown sugar
1 cup butter
1-1/3 cups heavy cream
1/2 cup Tortuga Dark Rum

Combine all ingredients in saucepan and bring to a boil over medium heat, stirring constantly. Cook 5 minutes or a little longer, until thickened and remove from heat. Can be refrigerated and warmed in microwave.

Rum Butterscotch

Serve over cakes, puddings or ice cream.

1 cup water
1 cup granulated sugar
1 cup light brown sugar
1 cup light corn syrup
1/2 cup sweetened condensed milk
2 tablespoons butter
1/2 of a 14.5 ounce can evaporated milk
1 teaspoon vanilla extract
1/3 cup Tortuga Gold Rum

In a medium saucepan, combine water, both sugars and corn syrup and stir well. Over medium heat, bring to a boil and continue cooking, stirring frequently, for 10 minutes. Stir in the condensed milk and butter and cool for five minutes, then stir in the evaporated milk, vanilla and rum and blend well. Refrigerate leftover sauce, covered.

Rum Cream Honey Dip

This is delicious with fresh fruit, as well as coconut shrimp and conch cakes.

2 cups heavy cream
1/4 cup Tortuga Dark Rum
1/4 cup Tortuga Wildflower Honey

Combine all ingredients and bring to a boil over medium heat, stirring constantly so cream does not scorch. Reduce heat to keep mixture at a simmer, stirring frequently, for about 10 minutes, until sauce has thickened and is reduced by a third. Let cool to room temperature and serve.

Rum Orange Cream

Delicious accent for fresh fruit, cheesecake or ice cream

2 cups sugar
1/2 cup water
3/4 cup heavy cream
2 tablespoons Tortuga Dark Rum
2 tablespoons Cointreau or Curacao

Combine sugar and water in medium saucepan and stir well. Heat over medium-low heat until sugar dissolves. Increase heat to medium and bring to a boil, swirling pan gently to avoid scorching, until sugar caramelizes (turns golden brown), about 10 minutes. Remove pan from heat and gradually stir in heavy cream (mixture will bubble rapidly) and return to low heat, stirring constantly until smooth. Remove from heat and whisk in the rum and liqueur. Cover and cool slightly. Sauce can be refrigerated and reheated over low heat.

Rummy Whipped Cream

You may never use plain old whipped cream again after tasting this.

2 cups chilled heavy cream
1/4 cup confectioner's sugar
2 tablespoons Tortuga 151 or Dark Rum

In a medium deep bowl, combine the heavy cream, sugar and rum and beat until soft peaks form. Can be made four hours ahead and refrigerated.

Tortuga Chantilly Cream

A Caribbean adaptation of an old Southern US favorite.

2/3 cup heavy cream
2 teaspoons Rum Vanilla
1 teaspoon Grand Mariner
1/4 cup confectioner's sugar
2 tablespoons sour cream

Chill a small deep mixing bowl and electric mixer beaters for an hour. Combine the heavy cream, rum vanilla, and Grand Marnier in the chilled bowl and beat on medium speed for 1 minute. Add the sugar and sour cream and beat on medium speed just until soft peaks form, about 3 minutes. Do not over beat. Makes about 2 cups. (**Variation**: If you haven't made Rum Vanilla yet, substitute 2 teaspoons Tortuga Dark Rum and 1 teaspoon vanilla extract. The flavor won't be exactly the same, but it will be close.)

Uncommon Condiments with Rum

Drunken Cranberry Sauce

Try this at your next Thanksgiving feast.

1 large unpeeled orange, seeds removed, cut into quarters
4 cups fresh whole cranberries
2 teaspoons Tortuga Hell-Fire Hot Pepper Sauce
1-2/3 cups sugar
1/4 cup Tortuga Dark Rum

Combine half the cranberries and half the orange in a food processor bowl and grind into coarse paste. Pour into a large bowl and repeat. Combine the fruit mixture with the pepper sauce, sugar and rum and stir well. Cover and refrigerate for 24 hours or longer.

Green Mango Mincemeat

1 pound ground beef
2-1/2 quarts chopped peeled firm green mango
2 /3 cup coarsely ground whole naval oranges, seeds removed
2 cups raisins
2 tablespoons fresh grated gingerroot
1 cup dark brown sugar, firmly packed
3/4 cup molasses
6 tablespoons cider vinegar
1 cup Tortuga Dark Rum
1 teaspoon cinnamon
1/2 teaspoon ground cloves
1/4 teaspoon ground allspice
1 teaspoon salt

Cook the ground beef in a 5 quart Dutch oven over medium heat, stirring frequently, for 3-4 minutes or until meat loses its pink color – do not brown. Add the mangoes, oranges, raisins, ginger, sugar, molasses, vinegar, rum, spices and salt to the meat and stir to mix well. Continue cooking over medium heat for about 30-35 minutes until most of liquid has evaporated, stirring often so mixture does not scorch. Remove from heat and cool slightly. Refrigerate in tightly sealed container if you plan to use within 4 days. Otherwise, freeze or can the mincemeat to store longer (use proper canning instructions and procedures.)

Green Mango Chutney

This is a basic Jamaican recipe with a hint of rum – and onion, which many recipes leave out. It's a bit more tart than most chutneys sold commercially, but the fresh, bold flavors are so much better.

2/3 cup golden or seedless raisins
1/4 cup Tortuga Dark Rum
12 cups peeled green mango (about 6 medium) cut into 1-1/2 inch chunks
1 medium onion, chopped
2 cups cider vinegar
1 cup light brown sugar, firmly packed
3 cloves garlic, minced
1 tablespoon Tortuga Hell-Fire Hot Pepper Sauce
OR 1/4th teaspoon minced, seeded Scotch Bonnet pepper
1/4 cup peeled and grated fresh gingerroot
1 teaspoon ground allspice
2 teaspoons salt

Combine the raisins and rum and soak for two hours until raisins have absorbed all the rum and are plump. In a large cooking pot or 6-quart Dutch oven, combine the mangoes, onions and vinegar and bring to a boil. Stir in the sugar, garlic, hot pepper sauce or Scotch bonnet, ginger, allspice, raisins and salt. Reduce heat to low and simmer uncovered, stirring occasionally, for about 30 to 40 minutes or until thick and syrupy but mango chunks are tender but still intact. Take a small sample and taste for seasonings. Add more hot pepper if desired. Cool and then store in clean glass jars and refrigerate up to two weeks. If you plan to store longer, follow directions for canning and sealing from your favorite cookbook. Makes about 10 cups.

Banana Chutney

Use the exotic small West Indian apple bananas for this recipe if you can.

1/4 cup raisins
3 tablespoons Tortuga Gold Rum
16 apple (finger) bananas, ripe but firm or 8 large bananas
3 cloves garlic, minced
1 large onion, sliced
1 tablespoon Tortuga Hell-Fire Hot Pepper Sauce
OR 1/4th teaspoon minced, seeded Scotch Bonnet pepper
3 tablespoons grated fresh gingerroot
1 cup cider vinegar
1-3/4 cups light brown sugar, packed
2 teaspoons salt

Combine the raisins and rum and stir well. Let the raisins soak for two hours to absorb the rum. In a large pot or Dutch oven, combine all ingredients and stir well. Bring to a boil over medium heat, stirring frequently, then reduce heat to simmer and cook, uncovered, for about 30 minutes or until thick. Store in a sealed container in the refrigerator for up to two weeks or seal the chutney in individual sterilized glass jars (I don't know how to can or pickle things, so I won't attempt to give you directions for this. Consult an expert.)

Rum Honey

1 cup Tortuga Wildflower or Citrus Honey (or any natural honey)
2 tablespoons Tortuga Gold or Dark Rum

In a small saucepan, warm the honey – this will make blending the ingredients easier. Combine the honey and rum and stir until well blended. Serve in place of regular honey –not recommended for children! Store in tightly sealed glass container. Stir before every use.

Rum Maple Syrup

1 cup pure maple syrup
2 tablespoons Tortuga Dark Rum (or more to taste, if desired)

In a small saucepan, warm the syrup slightly. Stir the rum into the maple syrup and mix well. Store any unused syrup in a tightly sealed container.

Sea Grape Jam

Sea grape jam used to be common on Cayman breakfast tables, but I had to really hunt for this recipe in East End, where the sea grapes still thrive along Grand Cayman's south coast.

5 pounds ripe sea grapes
3 cups sugar
1/4 cup Tortuga Gold Rum

The sea grapes must be very ripe for this recipe – purple and soft. Place about a cup of sea grapes at a time in a sieve or colander over a bowl and squash the grapes with your fingers to remove the skin and seeds and rub the pulp through holes into the bowl. (If you have an easier method, please let me know!) In a large heavy saucepan, combine the sea grape pulp and sugar and bring to a boil, stirring constantly. Stir in the rum and cook for five minutes longer, stirring constantly. Remove from heat and pour into sterilized glass jars and seal if you are planning to store it for longer than a few weeks in the refrigerator.

A Tortuga Rum Fête

The Cayman Islands is a tiny affluent British Overseas Territory 480 miles south of Miami, known primarily for thrilling scuba diving, glorious beaches and its role as the largest island offshore financial center in the world.

Each year this Western Caribbean island trio attracts over 1.3 million visitors by airline and cruise ships. Grand Cayman is home to more than 590 banks, 40,000 people (representing over 80 nationalities); 15,000 green sea turtles, Stingray City and a village called Hell. There isn't a canefield in sight, much less a rum distillery. Yet today Grand Cayman is the Rum Cake Capital of the world, thanks to Tortuga Rum Company.

Here is the short version of this unusual success story, the newest chapter in the history of Caribbean Rum.

TORTUGA
RUM COMPANY LIMITED

The Tortuga Rum Company Story

Meet the People who made Grand Cayman the Rum Cake Capital of the World

Cayman's Tortuga Rum Cake is better known worldwide than either this country's location or the proper spelling of its capital, George Town. Year round, Tortuga's rum-soaked confection sells by the thousands both locally and overseas. Such demand delights Captain Robert Hamaty and his wife, Carlene Jackson Hamaty, founders of Tortuga Rum Company Ltd. (Pictured below.) But the cake's status as one of the Caribbean's culinary legends often eclipses the company's fine rums, gourmet products – and unusual success story.

Tortuga Rum Company Ltd. has grown dramatically since it was started in 1984. The following year, owners Robert and Carlene Hamaty introduced Cayman's first private label rums: Tortuga Gold and Tortuga Light. Today, the family owned and operated company is the largest retail and duty free liquor business in the Cayman Islands with

17 Grand Cayman locations. The Tortuga Rum Company label has grown to include 11 quality registered blends, led by its Premium Label 12-Year Old Tortuga Rum for connoisseurs. Others include Tortuga Light, Gold, Dark, 151 Proof, Rum Cream Liqueur, Rum Liqueur, Coconut, Banana and Spiced Rums and Tortuga Coffee Liqueur.

The name Tortuga is a registered trademark in the US, UK and British Commonwealth countries and known internationally as one of the pioneers of the Caribbean's gourmet food industry. The Tortuga Rum Cake was introduced in October 1987 and now includes *five* varieties: original golden, rich chocolate, Blue Mountain Coffee, coconut and banana. Since then, Tortuga has also developed a growing line of private label gourmet products: Tortuga West Indian Rum Plum Pudding; five varieties of premium blended coffee (including three Tortuga Rum Coffees); two kinds of wildflower honey; Tortuga Rum Bar-B-Que Sauce; three varieties of Tortuga Rum Flavored gourmet chocolate fudge; Tortuga Gourmet Steak Sauce; Tortuga Jerk Sauce; Tortuga Hot Pepper Jelly: Tortuga Hell Fire Hot Pepper Sauce; chocolate rum mints and Tortuga Chocolate Rum Hazelnut Truffles.

Today the Tortuga Rum Cake is Cayman's top selling souvenir, number one export product and culinary signature. Publications including *Travel Weekly*, the leading North American travel industry news magazine, have featured articles about the Tortuga Rum Cake, calling it "a popular Cayman tourist attraction – along with Seven Mile Beach, wall diving, Stingray City and the Cayman Turtle Farm."

The Tortuga Trail

Green sea turtles, "las tortugas," were the creatures Columbus sighted on Cayman's coasts in 1503, earning the islands their first name. Turtles were also the treasure that enticed pirates ashore in 17th century Cayman, when Cuba and other neighbors were raising cane and refining rum. Onshore, Cayman had hardwoods, fresh water and thatch

palm for rope making, but unlike its nearest neighbor Jamaica, sugar has never been a cash crop. Here, the closest thing to molasses is the weekday traffic flow in and out of George Town. How did a rum company sprout and flourish on a flat coral island where cane is an oddity rather than a commodity?

This story began in 1948 when Robert Hamaty was born in Jamaica's sugar belt with rum in his blood – figuratively speaking. He grew up driving a tractor in his attorney-father's canefields, cutting sugar cane and hauling it to market. Even today, he admits "I never got the smell of pure molasses out of my nose."

But Robert's real passion was flying. After graduating from flight school he joined Air Jamaica and at age 24 became its youngest DC-9 Captain. A year later, he became Air Jamaica's youngest Captain flying a transatlantic route at the controls of a DC-8. In 1978 he joined Cayman Airways and rose to the rank of Chief Pilot. While flying charters on the Bermuda route, Captain Hamaty became intrigued by the number of bottles of duty free "Bermuda Rum" passengers carried onboard. Knowing that Bermuda, like Cayman, has no indigenous sugar industry or rum distilleries, he did some research. It turned out "Bermuda" rum was actually blended West Indian rum bottled elsewhere, imported to Bermuda and sold legally under a private label – a clever idea with tremendous appeal for tourists.

A Tortuga Rum Fête

About that time, he met Carlene Jackson, a Cayman Airways in-flight supervisor. This Caymanian lady shared his entrepreneurial spirit and business sense and became his wife and business partner in 1981. Carlene also had a generations-old family recipe for rum cake, which wasn't part of the original Tortuga business plan.

In 1984, while still with Cayman Airways, the couple ignored local skeptics and started Tortuga Rum Company Ltd. with Cayman's first private label rums: Tortuga Gold and Tortuga Light, both registered blends of fine Jamaican and Barbados rums. Prominent local merchants poured sarcasm on the venture, suggesting names like "Turtle Pee" would be more appropriate. They claimed a local Cayman rum would never fly in this devout Appleton and Bacardi market. Even close friends shook their heads at this risky venture. What their critics didn't understand: it wasn't the local market Tortuga was targeting – it was the potentially huge duty free liquor business. The Hamatys hoped to capitalize on Cayman's rapidly growing cruise ship tourism industry and lack of duty free liquor outlets for departing passengers. This was already a lucrative business in other Caribbean islands, yet practically untouched in Cayman.

The company started out in a tiny office on North Church Street without a warehouse, using Grand Cayman's Overton Traders as their distributor. The first Tortuga Duty Free Liquor store opened in 1987 in George Town within walking distance from the cruise ship terminal. By the end of that year, Tortuga had become a licensed wholesale distributor, established small bonded warehouse and opened a second duty free liquor store in George Town. The Tortuga Rum Cake story began later that year.

The Tortuga Rum Cake: Sweet Success

This is no Caribbean rum folklore. Unlike its local imitators, the original Tortuga Rum Cake recipe is a genuine family tradition, passed down through generations of Jacksons from Savannah, Grand Cayman. It was created long before modern kitchen conveniences and cake mixes, when Caymanians had Spartan pantries and relied on ingenuity and resourcefulness. For years, Carlene baked her rum cakes at home for special occasions. They were a pleasure enjoyed only by special friends and family.

Finally, friends who ran successful food-related businesses in other Caribbean countries convinced Carlene to test the local market and make the rum cake part of Tortuga's line. In October 1987 her cake appeared on the dessert menu of a local restaurant as Tortuga Rum Cake – and was instant hit.

Word spread rapidly and soon residents were ordering whole cakes for special occasions and gobbling up smaller portions as fast as they appeared on shelves. The demand became so great that by 1990, Tortuga expanded with a 1700- square foot commercial bakery at its small headquarters and bonded warehouse in Grand Cayman's Airport Industrial Park. The Tortuga Rum Cake earned a place in rum history as the Caribbean's first commercially produced rum cake.

The original recipe has never been revealed and has remained essentially unchanged for four generations. The Tortuga Rum Cake is made without preservatives from ingredients including fresh whole eggs, New Zealand Anchor butter, imported walnuts and a generous amount of premium five-year old, oak barrel aged Tortuga Gold Rum not sold to the public. Each cake is individually hand-glazed with a rich rum sauce before being vacuum packed.

In 1990 health problems forced Robert to retire from commercial flying. He took over as Tortuga's Managing Director, devoting his energy and entrepreneurial savvy to marketing, promotion and brand development. In 1991, the company achieved another milestone, introducing a unique custom vacuum-seal packaging machine, a process Robert helped develop. The packaging prolongs the cakes' shelf life to six months without preservatives – meaning they keep indefinitely if refrigerated or frozen.

From the day the Hamatys opened Tortuga Rum Company they faced and overcame incredible obstacles – but their greatest challenge began in 1991. Robert came down with a virus that attacked the heart muscles and resulted in cardiomyopathy, leaving him with a failing heart. For the next five years, he survived on determination and medication. Then in February 1996 he underwent a heart transplant in Miami. Uncanny as it sounds, the donor was a 27-year old pilot who died in a skydiving accident. Given Robert's impressive career as a pilot beginning at age 24, this was a strange coincidence. But not even that extraordinary operation slowed him or Tortuga's progress. Robert returned to work three months later ready to launch new projects and expand Tortuga's gourmet product line. He was determined to establish an identity in the marketplace not only beyond Cayman's coastline – but also far beyond the traditional scope of any other Caribbean rum company.

Since then, Tortuga Rum Company Ltd. has become a Caribbean success story, as one of the region's top duty-free businesses and producer of innovative gourmet products. In October 2001, Tortuga received its greatest recognition so far when President Robert Hamaty was named Caribbean Entrepreneur of the Year. This is the first time any individual or company from the Cayman Islands has received this prestigious award, considered the "Emmy of entrepreneurship" and one of the Caribbean business community's highest honors. Organized by Ernst & Young, Republic Bank Ltd. and CIBC West Indies Holdings Ltd., the annual event bases its five awards on selections by an independent panel of judges. Mr. Hamaty was selected from 41 nominees in the field of tourism, hospitality and entertainment for "his innovative business strategy" in creating a unique success story.

Yet the company remains a close-knit, family owned and operated business. Robert's wife and partner Carlene is Company Secretary and a Director. His son Basil has been involved as Director of Operations in Grand Cayman. In the USA, daughter Monique Hamaty Simmonds and her husband Marcus head the company's Miami office, Tortuga Imports Inc. Monique is International Marketing and Sales Director and Marcus is Chief Financial Officer. With a staff of 10, they coordinate the company's rapidly growing mail orders; e-commerce transactions and promotion and distribution in foreign markets.

Today, Rum Cake Lane and Tortuga Avenue are actual roads leading to the company's 10,000 square foot headquarters and main bakery in Grand Cayman's airport industrial park. Here, trays of fresh fragrant Tortuga Rum Cake samples tempt visitors as they watch hundreds of cakes being baked and vacuum packed. The state of the art facility with unique viewing windows can turn out up to 8,000 cakes a day. The company also operates two mini-bakeries, located next to the Turtle Farm in West Bay and on the waterfront in downtown George Town.

Tortuga is now a global brand name, appearing at retail outlets in over 400 cities in 28 states in the USA, including its exclusive Tortuga Rum Cake Company store in Key West. The Tortuga Rum Cake appears by name as a specialty dessert on menus at five star restaurants from Miami's South Beach to Manhattan and San Francisco. The cake is carried in boutiques onboard major cruise lines in the Caribbean, Alaska and Europe. In addition, Tortuga Rum Cakes and other Tortuga products are now available throughout the Caribbean and Mexico at leading retail shops in Antigua, Aruba, Tortola, St. Martin/Sint Maarten; Puerto Rico, Cozumel, Cancun and Mexico City; St. Thomas, Nevis (in the exclusive Four Seasons) and St. Barts. You'll also find Tortuga Rum Cakes at shops in San Juan, Puerto Rico's Luis Munoz Marin International Airport and at Houston International Airport. The company also has franchises in Jamaica and Barbados, where the Tortuga Rum Cake is sold as the Tortuga Caribbean Rum Cake.

Tortuga Rum Cake Lore

Like pirates, turtles and tax-haven status, the Tortuga Rum cake has inspired its own Cayman folklore. Sold with the slogan "a Slice of Heaven," its irresistible power over the palate tops the list. The cake has salvaged disastrous dinner parties, soothed family feuds and been the final course of many Cayman power lunches. Some say it takes only a taste to trigger impulsive desires and fantasies involving sultry nights. It can even elicit a sigh of pleasure from English bankers and Barristers. Substances this compelling usually aren't legal. The cake inspired a lively soca dance hit in 1999 by Cayman's Barefoot Man, aptly titled *Tortuga Rum Cake*, the lead track on his *Three Coconuts* CD.

● Political figures and pugilists, environmentalists and actors: a titillating list of celebrities and VIP's have tasted the Tortuga Rum Cake. Jamaican Prime Minister Rt. Hon. P.J. Patterson; Don King, Leslie Nielsen; Beau Bridges, Willie Nelson, Peter Benchley, Stan Waterman, Jean-Michel Cousteau; Burt Wolf, Eddie Murphy – even Mike Tyson – have sampled cakes of their own. Imagine the Tortuga punch lines inspired by that last one.

● The Tortuga Rum Cake was a big hit with the cast and crew of Paramount's *The Firm* in 1993 while on location in Grand Cayman. The film's unit publicist made sure a supply was readily available for Director Sydney Pollack as well as stars Tom Cruise, Gene Hackman, Jeanne Tripplehorn and Holly Hunter.

● During Cayman's **NFL Super Fish Bowl** blue marlin tournaments held from 1992-1994, 23 NFL players including Drew Bledsoe and Marcus Allen ate cakes like big donuts for snacks while trolling for marlin. It became a tournament tradition: the cakes had to be onboard for good luck.

● The Tortuga Rum Cake is a repeat TV star. In 1994, ABC's **Morton Dean** discovered the Tortuga Rum Cake while vacationing in Grand Cayman. He returned home to rave about it on *Good Morning America*, showing the cake to an audience of 200 million. NBC weatherman Al Roker, a diver and regular Cayman visitor, accepted a surprise Tortuga Cake from Cayman friends outside the NBC studio on NBC-TV's *TODAY Show,* June 1997.

● The Tortuga Rum Cake was seen by millions of viewers worldwide on NBC-TV's *TODAY Show* in December 1998. The cake was featured in a special 10-minute holiday gourmet segment hosted by NBC correspondent and syndicated food columnist **Phil Lempert**, who presented his picks for the holiday season's top fancy food gifts and entertaining. Tortuga's cake was the only Caribbean food item featured.

● In June 2000, the Tortuga Rum Cake became the first Caribbean gourmet food product ever featured on US cable TV's popular *Home Shopping Network*, viewed by millions throughout the continental USA. The segments also aired on *America's Store*, the *Home Shopping Network's* affiliate.

● At New York's prestigious **International Fancy Food and Confection Show** in July 2000, the Tortuga Rum Cake was in the TV spotlight again. During a live broadcast from the event, MSNBC's fine food correspondent Phil Lempert selected the cake from among thousands of products and showed it to the audience as one of his show favorites and the year's hottest gourmet items.

> You can have your cake—-and dance to it too! Cayman's popular confection inspired a local celebrity (and avid rum cake fan) to create a musical tribute that became a local hit. Legendary songwriter/ entertainer, George "Barefoot Man" Nowak salutes the Tortuga Rum Cake with a soca tune by that title, one of the top tracts on his *Three Coconuts* CD. It's one of more than 20 CD's featuring original and Caribbean music by Barefoot Man & Band, available throughout Grand Cayman including Tortuga's retail outlets. Or you can visit Barefoot at his website, www.barefootman.com for ordering information.

Exclusive:
<u>Tortuga Rum Cake Recipes!</u>

The Original Tortuga Rum Cake (1987®)

I have begged, bartered —even snooped for years around Tortuga's bakeries, but Carlene Jackson Hamaty refuses to share her original Tortuga Rum Cake recipe. After over 100 years, it remains a closely guarded family secret. Not even *Gourmet* magazine or the parade of celebrity chefs and food writers who have visited Cayman have been able to pry it from her.

However, as consolation for your disappointment, here are two unique and very different Tortuga rum cake recipes to keep you busy.

The Best Tortuga Rum Cake Ever

This is the rum cake recipe Tortuga leaks to spies from its competitors.

2 cups dried mixed fruits
1 or 2 quarts Tortuga Rum (any variety)
1 cup butter
1 cup granulated sugar
1 cup light brown sugar
4 large eggs
1 cup milk
2-3/4 cups flour
1 teaspoon baking powder
a few grains of salt
1 teaspoon vanilla extract
1 cup walnuts

Before you start, open a quart of Tortuga Rum and take a generous sample to check the quality. Good, isn't it? Carefully organize all ingredients. In a small bowl combine the dried fruit and 2 cups rum – take a sip first so you don't spill any – and stir well. Let the fruit soak for an hour. While waiting, open the other bottle of rum and check the quality. In a large mixing bowl, combine the butter and sugar. Taste the rum again. Pour into a meashuring cup and drink slowly to be sure it is at room temperature.

Find electric mixer, butt the beater and thugars until flight and luffy. If slow, check if mixer is on. Check rum again. Beat nuts until lumpy. Take another sip. Drop in heggs and bleat until high. Drain the froaked suit –remove excess rum by mouth. Throw rest into bowl and beat it. If it gets thtuck in beaters, pick out wif fingers and use hands instead. Check rum again for tonsisticity. Drop in 3 cups salt or anything , it doesn't really matter. Try to get it in the bowl. Add milk to rum and drink. Sift vanilla, chopped flour and nuts. Add babblespoon of blown fugar or any color around and wix mel. Pour into greased oven and turn pan to 350 gredees. Find rum. Set timer. When buzzing, wake up and find rum.

Tortuga West Indian Scripture Fruitcake

Variations of the recipe for Scripture Cake have been around since Colonial days and have appeared all over the world. However, the Tortuga version is the first to provide a Biblical reference to spirits, an essential ingredient in Caribbean Christmas Pudding and fruitcakes. Since it is derived from sugar cane, rum is included in the reference to sugar under Jeremiah 6:20.

1 cup raisins
 (Song of Solomon 2:5: "...sustain me with cakes of raisins...")
1 cup dried figs
(1 Samuel 30:12: "And they gave him a piece of cake of figs...")
1 cup chopped almonds
(Numbers 17:8: "...the rod of Aaron...yielded ripe almonds)
1 cup chopped dates
(Exodus 15:27: "...there were seventy palms.")
1/2 cup sweet red wine
(Deuteronomy 14:26 ".... And you shall spend that money for whatever your heart

desires...for wine or similar drink...)
1 cup Tortuga Dark Rum , divided
(Jeremiah 6:20, "...and the sweet cane from a far country")
3 large eggs
(Isaiah 10:14, "...as one gathereth eggs that are left, have I gathered all the earth....")
1 cup sugar
(Jeremiah 6:20, "...and the sweet cane from a far country.")
1/2 cup vegetable oil
(Numbers 11:8,"...and its taste was like the taste of pastry prepared with oil.")
1 tablespoon Tortuga Wildflower Honey
(Judges 14:18, "...what is sweeter than honey?")
1-3/4 cups flour
(1 Kings 4:22: "...and Solomon's provision for one day was thirty measures of fine flour..."
1/8 teaspoon salt
(Leviticus 2:13 "...shalt thou season with salt.")
1 teaspoon cinnamon
(Exodus 30:23, "Also take for yourself quality spices....much sweet smelling cinnamon...")
1/4 teaspoon nutmeg
1/2 teaspoon ginger
1/2 teaspoon ground allspice
1/2 teaspoon ground coriander
(Exodus 16:31 "...Manna: and it was like coriander seed...")
 2 teaspoons baking powder
(Amos 4:5, "Offer a sacrifice of thanksgiving with leaven...")

Combine the raisins, dates, almonds and figs in a bowl and pour the wine and 1/2 cup rum over them. Stir well and let the fruits soak for at least a week in the refrigerator. Preheat oven to 325 F. Lightly grease and flour or spray with Baker's Joy one 9 x 5 x 3" loaf pan. In a large bowl, beat the eggs until light. Gradually add the sugar and continue beating for 5 minutes. Slowly add the oil and honey and continue beating another 2 minutes until mixture is thoroughly blended. In a separate bowl, sift together the flour, salt, spices and baking powder. Add dry ingredients slowly to the egg mixture in two amounts, alternating with the remaining 1/2 cup rum, mixing well after each addition. Finally, fold in the soaked fruit and nuts. Pour the batter into the prepared pan and bake for 50 minutes to an hour, or until a toothpick inserted in center comes out clean. Remove pan from oven and cool for 10 minutes, then remove cake and cool on wire rack. The cake will keep for several weeks if tightly wrapped and stored in airtight container or refrigerator.

Party, Island Style — Any Time!

Wish you could run away to the sunny Caribbean? Even if you can't, Tortuga Rum Company can help you party island-style with friends any time. Wherever you are, you can turn any get-together into a real Caribbean jump up with a little help from this book and Tortuga Rum Company's products. But please-don't try to test *Tortuga Rum Fever's* 190 drink recipes all at the same party!

Of course, the best place to celebrate is right here in the Cayman Islands, where you can buy Tortuga liquors, Tortuga Rum Cakes and Tortuga gourmet label products to enjoy right away at Tortuga Rum Company's 18 retail and duty- free outlets island-wide. When you're leaving, stock up on Tortuga rums, liqueurs and other products at duty free prices at shops in the airport departure lounge. Cruise ship passengers can order duty-free liquor for easy delivery direct to their cruise ship. Tortuga rums come by the bottle and in Party Packs with Tortuga's Caribbean Rum Punch Mix.

You'll want lots of lively Caribbean music for your party. Tortuga's stores stock a large selection of reggae, soca and calypso tapes and CD's by the hottest island bands from Cayman and the rest of the Caribbean. You'll find CD's by top Caribbean artists like Byron Lee & the Dragonaires and The Mighty Sparrow along with Cayman's popular George "Barefoot Man" Nowak and Band; Lammie and Andy Martin, the original "Cayman Cowboy."

If island fever strikes when you're a long way from the Caribbean— "no problem!" You'll find a mini-Caribbean market just a mouse click away at Tortuga Rum Company's website, www.tortugarums.com, Order party supplies, gifts and the newest Tortuga gourmet products for prompt home delivery. Choose from all flavors and sizes of Tortuga Rum Cakes, coffees, rum fudge, Tortuga Hell-Fire Hot Pepper Sauce, Rum Plum Pudding, Caribbean Rum Punch mix-and much more. You can even order Caribbean music CD's and of course, more gift copies of *Tortuga Rum Fever & Caribbean Party*

Cookbook for friends. (Sorry— you can't order Tortuga Rums, liqueurs and flavored syrups online or by mail order.)

For mail orders by phone or fax, contact Tortuga Imports Inc. at 8781 SW 131st St., Miami, FL 33176. The toll free order numbers for North America are: phone: (800) 444-0625; Fax: (888) 440-2253; in Miami, (305) 378-6668 and Fax; (305) 378-0990. E-mail: service@tortugaimports.com In Grand Cayman, call (345) 949-7701/ 949-CAKE; fax: (345) 949-6322 or E-mail: tortuga@ candw.ky

INDEX

A

ackee
  about, history, 77-78
  Ackee Saute, 78
  Ackee and Saltfish, 97
  Ackee and Shrimp, 98
allspice (pimento)
  about, 71
  in jerk seasoning, 175-178
apple banana, 252
Arawak (Amerindian and Carib Indians), 29;77, 86,88-91; 175; 266
arrowroot, 73-74
avocado (pear)
  about, 77-78
  Avocado Rum Cream Soup, 198
  Pear, Grapefruit and Spinach Salad, 263

B

Bammy (cassava), 84-85
banana(s)
  Banana Chutney, 278
  Banana Mango Fritters, 259
  Banana Tortilla, 256
  Bananas Tortuga, 228
  Boiled Green Bananas, 101
  Cayman Apple Banana Nut Bread
  Cayman Banana Colada Pound Cake, 238
  Colada, 43
  Daiquiri, 33
  Green Banana Pudding, 79
  Rum Raisin Banana Bread, 252
  West Indian Banana Cream Pie, 246
Barbados, rum history in, 4-5; 28
barbecue (see also jerk)
  fish, 181-182
  ribs, 179-181
  sauces, 182-183
  tips and technique, 175-183
bartending
  mixing drinks, 18-21
  tips and methods, 14-21
Barefoot Man, 287
beans (and dried peas)
  soaking & cooking, 79-80
  Black Beans Borracho with Sour Cream, 81
  Honey Rum Spiced Beans, 80
  Rice and Beans, Honduran Style, 135

Rice N Peas, Cayman Style, 135
Rice and Pigeon Peas, 136
beef
  Christmas Beef, 117
  Jerk Burgers, 179
  Liver and Onions, 101
  Meat Patties, 103
  Oxtail, 107
  Rumhead Pot Roast, 186
  Steak with Rum Butter, 185
  Stew Beef, 108
  Tortuga Pepper Steak, 185
  West Indian Roast Beef, 184
  Wild West Indian Meatloaf, 187
bitters, Angostura, 20
Bligh, Capt. William, 81-82; 129
breads
  Bammy, 85
  Cayman Apple Banana Nut Bread, 252
  Cayman Mango Bread, 209
  Coconut Johnny Cakes, 254
  Easter Bun, 104-105
  Festival, 105
  Fresh Coconut Bread, 253
  Johnny Cakes, 101-102
  Pina Colada Bread, 251
  Rum Raisin Banana Bread, 252
  West Indian Pumpkin Bread, 254
breadfruit
  about, 81-82
  Breadfruit Chips, 82
  Breadfruit Salad, 106
  Breadfruit Vichyssoise, 203
bread pudding (see pudding)
breakfast dishes, Caribbean
  Ackee and Saltfish, 97
  Ackee and Shrimp, 98
  Boiled Green Bananas, 101
  Bun N Cheese, 104
  Easter Bun, 104
  Escoveitched Fish, 102
  Fish Tea, 94
  Johnny Cakes, 101
  Liver and Onions, 101
  Meat Patties, 103
  Pepperpot Soup, 96
  Pumpkin Soup, 97
  Red Bean Soup, 95
  Stamp & Go, 104
  Steamed Callaloo, 99
  Rundown, Cayman Style, 100
  Rundown, Mackerel, 99

breakfast dishes, with rum